D1363551

Legendary
Movies

Paolo D'Agostini

WHITE STAR PUBLISHERS

© 2008 White Star S.p.A.
Via Candido Sassone, 22/24
13100 Vercelli, Italy
www.whitestar.it

TRANSLATION
TEXT: Catherine Bolton
CAPTIONS: Erin Jennison

ISBN 978-88-544-0399-4

REPRINT:
1 2 3 4 5 6   12 11 10 09 08

Color separation: Chiaroscuro, Turin - Sogec, Turin
Printed in Italy, by G. Canale & C., Turin

PREFACE
Franco Zeffirelli

TEXT
Paolo D'Agostini

project editor **Valeria Manferto De Fabianis**

graphic design **Clara Zanotti**

editorial coordination **Laura Accomazzo**

I have spent a lifetime seeking beauty. Not the evident, garish and invasive sort, the type imposed on us by social roles or the kind that the beauty industry decides year by year, season by season. I have sought the beauty that lives in my dreams. In some way, have sought the magic of beauty. And I have learned, little by little and thanks to the friends I have had the good fortune to encounter along the way, how to recognize and reproduce what ultimately gives meaning to all of our lives. My films and, even before that, my set designs testify to this constant quest, which I have yet to abandon and which has a great deal to do with my own spiritual commitment.

When I debuted in cinema, I immediately understood that it was important to master the new and marvelous instruments available to me: film, lights, actors and so on. And I cannot deny that I learned the lessons rather well. Nor can I deny that used these tools to find my own personal art, my personal world of artistic expressions. This was a path on which I encountered other arts, from opera to literature, and I interpreted and even played with them. In my most recent films I 'played" with nostalgia and history. When we were shooting *Tea with Mussolini* I was literally paralyzed by my emotions. I was seeing scenes that I had really experienced, in a blend of embarrassment and nostalgia; I was trying to evoke memories as if they had not been my own. I believe that this is how each of us should look back on our lives: observing them as if they had pertained to someone else.

Cinema is a marvelous art form. It gives you the impression of re-experiencing events and emotions. As I relived that era I could recall even the smallest details. The faces were vivid to me and the streets were imbued with new life. In that film, I played with another instrument that cinema has to offer: the opportunity to blend fantasy and reality, because together they generate the magic of beauty. Indeed, I find that it is completely natural to mingle the two. If you close your eyes as you read a book, you create a new and utterly personal story. I did this with *Jane Eyre* and I cut an entire scene from *Otello*. Everyone has done this: Verdi himself betrayed Shakespeare. I cut, pasted and enriched my personal story with the many stories I heard from so many people during that period. In many cases I no longer even knew where the boundary between reality and fantasy lay.

For example, when I pondered a film on the golden age of the Renaissance, I liked to think that Leonardo painted to the sound of Michelangelo's chisel, as their workshops were just yards apart. Whether or not this actually happened was of little importance to me, nor is it important to the audience.

This is cinema: a mysterious toyland, as Fellini taught us, and a formidable stage for sentiments and passions, as Visconti believed. In any event, it is a splendid machine that brings to life the dreams and nostalgia we cultivate even as children, and it allows us to discover the beauty and truth within us.

FRANCO ZEFFIRELLI

All
Classifications
Are
Debatable.

All classifications are debatable. Such lists have been drawn up for decades, if not longer. A rapid glance at the Internet offers a dizzying number. Every list, regardless of whether it is the top 10, 100 or even 1000, is subject to objections, disappointment, indignation over the choices that have been made and to complaints that there are too many titles or too many oversights.

In choosing the films for this book, I attempted to respect a criterion. And I will explain it without offering any justification. After all, some will disagree regardless and not everyone will like my list.

Not all of the 140 "legendary" films presented here are masterpieces of cinema meriting a guaranteed and critically acclaimed place in the pantheon of the seventh art. They are ultimately films that reflect their times by interpreting the atmosphere of the era. They have marked an age, set fashions and influenced lifestyles. They have also become part of the heritage of common sentiment, the myths of the masses and widely shared points of reference. They are part of our general store of knowledge, basic culture and behavioral identification. They have become the objects of the same kind of "cult" that 20th-century society has reserved for songs and the figures from popular music.

Therefore, you will find not only some of the immortal and revolutionary cornerstones of cinematographic language – the notables of Expressionist German silent film, Italian Neo-Realism and France's New Wave, and monumental figures such as Orson Welles, Akira Kurosawa and Stanley Kubrick – but also titles that, in our collective memory, have marked the different stages in the common sentiment that we have been represented on the big screen, a sentiment that cinema alone has managed to convey to modernity. They parallel the stages in cinema's extraordinary capacity to communicate with us. In short, what you see influences you. It closely parallels your own life and is a dream that is within everyone's grasp because it recounts the stories, hopes, feelings and sadness each of us has experienced. Despite the fact that their popularity is not always matched by aesthetic and expressive merits, and that industrial, commercial and promotional strategies have almost always played a decisive role in their success, these films have gained such broad public acceptance that no historian – not even those who study cinema as an art form – can possibly ignore them. I am referring to works ranging from *Gone With the Wind* to *Doctor Zhivago*, from *Guess Who's Coming to Dinner?* to *Rambo*, and from the *Star Wars* adventures to Spielberg's fables.

Naturally, American works predominate and Hollywood films occupy a huge percentage of this list. Fourteen of the films are Italian (either by Italian directors or distinguished by a purely Italian cultural imprint, such as *Don Camillo*), eight are French, five are German (not counting Billy Wilder, one of the founding fathers of the Hollywood empire along with so many others who moved to the United States from Central Europe), two are Japanese and two are Spanish (if we consider Luis Buñuel's *Belle de jour* as hailing from Spain), one is Swedish, one is Russian and one is Chinese. An overwhelming majority is from the United States or, in any case, is represented by English-language films.

Our tally glaringly – and somewhat unjustly – reflects the relationships of power that the world capital of cinema has established with the rest of the planet. In this case, however, it would be simplistic to equate power with money. It also has to do with creative power and the invention of models of representation with which audiences from every corner of the globe can identify, not merely because they have been "colonized" or are obliged to embrace them.

When it comes to classifications – which are ultimately nothing more than the kind of game we would theoretically play if we were stranded on a desert island – and the concept of "Hollywood versus the rest of the globe" and specifically Europe, this rivalry has always existed. Cinema was born in Europe, as it was invented by the Lumière brothers and Georges Méliès. It was promoted to the rank of a phantasmagoric spectacle by the first Italian epics of the 1910s and rose to the highest formal levels thanks to the German and Soviet masters of the 1920s. But it was in America that it became the quintessential contemporary art, and it was in America that it acquired its specific definition as both an industrial and creative event, an "opus" but also simple and childlike entertainment, a hotbed of devices and circus tricks, and a venue for artists as well as financiers and profit seekers.

While Europe remains the guardian of *auteur* cinema, Hollywood has consolidated its role as the homeland of the cinema of producers and spectators, and this is reflected when it comes time to consecrate and celebrate its merits.

Yet the concept of the film festival is quintessentially European. The world's first was held in Venice in 1932, followed by Cannes and the Swiss festival in Locarno in 1946. It was conceived as a place of exploration and discovery, a showcase for new things that had never been seen before and were subjected to critical evaluation, examined first by selection committees and then by juries composed of "experts" representing a discriminating, avant-garde, competent, sophisticated and well-educated audience. The idea of awarding a prize a posteriori based on box-office success is purely American, however, and since 1929 it has been represented by the Oscar or Academy Award. It is no accident that the most coveted statuette, the Oscar for Best Picture, goes to the producer rather than the director.

Let's return to my reasons for choosing these works rather than others to represent the "best films of our lives." Naturally, it is a matter of taste, which is subjective, incontestable and imponderable. It is an element that slyly works its way into books such as this one, in which every effort has been made to portray and photograph something that is widely shared, albeit with the motivations and limitations set forth here. But along the way – in other words, when it painfully comes time to include or exclude a work – you realize that there are countless potential coordinates.

In the meantime, just like everything else and in particular just like other aspects related to the mass culture, cinematographic perception made a quantum leap between the period prior to World War II and the period after it. The very idea of a mythical, epochal or legendary cult object reflects a conceptual legacy rather than an imaginary watershed. Consequently, apart from very rare cases such as *Casablanca* or the eternal and universal appeal of Charlie Chaplin and Walt Disney, this is a parameter that is very difficult to apply to anything that predates the symbolic identification introduced by the new screen stars and the new anti-stars embodied by icons such as Marlon Brando, Marilyn Monroe and James Dean.

There is also the fact that while the global imagination is the one proposed by the American victors – victors on a military, economic and cultural level – each nation has its own imagination. Around the world, we find phenomena that have had enormous impact on a local level and popular stars who have never crossed borders or moved outside their specific location: Alberto Sordi in Italy and the comedian Louis de Funès in France, for example, not to the immense but circumscribed market targeted by India's Bollywood.

It must also be said that every national cinema puts an official stamp on its own pantheon and the film heritage it seeks to protect. In 1988 the United States established the National Film Registry at the Library of Congress. These archives contain films that have been acknowledged as "culturally, historically or aesthetically significant" and while they are not necessarily part of the mainstream industry, most of them are. Something similar is also being done now in Italy.

Lastly, there is a generational parameter and on this level it is difficult to find a "generalist" framework. Moviegoers who were 30 years old in the 1940s will always adore Greta Garbo and Marlene Dietrich, Clark Gable and James Stewart. Those who were 20 in the 1950s and 1960s will always have a special place in their hearts for cult films such as *On the Waterfront* and *Rebel Without a Cause*, and their idols are Jean-Paul Belmondo and Sean Connery, Audrey Hepburn and Brigitte Bardot. Today's teens are mad about Quentin Tarantino, Tim Burton, the Coen Brothers and films based on graphic novels such as *Sin City* and *300*. Forty years ago, young people who wanted to seem more sophisticated than their peers went into raptures over Ingmar Bergman and Michelangelo Antonioni; today their children hang on Lars von Trier's every word and are thrilled by the works of Korean filmmaker Park Chan-wook. Aside from the most knowledgeable movie buffs, there are few generational overlaps. It is rare that an 80-year-old moviegoer will share his great-grandson's excitement over *Kill Bill*. If asked to draw up a list of "must-sees," no teenager of the third millennium would contemplate including the Rooseveltian humanism of Frank Capra or the finely honed style of one of Ernst Lubitsch's sophisticated comedies, much less appreciate the elegant humor of Cary Grant and the subtly wicked perfection of Grace Kelly.

Naturally, there are evergreens. Opinions about Hitchcock are virtually unanimous, John Ford's spaces are the very essence of cinema for legions of people of all ages and nations, and around the world Federico Fellini's name will always be synonymous with boundlessly imaginative filmmaking. Marilyn Monroe is the icon that overcomes all barriers. In short, I have tried to come up with an average and achieve a respectable approximation, devising a potential list of unmissable films that will appeal to everyone.

The great adventure of silent cinema is illustrated in these pages by the first historical epic, the Italian film *Cabiria*, the masterpieces of the German directors Fritz Lang and F. W. Murnau, who laid the aesthetic groundwork for all future screen representations of disquietude, evil and fear, by the revolutionary lesson of Sergey Eisenstein and by the mastery of Charlie Chaplin, who remained faithful to silent cinema long after the advent of talkies, an era ushered in by *The Jazz Singer* in 1927. This summarizes the heroic season that saw the sweeping and revolutionary approach to serial production by a fledgling industry that had already gained enormous popular appeal, with short pie-in-the-face comedy films and the slapstick of Mack Sennett, Laurel and Hardy, Buster Keaton, the early Chaplin and the Marx Brothers. It was also the season that ushered in the first star system of Rudolph Valentino and the original United Artists, founded by Chaplin, Douglas Fairbanks, Mary Pickford and D.W. Griffith, Hollywood's first great director.

The two decades that followed were the golden years in which Hollywood affirmed its leadership in the industry through the diabolical well-oiled machine of its studios and the perfection of the star system. The great companies – the Majors – dominated the market, which brought a code of communication and system of signs around the world and triumphed everywhere: Metro-Goldwyn-Mayer, Warner Brothers, Paramount, Twentieth Century-Fox, Universal, RKO and Columbia.

Through their tycoons – Louis B. Mayer, Irving Thalberg, Arthur Freed, the Warner Brothers, Adolph Zukor, Jesse L. Lasky, William Fox, Darryl F. Zanuck, Carl Laemmle, Howard Hughes, Harry Cohn and David O. Selznick – the majors shaped a new and enormously successful symbolic universe. They invented the concept of film genres: the Western, the musical, the melodrama, the thriller, the comedy, the historical epic and the war movie. They created the universal stars of the 1930s and 1940s: Clark Gable, Greta Garbo, Jean Harlow, Spencer Tracy, Joan Crawford, James Stewart, Judy Garland, William Powell, Myrna Loy, Gene Kelly, Fred Astaire, Ginger Rogers, John Barrymore, James Cagney, Edward G. Robinson, Humphrey Bogart, Bette Davis, Ingrid Bergman, Gloria Swanson, Katharine Hepburn, Cary Grant, Jean Arthur, Carole Lombard, Claudette Colbert, Joan Fontaine, Rita Hayworth, Glenn Ford, William Holden, Judy Holliday, Kim Novak and Doris Day.

This was an era in which actors and actresses – in the roles of directors and screenwriters, as recounted by *A Star Is Born* and *Sunset Boulevard* – were under contract. The freedom of artists was strictly subjected to what can be defined as an employer-employee relationship, and the rules were ironclad. Each comma of the film scripts was subject to a strict system of self-regulation: the Hays Code, adopted in 1930.

The period after World War II and the 1950s brought new and irreversible technological changes akin to those of the transition from silent films to talkies, such as the affirmation and spread of color and widescreen formats. It also ushered in revolutions in terms of form and content. Italian Neorealism and the films of Vittorio De Sica, Roberto Rossellini and Luchino Visconti, immediately followed by those of Giuseppe De Santis, Michelangelo Antonioni and Federico Fellini, radically changed things. They demonstrated that another type of cinema was possible, that films could be made differently: that it was possible to emerge from studios and go to the streets and real places, shooting in natural light, and that screen stories and characters could be identical to those of real life.

This marked a watershed and nothing would ever be the same. It was a blow to Hollywood, but the United States did not lose its leadership in this industry. If anything, the country was strengthened by its military victory and the penetration of its culture, brought in by the liberating armies that made such an enormous contribution to restoring freedom and democracy to areas that had been oppressed by dictatorship. Hollywood reinvented itself by creating a new icon: youth. John Garfield, Montgomery Clift, Marlon Brando, James Dean, Paul Newman and Anthony Perkins embodied figures different from their fathers or older brothers, who were mature, adult and protective men, heroes like John Wayne in *Stagecoach* or criminals such as the mobsters in *Little Caesar*, *The Public Enemy* and *Scarface*. Instead, they interpreted the new season of uncertainty and resistance to the values of their fathers, who had freed the world from Nazism and Fascism, but had also invented and used the atom bomb. They were discontent, confused and rebellious, possibly without a sense of awareness and perhaps "without a cause" – but rebellious nonetheless. Immature and boastful, they rode their Harley-Davidsons, donned their leather jackets and were timid with girls, yet they were also violent and self-destructive, determined to live in a separate world.

Hollywood withstood beautifully and upped the ante, often coming to shoot epics in Rome's Cinecittà, transferring Hollywood to the Tiber and contributing to the real or alleged *dolce vita* of Via Veneto. But the pressure of the new giant, television, forced Hollywood to re-examine everything once more.

In the meantime, however, the new generation was coming to the fore around the world and, naturally, also in Hollywood. Figures such as John Cassavetes inherited, accompanied and anticipated the minor but important profile of inveterate characters who worked within yet also outside the "system": from John Huston to Orson Welles, Joseph Losey, Stanley Kubrick, Robert Altman and Woody Allen. These men were often more accepted, recognized and welcome in Europe than they were at home.

Above all, however, the "new cinema" movement developed elsewhere: in France with Jean-Luc Godard, François Truffaut and their numerous other companions (Louis Malle, Claude Chabrol, Eric Rohmer), as well as England (Tony Richardson, John Schlesinger, Richard Lester, Lindsay Anderson, Karel Reisz), Italy (Bernardo Bertolucci, Marco Bellocchio, Marco Ferreri, Pier Paolo Pasolini), Spain (Carlos Saura), Japan (Nagisa Oshima), Brazil (Glauber Rocha) and the Soviet capitals of Eastern Europe (Istvan Szabo in Budapest, Roman Polanski and Jerzy Skolimowski in Warsaw, Milos Forman in Prague).

The generation that emerged in the 1970s was influenced by them, but also by the preceding Italian lesson, including the glorious "Italian-style" comedy and popular low-budget movies, starting with Leone's spaghetti Westerns.

There was also the powerful albeit fleeting German meteor: Wim Wenders, Werner Herzog and Rainer Werner Fassbinder. Yet above all, this was the period of the American Renaissance: the "new Hollywood" with films such as *The Graduate* and directors such as Arthur Penn and Sydney Pollack. This was the generation that grew up in the 1950s and included figures of the caliber of Sidney Lumet, John Frankenheimer, Martin Ritt, Jules Dassin, Elia Kazan and Stanley Kramer, the generation that suffered the hysterical anti-Communist onslaught of Senator Joseph McCarthy and his witch hunt, and that learned Italy's lesson of social realism. It was a generation symbolically represented by seminal films such as *Easy Rider*, immediately followed by filmmakers who, rising to power and redesigning the imaginary universe of cinema, reestablished America's solid predominance: Brian De Palma, Michael Cimino, Martin Scorsese, Francis Ford Coppola, George Lucas and Steven Spielberg.

We have now reached the modern age and from past history we have come to current events. The past few decades have seen yet other changes. Powerful personalities and significant movements have emerged from settings that were once marginal or that, once great, had weakened: Pedro Almodóvar, Emir Kusturica, Ken Loach, Luc Besson, Nanni Moretti, Roberto Benigni and Giuseppe Tornatore. Some of the most significant examples have come from the Far East and Oceania: China, Hong Kong, Korea, Taiwan, Japan, India, Australia and New Zealand, with directors named Jane Campion, Peter Weir, Mira Nair, Chen Caige, Zhang Yimou, Wong Kar-wai, Ang Lee, Kim Ki-duk and Park Chan-wook.

The ways of producing and, above all, enjoying films have changed radically. Big movie theaters and enormous screens have not lost their appeal, but they have unquestionably become secondary. Creative processes have also changed, as has inspiration.

As always, the United States has not simply sat back and watched, and Hollywood has spawned inventors, geniuses and authors: Steven Soderbergh, David Lynch, Tim Burton (who in 2007 became the youngest director to be awarded an Honorary Leone d'Oro at the Venice Film Festival), Gus van Sant, Paul Thomas Anderson and *Magnolia*, Bryan Singer and *The Usual Suspects*, M. Night Shyamalan and *The Sixth Sense*, David Fincher and *Se7en*, the enigmatic Terrence Malick and *The Thin Red Line*, and the magnificent Clint Eastwood in his miraculous second childhood. We also find ambiguous geniuses of self-promotion such as Michael Moore, who succeeded in the seemingly impossible challenge of transforming a documentary into a blockbuster. But one of the most iconic is Quentin Tarantino, whose cinema full of references and allusions fearlessly proclaims that, in today's world, one can create things merely by recycling what has already been invented.

What remains, and what you will find in these pages – hopefully with some level of satisfaction between cries of "this is missing" and "that is missing" – is the miracle of creating, then and now, stories and characters that, like friends and family, have accompanied us and will continue to do so for the rest of our lives. Their names are Guido Orefice, Norman Bates, Ringo, Rick, Forrest Gump, Jules and Jim, Catherine, Marcello Rubini, Scarlett O'Hara, Norma Desmond, Sabrina, Frank Bullitt, Charles Foster Kane, Rocky Balboa, Lola Lola, Jacques Clouseau, Indiana Jones, Hannibal Lecter, Alex De Large, Jack Torrance, Tony Manero, Jim Stark and Vito Corleone. And they will never leave us.

▲1 ▲2

1914

1. 2. In 1914, Cabiria cost 1 million Italian lira; before then, no film had ever cost more than 50,000 lira.

[ITALY] Genre: **HISTORICAL**

CABIRIA

Cabiria, which was released in 1914, was the first epic as well as the first feature film in the history of cinema. It supposedly inspired both D. W. Griffith, the founder of Hollywood, and Cecil B. DeMille, the director whose name became linked to the very concept of epic films from the 1920s to the 1950s. *Cabiria* was directed by Giovanni Pastrone, who was born in Italy's Piedmont region in 1883 and went by the pseudonym of Piero Fosco. He began to work in silent film in 1905 as a factotum for a producer based in Turin, Italy's first film capital. In 1908 he founded Itala Film. As its head, he established important studios, invented and patented technical innovations, and created a circuit of film houses. In short, he became Italy's first movie tycoon. Although he made a number of ambitious motion pictures that always had historical or literary subjects, *Cabiria* is considered his masterpiece. Pastrone, who quit the film industry in 1919, died in 1959.

The film's most widely touted attribute at the time was the series of captions written in a pretentiously poetic, rhetorical and inflated style by Gabriele D'Annunzio, but today *Cabiria* is cited for more significant aspects. First of all, it was filmed using a dolly (a camera set on rails), placing it at the cutting edge in terms of both technology and expressiveness.

We should also try to imagine the effect of the lavishly staged première of this film – which was much longer than the standard works of the 1910s, although its original length is difficult to ascertain – held simultaneously at two enormous theaters in Milan and Turin, and accompanied by live orchestras playing a score that was specially composed by Ildebrando Pizzetti. This unprecedented event marked the first acknowledgment that cinema was no longer a fairground spectacle but entertainment that was worthy of the upper classes and that could compete with theater and opera in terms of appeal and prestige. Due to its ambitious approach and elaborate plot, the impressive and realistic impact of the special effects (the eruption of Mount Etna), the extravagant sets and costumes, and filming on location in Tunisia, the Alps and Sicily, the film cost

▲ 3   ▲ 4

Director: GIOVANNI PASTRONE

Cast: BARTOLOMEO PAGANO / LYDIA QUARANTA / UMBERTO MOZZATO

the astronomical sum of one million gold lire (50,000 of which supposedly went to D'Annunzio). It inaugurated what would be one of cinema's most successful genres for decades, the historical/mythological film, and immediately received international acclaim. One of the film's most memorable figures was the giant Bartolomeo Pagano, a longshoreman from the port of Genoa who was cast as the brawny Maciste, a character who was enormously popular for decades. Although the story was attributed to D'Annunzio, it was actually based on Emilio Salgari's novel *Cartagine in fiamme* and, in part, on Gustave Flaubert's *Salammbô*.

The story takes place during the Second Punic War (218-202 BC) and its complex plot mixes historical figures – the Carthaginians Hannibal, Hasdrubal and Sophonisba; the Numidian kings Massinissa and Syphax; and Archimedes and Scipio Africanus – with fictional figures who are actually the leading characters: little Cabiria, kidnapped and brought to Africa as a slave, and the Roman patrician Fulvius Axilla and his loyal servant Maciste, who are determined to save her. In the fledgling Italian film industry, which was a pioneer in terms of techniques and stylistic aspirations, above all in the field of historical extravaganzas, *Cabiria* was preceded by the 1912 film *Quo Vadis?*, directed by Enrico Guazzoni. The latter film was likewise intended as a celebration of the Roman spirit, victorious once more following the Italian-Turkish War of 1911-12. The same intent is evident in the 1937 film *Scipio Africanus* (although it was heavily influenced by Fascist propaganda) by Carmine Gallone, who also created another Italian epic with *The Last Days of Pompeii* (1926).

Not only did *Cabiria* anticipate the great Hollywood classics, but it was also the harbinger of the magniloquence of Abel Gance's *Napoléon* (1927), the French equivalent in terms of the spectacular, popular and patriotic grandeur of the silent film era. *Cabiria* was thus the first tangible affirmation that this new medium of expression and storytelling had truly come into its own. In short, it is a true monument.

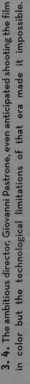

3. 4. The ambitious director, Giovanni Pastrone, even anticipated shooting the film in color but the technological limitations of that era made it impossible.

[GERMANY] **Genre: DRAMA / HORROR**

THE CABINET OF DR. CALIGARI

Director: ROBERT WIENE

Cast: WERNER KRAUß / CONRAD VEIDT / FRIEDRICH FEHÉR / LIL DAGOVER / HANS HEINRICH VON TWARDOWSKI

The Cabinet of Dr. Caligari is the silent classic that ushered in Expressionist cinema. It also became the prototype of future horror films, preceded only by Paul Wegener's *Der Golem* of 1915. Famous exclusively for this work, Robert Wiene was one of the directors who, along with masters such as Georg W. Pabst, Fritz Lang and F. W. Murnau, brought the Expressionist avant-garde to the screen. In fact, Lang was originally supposed to direct the film. In the prologue, a young man (Francis) begins to tell his story to an older man, in a setting that we later discover is an insane asylum. He talks about his hometown, his friendship with Alan, and their love for the same girl. A sinister-looking huckster shows up at the town fair, calling himself Dr. Caligari, and is given a place where he can display his attraction, Cesare (Conrad Veidt, who later starred in *The Student of Prague*, 1926, and *The Man Who Laughs*, 1928), whom he presents as a somnambulist. According to Dr. Caligari, Cesare has slept from the time he was born, but would wake up in front of the audience and respond to everyone's questions. In the meantime, the municipal secretary from whom Caligari finally managed to obtain a permit to participate in the fair is murdered. The show begins and Caligari orders Cesare to wake up from his eternal sleep. Held back by the wary Francis, Alan enthusiastically asks how long he has to live. The troubling answer is that the young man will die at dawn. That night a shadow enters Alan's house and kills him. Shocked, Francis exclaims that the somnambulist's prophecy has come true and runs to the police. He wants to discover the truth and examine the somnambulist. Meanwhile, a drifter tries to kill an old woman, but she cries out for help and manages to get him arrested. Francis and a doctor – the father of the woman he loves – pay a visit to Caligari, who introduces Cesare to them. At the same time, the arrested man confesses that he had nothing to do with the other murders and that he simply wanted to kill the old woman so that the murder would be blamed on the other assassin. That night Cesare sneaks into the girl's house to kill her in her sleep, but he is so dazzled by her beauty that he kidnaps her. Hunted, he abandons her on the side of the road. However, when Francis goes to Caligari with the police, he

1. 2. 3. 4. Here is the movie poster of the expressionist film par excellence. According to typical expressionist taste, the scenery emphasizes the artificiality of atmospheres with focal planes, angled surfaces, and acute angles everywhere, marked by the avant-garde artists Warm, Reimann, and Röhrig.

finds Cesare asleep. Unseen, Francis follows Caligari into an insane asylum. Troubled, the young man asks the doctors he meets if they have a patient by the name of Caligari. They say no and tell him he should talk to the director, who has just returned. As soon as he arrives, Frances is shocked to see that he is none other than Caligari. While the director is asleep, the other doctors help Francis by allowing him to search his office, where he discovers a document stating that, in 1703, a certain Dr. Caligari would visit town fairs with a somnambulist. The two sowed terror from city to city for months. According to the document, the obedient somnambulist committed a large number of murderers at his master's behest and, using a wax doll identical to him, Dr. Caligari managed to divert suspicion. Francis and the doctors also read the director's diary, which reports that he discovered and examined Cesare, and that his lifelong dream had come true, for he could finally discover the secrets of Caligari. Indeed, we see him prey to horrible hallucinations as he gradually begins to identify with Caligari. Francis finally unmasks and accuses the director/Caligari, who is immobilized in a straitjacket and carried off.

The epilogue brings us back to the opening scene and Francis is telling his story. As the shot widens, however, around him we see the entire cast, including Cesare and the girlfriend. They are all insane, including Francis, but he continues to protest, shouting that the director – not he – is the real madman. Naturally, the director is Caligari in his "respectable" guise. Francis is locked up

in the asylum and the director says that he finally understands the young man's madness: that Francis thinks the director is Caligari. Now that he knows what is troubling him, the director is convinced that he can finally cure him. Using the innovative flashback technique, the film proposes the same theme as *Frankenstein*: a scientist who steps outside the bounds of ethics and uses his power to enslave a patient. Although the film uses contrived and conventional twists, it can nevertheless be cited for its focus on dual personalities and the confusion between dreams and reality. The author expresses these elements by mingling the sensitivities of German Romanticism with the recent acquisitions of psychoanalysis, providing an allegorical interpretation. The premonitory shadows of a sense of aimlessness that will eventually transform men into robots (Lang's *Metropolis* takes up the same subject) emerge against the backdrop of the Weimar Republic and the troubles that would lead to Nazism. The film also stands out because of the extreme application of the aesthetic dictates of the Expressionist movement, evident in the harsh makeup, jerky performance, lighting and, above all, the set design – manifestly artificial, and provocatively asymmetrical and lopsided – that was the work of the artists from that movement. Screenwriter Carl Mayer and producer Erich Pommer played key roles in the making of this film. Interestingly, Pommer refused to let Mayer complete the film with a scene showing that Francis was sane and Caligari the madman.

In 1922 F. W. Murnau's *Nosferatu* – the full German title was *Nosferatu, eine Symphonie des Grauens* (*Nosferatu, a Symphony of Terror*) – ushered in the vampire genre and, in general, horror cinema. It was inspired by Bram Stoker's *Dracula* but the filmmaker never obtained the rights on the novel. Consequently, the production company was sued for copyright infringement, lost the case and was ordered to destroy every copy. Fortunately, however, the order was never fully carried out.

Along with Robert Weine's *The Cabinet of Doctor Caligari*, made two years earlier, and Fritz Lang's great films of the early 1920s, *Nosferatu* is considered one of the most representative works of the Expressionist movement. The Expressionist avant-garde – the term Expressionism reflects the use of drastically anti-naturalist and subjective approaches, with representation shaped by emotions and feelings, as a reaction against Impressionism – developed in Germany in the 1910s and 1920s. As was the case in all the other arts (painting, music and theater), in cinema it attracted prestigious disciples, notably Murnau and Lang. Nevertheless, in the dramatic but artistically lively climate of the postwar period in Germany, it influenced the entire Northern European season, which lent fundamental impetus to the seventh art. The movement involved an entire generation that, enticed by Hollywood and fleeing Nazism, emigrated en masse, bringing substance and depth to the golden age of the American film industry.

In order to get around copyright issues, *Dracula* became Count Orlok, while as far as the setting is concerned, Transylvania and the Carpathian Mountains are both cited, intentionally confusing the two. The year is 1838. The ambiguous realtor Knock receives orders from Count Orlok to find him a house in the German city of Bremen. Consequently, the realtor sends his young employee Hutter to visit the count, but the young man cockily scoffs at what he deems are ridiculous legends about the Count Orlok and his castle. When he arrives, however, he is forced to change his mind. In the meantime, back in Bremen Hutter's wife Ellen has a terrible premonitory dream.

After seeing with his own eyes that a set of coffins – including the one holding the vampire – is being prepared for shipment from the castle, Hutter flees in terror and heads home. Back in Bremen, the realtor Knock, who has actually been possessed by Orlok from afar, shows signs of insanity and is locked up in a psychiatric ward. The crew of the *Demeter*, the ship on which the coffins have been loaded to bring to Bremen, is killed by a mysterious "plague" that is documented in the logbook until the captain himself succumbs. Preceded by alarm signals, the vessel reaches the port, steered by the last survivor, and the city is immediately struck by a string of unexplainable deaths. It is Ellen who, after reading *The Book of the Vampires* despite the fact that her husband, now home, has forbidden it, finally understands what is happening. She discovers that only a woman can break the terrible spell: "a woman pure in heart who will offer her blood freely to Nosferatu and will keep the vampire by her side until after the cock has crowed."

1922
NOSFERATU

Director: FRIEDRICH WILHELM MURNAU
Cast: MAX SCHRECK / GUSTAV VON WANGENHEIM / GRETA SCHRÖDER

Here is the vampire, Nosferatu, in an image symbolic of the film. Even though Murnau's film fits the quintessential expressionist esthetic with its shot angles, horizontal beams of lights, and bad makeup, it breaks away from that sensibility through numerous innovative shots in realistic natural environments and sometimes even exterior settings.

The use of surrealistically artificial settings, with great emphasis on *mises en scène* (sharp and oblique camera angles, with stark chiaroscuro lighting), was typical of Expressionist cinema. Murnau moved away from this, using natural backgrounds and turning instead to specific filmmaking instruments and the resources distinctive of cinematographic language, which he exploited in a highly inventive way.

A powerfully evocative metaphorical and symbolic representation of absolute evil and its impending danger, the film has lent itself to numerous different interpretations.

The German director Werner Herzog remade this film, starring Klaus Kinski, in the late 1970s. *Shadow of the Vampire*, released in 2000, offers a fictionalized account of the making of Murnau's film, lending credence to the numerous legends that have surrounded it; John Malkovich plays the director and Willem Dafoe is Max Schreck, the actor who interpreted Orlok/Dracula and is described as a real vampire.

After all, Murnau himself (1888-1931) – whose real last name was Plumpe – was considered an eccentric figure. He left Europe for the United States, but quickly clashed with the Hollywood system. He then traveled to Polynesia with the great documentarian Robert Flaherty to work on a film about Bora Bora, but when the two had a falling out Murnau had to complete *Tabu* on his own. However, he did not live to see it released, as he was killed in a mysterious car accident. Declaredly homosexual, the director was driving with his extremely young chauffeur and lover, and the car supposedly went off the road while the director was performing fellatio on the driver, according to Kenneth Anger's book *Hollywood Babylon*, the 'gossip bible' on the subject.

Lang and Flaherty, as well as screenwriter Carl Mayer, actor Emil Jannings, filmmaker Georg W. Pabst (three of the leading figures of German Expressionist cinema of the 1920s) and Greta Garbo attended his funeral, which was held in Berlin.

24 [TOP]- Count Orlok gets ready to drown the puppies around Ellen Hutter's neck, but the first light of dawn kills them instead.

24 [BOTTOM] - Ellen, wife of Hutter (Gustav von Wangenheim) and the first to understand that Orlok is a vampire, tempts the count into a deadly trap.

The Battleship Potemkin is one of the most important and famous films in the history of cinema. It was made in 1925 by 27-year-old Sergey Eisenstein, who had debuted as a director that year with *Strike*. Naturally, it is a silent film in black and white.

The government of the young Soviet Union, which had lost its founder, Lenin, a year earlier, wanted to celebrate the 20th anniversary of the first Russian Revolution (1905) and commissioned the brilliant young revolutionary filmmaker to oversee a colossal venture to be completed in a very short time. Using this monumental project as his starting point, Eisenstein extracted a single episode (in the original script it barely took up 50 lines): the mutiny of the crew of the Battleship *Potemkin* in Odessa Harbor.

The director followed the precepts of classical tragedy, which allowed him to transform the chronicle of historical events – based on real episodes that were fictionalized only in part – into an epic, and the film is thus divided into five acts.

Act One: "The Men and the Maggots." The crewmen aboard the Battleship *Potemkin* refuse to eat their rations because the meat is rancid. They are headed by Vakulynchuk, their natural leader. When the officers ask the ship's doctor for his opinion, he shamelessly backs up those in command and negates the facts. Faced with the threat of punishment for insubordination, many of the men give in but others stand their ground.

Act Two: "Drama on the Quarterdeck." Those who have refused to eat the rotten food are arrested and condemned to death. They are dragged to the deck to face a firing squad, but when the riflemen are given the order to fire they refuse to shoot their companions. It is the signal to mutiny. The crew takes over, kills the officers and throws the doctor off the ship.

Act Three: "An Appeal from the Dead." During the revolt, Vakulynchuk is killed by an officer. The ship enters Odessa Harbor and the body of the heroic leader is laid out on the dock and honored by an enormous crowd that sympathizes with the mutineers.

Act Four: "The Odessa Steps." The Cossacks come to suppress the uprising, shooting at the defenseless crowd and killing men, women and children. In serried ranks, they advance down a monumental staircase. As the *Potemkin* fires its cannons against the Cossacks, the news arrives that a naval squadron is on its way to help put down the revolt.

1925

THE BATTLESHIP POTEMKIN

Director: SERGEJ MIKHAJLOVIČ EJZENSTEJN

Cast: ALEKSANDR ANTONOV / VLADIMIR BARSKIJ / GRIGORIJ ALEKSANDROV

▶ Here is the famous close-up of the face of the mother whom the Cossacks kill, leaving her baby carriage to roll down the huge steps on its own.

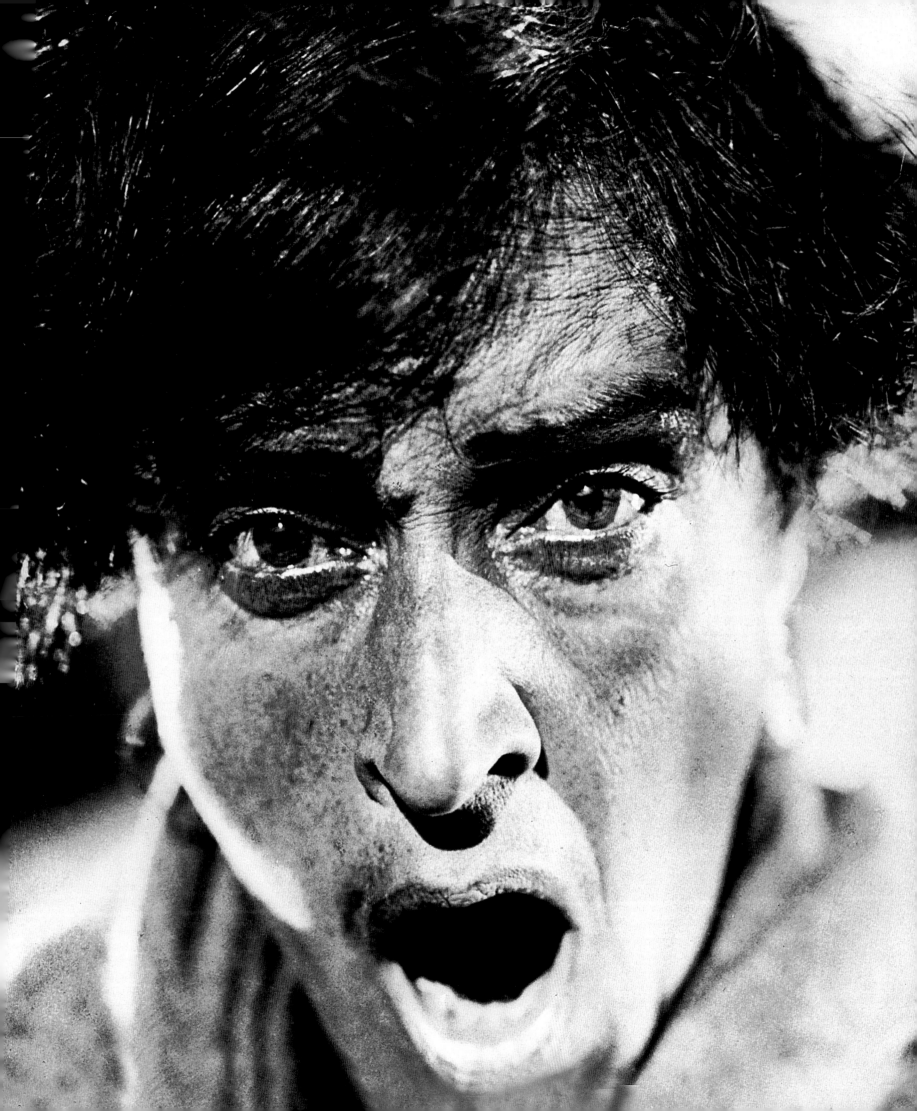

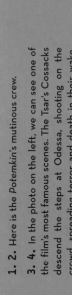

1. 2. Here is the *Potemkin*'s mutinous crew.
3. 4. In the photo on the left, we can see one of the film's most famous scenes. The Tsar's Cossacks descend the steps at Odessa, shooting on the crowd, spreading terror and death in their wake. After the mother's death, the baby carriage rolls down the steps without her.

Act Five: "Meeting the Squadron." The *Potemkin* and its mutineers, who hoist the red flag on the ship, set sail, ready to face the units sent to fight the rebels. However, when the revolutionaries cross paths with the Czarist squadron, they are welcomed by cries of solidarity and the *Potemkin* is allowed through without a single shot being fired.

An extraordinary example of the union of ideological motivations and stylistic innovation, between revolutionary propaganda and an equally revolutionary art form, *The Battleship Potemkin* is the exact opposite of the clichés that have been used to define it: heavy and dull. In reality, its pace and speed rival those of video clips that would be made 70 years later. Its pace can be attributed almost entirely to Eisenstein's powerful montage. With the exception of the compelling scenes on the Odessa Steps, filmed with traveling shots (and containing some of *The Battleship Potemkin*'s most celebrated mo-

▲ 4

▲ 5

ments, above all the vision of the baby carriage rolling down the stairs after the Czarist forces have shot the child's mother), most of the work was filmed with fixed shots. A sense of movement was thus created through montage. Another famous scene offers a shot of a sleeping stone lion, followed by one that is awake and then rampant: the symbolic meaning of this montage is self-evident.

It was first shown to the Soviet *nomenklatura* at the Bolshoi Theatre a few days before Christmas 1925 and premiered at Soviet cinemas in early 1926. It immediately became a classic, above all after it was presented in Berlin, which was Europe's leading cultural capital at the time. In the West, however, it did not circulate until much later, and only through experimental circuits, militants and film clubs. For example, it was not distributed in Italy until 1960. There are several versions that differ in length, music score and commentaries. *The Battleship Potemkin* influenced countless other films.

5. The style of this movie poster recalls the intimate relationship between Eisenstein and the avant-garde pictorials of the Twenties.

METROPOLIS

Director: FRITZ LANG
Cast: ALFRED ABEL / BRIGITTE HELM / RUDOLF KLEIN-ROGGE / GUSTAV FRÖHLICH

Fritz Lang's *Metropolis*, which took nearly all of 1926 to produce and officially premiered in Berlin in January 1927, is a prophetic, prodigious and monumental but profoundly contradictory work.

There are five key characters in the complex sequence of events taking place in Metropolis, a completely dehumanized claim first-century megalopolis where the rich live in luxury on the surface and workers live as slaves in the underground, at the mercy of the machines and grueling pace they are forced to maintain.

Fredersen *père* is the master of the workmen, the machines and the entire city. Rotwang is the brilliant scientist who invented the machines and he is perfecting a robot so that human labor will no longer be necessary. Rotwang works for Fredersen, but he is also his enemy because the woman he loved – now dead – left him for the master. Grot is the foreman, a responsible and proud man who not only rejects the rebellious and destructive hysteria of the masses, but also the principle of class struggles. Although he initially appears to be dominated by Fredersen, he will ultimately prove to be the man of constructive reconciliation. Maria – an eloquently symbolic name – is an angelic figure who secretly assembles the dehumanized workers in the catacombs, i.e. a third level of Metropolis. Her intent is not to foment rebellion but to urge them to wait patiently and faithfully for a messiah who will step in and resolve relations between them and their dictator and master. Lastly, there is Fredersen *fils*, who is presented as a fragile and easily influenced character, unlike his inflexible father. However, through his purifying descent into the underground, his growing awareness of the subhuman living conditions of the workers, which he experiences first-hand, and his devotion to Maria, which blossoms into love, he becomes the savior, the Mediator and peacemaker who establishes a new era of harmony and goodwill among men and social classes.

This process goes through many stages. Maria preaches peace and curbs the weak rebellious instincts of the workers, a social class that is in reality an anonymous herd without a conscience. Nevertheless, Fredersen, the father, decides to take action, as he considers Maria's sermons dangerous. Therefore, he tells the scientist to give his new invention Maria's likeness and sends the robot among the workmen to control them and repress their desire for freedom. The inventor, however, who is still deeply jealous of his rival over his lost love, instead programs the robot to incite the workers to destroy the machines and the city, a nihilistic and Luddite move that ultimately proves to be self-destructive. Maria's "double" personality causes countless complications, but everything is finally settled in the end with the message of peace that is conveyed when the elder Fredersen and the foreman shake hands, "officiated" by the younger Fredersen.

▶ The robot created by the scientist, Rotwang, in later years becomes the model for C-3PO in *Star Wars*.

32 - This image says a lot about the influence that Lang's masterpiece had on a future represented in film that would become a reality of sorts, later rendered inhumane by a "civilization" of machines. *Blade Runner* describes a similar type of metropolis.

33 - Drama, kindness, and social class conflicts distinguish the characters created by writer, Thea von Harbou, Lang's wife at the time when he created *Metropolis*.

34 and 35 - *Metropolis* is an experimental film setting with bold special effects achieved by combining scale models and life-sized sets. It took eighteen months to create with 30,000 appearances gone before they knew it. A blockbuster in its time, *Metropolis* recounts the delirious omnipotence of its political-financial-scientific power and the great director relied upon the same sort of delirium.

The film was influenced by the partnership between Lang and the author of the story, Thea von Harbou, who was the director's wife at the time and later joined the Nazi Party. Nevertheless, the strong point of *Metropolis* was neither its "message" nor its confusing ideological baggage, which Hitler found very appealing. Although its greatness may be difficult to grasp today, due to the fact that there are no extant versions that are philologically reliable in terms of length and editing, *Metropolis* is a timeless classic from a technical and stylistic standpoint.

Daring and futuristic in its approach, and enormously demanding from a production standpoint, thanks to its backdrops, special effects achieved mainly through scale models, lighting and geometric, imposing and patently artificial sets Lang's film is a flamboyant statement of expressionistic aesthetics in cinema. Received tepidly in Europe (the science-fiction writer H.G. Wells panned it, while Luis Buñuel's praised its form but criticized its content), it triumphed in New York, where it was paradoxically also accused of conveying a Communist message.

The film anticipated George Orwell's political fiction and was also the model for hits such as *Blade Runner*. Interestingly, in 1984 the composer Giorgio Moroder put together a fascination and arbitrarily edited shorter version of the film, with a rock soundtrack.

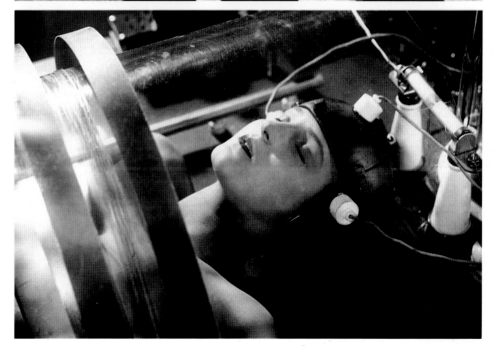

The Blue Angel (*Der blaue Engel*) was the first famous German sound film, although it was made in a dual version (German and English). It marked the international launch of Marlene Dietrich who, thanks to this film and the promising debut of her long-term collaboration with director Josef von Sternberg, came to be considered the female icon of lasciviousness and cynical sensuality. The erotic symbol immortalized here as Lola Lola wears only a corset and black stockings while, provocatively seated on a chair, she bewitchingly sings Frederick Hollander's song "Ich bin die fesche Lola."

Inspired by Heinrich Mann's novel *Professor Unrat*, the film recounts the decline – to the point of abjection – of a respected high-school professor, Immanuel Rath, played by the great actor Emil Jannings (who was memorable in Murnau's silent film *The Last Laugh*).

After discovering that his students go to the Blue Angel cabaret where the singer Lola Lola performs, the professor decides to go there in person, but strictly to catch his students *in flagrante delicto*. However, when he sees Lola's provocative show and the woman's wicked charm, he abandons every inhibition. Rath falls madly in love with the young singer and is willing to do anything to stay by her side. He leaves the school in the city, marries her and follows her in her bohemian lifestyle, which is completely different from the one to which he was accustomed.

His gradual decline toward losing his very soul is unstoppable. Despite the professor's regret over what he has done, he is unable to turn things around and faces all kinds of insults, terrible humiliation and derision. Destitute, he is forced to work as a clown in Lola's troupe, and when they return to his hometown the director of the company, a conjurer, forces him to perform a number that ridicules him. At the height of his mortification, Rath also discovers that another artist has become Lola's new lover. In a fit of jealousy – which marks a burst of dignity yet also proves his madness – he tries to kill her but is stopped and sent to jail. When he is released, he finds the courage to leave the Blue Angel to return to his old school and seek a place to die: his old desk.

1930
THE BLUE ANGEL

Director: JOSEF VON STERNBERG
Cast: MARLENE DIETRICH / EMIL JANNINGS

38 - Here's an image that's familiar to movie-goers of all ages everywhere. The alluring Lola Lola who performs in the seedy and smoky nightclub, Der Blaue Engel, boldly showing her shapely legs with black silk stockings clinging to them.

39 - Actor, Emil Jannings, played the distinguished high-school teacher, Immanuel Rath who fell hopelessly in love with Lola.

Dietrich's gelid and imperturbable demeanor is contrasted by her partner's baroque, grandly outmoded and heartrending performance. This contrast effectively reflected Jannings's background as a silent-film star, as opposed to Dietrich's different and more modern expressiveness. As a whole, the film shows rare power in conveying moral ruin, and the dark victory of vice over bourgeois decorum.

Its 1959 remake by Edward Dmytryck starred Curt Jurgens and May Britt.

Frankenstein was inspired by the novel written by Mary Shelley, wife of the poet Percy Bysshe Shelley. The novel, which was published in 1818, is set in Switzerland in the late 18th century.

One of the best-known and most widespread icons of the popular culture, thanks to 20th-century film adaptations "Frankenstein" became synonymous for monster, although this was actually the name of the scientist who created it.

This is not the only change or strained interpretation that can be found in the screen rendition with respect to the literary original. One example is the chronology, which was moved forward, as can be seen from the clothing, despite the fact that precise historical references are not provided. In any event, the 1931 film was just the first in a long series on the subject.

The boundlessly ambitious young Dr. Henry Frankenstein (Victor in the book; in the film his name is switched with that of his best friend) isolates himself from the scientific community and distances himself from his teacher, Professor Waldman, in order to pursue his mad project. He intends to create life in his laboratory, using his very own hands. In order to achieve this objective, he sets all ethics aside. With the help of his crippled assistant Fritz (transformed into Igor in other film versions), he obtains corpses to use in his experiments, stopping at nothing. He steals newly buried bodies from cemeteries and goes to the gallows to pull down the bodies of men who have been hanged. Moreover, he has Fritz go to the university classroom, where Waldman has just finished his lecture, to steal the brain of a dangerous criminal. The professor has just explained to his students the enormous differences between a "normal" brain – the first one that Fritz steals, but the jar slips from his hands and shatters on the floor – and an "abnormal" one.

Secretly withdrawing to a macabre old mill, Frankenstein is ready. He has built a human body using parts from different corpses and the "abnormal" brain. He is convinced that a complex series of electrical charges he has invented, strengthened by ideal atmospheric conditions (a violent storm is brewing), will breathe life into his "creature." At that very moment, however, his fiancée arrives, accompanied by his friend and his former teacher. Although the professor had banished the brilliant and promising Frankenstein from his classroom, the girl is so worried that she has convinced him to step in. She is convinced that, by going against nature, Frankenstein is exposing himself to enormous risks. In response, Frankenstein – whose plan has now been discovered – invites her to watch the birth of his creature. The monster comes alive, but it immediately becomes clear that the scientist's plan has gone awry.

1931
FRANKENSTEIN

Director: JAMES WHALE

Cast: BORIS KARLOF / COLIN CLIVE / MAE CLARKE / JOHN BOLES

Boris Karloff is the monster created by Doctor Frankenstein.

▶

42 [TOP] - The monster is about to come to life in Dr. Frankenstein's laboratory where his assistant, Fritz, stands by.

42 [CENTER] - After escaping, the monster is free, entering the room of Dr. Frankenstein's fiancé to terrorize her.

42 [BOTTOM] - The monster tries to kill his creator, Dr. Frankenstein.

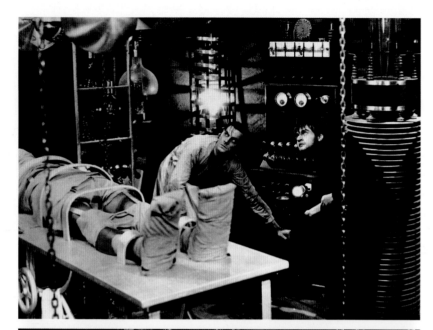

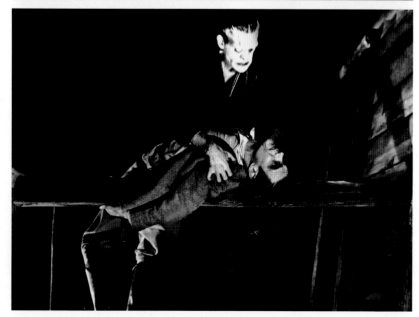

From this point on, the film glosses over the aspects probed by the novel. The violence that the monster perpetrates as he breaks away and flees from his creator is above all a result of fear. In a paradoxical demonstration of Frankenstein's success, the monster is aware and sensitive. He suffers because he realizes that he arouses fear and horror in people, as his appearance – effectively a human collage – terrifies people. As a result, he becomes aggressive and dangerous. When a little girl who trustingly allowed him to approach her and asked him to play drowns, the manhunt launched by the entire village closes in around the creature, ultimately neutralizing it and bringing peace to the population, including Frankenstein, who can finally marry his fiancée.

Produced by Carl Laemmle and Universal Studios the same year as Tod Browning's *Dracula* starring Bela Lugosi, James Whale's film – like *Dracula* – moved beyond the important precedents of silent film (the first version of *The Hunchback of Notre Dame* and *The Phantom of the Opera* starring Lon Chaney) to launch a genre and trademark, a series that would flourish in the 1930s and 1940s. It would become successful again between the 1950s and the 1960s, not only in Hollywood but also Europe (in England with Hammer productions; in Italy with directors Riccardo Freda and Mario Bava), and it ushered in a generational changeover in the star system. Frankenstein, Dracula, the Mummy, the Invisible Man and the Wolf Man were the most famous and successful monsters of the silver screen (and of Universal Studios), and the most important stars connected with horror and monster movies were Boris Karloff (Frankenstein and the Mummy), Bela Lugosi (Dracula), Claude Rains and Lon Chaney, John Carradine, Vincent Price, Peter Cushing and Christopher Lee. There have been numerous parodies, from *Bud Abbott and Lou Costello Meet Frankenstein* (1948) to the 1974 classic by Mel Brooks, *Young Frankenstein*, starring Gene Wilder as the doctor.

It is interesting to note that Boris Karloff's name does not appear in the titles of this version of *Frankenstein*, released in 1931. The name of each character appears next to the name of the actor or actress cast in the role, but the only thing listed next to the word "Creature" is a question mark.

With a skillful play of contrasting light and shadow, and careful dosage of the dual reaction that it inspires in the audience, somewhere between loathing and compassion for his state of unhappiness, the monster is finally neutralized and the village liberated from its nightmare.

Grand Hotel is the mother of the "all-star" scenario and the archetype of films in which several stories are interwoven.

The setting is the Grand Hotel in Berlin in the 1920s. There are six characters, two women and four men. Madame Grusinskaya (Greta Garbo) is a Russian ballet star whose career is waning. Capricious, aloof and volatile, we constantly hear her repeat the order, "Mme Grusinskaya's car is to be brought" – followed by the counter-order, "Mme Grusinskaya's car is not to be brought." The other woman is Flaemmchen (a marvelously sensual Joan Crawford), a modest stenographer who dreams about being a model because she is well aware of her beauty.

Baron von Geigern (John Barrymore) is a penniless aristocrat who is forced to become a hotel thief yet maintains his gentlemanly style. He constantly wanders around the hotel, staying there without ever paying the bill, and awaits his next dupe because ill-intentioned creditors are after him. Regardless of who is involved, however, he always offers a touch of class.

Preysing (Wallace Beery) is a German textile industrialist who is anxiously trying to complete a vital merger in order to save his failing company. An authoritarian and rather uncouth boss, he also appears to be an upright family man. In these circumstances, however, he is at his very worst. Otto Kringelein (Lionel Barrymore) is Preysing's humble employee and has discovered that he is terminally ill. Consequently, he has decided to spend every last cent of his savings to enjoy the kind of life he has never had. Although he is loud, clumsy and pathetic, a climate of sympathy and solidarity is arisen around him.

Lastly, there is the unflappable Dr. Otternschlag (Lewis Stone), who has a burn mark on his handsome face, a reminder of the Great War. He serves as the narrator and conscience of the story, and his is the voice we hear in the famous prologue and, again, in the epilogue: "Grand Hotel. People come, people go. Nothing ever happens."

The characters' destinies cross at the hotel. Grusinskaya, whose fans are turning their backs on her, is theatrically about to give in to disappointment and solitude. But when the baron sneaks into her suite to steal her pearl necklace, he distracts her from her suicidal thoughts and gives her hope, for she falls in love with him and he, in turn, is saved because he returns her feelings. The beautiful stenographer, who was originally courted by the baron, is infatuated with him, but then gives in to the industrialist, who has hired her for the important meeting to finalize the merger. In the end, she too will redeem herself by heading to Paris with Kringelein (and his money).

1932

GRAND HOTEL

Director: EDMUND GOULDING

Cast: GRETA GARBO / JOAN CRAWFORD / JOHN BARRYMORE /
WALLACE BEERY / LIONEL BARRYMORE

"The Grand Hotel: people who come and go, without any purpose at all."

From today's perspective, the confrontation and rivalry between Greta Garbo (above, with John Barrymore) and Joan Crawford (at center, between Lionel Barrymore and Wallace Beery) is resolved clearly in favor of the latter, whose acting is more straightforward, less affected, and more modern.

After Madame Grusinskaya tells the baron that she loves him and asks him to go to Vienna with her, naturally he does not rob her. Still short of money, however, he heads to Preysing's room, where he is caught in the act and killed. Preysing points to his employee as an accomplice – he wants to cover up the murder as well as his dalliance with the stenographer, to which Kringelein has been privy – but finally gets his comeuppance. Once the victim of his boss's arrogance, Kringelein, who had unjustly been fired, gets his revenge by bringing Preysing to justice.

The plot reveals a circular structure: like the revolving doors of the Grand Hotel. This flamboyant melodrama brought Metro-Goldwyn-Mayer enormous fame. It offers a parade of stars whose presence is very carefully dosed. For example, the two leading ladies never appear in the same scene. However, Garbo overacts almost to the point of being ridiculous and, regardless of her dazzling charm, Crawford bests her in terms of controlled gestures and a modern acting style. The two Barrymores use opposite approaches to their characters: John is low-key, whereas Lionel exaggerates. The film is based Vicki Baum's bestseller, *People in a Hotel,* and was personally overseen by MGM tycoon Irving Thalberg. It won the Academy Award for Best Picture.

KING KONG

Director: ERNEST B. SCHOEDSACK

Cast: FAY WRAY /
ROBERT ARMSTRONG / BRUCE CABOT

A film crew headed by director Carl Denham (Robert Armstrong) goes to tropical Skull Island (Sumatra) to make a film in this mysterious setting. The group includes the actress Ann Darrow (Fay Wray). When they arrive, she is kidnapped by the natives, who plan to sacrifice her to the island's enormous gorilla, the last member of a prehistoric species that they worship as a god. The giant gorilla seems pleased with their "gift" and protects her from the threat of other prehistoric animals living on the island.

John Driscoll (Bruce Cabot), the intrepid first mate on the expedition's ship, rescues Ann and Kong is captured, drugged, immobilized and brought to New York to be exhibited as an extraordinary attraction. But Kong manages to break out of the enormous cage in which he is chained, grabs "his" Ann and climbs to the top of the Empire State Building, the city's tallest skyscraper, from which he terrorizes New York until he is finally shot down by an air squadron.

King Kong is one of RKO's most famous films. The corporation, established in the 1920s, prospered during the 1930s and 1940s, but the capricious and volatile management of the extravagant tycoon Howard Hughes marked its final period and the company was dissolved 30 years after it was founded. Along with MGM, Paramount, Warner and Fox it was one of the Big Five; Columbia, Universal and United Artists were known as the Little Three. RKO's fame was tied to prestigious names such as Katharine Hepburn, Fred Astaire and Ginger Rogers, Orson Welles, Alfred Hitchcock and Nicholas Ray, and particularly to Val Lewton's horror films, notably *Cat People* and *The Body Snatcher*.

King Kong was created by Edgar Wallace, an extremely prolific writer who, with Arthur Conan Doyle and Agatha Christie, helped established England's preeminence in the detective and mystery fiction in the early 20th century.

The gigantic prehistoric gorilla, King Kong, captures the beautiful actress, Ann. ▶

The natives on the tropical island, where Ann has arrived with a film crew, abduct her. They intend to sacrifice her to King Kong, whom they venerate as a god.

The film by Merian C. Cooper and Ernest B. Schoedsack represented a new frontier in adventure and fantasy films, thanks to the surprising use of elaborate and innovative special effects; the giant ape was the work of Willis O'Brien. At the same time, it also represented an expressive and poetic apex that reinterpreted the fable of Beauty and the Beast, cogently absorbing the concepts of psychoanalysis albeit in a language targeting the masses. In fact, although its erotic symbolism may have escaped the audiences and critics of the era, this aspect plays a leading role and, amidst exoticism and adventure, it inspires the contradictory blend of terror and attraction evident in the relationship between the damsel and the monster. The film is also a powerful critique of Western imperialism. Despite its civilized appearance, represented by the skyscraper climbed by Kong, the aggressive and essentially savage nature of Western society makes it too a dangerous and impenetrable jungle. The film also lampooned the cynicism of cinema and show business.

There are two mediocre remakes of this marvelous tale: one released in 1976 (with Jessica Lange, with effects by Carlo Rambaldi and produced by Dino De Laurentiis) and a slightly better version made in 2005 (by Peter Jackson and starring Naomi Watts).

51 - This film marks a historical milestone in the invention of special effects with highly spectacular results.

1 ▲
2 ▲
3 ▲

1. 2. 3. Willis O'Brien was the "architect of tricks" who automated King Kong, making actors in ape suits completely unnecessary. He employed a recorded lion's roar for King Kong's howl.

4. 5. 6. In the celebrated finale at the top of the Empire State Building, then the tallest skyscraper in New York, the ape took refuge after abducting Ann, enduring an attack by a squadron of airplanes.

1934

[USA]   Genre: ROMANTIC COMEDY / ROMANCE

IT HAPPENED ONE NIGHT

Director: FRANK CAPRA

Cast: CLARK GABLE / CLAUDETTE COLBERT

It Happened One Night is a veritable gold mine, an archetype and the inspiration for countless imitations and variations on the screwball comedy theme. The capricious heiress Ellie Andrews (Claudette Colbert) jumps off the family yacht and runs away as a protest, because her father is against her marriage to King Westley (Jameson Thomas). Her crusty, authoritarian parent (Walter Connolly) happens to be right, however, because Westley is simply a playboy after her money, but Ellie will not realize this until much later.

Virtually penniless, she boards a Greyhound bus from Miami to New York to meet her beau and during the ride she meets Peter Warne (Clark Gable). Warner, a reporter who has just been fired for drinking on the job and telling his greedy boss exactly what he thinks of him, is well aware that freedom is priceless. Sparks fly as soon as the two meet. Together they will embark on a long and adventurous journey after making a deal: although he treats her like a spoiled young woman, he will help and protect her in exchange for exclusive rights to her story (but the collect telegram he sends his boss is promptly tossed into the wastebasket without even being read). They travel by bus, hitchhike and then steal a car from the person who gave them a ride but the robbed them. In a classic scene, the car stops when she lifts her skirt to show off her legs, although Peter is the one who claims to be an expert on hitchhiking. They sleep in motels and at campsites, dividing the space between their beds by hanging a blanket over a clothesline. These "walls of Jericho" are sacred for someone like Peter who, despite his gruffness, claims to be a gentleman.

During their last overnight stop, when they are just hours away from their destination, Ellie tells him that she loves him. Skeptical, Peter reacts by discouraging her, only to change his mind a short time later, but by this time Ellie has fallen asleep. Peter, who needs money not only to pay for the room but also in order to marry her, leaves her sleeping and heads to New York to write the article for the paper, get paid for it and then return to her. However, just when the happy ending seems to be around the corner, the classic misunderstanding occurs. Ellie is roused by the motel owner and kicked out. Thinking that Peter has left her, she calls her father who, overjoyed to have her back, has decided to let her marry Westley after all, despite his intense dislike for the man. As Peter euphorically heads back to get her, he encounters the convoy of luxury cars that have come to take Ellie home, and in turn is convinced that she has double-crossed and used him. As soon as his editor in chief finds out, he takes Peter's article off the front page and replaces it with another piece, cursing him once again for his shoddy work. As Ellie prepares for her wedding, honest Peter returns his advance to the paper and contacts Ellie's father. He is not interested in the $10,000 dollar reward Mr. Andrews promised to the person who found her, but simply wants to be reimbursed for his expenses during the trip: $39.60. Realizing that the two are in love, the gruff old millionaire will be the one to convince his daughter to leave her fortune hunter before her second wedding and go to the man she truly loves. And, naturally, he suggests that she tear down "the walls of Jericho."

The journalist, Peter Warne (Clark Gable) and the heiress, Ellie Andrews (Claudette Colbert), await transit to New York.

The entire film, and the journey around which it is structured, is dotted with social and human cross-sections of America during the Great Depression. It also mocks moral standards: when Gable undresses we discover that he is not wearing an undershirt and his bare-chested figure – shocking at the time – made him a new male icon. Ellie's wealthy father, conservative in business but modern when happiness is at stake, proves to be more advanced than his daughter when it comes to sentiments and sexual mores, urging her to marry for love and tear down the "walls of Jericho."

1. The beautiful and unpredictable Ellie at a party in her honor.

2. Ellie and Peter find shelter in a motel where they stay in the same room and improvise separate sleeping arrangements.

3. Bundt cake and coffee is the well-known Ellie and Peter breakfast scene.

4. Ellie falls asleep on Peter's shoulder as the first sign of a blossoming love.

▲ 3

▲ 4

There are also many other modern elements, such as motels, buses and hitchhiking, as well as hints of freedom of information – but also the aggressive way in which it is obtained.With its fast pace and brilliant uninhibited dialogue (scripted by Robert Riskin), the film was a model for the golden age of American comedy. It was also an extraordinary personal success for Frank Capra, who fully expressed his optimistic ideology as a "dreamer with his feet on the ground," an approach he spearheaded throughout the Roosevelt era. *It Happened One Night* was the first film in history to win all five major Academy Awards: Best Picture, Best Director, Best Screenplay, Best Actor and Best Actress. It would be impossible to cite all the films that were influenced by it, but two of the most notable examples are *Roman Holiday*, in which the reporter gives up his exclusive story for love, and the wedding scene in *The Graduate*.

1936

MODERN TIMES

Director: CHARLIE CHAPLIN

Cast: CHARLIE CHAPLIN / PAULETTE GODDARD

When *Modern Times* was released in 1936, Charlie Chaplin and his Little Tramp character could already boast not only an endless string of films (starting in 1914) but also at three masterpieces: *The Kid* (1921), *The Gold Rush* (1925) and *City Lights* (1931). Chaplin was already considered an unparalleled figure in cinema – and would remain so – and he masterfully embodied the union of art and popularity, without any class, age or language barriers.

The plot of the film revolves around a complex series of situations. Chaplin plays a factory worker who works on an assembly line. Not only is he subjected to the inhumane and stultifying repetitiveness of the actions he is forced to perform to maintain the production rate, but he is also chosen as a human guinea pig to test a new feeding machine designed to streamline mealtimes as well. The effect is tragicomic.

The nightmare of nuts to tighten – his job – convinces him to tamper with the central parts of the assembly line, blocking it and ultimately getting trapped in its mechanisms. Once he is released from it, he mocks the factory owner and gets sent to an insane asylum.

Finally released from the hospital, he picks up a signal flag that fell off a truck and starts to flutter it to catch the driver's attention, but fails to realize that he has inadvertently placed himself at the head of a march of unemployed workers who are also waving flags (presumably red, like the signal flag, although the film is in black and white). Identified as the demonstrators' leader, he is arrested by the police.

In prison he happens to foil an attempted revolt by the inmates. As a reward, he is pardoned and is given a certificate that should help him get a new job.

Thanks to these credentials, he finds a job at a shipyard. Nevertheless, this position is not destined to last, because he launches an unfinished ship. There is no need to fire him, as he leaves on his own. In his subsequent wandering, he runs into a girl (Paulette Goddard) – the gamine – who lives by her wits after running away from an orphanage, to which she was sent after her unemployed father was killed during a demonstration. In an attempt to get himself arrested so that at least the government will be forced to feed him, when the gamine steals a loaf of bread he takes the blame for it. As a result, both of them are arrested. However, when the paddy wagon transporting them crashes, they run away together.

Victim to hellish machinations, Chaplin is making fun of them. ▶

He finds a job as a night watchman at a department store. During his shift, he lets the gamine in and, undisturbed, the two have a feast in the bakery department. The arrival of three thieves, one of whom a former colleague from the factory who is now unemployed and steals out of need, convinces him to sympathize with them and the thieves join in the feast. Found fast asleep in the clothing department the following day, he is fired and arrested again.

When he is released from jail, he finds the gamine waiting for him, and she invites him back to the shack she has found in the meantime. Reading the paper, he finds out that the factory has opened again, so he returns and is rehired. Once again, however, he gets into trouble, only this time he manages to get his boss trapped in the machinery. He is arrested again and, once more, the gamine is there waiting for him when he is released. The girl has found a job at a restaurant and manages to get him hired as a waiter.

As part of his job, he must also perform as a singer. Terrified that he will not remember the words, he writes them on his cuffs, which he promptly loses. Therefore, he must improvise but his performance is surprisingly a success. Just when things seem to be looking up, two officers come to take the gamine away, as she is still a ward of the state, but he helps her escape. Hand in hand, the two head off for a future together.

The film, which Chaplin had already contemplated making in 1933, after an extremely long tour following the release of *City Lights*, shows the powerful influence of the dire social problems that arose following the stock-market crash of 1929 and that had profoundly disturbed him. In his own way, however, Chaplin also interprets not only the political winds of Europe, in which worrisome dictatorships were gaining power, but also Roosevelt's New Deal. This film was his contribution in favor of the disinherited and it reflects a childlike, fairytale hope for the equitable redistribution of wealth. At the same time, it also shows ironic mistrust of the organized forms of redemption inspired by the Marxist ideology.

In *Modern Times*, made in the second half of the 1930s, Chaplin remains loyal to silent cinema, save the part in which he improvises the words of "Je cherche après Titine" in a sort of Esperanto, blending sounds from French, Spanish and Italian.

60 and 61 - Whether purely as a sign of mistrust or diffidence toward Marxists in the struggle for social class, Chaplin takes a strong stance against capitalism as the source of poverty and unemployment. The U.S. does not welcome the film with open arms and Nazi Germany bans it.

1. 2. Paulette Goddard (1911-1990) becomes Mrs. Chaplin the same year as the film is released. She would divorce him and first marry actor, Burgess Meredith, then writer, Erich Maria Remarque. She would be remembered as one of the actresses who screen- tested for the role of Scarlet O'Hara.

64 - The factory and machines are not in service to man. And the police force is in service to the owners.

1. 2. As the "Tramp," Charlie Chaplin succeeds after an attempted prison escape by receiving a pardon that takes him home, poor but free.

3. In the final image, the Tramp moves away toward the horizon with his comical yet solemn gait, accompanied by the street urchin. That scene motivated generations of people worldwide to perceive it as quintessentially "Chaplinesque." There is still hope for the future despite everything that has transpired in the past.

The action in *Grand Illusion* (*La Grande Illusion*) takes place at the Franco-German front during World War I. Two aviators, Captain de Boeldieu (Pierre Fresnay) and Lieutenant Maréchal (Jean Gabin), the former an aristocrat and the latter a lower-class Parisian, are captured while on a mission. They are gallantly "received" by Captain von Rauffenstein (Eric von Stroheim), who promptly recognizes de Boeldieu as his equal in education and social status. The two French officers, as well as other French soldiers, are sent to a prison camp, where they find other Russian and English prisoners of war.

After spending weeks trying to dig a tunnel, just as they are about to escape they are transferred from this prison. Their new destination is an old fortress from which escape seemed impossible, and the commander here is none other than von Rauffenstein. Although he is disabled and forced to wear a corset, the German officer never forgets the utmost decorum and protocol. At the prison camp, von Rauffenstein attributes the honors of rank to de Boeldieu but overlooks the other prisoners, and does nothing to dissemble his feelings and class prejudices. But the prisoners' goal never changes: escape. De Boeldieu will be the one to come up with a plan, organizing a concert that throws everything into disarray, initially with impromptu flutes (which are confiscated) and then with pots and pans, finally drawing the guards' attention to himself. He thus allows Maréchal and Lieutenant Rosenthal to escape by sacrificing his own life. Indeed, he is killed by none other than von Rauffenstein – the unbending soldier – who begs his forgiveness on his deathbed and honors him with a flower.

Taken in by a peasant, Elsa (Dita Parlo), who has been left alone with her little daughter, the two soldiers continue their journey yet leave their hearts at that farmhouse. They are close to the Swiss border and, by the time an enemy patrol finally sees them, it is too late, as they are already on the other side. Will they return? Maréchal hopes to go back to Elsa as soon as peace is restored, but the war is still far from over.

1937
GRAND ILLUSION

Director: JEAN RENOIR

Cast: PIERRE FRESNAY / JEAN GABIN / ERIC VON STROHEIM / DITA PARLO

The lieutenant marshal (Jean Gabin) is captured during the First World War and is portrayed here in the first days of his imprisonment.

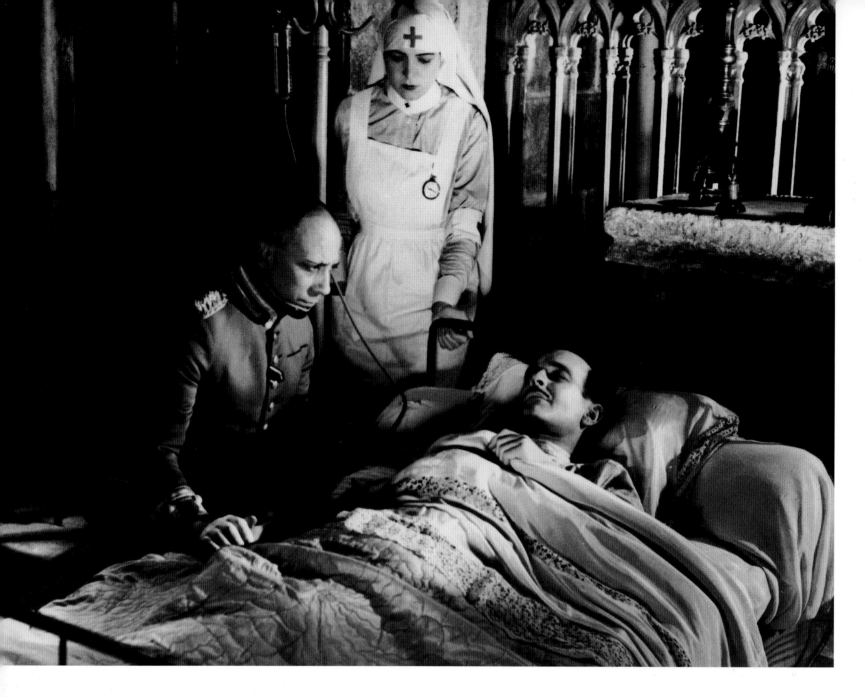

68 - Captain de Boeldieu (Pierre Fresnay) is on his deathbed here, attended by his great enemy, von Rauffenstein (Eric von Stroheim).

Jean Renoir's masterpiece is a classic of pacifism. It was powerfully influenced by the climate in which it was conceived, that of the Front Populaire, but there were unfortunately insinuations about its ambiguity and even suspicions of collaborationism. The director's special touch probed an array of concepts, such as patriotism. For example, Maréchal ends up in isolation for singing "La Marseillaise" while dressed as a woman during a prison-camp play. This is one of the film's most unforgettable scenes, as its power resides in the contrast between ridicule and emotion. Renoir also examined military duty, the solidarity of fellow soldiers, coexistence with prisoners of other nationalities, human compassion, the hatred of war, the futility of boundaries, and the demolition of class, language, religion and racial barriers (Rosenthal is Jewish and another fellow prisoner is black). De Boeldieu and von Rauffenstein represent and defend a world based on the inviolability of these barriers. Yet at the same time they also realize – the Frenchman fatalistic, the German contemptuous – that these barriers are destined to fall.

The film's enormous power stems from the fact that it strives to maintain a positive atmosphere and never gives in to rhetoric.

69 - The dignity and the honor of French prisoners, among whom is the marshal, stands out when faced with incarceration in German prisons.

1939

[USA]   Genre: FANTASY

THE WIZARD OF OZ

Director: VICTOR FLEMING

Cast: JUDY GARLAND / FRANK MORGAN /

RAY BOLGER / JACK HALEY / BERT LAHR / BILLIE BURKE /

MARGARET HAMILTON

Dorothy's crotchety neighbor hates her dog, Toto, so Dorothy (Judy Garland) complains to the entire household, composed of Aunt Em, Uncle Henry and three farmhands. In fact, that very evening the neighbor, Miss Gulch (Margaret Hamilton), comes over on her bicycle to take the dog away with the sheriff's permission. The dog manages to escape and returns to Dorothy, who decides that they must run away from this danger and find the fantastic places she is convinced must lie somewhere over the rainbow.

They promptly encounter Professor Marvel, who tells the girl a white lie and convinces her to go home to her worried aunt. On the way home, however, Dorothy and Toto encounter a tornado. They manage to reach the farm, but by the time they get there everyone else is already in the storm cellar and the doors are locked. They run into the house, but something hits Dorothy on the head and knocks her out.

When she comes to, she discovers that the house is flying through the air because they are in the eye of the tornado. As soon as it lands, Dorothy opens the door and suddenly her entire black-and-white world is transformed into color. In front of her is an extraordinarily beautiful park populated by odd-looking dwarfs called Munchkins. Glinda, the Good Witch of the North (Billie Burke), is the one who tells her what has happened and why everyone is so grateful to her. Dorothy's house landed on the Wicked Witch of the East, killing her and leaving only her ruby slippers intact. Everyone welcomes her, singing and celebrating, until the arrival of the dead witch's sister, the Wicked Witch of the West. The green witch wants the ruby slippers, but they magically land on Dorothy's feet and the woman flies off on her broomstick, swearing that she will get revenge. The only way that Dorothy can escape the witch is to return whence she came, Kansas, and Glinda explains that to get there she must follow the yellow brick road to the Emerald City, the home of the Wizard of Oz, who can help her get home.

There is only one proviso: Dorothy must never take off the ruby slippers. Dorothy and Toto thus set out on their journey through this fantastic world populated by talking trees. The little group grows along the way. The girl and her dog are joined by a Scarecrow (Ray Bolger) who wants to ask the wizard for a brain, a rusty Tin Man (Jack Haley) who wants a heart, and a Cowardly Lion (Bert Lahr) who is unable to sleep because he is even afraid of counting sheep. All five go to ask the great wizard to grant them their wishes. The Wicked Witch of the West tries to obstruct their journey, forcing them to cross a field of poisonous poppies. However, the little group is saved by Glinda, who makes it snow and cancels the spell of the flowers. They finally reach the Emerald City, whose green citizens lead a happy and leisurely life. The population welcomes the group, but then the Wicked Witch of the West arrives and skywrites "Surrender Dorothy" with the smoke from her broomstick. The group knocks on the wizard's door, but he is unwilling to receive anyone. They are finally helped by the guard, who is moved by the story of how young Dorothy was separated from her family.

The wizard (Frank Morgan) humiliates them by sarcastically listing their requests and tells them that he will only help them if they kill the Wicked Witch of the West and bring him her broomstick.

It seems like an impossible task, but the five show their determination and manage to reach the witch's castle, which is protected by an army of flying monkeys. After Dorothy's three companions save her from the clutches of the witch, who is about to kill her, it is Dorothy who, in turn, kills the witch by pouring a bucket of water over her.

72 - *The Wizard of Oz* is celebrated for many things but especially its musical aspect that finds its heart in the song, "Over the Rainbow."

73 - This film was significant for its exaggerated, extreme, and surreal coloration when audiences were still quite unused to film in color, only firmly established later during the decade of the Fifties, with many films still made in black and white through the Sixties. Dorothy's famous ruby slippers are in the photograph below.

They return triumphantly to Oz carrying a broomstick, only to discover that the wizard is actually an imposter. However, he is a goodhearted man who shows the Scarecrow, the Tin Man and the Cowardly Lion that they respectively have a brain, heart and courage.

The wizard promises that he will personally accompany Dorothy to Kansas in his hot-air balloon, but a sudden gust of wind carries him off, leaving the girl behind. Glinda appears and consoles the girl, explaining that she doesn't need anyone's help to go home. Dorothy finally understands her mistake and muses, "If you can't find your heart's desire in your own backyard, then you never really lost it to begin with." To get back to the farm, all she needs to do is close her eyes, click her heels together three times and repeat the words, "There's no place like home." Dorothy reawakens in her bed and her black-and-white world, surrounded by her loved ones. She realizes that the three farmhands have the faces of her three marvelous travel companions and, despite the fact that everyone repeats that she simply had a bad dream after hitting her head, she continues to tell them that everything was real.

Inspired by the children's classic *The Wonderful Wizard of Oz* published by L. Frank Baum in 1900, the first in a long series of Oz books written by Baum and then other authors, the film launched the fantasy genre. Directed by Victor Fleming in 1939, the same year he directed *Gone With the Wind* (in both cases he replaced George Cukor), *The Wizard of Oz* is a landmark in Hollywood superproduction and was released by MGM, the major specializing in musical cinema. It required an enormous investment and the filming was fraught with hundreds of complications, some true and others legendary, but it was destined to become a blockbuster. The film's ambitions are particularly evident in the use of color (Technicolor) - as was also the case with *Gone With the Wind* - and special effects. *The Wizard of Oz* was an enormous personal success for the teenage actress Judy Garland, who was born in 1922. In the casting phase, Garland competed with Shirley Temple - the quintessential child star - and Deanna Durbin for the role. Her rendition of "Over the Rainbow" went on to become famous and has since been reinterpreted in countless versions. The film won two Oscars (Best Song and Best Original Score) in 1940, the year in which the Academy Awards were dominated by *Gone With the Wind*.

NINOTCHKA

Director: ERNST LUBITSCH
Cast: GRETA GARBO / MELVYN DOUGLAS / BELA LUGOSI

Ninotchka, the next-to-last film made by the "divine" Greta Garbo, was released in 1939. Two years later, at the age of just 36, the actress decided to retire after starring in *Two-Faced Woman*. The famous comedy by the Berlin-born Jewish director Ernst Lubitsch, who emigrated to Hollywood in the 1920s and was one of the many Mittel-European actors, directors and screenwriters who fled from Hitler's anti-Semitic rule and bolstered the American film industry.

The tagline "Garbo talks!" was coined when she starred in Lubitsch's first sound film, *Anna Christie* (1930). This time, to underscore the first and only comic role ever played by the Swedish star, the ads announced, "Garbo laughs!"

In the story, the Soviet authorities have confiscated a noblewoman's jewels in order to sell them. Consequently, three officials are sent to Paris to negotiate the sale. However, the owner of the jewels refuses to resign herself and asks her friend Léon, an aristocratic bon vivant (Melvyn Douglas), to corrupt the three coarse and clumsy agents by introducing them to the pleasures and luxuries of bourgeois society. He is so successful that Moscow, represented by the stern People's Commissar (Bela Lugosi, a Hungarian actor who arrived in the United States with the same wave of immigration as Lubitsch and was cast as the first Dracula in 1931), decides to send in a much more inflexible representative than the first three to take charge of the situation.

Thus Nina Ivanovna – or Ninotchka (Garbo) – arrives in Paris. Now the fascinating Léon must lavish his attention on her to soften her stern and scornful demeanor. The beautiful Ninotchka does not give in because she has renounced her ideology but out of love for Léon. And out of love for Léon she also gains a taste for frivolity, such as the little hat she had originally refused to accept.

Indeed, it would be straining things to think that the director's goal was political satire, as this work is a provocative and alluring *divertissement*. Following the advent of sound film, the 1930s marked the golden age of Lubitsch's comedies and his elegant sense of humor, conveyed through brilliant dialogue and repartee, and the art of subtly mischievous situations and piquantly erotic allusions. In short, it encompassed what came to be defined as the inimitable "Lubitsch touch."

Although she would never have been a comedienne, Garbo's performance left audiences with a sense of regret over the many lost opportunities, before and after, to play roles other than the typecast *femme fatale* role created by film studios – much to Garbo's own chagrin.

The screenplay was written by Charles Brackett and Billy Wilder. The latter would prove to be the most important heir of Lubitsch's light and pungent art, though he was ultimately less light-hearted and far more scathing.

"Garbo laughs!" was the campaign slogan for the goddess' penultimate performance on the silver screen.

76 - A beautiful inspector and Bolshevik all in one package, the "associate," Ninotchka, goes from Moscow down to Paris to manage operations of three Soviet agents who have allowed themselves to be seduced by capitalist pleasures.

1. 2. 3. Unlike her greedy and corruptible partners, Ninotchka does not resist love and gives in to the charms of Count Leon (Melvyn Douglas) with whom she falls in love, despite opposing ideologies. Ernst Lubitsch plus Charles Brackett and Billy Wilder complete the perfect ensemble for comedy.

19**39**

[USA]   Genre: **WESTERN**

STAGECOACH

Director: **JOHN FORD**

Cast: **THOMAS MITCHELL / JOHN WAYNE / JOHN CARRADINE / CLAIRE TREVOR**

Stagecoach is the mother of all Westerns, or rather of all "mature" Westerns, those from the genre's golden age, which lasted approximately 20 years. In fact, the genre had already flourished during the "childhood" of cinema, thanks above all to rich serial productions in the style of Tom Mix.

The year is 1880. Traveling on a stagecoach that is going from the little town of Tonto, Arizona, to Lordsburg, crossing dangerous and treacherous areas with hostile Indians, is a small but varied group of people who programmatically seem to exemplify the society of the era. Yet perhaps this social cross-section of conformism and prejudices, solidarity and emotions, also reflects society of all eras. In effect, John Ford directed his masterpiece in 1939, at the height of the New Deal, and the philosophy that runs through the most classic example of the most classic American genre is powerfully permeated by the Roosevelt spirit.

Seven men and women gradually get into the stagecoach. One is the pregnant wife a cavalry officer. Hatfield is a professional gambler and a Southern gentleman. We also find a timid whiskey salesman, a marshal, the prostitute Dallas, who has been run out of town for offending decency and morality, the alcoholic doctor Boone and a dishonest banker. The seven are finally joined by Ringo, who has been accused of a crime he did not commit and is on his way to Lordsburg to avenge his father and brother by killing their murderers, the three Plummer Brothers.

1. 2. 3. An unjustly hunted gunman and a prostitute with a good heart, the boundless prairie, armed confrontation and a handful of pursuers against the overpowering Indian forces, a reversal in the desperate situation thanks to "our guys" arriving unexpectedly at a gallop among flags flying and bugles announcing the charge. This is the archetype of the western, diligently conveying a microcosm of weaknesses and heroic acts at its heart.

The stagecoach sets out despite the news of an imminent Indian attack, underestimating the true risk involved. It is destined to be a very intense and metaphorical journey that will reveal the true nature of each of the travelers. Above all, it will allow the outcasts to redeem themselves and the others – at least those in good faith – to see them in a new light. When the pregnant woman gives birth in a situation of extreme hardship, she is assisted and saved by the prostitute and the alcoholic doctor, two figures who would become iconic in the history of Westerns and would be replicated time and again. When it comes time to face the Indian attack before the cavalry comes in to save the group, the outlaw Ringo and the scornfully cynical Southern gentleman – who gets killed in the process – are the ones who instill courage.

When they reach their destination, the marshal allows Ringo to carry out his vendetta and escape to Mexico with Dallas, the prostitute.

The film's most memorable moment is the sweeping sequence of the Indian attack, the pursuit of the stagecoach and the arrival of the cavalry. It is a demonstration of virtuoso technical skill, shot from a camera car running parallel to the stagecoach and supposedly moving at a speed of about 38 mph. This famous sequence was shot in Monument Valley, which became the sanctuary and quintessence of the Western epic thanks to this film.

Written by Dudley Nichols based on a story that, in turn, was inspired by one of Guy de Maupassant's short stories, *Stagecoach* won two Academy Awards. Thomas Mitchell was awarded the Oscar for Best Supporting Actor (he played the drunken physician, the "Doc" character who, in countless guises, would appear many later Westerns). The other Oscar was for Best Music; the score was based on traditional folk tunes.

Ford had not made a Western since the mid-1920s and, thanks to *Stagecoach*, he would enjoy a prolific and glorious season as the bard of the American frontier.

Gone With the Wind is not simply a movie: it is a monument. The figures speak for themselves. It is 3 hours and 40 minutes long and cost $4 million to make – in the late 1930s! Until the 1970s it held the record in terms of box-office receipts and has yet to be beaten when it comes to the number of viewers. Margaret Mitchell's bestseller (1936), on which it was based, has sold 60 million copies thanks to the fame of this motion picture, and Mitchell received $50,000 for the film adaptation rights. It won 8 Academy Awards, including Best Supporting Actress, which went to Hattie McDaniel (who played Mammy) and was the first Oscar ever awarded to an African-American. Nevertheless, for racial reasons the actress was not invited to the gala première, held in Atlanta – in segregated Georgia – on December 15, 1939.

Despite the fact that a dozen authors were involved in adapting the novel and penning the screenplay (most of whom, including F. Scott Fitzgerald, were not listed in the credits) the true author and tyrannical master of the film was David O. Selznick. It was "officially" directed by Victor Fleming, stepping in to replace George Cukor, who had already started filming. However, it was also the handiwork of screenwriter William Cameron Menzies, who had a profound influence on the final work as well as the dazzling Technicolor photography.

Before the unknown English actress Vivien Leigh (Sir Laurence Olivier's future wife) was chosen for the role of Scarlett O'Hara, other notables were considered, including Paulette Goddard, Susan Hayward, Miriam Hopkins, Katharine Hepburn, Carole Lombard, Jean Arthur, Joan Crawford and Tallulah Bankhead. Clark Gable was cast as Rhett Butler, supposedly for the sum of $120,000, but one of the candidates before him was Errol Flynn, who would have been paired with Bette Davis as Scarlett.

It is the epic and melodramatic story of Scarlett O'Hara, a strong-willed, independent and fickle young landowner who lives through the American Civil War and the ensuing catastrophe that destroyed the Confederate Army, and the Southern economy and way of life. She is in love with the fragile Ashley (Leslie Howard), but he marries the gentle Melanie (Olivia de Havilland) instead.

Meanwhile, between one loveless marriage and the next, Scarlett continues to play cat and mouse with the manly and arrogant adventurer, Rhett Butler. Despite their mutual attraction, they will never understand each other and are condemned to endless cycles of love and hatred that never mesh. Both are too strong-willed and this ultimately undermines any chance for happiness. When the tearful Scarlett begs him – too late – not to leave, pleading, "Rhett, if you go, where shall I go? What shall I do?" he responds with one of the cinema's most memorable lines: "Frankly, my dear, I don't give a damn." The unforgettable and timeless last scene of the film is accompanied by Scarlett's legendary words, "I'll think of some way to get him back. After all, tomorrow is another day!"

1939
GONE WITH THE WIND

Director: **VICTOR FLEMING**

Cast: **VIVIEN LEIGH / CLARK GABLE / HATTIE MCDANIEL / LESLIE HOWARD / OLIVIA DE HAVILLAND**

This is certainly the most famous frame in all the history of film. Rhett holds the spirited Scarlet in his manly arms.

Against the backdrop of an ultraconservative and traditionalistic story that is a deplorable manifesto of racism and slavery, a nostalgic tableau of values that have rightfully been condemned by history, these closing words recap the invincible strength and modernity of the film's leading character. Her words are also emblematic of the power and sheer longevity of a film that has become the quintessence of America's culture, spirit and history. Indeed, it is the highest and most genuine expression of American cinema: a true legend.

83 - Leslie Howard is Ashley, the fragile Southern gentleman who is loved by Scarlet but who marries the meek and mild Melanie (below) instead, played by Olivia de Havilland.

84 and 85 - The epic film, *Gone With the Wind* is also holds one of the most impressive records. It lasts 3 hours and 40 minutes and had a $4 million budget (in 1939). With the highest box-office receipts until the Sixties, *Gone With the Wind* had no match in the minds of a great number of spectators.

86 and 87 - The conflicted love between Rhett Butler and Scarlett O'Hara seems to thrive throughout the entire film with both of them failing to ever be on the same wavelength. Their respective pride and mutual show of contempt for each other lead Rhett to respond to a late demand that she needed him with a cocky, "Frankly, my dear, I don't give a damn." But Scarlet would recover from these breakups; in the end she reacts with "I'll think about that tomorrow." "After all, tomorrow's another day."

< After all, tomorrow is another day! >

Citizen Kane can truly be defined as legendary: the most legendary film in the history of cinema. Nevertheless, it was only with time that it was finally acknowledged as such, demonstrating that this status becomes evident only in retrospect. It was not immediately understood, and was opposed and criticized above all in United States. Europe did not acknowledge its importance until after World War II, thanks also to the illustrious opinions of notables such as Jorge Luis Borges and Jean-Paul Sartre.

Orson Welles was just 26 years old when the film was released in May 1941, but he was already cloaked in the aura of the "baroque" genius. This work – colossal in every sense – would merely serve to enhance his reputation. His extraordinary cinema debut was preceded by the early fame of his daring theatrical productions and, above all, the sensationalism surrounding his 1938 CBS radio adaptation of H.G. Wells' science-fiction novel *The War of the Worlds*. The horrifying simulated chronicle of a Martian invasion of Earth panicked listeners across the country, giving the 23-year-old *enfant terrible* widespread notoriety. Thanks to the fame of this episode, Welles was given a contract by the RKO film production company, guaranteeing him extraordinary independence with respect to the rules of the studio system, which were extremely rigid at the time. Granting a director control over his film was virtually unheard of.

Orson Welles' debut and the creation of his masterpiece also represent Hollywood's historical first step toward what would become the modern concept of auteur cinema.

The film investigates the character of Charles Foster Kane, played by Welles and manifestly inspired by media tycoon William Randolph Hearst, who owned a vast empire in the field of mass communications, and it commences with Kane's desperate, lonely death.

Following an initial sequence that introduces us to the mansion – as gloomy and monumental as a mausoleum – that Kane has built to crown his delusions of grandeur (it is called Xanadu), we are shown his deathbed. As he dies, he drops a glass snowball containing a little cottage and utters an enigmatic last word: Rosebud.

This inspires a journalist to examine Kane's life and, based on that last word (although only the audience heard it; this marks is one of the many challenges contained in the film), he decides to talk to the people closest to him.

ntrepreneur Charles Foster Kane (Orson Welles) acts as an aggressive editor and unscrupulous manager, impulsively times ownership of the "New York Enquirer," a failing newspaper, bringing it to inconceivable levels of distribution.

1941
CITIZEN KANE

Director: ORSON WELLES

Cast: ORSON WELLES / JOSEPH COTTEN

The reporter speaks to Kane's second wife, a mediocre opera singer, as well as his butler and his two closest assistants in the unscrupulous journalistic venture of the *New York Inquirer*, a prestigious and professional but failing newspaper that Kane buys on a whim and, through gossip columns and political blackmail, transforms into a national chain and money machine. The reporter's goal is to discover the meaning of Rosebud, which may be a key to revealing Kane's secret and penetrating the enigma of a life of immense ambition, daring projects, tenacious and peremptory self-affirmation, and reckless competitiveness in business, politics and emotions. Yet Kane's life ends ingloriously through his own selfishness: in the end Kane's last nostalgic thought is for his humble origins. Rosebud was the name of a small sled, the only toy that, as a child, he had enjoyed before an unexpected legacy took him away from his natural family to deliver him to his fate of wealth and power.

Citizen Kane had an enormous and scandalous impact in terms of content. Its air of condemnation, an apologue of the American way of exploiting the power of money, was so incisive that Hearst's newspaper and radio network completely boycotted the film, and there was a very heavy-handed attempt not only to block the film but also to discredit the director. Although it was nominated for nine Academy Awards, it only won the Oscar for Best Original Screenplay, which was written by Welles with Herman J. Mankiewicz.

On a stylistic level, it is as revolutionary as the Russian classics and German expressionist films had been and as the masterpieces of Italian Neorealism were destined to be. Through the eye of cinematographer Gregg Toland and his choice of lenses creating greater depth of field, using "Expressionist" lighting and low-angle shots, the film attempted solutions so daring that they broke the established rules of the grammar and syntax of cinema.

1. 2. 3. The debut film of the young genius, Orson Welles, encounters many obstacles because his Charles Foster Kane is a transparent allusion to the mass media magnate, William Randolph Hearst, who made every effort to stop the release of this cruel portrait of a devious man.

1 ▶

2 ▶

3 ▶

92 [LEFT] - In despair, Kane dies alone in the lavish Xanadu residence where he lives with his second wife, invoking the unhappy childhood memory of "Rosebud." However, no one realizes that this was the name of the small sled with which he played as a child.

92 [RIGHT] - Kane's right-hand man (Joseph Cotten) is also his conscience and the only one who dared to oppose him.

Dorothy Comingore interprets the role of the ruthless Kane's second wife, a mediocre opera singer. ▶

CASABLANCA

Director: MICHAEL CURTIZ

Cast: HUMPHREY BOGART / INGRID BERGMAN /
PAUL HENREID / DOOLEY WILSON / CONRAD VEIDT / CLAUDE RAINS

If the term "legendary" were not a meaningless cliché, *Casablanca* could be defined as the quintessential legend. Indeed, it is likely that no other film fits the bill this well.

Made in 1941 and released in 1942, it represents the film industry's most extraordinary and effective contribution to the anti-Nazi and anti-Fascist cause and to promoting the democratic patriotism of the Allies. Indeed, cinema is a language accessible to immense numbers of people and, in this case, it was used to create a miraculous mélange of adventure, espionage and romance.

During World War II, the Moroccan port of Casablanca was a crossroads of adventurers and a den of spies. In this setting, the American Rick Blaine (Humphrey Bogart) is a voluntary expatriate, fleeing from a past – about which we can only guess – of broken romances and freedom fighting. His nightclub, Rick's Bar, attracts all and sundry: German officers such as Strasser (Conrad Veidt) and French policemen such as Renault (Claude Rains). After all, Morocco was a French colony and a collaborationist government was set up after France was occupied by the Third Reich in 1940. Consequently, Renault is Strasser's reluctant "friend." Ambiguous figures of all kinds patronize the club: dealers in arms and documents, profiteers, people trying to make easy money and gamblers (the minor characters played by Sydney Greenstreet and Peter Lorre are memorable), but also anti-Fascist patriots and resistance fighters.

One of them is Victor Laszlo (Paul Henreid), who heads the Czech Resistance and has illegally arrived in Casablanca with his wife Ilsa (Ingrid Bergman). He desperately needs a letter of transit that will allow him to go somewhere safe so that he can continue his work.

As destiny would have it, Rick has two of these safe-conducts, but Ilsa also happens to be the woman who jilted him in Paris but with whom he is still in love. In the name of that love, now over, he has donned the mask of the cynical loner. But in the name of a love that might be rekindled, Rick is prepared to use the safe-conducts for himself and for her. Indeed, was that love ever really over in the first place? No: Ilsa had her own good reasons for pretending it was. He wants them to leave together, start living again and perhaps even fight for this noble cause.

None of this is meant to be. Rick will ultimately redeem himself, acting like a true hero, but relinquishing love in the process. He understands that he must step aside, that Ilsa – who is ready to go away with him – must stay with Victor, and that Victors needs both Ilsa and the safe-conduct more than he does. And so we come to the poignant final scene: the airport, a plane on the runway, a foggy night, lights that slice through the inky darkness, raincoats and broad-rimmed hats. All of these elements have become iconic. (Woody Allen's *Play It Again, Sam* is one of the most notable tributes and allusions to the film.)

The disenchanted Rick found refuge in Casablanca, but events in his past soon catch up to him. ▶

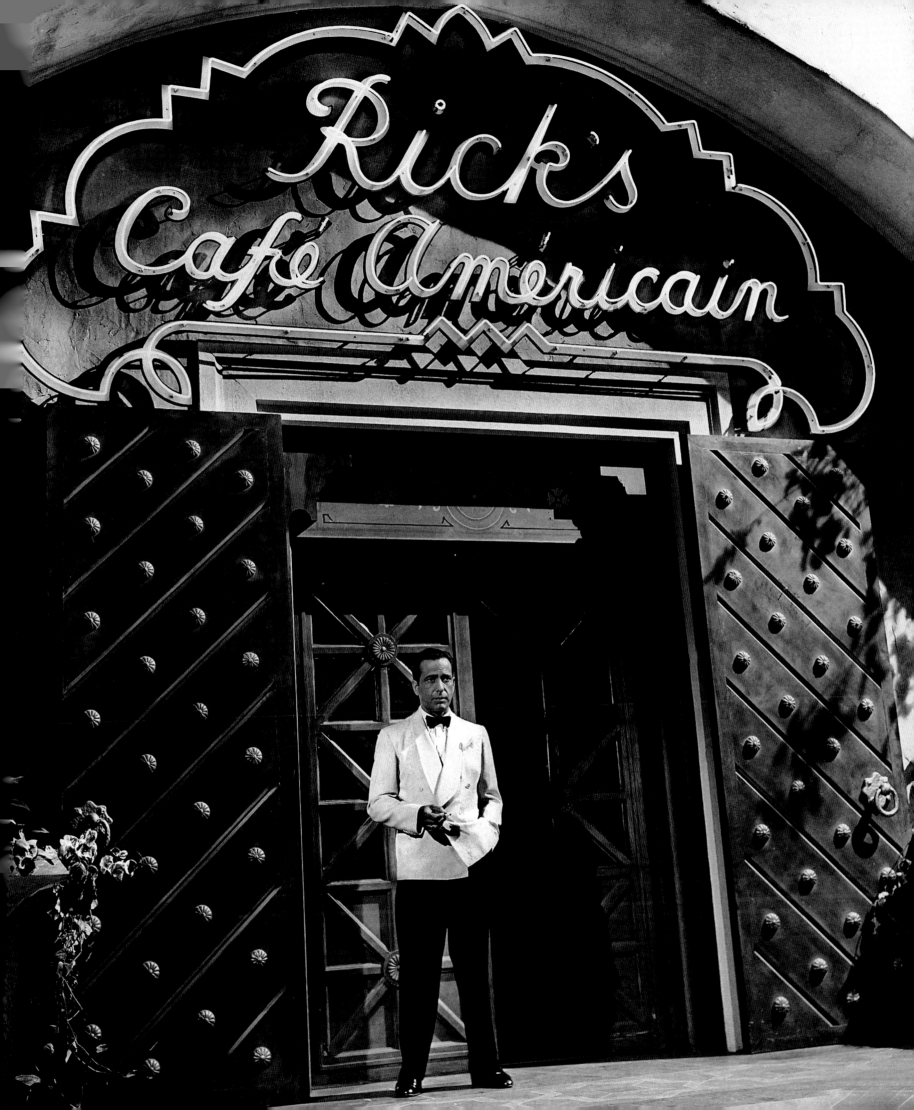

After saying goodbye to Ilsa, who leaves with Victor, Rick and Captain Renault are ready to set aside their bitterness and failures, and make every effort to ensure that democracy and good can ultimately triumph.

One of the elements that made the film so famous is "As Time Goes By," the song that the pianist Sam (Dooley Wilson) plays and that Ilsa and Rick consider "their" song. Umberto Eco's trenchant comment says it all. "When all the archetypes burst out shamelessly, we plumb the depths of Homeric profundity. Two clichés make us laugh but a hundred clichés move us."

The film won three Academy Awards in 1944: Best Picture, Best Director and Best Adapted Screenplay.

96 - After procuring a permit for Ilsa and Victor, "a beautiful friendship is born" between Rick and Captain Renault." Overcoming their respective skepticism, they fulfill their duty with a final victory in democracy.

<Play It Again, Sam>

97 - "Play It Again, Sam," still plays
our song, "As Time Goes By."
There is still a great love between Ilsa
and Rick, sacrificed on the altar of
loyalty to the ideals of the Resistance.

98-99 - The farewell between the two,
Humphrey "Bogey" Bogart and Ingrid
Bergman, breaks our hearts but we
know that it's for a good cause. When
the outcome of the war against Hitler
was still uncertain, Casablanca was a
powerful vehicle for war propaganda.

Although it was made in 1941, *Arsenic and Old Lace* was not released until 1944 in order to avoid detracting from the enormous Broadway success of Joseph Kesselring's comedy, on which it is based. Frank Capra's famous film is exemplary in the history of the great comedy of Hollywood's golden age, despite the fact that diverges enormously from the fundamental ideological inspiration and populist optimism that characterized the enormous contribution made by the Italian-American director during the period of the Great Depression and Roosevelt's New Deal.

The story, which is set entirely in the old Brewster house, revolves around a brilliant theater critic Mortimer Brewster (Cary Grant), who – going against his profound convictions against marriage – has fallen in love with and married Elaine (Priscilla Lane). Immediately after the wedding, the couple decides to go visit his two elderly and extravagant aunts, Abby and Martha, who live with their other nephew, Mortimer's brother Teddy. Teddy, who is somewhat unbalanced, thinks he is President Theodore Roosevelt and, wearing a helmet, every so often he shouts "Charge!" and dashes down to the basement, where he says he's digging the Panama Canal.

Mortimer discovers a corpse in one of the chests and immediately blames Teddy's madness, deciding that his brother must immediately be sent to an asylum. However, the sweet old aunts guilelessly explain that it was all their doing and that this was not the first victim of their "charities." In fact, the old women gently put an end to the lonely lives of elderly men by giving them a poisonous cocktail. The corpse that Mortimer found, like all the previous corpses, is in the basement until Teddy can bury them, as the aunts take advantage of his conviction that he is digging the Panama Canal.

Mortimer is unable to find a solution to the dilemma and to complicate matters even further another brother, the despicable Jonathan, arrives in the company of an alcoholic plastic surgeon, Dr. Einstein. The latter are played by Peter Lorre (Einstein) and Raymond Massey (Jonathan), whom the doctor has disfigured. As a result, Jonathan closely resembles the quintessential Hollywood monster, Boris Karloff in his makeup (the most famous Frankenstein on the screen and later Imhotep in *The Mummy*), a resemblance that sparks fits of anger whenever it is mentioned to Jonathan. In the theater version it was Boris Karloff who played the role of Jonathan, poking fun at himself, but Karloff was unavailable for the film and the director was forced to cast someone else. In any event, the two have arrived with their own corpse to dispose of, so they decide to use the aunts' strategy. The women, however, are against this, claiming that their corpses are of a different caliber than the one their killer nephew wants to conceal.

1944

ARSENIC AND OLD LACE

Director: FRANK CAPRA

Cast:

CARY GRANT / PRISCILLA LANE /

PETER LORRE / RAYMOND MASSEY /

JOSEPHINE HULL / JEAN ADAIR

The brilliant drama critic and previously confirmed bachelor, Mortimer Brewster, discovers the horrible traffic of corpses in the home of his pure and innocent little old aunts.

1. 2. 3. 4. Masterpiece of "screwball" comedy (not exactly typical of Frank Capra but still unique and formidable), *Arsenic and Old Lace* unites an ensemble of top-notch actors and character actors: Cary Grant, Edward Everett Horton (the director of the mental hospital), Raymond Massey, Peter Lorre (Mortimer's evil brother and his disreputable plastic surgeon), and the two unforgettable little old ladies, Josephine Hull and Jean Adair.

In the meantime, Mortimer – who risks being killed by the irascible Jonathan – has no idea how to proceed, and the head of the asylum (the outstanding character actor Edward Everett Horton), who was called in by Mortimer, also runs the risk of being poisoned. Desperately convinced that he belongs to a family of lunatics, Mortimer sends his wife away for her own good. In the end, however, after he manages to consign the criminals to the police and the lunatics to the asylum, Mortimer can finally heave a sigh of relief when his aunts inform him that he is not really a Brewster but a "bastard."

In addition to being a veritable gold mine of ideas in the areas of drama, writing, acting and *mise en scène* – a gold mine that makes this brilliant work one of the finest examples of what is known as "screwball comedy" – *Arsenic and Old Lace* is also a demonstration of sly anti-conformism, dark humor and macabre entertainment that pokes fun at priggish clichés regarding love, marriage and family.

5. Among many, the most amusing thing in this film is that Capra cannot get Boris Karloff (Frankenstein) from the previous theatrical version on set, so has Raymond Massey made up to look as much like Karloff's Frankenstein as possible. However, the character of Jonathan is a brutal assassin, has his physical characteristics altered in order to escape justice, yet the surgeon's error has made him horribly similar to Frankenstein, and he becomes a beast when reminded of his unwanted resemblance to the monster.

ROME, OPEN CITY

Director: ROBERTO ROSSELLINI
Cast: ANNA MAGNANI / ALDO FABRIZI / MARCELLO PAGLIERO

Roberto Rossellini's *Rome, Open City* (*Roma città aperta*) is the emblem of the Neorealist movement and of the revival of Italian democracy following the fall of Mussolini. However, it also marks a historical watershed in cinematographic language: Hollywood itself has acknowledged that the history of cinema can be divided into a "before" and "after" *Rome, Open City*. Its unprecedented sense of immediacy and truthfulness is due in part to choices made in the field, but can also be attributed to the sheer lack of equipment, as the film was adventurously made immediately after the liberation of Rome (June 1944), at a time when other parts of Italy were still controlled by the enemy.

There are three main characters: Pina, a lower-class Roman widow about to be remarried, the priest Don Pietro (Aldo Fabrizi) and the Communist engineer Manfredi, a Resistance leader in Rome (Marcello Pagliero). Their destinies entwine during the nine months of the German occupation of the capital, declared an "open city" due to the presence of the Holy See, following the bombing of San Lorenzo in July 1943 and the appalling massacre of the Ardeatine Caves (March 1944).

Manfredi needs to hide and he gets help from Don Pietro and Pina's proletarian family. Pina's fiancé is captured and – in a scene etched in our collective memory – as she runs after him she is shot down by the Germans in front of her young son. The priest, arrested and tortured by the Gestapo, is brought before a firing squad and Manfredi, who has been handed over to the Germans by an informer, is tortured to death in front of the priest, who curses their persecutors. Despite their sacrifice – or possibly because of it – the struggle will continue after them and in their name.

The enormous importance of this film is paralleled by the debate that it has sparked over time. Objections and observations, all of which revolve around the idea that the work is based on compromises, have been posited not only on aesthetic grounds but also on political and ideological ones.

First of all, *Rome, Open City* necessarily represents a transition. The presence of two highly recognizable stars – Fabrizi and Magnani – who had already gained enormous fame, and the choice of a tone that encompasses both melodramatic and lighter elements link the film to the previous season. Only in part does it anticipate the radicalization of Rossellini's other two masterpieces in the "war trilogy" (*Paisà* and *Germany Year Zero*) or the extreme austerity of De Sica's *Umberto D*. The fact that Pina, who already has a child, is living with a man and is compelled to legalize their relationship represents a fascinating aside in this film, underscoring the nonconformism of the lower classes and of those who fought against tyranny.

From a political and ethical standpoint, the film is indeed the outcome of compromise, but one that reflects the director's philosophy rather than mere opportunism. While the character played by Magnani was directly inspired by the case of the anti-Fascist martyr Teresa Gullace, Fabrizi's combines the true stories of Don Morosini and Don Pappagallo, priests who were arrested and killed by the occupying forces because they collaborated with the Resistance. However, the film character accentuates unarmed Christian testimony and overlooks

1. 2. 3. This is the most famous sequence in the film and in all of Italian neorealistic cinema. Pina rebels against the Germans that are searching the apartment building where the woman lives. They capture her man, Francesco, and take him away as she calls out his name, following the truck as it moves away. A spray of sub-machine gunfire brutally stops her when her young son Marcello runs to embrace his mother, who is now dead. This image has traveled around the world, establishing Anna Magnani as a symbol of a film genre that is not just Italian.

the fact that the reference models were active freedom fighters. The voice of screenwriter Sergio Amidei, a Communist who was in close contact with the party's clandestine leaders, carried enormous weight in the conception of *Rome, Open City*, as his goal with the story was to exalt and praise the Communist contribution to the liberation effort. Rossellini, who had different political viewpoints that were unquestionably less rigid from an ideological standpoint and possibly more in favor of populism, instead sought a balance that prefigures the political equilibrium of the postwar and post-Mussolini period. This balance was founded on the collaboration but also the difficult coexistence of two cultures and "families" that played a leading role in Italy: Catholicism and Marxism. Furthermore, Rossellini "altered" real events, downplaying the active and bloody participation of Fascist soldiers and placing all the blame on the Germans. This decision portended the hope of national pacification and a way to overcome the trauma of civil war.

Nevertheless, these debates are confined to the arena of film studies and have never tarnished the power of this film, nor its aesthetic and civic message.

It won the Grand Prix at the first Cannes Film Festival in 1946, and the screenplay by Sergio Amidei, who also relied on numerous assistants (including Fellini), was nominated for an Academy Award.

19 46

GILDA

Director: CHARLES VIDOR

Cast: RITA HAYWORTH / GLENN FORD

Gilda is set in Buenos Aires: Johnny Farrell (Glenn Ford), an adventurer with a mysterious past, is attacked in a dark corner of the port and saved by the cold, enigmatic Ballin Mundson (George Macready), who always carries an elegant cane that conceals a lethal steel blade. The two men make a deal and Farrell now owes his life to Mundson. They meet at Mundson's luxurious illegal casino, to which the authorities turn a blind eye. The two get into a fight when Mundson discovers that Farrell won by cheating, but then they become inseparable. Nevertheless, Mundson is the master and Farrell his guard dog, albeit one in a tuxedo. The story plays out in front of a wily and philosophical casino employee, Uncle Pio (Steven Geray), who called Farrell "a peasant" the first time the two met but would watch over him and providentially save his life a second time – this time protecting him from none other than his initial benefactor.

Mundson is actually using the casino as a cover for trafficking in tungsten, in which he is working with ex-Nazis. He is being investigated by the policeman Obregon (Joseph Calleia), likewise a philosopher and, in the end just as providential as Uncle Pio. Returning from a mysterious trip, Mundson is accompanied by a woman he introduces to Farrell as his wife. Gilda (Rita Hayworth), a stunning nightclub singer, turns out to be the woman who made Farrell's life so unhappy and she represents everything from which he is trying to escape. Mundson, who notices the palpable mutual hostility between the two, puts Farrell's loyalty to the test by assigning him to follow and protect Gilda. Johnny performs his assignment, loyal to his friend and boss, contemptuous towards the woman. Yet passion still lurks beneath the surface, despite the fact that he does everything to punish her by punishing himself.

Forced to flee, Mundson – unseen – catches them embracing before he stages his own disappearance. He plans a fake plane accident and his scheme succeeds, as everyone believes he is dead. Farrell comes forward to take his place – also as Gilda's husband – but continues to punish her as well as himself. It is Obregon who finally opens his eyes and helps him understand that Gilda has always loved him and that, despite appearances, she has always been faithful to him. At this point, however, Mundson reappears to take revenge but, thanks to Uncle Pio, he is betrayed by his deadly cane. This weapon acquires unexpected significance and reflects the cynical prophecy uttered by Farrell at the very beginning: that the dagger is like a woman. "It looks like one thing, and then right in front of your eyes, it becomes another thing."

Rita Hayworth's poignantly ingratiating sensuality is the secret to the enormous success of this film. ▷

108 - When Gilda sings "Put the Blame on Mame," slipping off her black satin glove, the atomic bomb explodes.

109 - At left, the famous scene of the barely suggestive yet explosive striptease. Erotic promise and purity, cynicism and innocence, naïveté and enchanting expressions, all belie an undercurrent of perversion and corruption. Despite the precarious and unstable balance of the film's plotline, this blend is really what makes Gilda an unforgettable character and an incredible symbol of a post-war period full of opposing sentiment, somewhere between disenchantment and a hope for something better. Gilda's complex character truly launched the career of this famous actress.

Despite a feverish and incredibly muddled plot full of overblown baroque twists - the exact opposite of the linearity of a previous but closely related film, *Casablanca* - the aesthetic and visual expressiveness of Charles Vidor's film emerges thanks to the extraordinary *noir* aura achieved by Rudolph Maté's stunning photography, and it is considered a Hollywood legend.

The character of Gilda, one of the film industry's most memorable dark ladies, turned Rita Hayworth (married to Orson Welles at the time) into a superstar and the embodiment of a powerful blend of intriguing cynicism, childlike innocence and explosive sensuality: a true bombshell. Hayworth was dubbed by Anita Ellis when she sang "Put the Blame on Mame" and "Amado mio," although we hear her own voice in the version she sings accompanied by a guitar. Nevertheless, her seductive moves and, above all, her enticing air of expectation as she languidly pulls off her black satin glove during the casino performance have become the unforgettable icons of pure eroticism on the screen.

▶

Glenn Ford is Farrell. Gilda would like to give him her body and soul to and he also desires her above anything else. Life seems to have decided otherwise.

110 - Gilda knew how to be bitter, cynical, and callous, but also tender and defenseless like a child. She plays the guitar, regretting a time when, before marrying the rich and shady Mundson, she was simply a singer and dancer, engaging in conversation with the waiter-philosopher, "Uncle Pio," and when she abandoned Mundson, not deserving him yet still finding a safe harbor in him. However, the flame of contradictory passion between her and Farrell was about to re-ignite.

IT'S A WONDERFUL LIFE

Director: FRANK CAPRA

Cast: JAMES STEWART / HENRY TRAVERS / DONNA REED / THOMAS MITCHELL / LIONEL BARRYMORE

It's a Wonderful Life is pure perfection. It is one of those extremely rare cases in which a masterpiece is also an enormously popular hit that is accessible to all audiences. At the same time it is the greatest and most faithful representation of the American ideology.

It is Christmas Eve and the life of George Bailey (James Stewart) hangs by a thread. Help from "up there" is the only thing that can save him. God and St. Joseph assign the next available angel to the job, Angel Second Class Clarence Odbody, who has not earned his wings yet. In order to prepare for his assignment, Clarence reviews George's entire life.

In 1919, twelve-year-old George is playing with his friends on a frozen pond when his little brother Harry falls in, but George saves him. A few years later, he works for a local pharmacist who, crazed with grief over the death of his son, makes a terrible mistake and prepares a pre-scription with poisonous ingredients. But George takes all the blame, preventing terrible consequences. These are the portents of his fate as a man with a heavy load to bear. Although his only ambition is to leave the small town of Bedford to study engineering, in order to put into prac-tice his modern ideas on low-cost housing, and travel around the world, George must bear the responsibility of using his talents to help his hometown. And Frank Capra turns all this into a marvelous fairytale.

George's father and Uncle Billy (Thomas Mitchell) have set up a company that offers mortgages, taking all the risks but allowing the local population to avoid being extorted by the greedy and Dickensian Mr. Potter (Lionel Barrymore). Potter is the cynical and opportunistic master of the town. He considers George's father a failure and an idealistic dreamer, and certainly not a savvy businessman like him. However, it is his father's example that inspires George to continue his undertaking after his death. Mary (Donna Reed), his childhood sweetheart who has wait-ed for him and would become his wife, bearing him 4 children, supports him in everything. George understands that his father was a little big man and relinquishes his own ambitions to devote himself to this mission. He manages to deal with every difficulty, even the seemingly insur-mountable ones of the Great Depression, and he withstands all of Potter's threats and cajolery, despite the fact that Potter is the richest and stingiest man in the country. In bad times he manages to endure the pressure put on him by Potter, who is also a shareholder in Bailey's compa-ny, to ruin all the lower-class citizens indebted to banks. Potter refers to them as the riffraff, but George Bailey, the model American citizen, points out that housing loans improve their lives. "Doesn't it make them better citizens? Doesn't it make them better customers?" In short, the film extols pure American values: the spirit of initiative and risk, which are never separated from the awareness of personal freedom.

Nevertheless, that first Christmas after the end of World War II, the difficulties truly seem to be insurmountable.

Frank Capra and James Stewart are the perfect combination to represent the best in the American spirit. ▶

Uncle Billy absentmindedly loses the entire company capital, which ends up in the hands of none other than Potter, who takes advantage to exact his revenge on the Bailey family (although Uncle Billy finally has the chance to tell Potter exactly what he thinks of him). Indeed, in the past George had scornfully turned down Potter's highly profitable offers, because the price would have been George's freedom. He is on the verge of ruin. The only thing George has left is his life-insurance policy, but the old miser laughs in his face when George goes to ask him for help: "You're worth more dead than alive!"

And so that Christmas Eve George is about to jump off a bridge into the freezing river, but this is where the angel Clarence appears. To demonstrate everything that George has done, he shows him the nightmare of what would have happened if he had never been born. George sees the spectacle of a city called Potterville that is prey to the selfishness and hostility of the entire population and has led the poorest to ruin. "Each man's life touches so many other lives," the angel tells him.

Having learned his lesson, George goes back to his family and the entire town demonstrates to him that his sacrifice and dedication have not been in vain, and that giving friendship, solidarity and love is the best investment of all. During their celebration, he happens to find a copy of *Tom Sawyer*, Clarence's favorite novel, with this dedication: "Remember, no man is a failure who has friends. Thank you for the wings." In the end, the two have helped each other because, after finally doing a good deed, Clarence has earned his wings and is promoted.

Moral of the story: faith counts more than intelligence, astuteness and cunning. Particularly the pure and unspoiled faith of a child.

115 [TOP]- Despite his predicament when for a moment he's led astray, George refuses a bad-intentioned handout from the profiteer, Potter (Lionel Barrymore).

115 [CENTER] - George is desperate and everything is going badly when the good-intentioned angel demonstrates how reality could be more dismal if the small town of Bedford didn't have George as its citizen.

115 [BOTTOM] - All misunderstanding is finally cleared up and the whole town, confronting the infamous Potter, celebrates George's courage and moral fortitude. Everyone runs into the house, happy for the family of George Bailey (at far left, Ward Bond is the town's policeman; at far right with his hat, Thomas Mitchell is George's Uncle Billy). Life, after all, is truly wonderful.

George doesn't believe but Clarence is truly an angel and was sent to Earth on Christmas night to help him find his way back to moral redemption.

1 ▲

1948

[ITALY] Genre: DRAMA

THE BICYCLE THIEF

Director: VITTORIO DE SICA

Cast: LAMBERTO MAGGIORANI / ENZO STAIOLA

There is something important that must be understood in order to grasp the revolutionariness of *The Bicycle Thief* (*Ladri di biciclette*) and the choices that, even before making this film, its director Vittorio De Sica had made in *Shoeshine* (1946) and would later confirm with *Umberto D.* (1952).

In the Thirties and early Forties De Sica was an extremely popular Italian actor who not only starred in numerous comedies (particularly those directed Mario Camerini) but also recorded famous songs. In the petit bourgeois society that distinguished the country during this period, De Sica was the Italian equivalent of the brilliant and carefree figure of Cary Grant. Consequently, his decision during the postwar period to embark on a completely different course and become a film director was not only unexpected but extremely bold, as he risked his firmly established reputation. A man and artist who was intuitive rather than cultured, who was guided by infallible instinct rather than ideology, De Sica felt that it was his ethical mission to describe the country during this dramatic period of poverty and uncertainty.

The film recounts a day in the life of a Roman lumpenprole, Antonio Ricci. Unemployed and – like so many others living in the same condition in postwar Rome – worried about feeding his family, Antonio manages to find work as a billposter. However, he needs a bicycle for the job. His is at a pawnshop, and so in order to redeem it his wife brings in their bed linens. Antonio has barely started his rounds when his precious vehicle is stolen.

This is the beginning of his ordeal, as Antonio goes to the police, who prove to be powerless, and then turns to his friends, garbage collectors, em-

1. 2. 3. Antonio and son, little Bruno (Lamberto Maggiorani, Enzo Staiola) who assists his father on a distressing day when his bicycle's stolen. The bicycle is their only means of support, however Antonio had previously stolen it from someone else out of desperation. An awkward situation, he is quickly found out, chased, and humiliated. So distant from the typical Hollywood model, this film demonstrates to the entire world that the screen can also tell the life story of common men and women.

barking on an odyssey that takes him from Piazza Vittorio to Porta Portese, the historical markets in Rome's lower-class neighborhoods. Out of desperation, he even turns to a fortune-teller. When he finally identifies the thief and follows him into a poor neighborhood, he is forced to give in to a wall of hostility and a code of silence, and the lack of proof or witnesses prevents him from reporting the thief.

Silently and apprehensively accompanied everywhere by his little son Bruno, Antonio is about to give up when he sees an unattended bicycle and gives in to the temptation to do exactly what had been done to him. However, he is caught in the act and, surrounded by an angry crowd, Antonio is spared only by the fact that his son has burst into tears. The bicycle owner decides not to press charges and Antonio avoids getting arrested, but he is not spared humiliation in front of his son. Nevertheless, in the film's poignant last scene he is redeemed by Bruno's loving gesture, as the boy squeezes his father's hand to console him and convey a silent message of faith and hope. The two head home at the end of a day that has been dramatic for both, but that may also mark a new beginning. Everything revolves around the fundamental narrative element of the bicycle, an object whose value – so precious in that impoverished era and society – is hard to grasp today. Yet the film maintains its universal significance as a manifesto of the human condition in situations of extreme hardship and poverty. Although numerous writers were involved in the script, the final film version can be attributed to the work of screenwriter Cesare Zavattini, De Sica's sensitivity and the revolutionary technique of Neorealism – of which *The Bicycle Thief* is the best-known example – distinguished by outdoor shooting, improvised dialogue and the inexperience of amateur actors (Lamberto Maggiorani as Antonio and Enzo Staiola as his son). De Sica received enticing offers of financial backing from the United States, but he turned them down as their proviso was that a famous actor – Cary Grant – play the leading role. Along with De Sica's *Shoeshine* and Roberto Rossellini's films *Rome, Open City* and *Paisà*, *The Bicycle Thief* was acclaimed by international artistic and intellectual circles (the film was touted by René Clair), marking a radical turning point in the very concept of cinema for all the films that followed. In 1949 it won a Special Award; the Academy Award category of Best Foreign Language Film was not introduced until 1956.

The Asphalt Jungle probes the preparation, execution and consequences of a jewelry-store robbery. "Doc" Erwin Riedenschneider (Sam Jaffe), a famous burglar who has just gotten out of prison, is the perfect man to pull off a big job. Through the complicity of a dishonest lawyer, Alonzo Emmerich (Louis Calhern), he assembles a group of seasoned criminals to prepare the heist. Dix Handley (Sterling Hayden) dreams of using the proceeds to get back the horse farm he lost during the Great Depression. The hunchback Gus Minissi (James Whitmore) is hired as the driver. Louis Ciavelli (Anthony Caruso) is an expert safecracker and, lastly, there is the bookie Cobby (Marc Lawrence).

The plan has been laid out down to the last detail and is carried off efficiently and with professional aplomb. Everything goes smoothly until the nitroglycerin used for the safe explodes and sets off the alarm, alerting the police earlier than planned. A run-in with one of the guards leaves Ciavelli wounded.

Despite the incident, the men pull off the heist and escape. However, when the corrupt cop Ditrich (Barry Kelley) steps in, angry that his contact in the gang, Cobby, did not involve him in the heist, he triggers a chain reaction and the group begins to fall apart. One by one, the members of the gang are captured and killed by the police.

All critics emphasize that one of the key elements in the film's finely balanced and terse narration is the allegorical power of the story, which does not favor one character over another. It is a story without heroes or traitors, an allegory of greed. Despite the fact that the film is about a group, it is effectively a gallery of individual characters sketched out skillfully and in depth. One of the most striking is Dix, and one of the film's most classic scenes is about him: his death among his horses.

1950
THE ASPHALT JUNGLE

Director: JOHN HUSTON

Cast: STERLING HAYDEN / LOUIS CALHERN / JEAN HAGEN /
JAMES WHITMORE / SAM JAFFE / MARILYN MONROE

Marine Sterling Hayden as a "confessed criminal" communist appearing before Senator McCarthy's "House Committee on Un-American Activities," had a promising presence but was neve true protagonist despite great opportunities for such. Here are *Johnny Guitar*, directed by Nicholas Ray, *The Killing* and *Doctor Strangelove* by Kubrick, *The Long Goodbye* by Altman nd *1900* (Novecento) by Bertolucci.

▲1

▲2

One of John Huston's most celebrated and successful films, *The Asphalt Jungle* is based on the novel by the same name. Huston transformed it into a new classic in the tradition of gangster movies, using the noir atmospheres of the thrillers of the 1940s and 1950s, one of the most classic of which was directed by Huston himself: *The Maltese Falcon* (1941). It was also the trailblazer and paradigm of the subgenre of films revolving around the dynamics of the perfect heist. There are two famous French variations on this theme, *Touchez pas au Grisbi* and *Rififi*, both made in 1954, not to mention a worthy successor, Stanley Kubrick's *The Killing* (1956), also starring Sterling Hayden, and Quentin Tarantino's tribute in *Reservoir Dogs*. The film also inspired brilliant variations and parodies.

The 24-year-old Marilyn Monroe played the girlfriend of one of the gangsters, her first major film role.

▲ **3**

1. 2. 3. Key chapter in the evolution of the American film noir genre and in the artistic path of its director, John Huston, this film portrays the strength of unanimity and failure of humanity, the exact opposite of an amazingly efficient criminal exploit. Sterling Hayden's character becomes a criminal against his will, a man tormented by nostalgia for the lost harmony of the countryside. At center, twenty-four year old Marilyn Monroe plays a very small part, beginning her very quick path to stardom with this film.

When Billy Wilder directed *Sunset Boulevard* in 1950, he had already written the screenplay for *Ninotchka* and directed *Double Indemnity* and *The Lost Weekend*. And he had already won two Oscars. Forty-four years old, he was the preeminent pupil of Ernst Lubitsch, who – like him – had also emigrated from Europe, but Wilder had not yet gained a reputation as a genius of comedy. At this point in his career, he was still making dramatic films and *Sunset Boulevard* contributed decisively to defining the *noir* genre.

Joe Gillis, a penniless young screenwriter who is being chased by repossession agents, finds shelter in the sumptuous but dilapidated mansion owned by Norma Desmond, a former silent-screen star. Desmond lives there with her faithful but dour butler (Eric von Stroheim), who is actually her ex-husband and former director. Norma and Joe enter into an ambiguous and morbid relationship. More than anything else, Norma wants to return to the silver screen and would like Joe, whom she turns into her lover, gigolo and instrument, to write the script for her great comeback. Joe is torn between disgust, the unscrupulous temptation to take advantage of the situation, and true attraction.

In the end, however, driven by his feelings for another young screenwriter, he rebels, but it costs him his life. When the police arrive, bursting into the mansion to arrest the actress – now delirious – for murder, Norma plays her final, grotesque climatic scene, descending the staircase like a true movie star. In the meantime, Max, who has always remained at her side and worshipped her, steps into his old role as director and pretends to film her. Naturally, however, everyone is there not to celebrate the reborn star but for a very different reason.

The entire story is narrated as a flashback by the dead man, Joe, whose corpse we see floating in the swimming pool at the beginning of the film. However, this opening scene is different than had originally been planned. After the first solution had been filmed, it was shown to a test audience, as was customary among Hollywood studios at the time, but it met with gales of laughter, as it portrayed the talking corpse lying on a table in the morgue.

In reality, the cast was the outcome of a series of turndowns. Montgomery Clift was initially asked to play Joe. However, he decided not to risk being identified with such an ambiguous character, and Fred MacMurray turned it down for the same reason. Marlon Brando was also considered, but was thought to be too little known.

1950
SUNSET BOULEVARD

Director: BILLY WILDER

Cast: GLORIA SWANSON / WILLIAM HOLDEN / ERICH VON STROHEIM

124 [LEFT] – Appropriately clad in leopardskin with large dark sunglasses and large hat, the star who refutes her declining popularity engages the young scriptwriter, Joe Gillis, in conversation by the pool of her Hollywood mansion. If at first he believed that he could take advantage of this unlikely relationship, he would soon be disgusted and finally overwhelmed by it.

124 [RIGHT] – The erratic yet divine Norma goes to visit the great director of the golden age, Cecil B. De Mille, at Paramount Studios. The woman is convinced of her certain *rentrée*, that all would welcome her with open arms, and again pay her homage as a great star. Unfortunate for her, De Mille is just pretending in pity and deference to the memory of her former celebrity.

Norma cannot tolerate that her "protector" loves another woman, a woman as young as he is, so she slaps him

William Holden was finally chosen and Wilder would subsequently cast him repeatedly in his films.

The female lead, for which a true silent-screen star was sought, was also offered to Mary Pickford, Pola Negri and Greta Garbo. Gloria Swanson, who was finally chosen to play Norma Desmond, had also been a celebrity in the 1920s, as was Stroheim, who also happened to be the author of the "cursed" film *Queen Kelly* (work on it stopped and he was dismissed). The latter film had starred none other than Gloria Swanson and in *Sunset Boulevard* we see an eloquent example of the great past of a film star and of her former director and husband turned manservant. These are not the only figures in the film recalling the glorious early days of cinema: Buster Keaton and filmmaker Cecil B. De Mille also make cameo appearances.

Wilder surrounded his leading character with an array of eccentric touches and luxuries, from the monkey for which Norma stages a funeral to the majestic vintage Isotta Fraschini in which she drives to the Paramount Studios.

A savage and dark portrait of the world of Hollywood, the film also triggered a number of negative and shocked reactions. It received 11 nominations and won 3 Oscars, notably the well-deserved and exemplary Academy Award for the screenplay, which Wilder wrote with Charles Brackett and D.M. Marshman, Jr. Considering the subject of the film and Wilder's own experience working in the profession of his character, Joe Gillis, the latter award is also highly symbolic.

1 ▲   2 ▲

1952

[USA] Genre: MUSICAL

SINGIN' IN THE RAIN

Directors: STANLEY DONEN, GENE KELLY
Cast: GENE KELLY / DONALD O'CONNOR / DEBBIE REYNOLDS

The year is 1927 and the movie industry's most important innovation is about to be introduced: talking pictures. Following the release of *The Jazz Singer*, the first talkie in history, production companies are facing a major crisis because they must incorporate this change.

Singin' in the Rain tells the story of Monumental Films, whose biggest stars are Don (Gene Kelly) and Lina (Jean Hagen). The event is the première of their latest silent epic. Interviewed by a journalist, Don recounts his brilliant career, from his earliest works to his rise to fame and fortune, but he is making everything up. Indeed, the images tell us a completely different story. But this is a movie star's life, and appearance is everything. If glossy magazines want a nice story, that is what they get. However, when the journalist asks him if he and Lina will ever get married, Don is quick to respond that they are just friends.

At the end of the screening, the audience is ecstatic. The couple symbolizes the glittering world of Hollywood – based strictly on appearance, of course.

1. 2. 3. This sequence is the most famous one in the film. Gene Kelly dances and sings "Singin' in the Rain," the song that lends its name to the film, at perhaps the moment that is the most representative (with some passages by Fred Astaire and Ginger Rogers in *Top Hat* equally symbolic) of the classic Hollywood musical epic. The number expresses the big city dreams of a country boy upon arrival in New York.

On his way to the production party, in order to escape from fans who have recognized him Don gets into a passing car, driven by pretty young Kathy (Debbie Reynolds). When he makes a pass at her, to put him off she makes fun of his pantomimes as a silent actor. She tells him that she is a theater actress, commenting that real talent is seen only on stage and that he is merely a shadow on the screen.

At the party, the producer shows the guests a clip from a talkie and everyone is shocked. Recalling what Kathy said to him, Don starts to doubt his own talent, but his best friend, Cosmo Brown (Donald O'Connor), tries to encourage him. To entertain his party guests, the producer has hired a dance troupe and, much to Don's surprise, Kathy is in the front row. She is not a theater actress after all, but merely a chorus girl! Don pokes fun at her and the girl angrily throws a pie at him, missing him and hitting Lina in the face instead. Kathy is fired on the spot.

A month goes by and Don starts filming a new movie, but he cannot get the dancer out of his head. During a love scene with Lina, he discovers that she is the one who got Kathy fired. As he kisses her, he tells her that he loathes her. Suddenly, the filming stops. Given the enormous success of *The Jazz Singer*, the producer has now decided that the new film should be a talkie.

In the meantime, during screen tests the director decides to offer one of dancers a minor role. Don immediately recognizes Kathy and begs her to accept the part. Then he takes her to an empty studio, "turns on" a sunset, creates a light breeze and wins her over with a love song.

The preparation of the film continues with speech lessons. Don does very well, but Lina is terrible. The shooting is finished but the outcome is a disaster. At the premiere, the entire audience bursts out laughing as soon as the diva opens her mouth.

1. 2. 3. This story recounts the trauma of the transition from silent films to "talkies." Gene Kelly is coupled with a bad actress, an absolute diva whose fame is at an end. In these new times, only those with true talent can survive. This is precisely when the young Debbie Reynolds is discovered and launches her career (also being courted by her future partner) when she attempts to rescue the bad actress by dubbing her unpleasant voice. A path to brilliant success then opens for the new couple.

Don is crushed: Kathy was right. He is a second-rate actor and the film is bound to ruin him. She tells him that he's wrong and, with Cosmo, tries to cheer him up. Then they have an idea. Why not turn the film into a musical? They have nothing to lose by having Don do what he does best: singing and dancing. And Lina will be overdubbed by Kathy. The producer is enthusiastic and his only proviso is that Lina must not be told until the filming is over. Don's delight over the turn of events is evident in the film's most famous scene, in which he sings and dances in a deserted street on a rainy night.

Everything seems to be going smoothly and it is clear that the film will be a hit. The producer has already prepared the ad campaign. But a few days before the film is scheduled to premiere Lina finds out about the overdubbing and threatens to sue the production company. No one must know that her "voice" is actually Kathy's.

The premiere is a triumph and Lina insists on thanking the audience. Alone on stage she utters a few inanities, but then the spectators beg her to sing a song. She doesn't know what to do, but Don takes care of everything. He tells Kathy to stand behind the curtain and sing while Lina lip syncs. Kathy has no choice, as she must honor her contract. The song starts and in the very middle Don, Cosmo and the producer raise the curtain to show the real singer. Kathy tries to run off, but Don stops her and introduces the new star of Monumental Films.

Conceived as a simple vehicle for songs, recapping – if not recycling – MGM's notable tradition of musicals, it is effectively a monument to this genre, one of Hollywood's most iconic along with Westerns, and has become a cult object for enthusiasts. Gene Kelly worked with Stanley Donen not only as co-director but also as choreographer.

1. 3. Donald O'Connor plays Cosmo Brown, incomparable right hand man to Don played by Gene Kelly.

2. Cyd Charisse has a non-central but developing role in this film and would become one of the most appreciated actress-dancers of American Fifties' musicals, especially in *Brigadoon* and *The Band Wagon*, both directed by Vincent Minnelli.

1952

[USA] Genre: **WESTERN**

HIGH NOON

Director: FRED ZINNEMANN

High Noon is a powerful but – by today's standards – schematic civic metaphor in the form of a Western. It was produced by Stanley Kramer (who would later direct *Guess Who's Coming to Dinner?*), written by Carl Foreman, a screenwriter blacklisted by the McCarthy Commission for alleged anti-American activities, and directed by the Jewish-Viennese émigré Fred Zinnemann. And it cast Gary Cooper, a star who was an icon of Roosevelt's America and the New Deal.

A fast-paced marvel of suspense, *High Noon* recounts a story that effectively unfolds in real time.

It is set in Hadleyville, Kansas, shortly after the Civil War. The time is 10:30 a.m. and Marshal Will Kane (Cooper) has just married the Quaker Amy (Grace Kelly) and resigned from his post. However, we learn that Frank Miller, a criminal that Kane arrested and sent to jail a few years earlier, has been released by a corrupt judge and is coming to town on the noon train. Three of Miller's men (one of whom played by the then-unknown Lee van Cleef) will be waiting for him at the station to help him hunt down the marshal, as the criminal has vowed to get revenge.

His wife insists that they leave anyway. Because of her religious beliefs, she is against any form of violence, an attitude that places her in an ambiguous position throughout much of the film and effectively reflects the townspeople's cowardice. Nevertheless, Kane decides that he will postpone

**Cast: GARY COOPER / GRACE KELLY /
LEE VAN CLEEF / KATY JURADO**

1. 2. 3. 4. Gary Cooper is here with Grace Kelly who is still a long way from becoming the Princess of Monaco. Here is the gang of men that Sheriff Kane would have to face alone at high noon (the second to last on the right is Lee van Cleef, future mainstay of the Italian "spaghetti" western). Sheriff Kane confronts the danger victoriously, but disappointment in his peers motivates him to discard his sheriff's star in the dust and abandon the countryside with his wife, Amy, although she herself would withdraw her support in a temporary moment of confusion and upset.

their departure by a few hours because his sense of honor, dignity and respect for the law forces him to face the situation.

Kane, who has no intention whatsoever of being a hero, tries to assemble a group of volunteers but the townspeople find an excuse not to help, leaving him completely on his own. At the final showdown, Kane will vanquish the bandits, thanks also to the providential help he gets from Amy, whom the marshal's ex-lover (Katy Jurado) convinced to stay behind.

The final scene is marvelous: a tracking shot shows us the town from above as people reemerge, while Kane bitterly throws his marshal's star in the dust, gets into his buggy with his bride and leaves forever. At the time, this gesture must have appeared to go against America's obsession with the ideals of law enforcement and purity.

Without reading too much into the filmmakers' intentions, it is clear that the goal of the film is to affirm individual responsibility and freedom (concepts that also reflect the noblest underpinnings of the American spirit) against all types of conformism and obtuseness.

Although it differs enormously from standards of the quintessential American film genre, *High Noon* is nevertheless considered one of the greatest Westerns ever made.

The Cooper-Kelly duo is somewhat incongruous, as in 1952 he was 51 and she was 23.

The film won four Academy Awards in 1953, including Best Actor (Cooper's second Oscar, after *Sergeant York*), Best Music and Best Song, the unforgettable "Do Not Forsake Me, Oh My Darling," by Dimitri Tiomkin and Ned Washington, performed by Tex Ritter and later turned into a popular hit by Frankie Laine.

1952

DON CAMILLO

Director: JULIEN DUVIVIER

Cast: FERNANDEL / GINO CERVI

The five titles of the saga launched in 1952 by the film *Don Camillo* (by French director Julien Duvivier and Italian producer Angelo Rizzoli), all of which starring Italian actor Gino Cervi and French actor Fernandel, were adaptations of the stories written by Giovannino Guareschi. Initially published in newspapers and magazines (above all the humor weekly *Candido*), they were later collected in numerous volumes starting in 1948. Only three of the films were released during the author's lifetime.

Giovannino Guareschi (1908–1968) was a famous Italian journalist, writer and satirical illustrator. Rebellious, irreverent and anarchical, from 1936 to 1943 he was editor in chief of *Bertoldo*, a popular satire/humor magazine published by Rizzoli and directed by Cesare Zavattini. Originally a fortnightly and later a weekly, it competed with the equally popular periodical *Marc'Aurelio*. Despite the Fascist regime and censorship, these two hotbeds of talent ultimately stimulated Italian cinema, literature and journalism in the postwar period. Following World War II Guareschi founded *Candido*, which he headed until 1957.

The author was a fiery and controversial figure. In 1938 he signed the "Racial Manifesto" supporting Mussolini's anti-Semitic laws. Following the armistice of September 8, 1943, out of loyalty to the House of Savoy he refused to adhere to the Italian Social Republic and was sent to a German prison camp. Despite his monarchic sentiments, his violent aversion for Communism brought him to the forefront of the Christian Democrats (CD) in the tough electoral battle of 1948. He was the one who created the cruel satirical cartoons that became famous as *trinariciuti* or party-liners (the term means "three-nostriled": he sketched Communists as having an extra nostril in order to clear their brains, clouded by party policy). He also coined effective propagandistic formulas for the electoral campaign, which the CD won against the leftist Popular Democratic Front. One example is his line, "In the privacy of the voting booth, God can see you but Stalin can't." However, his diehard individualism is demonstrated by the fact that he faced serious legal problems after he opposed the CD party leader Alcide De Gasperi. Lastly, although his actions demonstrated that he was against Fascism, in the last decade of his life he embraced the ultra-rightwing neo-Fascist movement.

Guareschi owed his fame above all to his invention of the characters of Don Camillo and his rival Peppone. In the intense climate of the Cold War he created a story – set it in a small town in the Po valley, an area that had just emerged from some of the bloodiest episodes of the war – about the seemingly discordant but essentially sympathetic and friendly rapport between a Communist mayor and a harshly anti-Communist pastor. Guareschi thus contributed decisively to establishing the idea of the folksy affability and gruff cordiality of the people of this area. At the same time, he helped create a mass subculture that was destined to endure for several decades, reflecting the long-term coexistence of the two major powers on the Italian political scene: the Communist Party and the Christian Democrats. His use of parody guaranteed widespread appeal and recognition not only in Italy but in all areas in which the input of Communist parties and their resistance against Nazism

1. Don Camillo is the popular French comic, Fernandel. Peppone is Gino Cervi, an already very popular Italian film actor, primarily playing roles with director, Alessandro Blasetti, in the latter Thirties. This character and Inspector Maigret whom he embodied for television in the Sixties represent the two happiest time periods in his long career.

2. 3. This is the story of two friends and enemies, the conservative yet quick-tempered priest who talks with the crucifix and the Stalinist mayor of a Lombardian "red" town against the backdrop of the Cold War, penned by journalist-writer, Giovannino Guareschi. This and other films that followed would be benchmarks for rewarding experimental Franco-Italian co-productions.

was fundamental, as testified by the enormous success of these films.

The idea of bringing this "little world" to the screen – Guareschi used the term in his stories, but in the film it became the town of Brescello – and of using Gino Cervi, a top name since the 1930s, and the comedian Fernandel to play the leading characters proved to be a winning one. In the role of Don Camillo, Fernandel turns to a talking crucifix for advice on how to oppose his rival for power (albeit on a local level) and for help in restraining his own character, as impulsive as his adversary's.

The first and second films (*Don Camillo*, 1952, and *The Return of Don Camillo*, 1953) were directed by Duvivier; the third (*Don Camillo's Last Round*, 1955) and fourth (*Don Camillo: Monsignor*, 1961) by Carmine Gallone; the fifth (*Don Camillo in Moscow*, 1965) by Luigi Comencini. Two other films were made later, but with different actors: in 1972 with Gastone Moschin and Lionel Stander, and in 1983 with Terence Hill and Colin Blakely. The two characters were so popular that the film spawned television series in Brazil and England. In the latter, Mario Adorf played Don Camillo.

THE WILD ONE

Director: LÁSZLÓ BENEDEK

Cast: MARLON BRANDO /

LEE MARVIN / MARY MURPHY / ROBERT KEITH

The qualities of László Benedek's *The Wild One* emerge above all, if not exclusively, in the visual impact of its opening scene, with the onscreen voice that introduces the story as the camera shows an extremely long straightaway and the arrival of the gang of the Black Rebels, thuggish bikers led by the glowering and taciturn Johnny (Marlon Brando).

The group of young drifters initially stops and breaks up a bike race, stealing the trophy that Johnny then boldly displays on his motorcycle. The drifters go on their way, stopping in a sleepy little town that they turn upside down with their raucous behavior. They hang out at the local bar, to the joy of its owner because they consume enormous amounts of beer, but they worry the aging sheriff. Despite the indignation and protests of upright citizens, the sheriff seems to be willing to reach a compromise, initially out of opportunism. In the meantime, the rough-mannered Johnny courts the barmaid, who turns out to be the sheriff's daughter.

A rival gang, led by Chino (Lee Marvin), once Johnny's friend but now his adversary, arrives. Mayhem and brawls escalate, disturbing the town and exasperating the population. A group of citizens determined to take the law into their own hands closes in on Johnny, who accidentally kills an elderly man with his motorbike and lands in jail. Johnny gets off with a reprimand and the gang leaves again, but not before Johnny – hardened by life – makes an unsuccessful attempt to apologize. But the only thing he manages to leave behind for the girl is the famous trophy and the memory of his smile.

Following *A Streetcar Named Desire*, *Viva Zapata!* and *Julius Caesar*, and before his consecration as a major star in *On the Waterfront*, Brando, in his leather jacket, became the leading youth icon, preceding James Dean's exploits in *Rebel Without a Cause* by very little but arriving years ahead of the films on gangs and motorcycles that became popular in the Sixties and Seventies.

Wearing a cap, leather jacket, and expression somewhere between hard and devious, he sits on his motorcycle. This is the get-up and persona of Marlon Brando's "tough guy." ▶

Today it may seem laughable that the innocuous rebelliousness of these "thugs" caused such a scandal. And yet the film, which was not a big hit, was considered dangerous and antisocial at the time. It was effectively a symptom and a warning bell, the first film of unprecedented generational unrest, paralleling what was occurring in literature and music with Jack Kerouac's Beat Generation, Charlie Parker's jazz and nascent rock and roll. As a result, it was destined to it to be imitated endlessly.

1. 2. 3. 4. The arrival of the "wild ones" in the peaceful town occurs with short-lived moments of crude flirting, abandoning any tenderness toward the girl tending bar, also the daughter of the local sheriff. Here is the whole gang of Black Rebels posing with their head honcho, Johnny, at center. *The Savage* leads the pack with derivative films following suit in a cascade of "rebels without a cause" productions to 1968 and beyond.

▼ 3

▼ 4

It captured a sense of confused intolerance toward the adult lifestyle, the conformism of the middle class, and the values of an America that had emerged victorious from World War II but had paid an enormous prize and suffered irreversible trauma.

The film was produced by Stanley Kramer, who years later would direct blockbusters such as *Guess Who's Coming to Dinner?* and *Judgment at Nuremberg*.

The runaway success of *Roman Holiday* owes everything to Audrey Hepburn's unique and inimitable charm. In 1952, when William Wyler's film was made – shot on location entirely in Rome – she was not a debutante as she had already been in a number of films, albeit only in minor roles. This one, however, represented her breakthrough performance.

A mediocre and superficial work, *Roman Holiday* is nevertheless a landmark. This was due first of all to the fact that it revealed the talent, style and fresh charm of the 23-year-old actress, who immediately became a film and fashion star: a new female icon. The following year she would star in *Sabrina*, and it is interesting to note the number of times she starred with much older male partners, from Gregory Peck in *Roman Holiday* to the duo of William Holden and Humphrey Bogart in *Sabrina*, and Cary Grant in *Charade*.

Clearly inspired by the story of Cinderella – although here the roles are reversed (this is one of the film's pluses) – *Roman Holiday* would later serve as the starting point for *Pretty Woman* and the superstardom of Julia Roberts.

The story was written by Dalton Trumbo, a famous screenwriter who had been one of the Hollywood Ten blacklisted during the McCarthy era as Communist sympathizers.

The view of Rome was unquestionably toned down, although no more than the Italian film *Poveri ma belli* (*Poor but Handsome*) made several years later. Nevertheless, it is moving to watch this movie today, with the reconstruction of Via Margutta and its crowded stalls and crafts shops.

Princess Ann, the heir to the throne of a small kingdom, arrives for an official visit. However, the young woman is forced to adhere to a very tight schedule and strict protocol. The enormous demands that are placed on her lead to a breakdown and her doctor gives her a sedative, but that night Ann flees the palace – effectively a gilded cage – and, enthralled, explores the streets of Rome. However, the sedative makes her drowsy and she falls asleep on a public bench. An American journalist, Joe Bradley (Gregory Peck), happens to find her but does not recognize her and, feeling sorry for her, takes her back to his bohemian flat in Via Margutta.

1953
ROMAN HOLIDAY

Director: WILLIAM WYLER

Cast: GREGORY PECK / AUDREY HEPBURN / EDDIE ALBERT

The unhappy princess experiences the thrill of freedom, zigzagging on a Vespa through the alleyways of Rome.

140 - Trusting and naïve, Anna places her confidence in journalist, Bradley who is a bit like Clark Gable in *It Happened One Night*, sniffing out an exclusive scoop with the discovery of the princess's escapade while visiting Rome. But along the way, things change and the two fall in love. Unlike Capra's masterpiece, it's a shame that they must part ways when royal duties beckon, yet before taking her leave, the girl still has the time to assure herself of the journalist's fidelity.

During an unforgettable day spent with the delightful princess, Gregory Peck/Joe Bradley takes her to visit all of the tourist attractions in the Eternal City, including the famous Mouth of Truth statue.

The following morning the princess wakes up, dazed but pleased to see the man who has put her up for the night.

While she was sleeping, however, Joe managed to slip out to go to the office, where his boss promptly reprimands him. The editor is angry that the journalist has not heard the latest about the disappearance of the princess, whom he was supposed to interview that morning. When he sees the photographs published in the papers, Joe realizes who is guest is and does everything he can to keep her there, determined to get an exclusive story. But the day is destined to go differently.

Although he initially indulges the princess's desire to enjoy a day like any ordinary girl out of purely opportunistic reasons, as they spend time together Joe falls in love with her. The scene in which Peck and Hepburn zip around Rome on a Vespa is a classic and it gave the Italian scooter enormous publicity.

At the end of the day, he takes her back – neither of them revealing their true identities – and reluctantly says goodbye to her, relinquishing his scoop. He surprises her the next day when he shows up at the press conference, but lets her know that he will not publish anything about the time they spent together: precious hours – but not for professional reasons.

The film launched the season known as "Hollywood on the Tiber," destined to endure for the entire decade, thanks also to the American stars who were cast in Vittorio De Sica's *Stazione Termini* the following year.

From Here to Eternity examines the lives of six characters – four men and two women – at an American army base in Hawaii just before December 7, 1941 and the Japanese attack on Pearl Harbor that drew the United States into World War II.

Burt Lancaster is Sergeant Warden and Montgomery Clift is Private Prewitt, who had been a boxer. Frank Sinatra plays the cheerful Private Angelo Maggio. Ernest Borgnine is the ruthless Sergeant Judson, in charge of discipline. Deborah Kerr is the adulterous wife of one of the captains and she is secretly involved with Warden. Donna Reed plays Alma, a call girl.

Prewitt is targeted when he flatly refuses to join the base's boxing club to entertain the enlisted men. After injuring a friend in the last match he had ever played, he swore that he would never box again. He is protected by Sergeant Warden, comforted by Alma and supported by his colleague, the Italian-American Maggio.

Maggio is the one who, rebelling against injustice, is destined to fare worse than anyone. Locked up in a stockade, he is beaten to death.

Furious over his friend's death, Prewitt resorts to violence to avenge him, but his escape from sure punishment is dwarfed by the emergency of the Japanese attack. None of their lives will ever be the same again.

Reflecting the atmosphere and colors of the shocking melodrama of the novel by James Jones, the film directed by Fred Zinnemann (who had just finished *High Noon*) is a powerful accusation against narrow-minded militarism. Given the climate in the United States at the time (1953) – this was a period of widespread fear of Communist attacks – the film's anti-military stance aroused great hostility. Nevertheless, it was enormously popular with audiences, winning an award at the Cannes Film Festival and eight Oscars. Among the cast, Sinatra and Reed won Academy Awards, respectively for Best Supporting Actor and Actress, whereas the outstanding Clift, Lancaster and Kerr, nominated in the categories of Best Actor and Actress, lost to William Holden for *Stalag 17* and Audrey Hepburn for *Roman Holiday*. The film's most memorable and iconic scene is that of Lancaster and Kerr's long, passionate and – for the era – scandalously explicit kiss on the beach.

1953

FROM HERE TO ETERNITY

Director: FRED ZINNEMANN

**Cast: BURT LANCASTER / MONTGOMERY CLIFT /
DEBORAH KERR / DONNA REED / FRANK SINATRA /
ERNEST BORGNINE / PHILIP OBER**

Burt Lancaster and Deborah Kerr are a beautiful couple with a long sequence of kisses on the beach, however in the end, their passion does not serve to build their happiness.

144 - The kind Italian-American soldier, Angelo Maggio (Sinatra), was beaten to death by the iron fisted sergeant, Judson (Ernest Borgnine), but would eventually be avenged.

145 - The two sergeants confront each other, the more humanitarian Warden (Lancaster) and the implacable Judson (Borgnine). It would be the soldier, Prewitt (Montgomery Clift), a boxer who no longer wants to fight after inadvertently blinding an adversary, that restores integrity to the memory of his friend, Maggio, putting an end to the injustice and oppression by killing Judson and taking the blame. However, the attack on Pearl Harbor had already occurred by that time and everyone's lives would be at total risk.

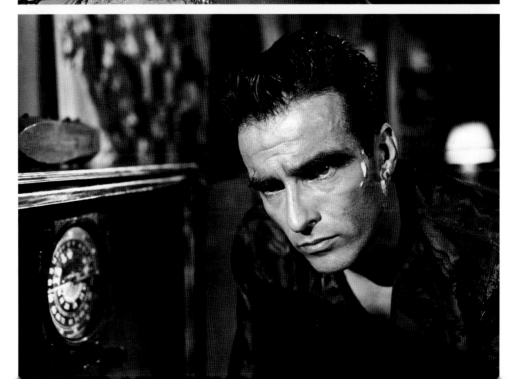

A Star is Born is the quintessential Hollywood story, as the film is about Hollywood itself. It is an extraordinary interweaving of creativity and creative influences, a chain that is something more than an ordinary remake.

Everything started with George Cuckor's 1932 film *What Price Hollywood?*, in which a waitress becomes a movie star after being discovered by director who, in turn, destroys himself with alcohol and ultimately commits suicide. In 1937 William Wellman directed the first version of *A Star is Born* (screenplay by Alan Campbell, Dorothy Parker and Robert Carson, produced by David O. Selznick, who would become most famous for *Gone With the Wind*), which drew enormously on Cuckor's film. In 1937 version starred Fredric March as the actor Norman Maine, Janet Gaynor as the small-town girl Esther Blodgett who, thanks to him, becomes the successful actress Vicki Lester, Adolphe Menjou as the producer Oliver Niles and Lionel Stander as the treacherous publicist Matt Libby.

In 1954, working with screenwriter Moss Hart, Cukor thus directed the remake of a movie that, in turn, had been inspired by his own film. In the 1954 version, James Mason and Judy Garland played the two leading roles. Nevertheless, there are several decisive differences. First of all, it was transformed from a melodrama with moments of light comedy (albeit with a tragic ending) into a far more dramatic work with musical scenes. There is also an enormous difference between Mason, who would go on to play Humbert in *Lolita*, and March, who was cinema's first Dr. Jekyll/Mr. Hyde in 1932. Furthermore, Garland, who was above all a singer, brought a touch of intimate truth to the character. Her personal life effectively paralleled that of her screen partner's character, as both were self-destructive alcoholics.

Despite the numerous cuts that were made, the second film is much longer than the first. Unlike the first film, the 1954 version was made in color and CinemaScope. In fact, it was Cukor's first color film, and rich and warm color effectively plays an important narrative role in the film. The second film also examines its subject in a harsher light, taking a more realistic look at the other side of celluloid dreams and illusions.

▶ Despite being still young, at 32, Judy Garland was already deeply troubled in her mind, and her body manifested signs of that disturbance.

1954
A STAR IS BORN

Director: **GEORGE CUKOR**

Cast: **JUDY GARLAND / JAMES MASON / JACK CARSON**

The young and ambitious Esther, backed solely by her grandmother's unsophisticated help and wholesome teachings, boldly sets off to take Hollywood by storm. She moves into a boarding house and has just one friend, a young and unemployed assistant director who is as broke as she is. When her friend manages to get her a job that will allow her to enter the glittering world of Hollywood through the back door, Esther is noticed by the famous actor Norman Maine. The two fall in love and he becomes her Pygmalion. However, her meteoric rise to fame with the stage name of Vicki Lester coincides with his decline. His popularity wanes and he becomes increasingly depressed, drinking more and more. When Norman exceeds all limits Esther/Vicki decides to give up her career to help the man she loves. Seemingly reassured, Norman instead drowns himself. Devastated, Esther decides to leave Hollywood and return to her hometown, but her grandmother, who is proud of what the girl has achieved through so much sacrifice and determination, convinces her that she must stay there not only for herself, but above all as a tribute to Norman.

Cukor's film uses the same powerful scenes as Wellman's version, such as the one of the Academy Awards ceremony, when Norman - drunk - accidentally hits Esther in the face while she is accepting her Oscar. Another parallel can be found in the lecture by the judge, who decides not to sentence and humiliate Norman after the actor is arrested for getting into a fight that is actually the fault of the unctuous Libby, the archetypal servant who turns against an employer who has fallen into disgrace. The judge decides to believe Vicki's heartfelt words and allows her to take her husband home. And there is the final classic scene when, after Norman's death, Vicki decides to return to the stage for a charity function and introduces herself as Mrs. Norman Maine.

Yet another remake was released in 1976 starring Barbra Streisand and Kris Kristofferson, in which the events are transferred to the world of rock music and drugs replace alcohol.

149 - *A Star Is Born* is the universal story of a rising star and the birth of another. Below, the scene of the unintentional slap that Norman Maine gives to Vicky Lester when bursting in drunk to the Oscar Awards ceremony.
Although the actress/singer interpreted the role of the burgeoning star, Garland's true personality is still reflected in the inebriated celebrity, her performance derives from that character, and contributes to deepening the dramatic strength of this atypical musical.

Cloaked in an aura of ambiguity – as was its director, Elia Kazan – *On the Waterfront* is enormously powerful even today.

The story takes place on the docks of New York and in the poor neighborhoods where stevedores live. The film was shot on site. The workers live in fear of a trade unionist (Lee J. Cobb), who is more of a mobster than a defender of worker rights, just as his gang of disciples resembles a racket rather than a union that organizes and protects laborers. No one works without the approval of Johnny Friendly, and anyone who rebels or thinks of reporting the protection money extracted by Johnny, who gets rich by exploiting the poor, faces serious trouble. His right-hand man Charley Malloy (Rod Steiger) has a brother, Terry (Marlon Brando), a promising ex-prizefighter who was sacrificed to betting and the interests of the local bosses. He is a man who is unable to develop his own sense of awareness and goes with the status quo, more out of laziness than cowardice. After the "accidental" death of one of his colleagues who was about to report the racket – a murder in which Terry took part – he meets Edie (Eva Marie Saint), the dead man's sister and the daughter of an old dockhand. Despite his hesitation and braggadocio, Terry finally opens his eyes, redeemed by love.

When a second murder is followed by the death of his brother Charley, considered a traitor precisely because of Terry, he no longer has any doubts. But does his change of heart reflect a thirst for revenge or a sense of justice and respect for legality and dignity? This is the dilemma and a key figure in solving it is the Catholic priest, Father Barry (Karl Malden), who emerges as the champion of the oppressed, urging them to come out in the open and overcome not only their fear but also the deep-rooted prejudice whereby anyone who "talks" is a contemptible spy. The vibrant monologue of this "waterfront priest" is memorable. After relinquishing the idea of making his parish the organizational center to save these workers, he risks his own safety by going among the dockhands and, descending into the hold of a ship where they are unloading cargo, he bends over the corpse of the latest victim of violence, replacing the moderate, ambiguous words and gestures of a priest with a combative and threatening tone: "Boys, this is my church!"

Convinced now about the right thing to do, Terry goes before the Committee of Inquiry that is investigating this abuse, putting an end to Johnny's enormous power. But this does not settle the matter and there will be a final confrontation between the two sides. Beaten in front of the complacent companions for which he risked everything, urged on by the priest Terry finds the strength to get up and go to work, demonstrating that Johnny and his gang are ultimately impotent. In the end, the other men will ultimately follow him, but only because he has paved the way.

1954

ON THE WATERFRONT

Director: ELIA KAZAN

Cast: MARLON BRANDO / EVA MARIE SAINT /

ROD STEIGER / LEE J. COBB / KARL MALDEN

1. 2. 3. Terry (Brando) is still a hoodlum on the waterfront but dates Edie (Eva Marie Saint), sister to a rebellious worker against the racket who Terry himself contributed to killing, and a seed of understanding begins to grow in him. He then begins to argue about the rules of engagement with his brother, Charley (Rod Steiger), the boss's right hand.
The day of reckoning occurs in court when Terry decides to expose the trafficking of Johnny (Lee J. Cobb), the union mafia boss at the docks.

Inspired by an investigative report that won the Pulitzer Prize, the film came in the wake of Kazan's testimony before the House Committee on Un-American Activities, the body coordinated by Senator McCarthy, the Republican senator (1947–57) who came to symbolize the Cold War. McCarthy launched a high-profile witch hunt designed to expel Communist sympathizers from intellectual circles and the film industry. The director named colleagues and artists with Communist leanings. Before achieving enormous fame in the film industry in the early 1950s, in the 1930s – the era of the New Deal and solidarity with the Spanish Republic – Kazan was a theater director committed to social issues. He founded the Group Theatre and, in the postwar period, he and Lee Strasberg founded the Actors Studio, the hotbed of thespian renewal. In short, he fully pertained to New York's left-wing intellectual elite before anti-Communist sentiment broke out. For a brief period before the war, he had even been a militant in America's small and illegal Communist Party.

Therefore, he was singled out as an ambiguous figure if not a traitor, and this reputation would follow him for decades, despite his undisputed artistic stature. One of those he reported was the playwright Arthur Miller, with whom he had worked closely as he had directed Miller's masterpieces on stage, notably *Death of a Salesman*.

153 - Giving testimony against Johnny carries such a high price that Terry pays, still
under the watchful eyes of the still frightened workers and their conspiracy of silence.

The first screenplay of *On the Waterfront* was penned by Miller, but was then replaced by another version by Budd Schulberg. Miller supposedly wrote *A View from the Bridge* in response to *On the Waterfront* and its views on union corruption.

In the film, Brando's character tends to go to the rooftop of his building – also the home of the childhood friend killed toward the beginning of the film – to meditate. Following his death, Terry takes care of the pigeons he is breeding and starts to talk about the innocent birds threatened by predatory hawks; when he decides to go before the Waterfront Crime Commission, a group of thugs kills his birds as a sign that they consider him a spy. It is likely that, between the lines, Kazan was making an autobiographical reference.

The directing concept is extremely modern, placing great importance on noises and music (Leonard Bernstein). Brando's checked jacket became a classic and Brando himself is extraordinary in the film, putting method acting into practice but without overdoing it as he had done in Kazan's *Viva Zapata!* The film won 8 Academy Awards, including the Oscar for Best Black-and-White Cinematography, which went to Boris Kaufman. All three of the actors in secondary roles – Cobb, Malden and Steiger – were nominated for the award of Best Supporting Actor.

Larrabee brothers, the conceited playboy David (William Holden), but he never noticed her. In fact, the girl attempted to commit suicide – somewhat ridiculously – by closing herself in the garage and turning on all the engines of the Larrabees' eight cars. This is the pendent to the philosophy of her father, the chauffeur: "I like to think of life as a limousine. We're all riding together, but there's a front seat, a back seat and a window in between."

To avoid an embarrassing and inappropriate situation, the girl is sent to Paris for two years at the Larrabees' expense. When she returns, however, the gawky teenager has been transformed into a fascinating and sophisticated young woman whom David barely recognizes. Once he does, however, he is the one who begins to court her.

His older brother Linus (Humphrey Bogart) who, unlike David, is concerned only with his responsibilities and the family business, is worried that this will endanger David's upcoming marriage to a wealthy heiress, which is important for the Larrabees' interests. Therefore, to distract her, he clumsily begins to lavish attention on the girl.

Through a series of misunderstandings, changes and unexpected turns of events, David discovers that he is in love with his fiancée, whereas Linus and Sabrina realize that they have fallen in love with each other. But their happiness will require some effort.

The *coup de théâtre* comes when the Larrabee family gathers to sign an important industrial agreement with the family of David's fiancée. In the meantime, Sabrina has been sent off on a steamship to Europe – this time by Linus himself – so that she cannot interfere with the family's plans. Suddenly, however, Linus decides to give up everything and acts impulsively for the first time in his life. He races to the ship, and once he is aboard – remembering the lesson that Sabrina had taught him about how one should wear a hat in Paris – he has a servant bring his hat to the girl who is sunbathing on deck to ask her to fix it properly: "Il y a un monsieur sur le bâteau qui voudrait bien que vous lui arrangiez son chapeau." This is a sign that all the problems have been solved and is the promise of the inevitable happy ending.

1954
SABRINA

Director: BILLY WILDER
Cast: AUDREY HEPBURN / HUMPHREY BOGART / WILLIAM HOLDEN

▶ After playing in *Roman Holiday* and *Sabrina*, Audrey Hepburn achieved a central role in the make-believe world of the Fifties with her petite, agile, svelte, and elegant figure

▲ 1
▲ 2

▲ 3
▲ 4

1. 2. 3. 4. Sabrina is the daughter of the chauffeur to the Larrabee family and finds herself divided between the destiny of social classes, respect for her own status and that of her father, the pressing emergence of her own talent, and the intersecting attentions of the two Larrabee heirs, interpreted by William Holden and Humphrey Bogart.

157 - Here are irresponsible Larrabee playboy, handsome sophisticated David (Holden), and Sabrina, a new woman after Parisian therapy.

It has been objected that the type of romantic and sentimental comedy that inspired this film does not have the mordant wit that would distinguish Wilder's later well-known works. This may be true, but it is equally evident that underlying his breezy lighthearted tone is a harsh critique of this social model and the fact that it is impossible to break down class barriers - except in a fairytale.

Although Hepburn is extraordinary in *Sabrina* - and with this role she established her inimitable style - the other two stars are not at their best. Holden's performance is passable, but Bogart is clearly miscast. Unsurprisingly, he played a role that was supposed to go to Cary Grant and was effectively tailor-made for him.

In 1995 Sydney Pollack produced a respectable remake starring Julia Ormond, Harrison Ford in the role played by Bogart, and Greg Kinnear.

158 and 159 - It is with the older Linns (Bogart) that Sabrina would discover true love. He would reveal some feelings as well yet, too occupied by responsibility and business affairs, he would never have the time to devote himself completely to returning them. An exemplary Wilder artistic comedy of harmonious perfection and pleasant dilemmas, not only is it much heavier than it seems, the film was also shot on a set where rivalry reigned.

1▲

1954

[JAPAN] Genre: ADVENTURE

SEVEN SAMURAI

Director: AKIRA KUROSAWA

Cast: TAKASHI SHIMURA / TOSHIRO MIFUNE

No one should make the mistake of comparing *Seven Samurai* with its American remake, *The Magnificent Seven*, as the latter would unquestionably fare very poorly.

In 17th-century Japan, rife with anarchy and disruption, a poverty-stricken mountain village is constantly raided by outlaws and drifters who steal the unarmed peasants' harvest and leave them to starve. Consequently, they decide to follow the advice of the village elder and go into the city to find a samurai, a member of the noble class of mercenary warriors, to obtain help and protection. Their search proves to be difficult. The villagers have no reward to offer and can barely even feed their defenders. They cannot spend much time in the city and it is difficult to find a proud but masterless samurai willing to accept such a lowly undertaking with no prospects for glory.

Nevertheless, they manage to convince an aging, disenchanted and sympathetic samurai, Kambei, after they see him fight shrewdly and skillfully to liberate a little boy kidnapped by a thief. Kambei accepts the proposal and, as the villagers look on, he begins to recruit samurai to accompany him. Kambei forms a group of six, including himself, and each one has a different personality and different skills. In the end, however, there will be seven of them to defend the village because the group is joined by the irascible and clownish drunk Kikuchiyo (played by Toshiro Mifune, Kurosawa's favorite actor, who magnificently starred in his 1950 masterpiece *Rashomon*; Mifune went on to become an international movie star).

2 ▲   3 ▲

1. 2. 3. Toshiro Mifune is an ostentatious and ridiculous braggart, a self-styled samurai who succeeds in including himself among six other authentic samurai with whom he would valiantly fight. The actor would become an international star and Kurosawa's film would directly inspire the western, *The Magnificent Seven.*

In reality, he too has peasant roots, but wants to stand out among the samurai for his valor. The scope and stature of this film cannot be rivaled by its enormously popular Hollywood remake. Indeed, *Seven Samurai* is unquestionably an action film that expresses far more and lends itself to extraordinarily rich and complex interpretations. The undertaking that unites the samurai and the villagers represents a gesture that breaks down seemingly insurmountable caste and class barriers. It depicts solidarity and a spirit of sacrifice in the name of an intangible reward: honor. From the viewpoint of the weak – the peasants – it also illustrates how people react to a destiny of subjugation and injustice. The entire film, from the prologue to the epilogue, and from the meticulous observation of individual personalities in the construction of the "team" to the epic fight, is illuminated by skillful direction that probes every detail yet adds nothing superfluous (the original version, which is 200 minutes long, should be viewed in order to appreciate it fully).

As to the epilogue, we can quote the Italian critic Morando Morandini. "It ends on a note of virile melancholy: Kamei says that the samurai are like the wind that passes swiftly over the earth, but the earth remains and belongs to the peasants. The peasants are the true victors and the samurai the vanquished."

The words from the epilogue are an example of the many parts that were repeated virtually verbatim in John Sturges' remake, although the latter does not capture the power of these words, nor the depth of their moral lesson. The American director instead merged the figure of the peasant samurai, played by Mifune, with that of the inexperienced boy and aspiring samurai who is benevolently and paternally put to the test in Kurosawa's version, to create the character of the half-blood portrayed in *The Magnificent Seven* by the up-and-coming actor Horst Buchholz.

James Stewart plays L.B. "Jeff" Jeffries, a photo reporter is confined to a wheelchair after breaking his leg while on the job. To pass the time, he starts spying on his neighbors with his telephoto lens.

The apartment house hosts a wide variety of people, from a newlywed couple to a dancer, a struggling musician, "Miss Lonelyhearts," a single woman who is convinced she is an artist and a couple that cannot bear the summer heat. In fact, it is summer and the windows are open onto the courtyard of this apartment house that is home to the denizens of Greenwich Village, New York's bohemian district in the 1950s. And there is also a quarrelsome married couple.

Jeff, who is visited by his girlfriend Lisa (Grace Kelly), his nurse Stella (Thelma Ritter) and a detective friend, gradually becomes convinced that the woman has been murdered by her husband (Raymond Burr, who shortly thereafter went on to become famous in the television series *Perry Mason*). In a crescendo of tension, what the people around Jeff originally thought was a ridiculous obsession proves to be true. There is an animated confrontation during which Lisa shows her courage and sangfroid, and Jeff breaks his other leg.

Considered the perfect film, *Rear Window* is rightly praised as one of the finest works of Alfred Hitchcock, the English director who moved to Hollywood in the early 1940s. It also lends itself to a wide array of comments, analyses and observations, like all of the director's masterpieces. Nonetheless, Hitchcock never overlooks the essence of his self-assigned task as an entertainer and refuses to be overshadowed by the deliberate goal of proving his hypotheses.

Jeff's voyeurism engenders numerous reflections. First of all, it is a metaphor for his profession. The *mise en scène* – the relationship established between the eye, in this case the leading character's point of view as represented by the lens of the camera, the point of view of the director (and thus of the audience), the courtyard and the daily lives being led behind the windows, i.e., the stage or the screen – is a metaphor for entertainment, theater and cinema itself.

Secondly, the spats between the immobilized and irritable Jeff and his fiancée tell us that she wants to get married. She wants him to settle down and give up his chaotic bohemian lifestyle, but he is reluctant to do so. In this sense, his peering into other lives, particularly those of couples, and discovering nastiness in one of them may be his way of justifying his doubts about the institution of marriage.

1954
REAR WINDOW

Director: **ALFRED HITCHCOCK**

Cast: **JAMES STEWART / GRACE KELLY / THELMA RITTER / RAYMOND BURR**

Here are Jeff, disabled photojournalist tempted into voyeurism, and his persistent fiancée, Lisa.

164 - Disabled after an accident, Jeff kills time looking through his rear window, spying on the courtyard of his apartment complex. He uncovers a homicide but above all discovers the joy and pain of life as a couple, and impending marriage of which his attentive and a bit authoritarian fiancée, Lisa, does everything to convince him.

1. 2. 3. 4. 5. Among the diverse scenes of life that Jeff witnesses from both his sacrificial and privileged position, is the murder of his neighbor's wife by her husband played, by Raymond Burr (in the first image above left, Raymond Burr, the future Perry Mason, here a killer).

It has been asserted and reasserted but still worth repeating. The window is the screen, Jeff's eyes are the camera therefore the director's eyes, which become the audience's eyes. In other words, we all become voyeurs by seeing this film. More than just the perfect thriller, this film is a poignant reflection (a word that would probably have horrified Hitch as it's generally recognized that films were not "pieces of life" but "pieces of cake" to him) on the male-female relationship, cohabitation, conflicts in understanding, and marriage considered as a loss of individual freedom.

Lisa is dangerously and courageously putting her own personal safety at great risk. Thinking he's discovered, the assassin might react.

François Truffaut, the most important exegete of Hitchcock's work, commented that *Rear Window* is a film about indiscretion, violated intimacy, the most ignoble side of surprise and the impossibility of achieving happiness. It is "about dirty linen that gets washed in the courtyard, about moral solitude, an extraordinary symphony of daily life and ruined dreams."

In 1954, the year the film was released, Hitchcock was 55 years old and, between silent films and "talkies," he had already directed more than 40 films, including *Spellbound, Notorious* and *Dial M for Murder*.

James Stewart was 46, 21 years older than his costar, had already won an Oscar and would later work with Hitchcock in *The Man Who Knew Too Much* and *Vertigo*. Grace Kelly worked with Hitchcock in three films made one after the other in the same year: *Dial M for Murder, Rear Window* and *To Catch a Thief*.

Based on the novel *It Had to Be Murder* by mystery writer Cornell Woolrich, *Rear Window* sensationally anticipates many television fads, from candid camera to reality shows. Enormous attention was paid to preparing the set, which was completely artificial and was built at Paramount Studios.

In 1998, the former Superman, Christopher Reeve, who was confined to a wheelchair in real life following a terrible accident, starred in a mediocre remake. An episode of *The Simpsons*, the famous cartoon series, parodies the film when little Bart spies on his neighbor Ned Flanders.

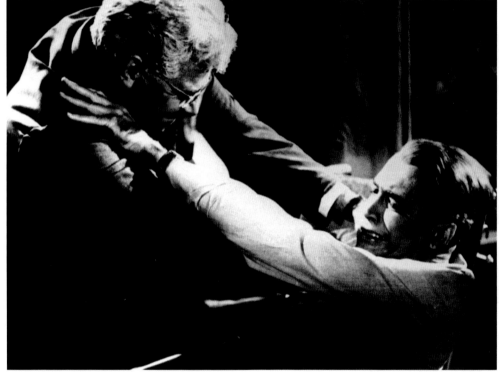

167 - Jeff involves Lisa and his nurse, Stella (the great Thelma Ritter), in his espionage activities and conjecture about events outside his window. The assassin risks everything and makes contact with Jeff in his apartment. Defenseless from the disability forced upon him, Jeff is compelled to endure his threats. People say that *Rear Window* was the director's favorite among all his films. James Stewart was 46 years old and Grace Kelly was only 25 at the time. She shot three back-to-back films with Hitchcock who adored her icy sensuality in *Dial M for Murder, Rear Window*, and *To Catch a Thief*. Her last film would be *High Society*. In 1956, she married Prince Rainier and became the Princess of Monaco.

1955

REBEL WITHOUT A CAUSE

Director: NICHOLAS RAY

Cast: JAMES DEAN / NATALIE WOOD / SAL MINEO

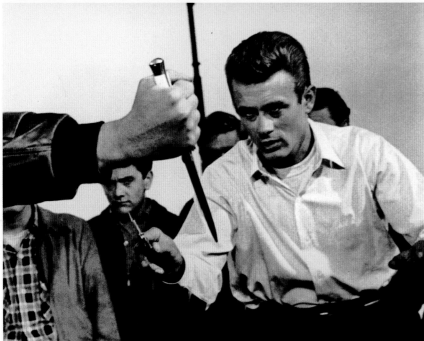

Dean greatly admired Brando, who was six years his elder and already a box-office attraction. Unlike him, however, James Dean's life and career were destined to be extremely short. *Rebel Without a Cause*, his second film, was released in 1955 (October 27), as was *East of Eden*, which premiered in New York in March and was released nationally in April. Dean's third and final film, *Giant*, was released the following year, when Dean was already dead. He was killed in 1955, at the age of just 24, following a car accident in his Porsche.

Dean – even more so than Brando – would immediately become an icon for youthful rebellion and would be imitated by millions. His short life and the moody, disenchanted air to which his image would be tied forever have made him a legend for all the generations of teenagers that followed. He was the first hero – or antihero – of a mass consumer society. The legend of James Dean was rivaled only by those of Marilyn Monroe, Elvis Presley, the Beatles and Che Guevara.

1. 2. 3. 1955 was a fatal year. Between March and April, Elia Kazan's *East of Eden* from the novel by John Steinbeck was released. In October, Nicholas Ray's *Rebel Without a Cause* was released. James Dean (turning 24 on February 8th) had already died in a car accident on September 30th while driving his Porsche. More than a year later, *Giant* would be released, the third and final film that the young actor did not even have time to finish shooting. The legend of the young hero lives on forever throughout the world, even in the few roles he had a chance to play.
Hardly more than ten years later, Ernesto "Che" Guevara (who died when only 15 years older than James Dean had been) would be as powerful and eloquent on screen.

And God Created Woman (Et Dieu ... créa la femme) is a classic example of the hype that has often surrounded French cinema. In this case, the film was overrated in every aspect but one: the erotic potential of Brigitte Bardot in her début role. The film was made not long after the era of seductive screen icons Rita Hayworth and Silvana Mangano, and essentially at the same time as the provocative Marilyn Monroe became a star. BB was 22 when the film was made - she was born in 1934, the same year as another symbol of femininity of the era, Sophia Loren – and the mambo-dancing sex symbol became an overnight sensation. Indeed, the film is titillating even by today's standards.

The film is set in a picturesque fishing village that would soon become famous: Saint-Tropez. Kind-hearted Michel (Jean-Louis Trintignant), his older brother Antoine (Christian Marquand), decidedly less reliable, and an older nightclub owner (Curd Jurgens) lust after the orphan Juliette. Frivolous and sultry, the girl seduces all the men she meets. She marries Michel, takes off with his scoundrel brother and spurns the third man. In the end, however, she discovers that she truly loves Michel.

In short, the film is completely vacuous and, despite the fact that it is no better than some of the other ho-hum comedies of the era, it became an international sensation. BB, an ingenuous and amoral Lolita, and an icon that would be examined in depth by intellectuals such as Simone de Beauvoir and Françoise Sagan, was the epochal forerunner of the libertarian 1960s who came to represent modern beauty and women's liberation.

Director Roger Vadim was insignificant from an artistic standpoint and his main claim to fame was the fact that he was Bardot's husband. The two were married from 1952 to 1957, after which he went on to marry a string of beautiful women, including Jane Fonda, who starred in his film *Barbarella*. Nevertheless, he showed shrewd insight into a changing era and benefited enormously from his "discovery" (although BB had already starred in a number of films). According to the Italian critic Morando Morandini, "She was his Pygmalion rather than the other way around."

The film turned the French Riviera, where it was set and filmed, into an internationally famous destination and popular jet-set resort. Bardot moved to the area when, increasingly misanthropic, she retired from acting to devote her time to protecting her beloved animals.

Brigitte Bardot, then only 22, was emerging as a new sex symbol.

1956
AND GOD
CREATED WOMAN

Director: ROGER VADIM

Cast: BRIGITTE BARDOT / JEAN-LOUIS TRINTIGNANT / CHRISTIAN MARQUAND / CURD JÜRGENS

174 - Born in Paris in 1934 to a middle-class family, Brigitte Bardot posed for the cover of Elle at 15 years old and acted in her first film at 18. That same year she married Roger Vadim who would be her Pygmalion. By 1956 when Vadim built "*Et Dieu...créa la femme*" ("...And God Created Woman") around her, she had already participated in numerous films, even some important ones like The *Grand Maneuver*, directed by René Clair, becoming from that point on the "Brigitte Bardot phenomenon."

175 - Brigitte Bardot is the prototype for Lolita, the sulking and sensuous teen, naïve and corrupted, provocative and natural, innocent and bold, unscrupulous and submissive all at the same time. She was an earthquake to weak masculine defenses and one of the very few true diva phenomena, perhaps one of the only with such intensity born outside of the Hollywood machine.

be killed. Little Moses is saved and placed in a basket that is set afloat on the Nile. He is found by Bithiah, the pharaoh's daughter, who adopts the child and raises him as a royal prince, sharing the secret of his provenance only with her slave, who would betray this secret years later.

Bithiah's brother Seti, who has become pharaoh in the meantime, loves Moses like a son, preferring him to his own son (the future Rameses II) as the heir to the throne and the husband of Nefertari, who has been chosen to marry his successor. This sparks the rivalry between Rameses and Moses. Valiant and loyal – and unaware that he is not Egyptian but Hebrew – Moses wants to treat Hebrew slaves more humanely and is backed in this by the pharaoh, who considers this population a resource that should not be wasted simply out of futile rage.

1956
THE TEN COMMANDMENTS

Director: CECIL B. DEMILLE
Cast: CHARLTON HESTON / YUL BRYNNER / ANNE BAXTER / EDWARD G. ROBINSON

Charlton Heston, actor and symbol of the blockbuster Hollywood epic film

Cecil B. DeMille, the Hollywood director most identified with the epic format, remade the same film that he'd previously done as a silent film in 1923, lavishing a wealth of unprecedented production resources never before seen in the history of historical Biblical film and absolute cinema, taking full advantage of the potential of Cinemascope and projection on a panoramic wide screen.

The revelation of Moses' true origins upsets this balance, but Rameses rejoices over what he thought he had lost. He becomes pharaoh and convinces Seti – on his deathbed – to reject Moses.

Moses, in turn, has had a divine revelation and accepts his destiny as the leader of the Hebrew people. He will ultimately show Rameses the power he holds. Transforming his rod into a cobra, he inflicts ten plagues on Egypt, from the turning the waters of the Nile to blood to the disease that strikes all the firstborn, including the son born to the pharaoh and Nefertari. Lastly, he parts the Red Sea to allow his people – pursued by the pharaoh's army – to cross it to reach Mount Sinai on the opposite shore. It is here, that, despite all the discontent and temptations that spread through his people during their long wait, God finally reveals the Ten Commandments.

1. 2. 3. As in *Intolerance*, directed by D.W. Griffith, the project anticipated alternating and running one period scene parallel to a modern one. However, it did not work and he chose to photograph everything on film with actors in costume using spectacular exterior shots in Egypt. Because of the stylized historical Biblical subject matter, the success of this film resulted in the frequent transfers of American film crews to the Mediterranean and Italy and the birth of a flourishing historical fiction tradition of B movies in Italian cinema, from the end of the Fifties on.

180 and 181 - Charlton Heston as Moses is flanked by Yul Brynner as Ramses, his archrival, Anne Baxter, Edward G. Robinson, Yvonne De Carlo, Debra Paget, John Derek, Nina Foch, Vincent Price, and John Carradine.

Naturally, with a length of 3 hours and 40 minutes the film also probes other events and features countless characters. Charlton Heston was chosen for the leading role because of his resemblance to Michelangelo's Moses. The bald and muscular Yul Brynner played his rival, Rameses II. Edward G. Robinson, the legendary "bad guy" in gangster movies, was cast as the Hebrew traitor and slave driver during construction of the city in honor of the pharaoh. Anne Baxter played Nefertari and Yvonne De Carlo the Bedouin shepherdess Sephora, who married Moses after her tribe took him in when Rameses II ordered that he be abandoned in the desert. Debra Paget, John Derek, John Carradine and Vincent Price complete the main cast. The film, which was made and projected with VistaVision, won the 1957 Academy Award for Special Effects.

182 and 183 - Charlton Heston (1923-2008)
primarily owes his great fame to *The Ten
Commandments* and to *Ben-Hur* in the three
years following. However, he also
participated in two very stunning films,
Touch of Evil by Orson Welles and *Major
Dundee* by Sam Peckinpah. In addition,
he played roles in other movies within
the same epic film genre like the historical
El Cid, the fictionalized biography of
Michelangelo — *The Agony and the Ecstasy*,
and the science-fiction *Planet of the Apes*.
A politically controversial personality for
his vigorous defense of citizens' right
to bear arms, he was thus the target of
documentary filmmaker, Michael Moore,
in *Bowling for Columbine*.

19**57**

[SWEDEN]   Genre: **DRAMA**

THE SEVENTH SEAL

Director: INGMAR BERGMAN

The Seventh Seal is the film that won the Special Jury Prize at the 1957 Cannes Film Festival, revealing to the world the powerful artistic personality of Swedish director Ingmar Bergman. When he made the film (based on his own play) in 1956, he was 38 years old and, in addition a prestigious career in theater, he had already made numerous films, including *Smiles of a Summer Night* (1955).

Bergman emerged on the film scene in the 1950s, the same period that saw the domination of Luis Buñuel, Akira Kurosawa, Roberto Rossellini, Luchino Visconti, Federico Fellini and Michelangelo Antonioni in *auteur* cinema, influencing directors around the world, from Stanley Kubrick to Woody Allen. These pioneers – each in his own part of the world and according to his own style – led to a dramatic change from naturalistic realism to the investigation of interiority, conscience and angst.

Set in the Middle Ages, in an era of plagues and apocalyptic terrors, the film describes the return from the Crusades of the Danish knight (Max von Sydow), accompanied by his squire Jons (Gunnar Björnstrand). The latter is skeptical and tied to the immediacy of life and its material precariousness, whereas the former is overcome with doubt, disappointment and questions about the mystery of life and death, and the faith he fears he has lost.

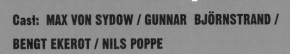

**Cast: MAX VON SYDOW / GUNNAR BJÖRNSTRAND /
BENGT EKEROT / NILS POPPE**

1. 2. 3. Apart from theatrical work that preceded his films, Bergman's sources were particularly pictorial, from Dürer's paintings on panels in medieval churches as well as from "The Apocalypse" by St John; verses from this biblical book were recited in the film. The *angst* that pervaded the world of the Fifties probably came from more than just this director's Swedish background in his ideological juxtapositions and tension that agitated the scarecrow to a third and final world war. Bergman had an extraordinary fascination with sharp, clean, black-and-white photography.

In a world in which everyone seems to have gone astray (around him, some try to expiate their sins while others turn to pleasure and revelry), the knight's return is influenced by two encounters, one with a priest who is actually Death in disguise and the other with a roving company of acrobats, who manage to convey the meaning of love and give him faith in life. The knight plays the famous chess game – the leitmotif of the film – with Death and his very life at stake.

Despite the fact that the film's overly programmatic and schematic metaphysical research has been criticized over the years, *The Seventh Seal* is nevertheless one of the finest examples of philosophical cinema and is imbued with enormous visual power. It is the quintessence of Bergman's approach. One of its most notable aspects is the existential crisis faced by the Scandinavian Protestant knight, who is torn between his profound sense of sin and guilt and his lack of faith, and thus his agonizing inability to find eternal meaning in human destiny. Therefore, he is gripped with terror in the face of a grim afterlife without any possibility of redemption or salvation.

The cast features many of the great actors who were regulars in Bergman's works: the two leading players and Bibi Andersson, who plays the wife of the acrobat Jof (Nils Poppe). The following year Andersson would star in another Bergman masterpiece, *Wild Strawberries*.

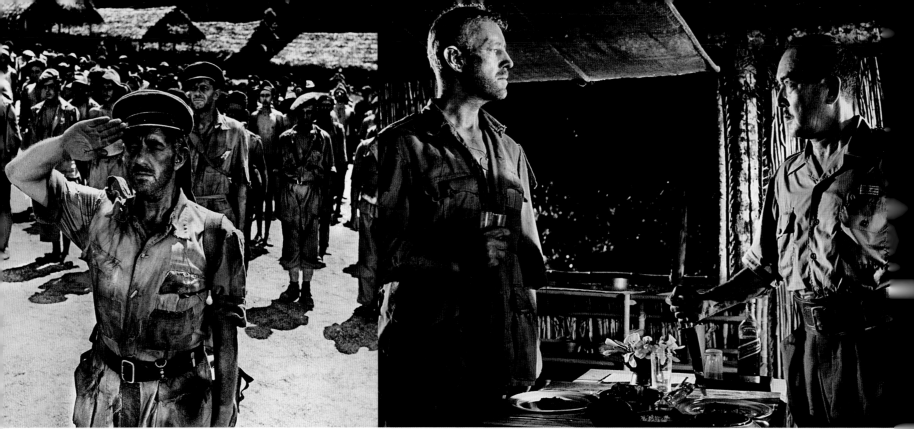

1 ▲

2 ▲

1957
[UK / USA] Genre: **WAR**

THE BRIDGE ON THE RIVER KWAI

Director: **DAVID LEAN**

The first of the three major films by the English director David Lean – it would be followed by *Lawrence of Arabia* and *Doctor Zhivago* – *The Bridge on the River Kwai* is also the best of the trio.

The story is set in the Asia-Pacific Theater during World War II. The British regiment, commanded by Colonel Nicholson (Alec Guinness), receives orders to surrender to the Japanese, who are occupying vast areas in Southeast Asia. Nicholson's men are captured and brought to a prison camp in the Burmese jungle commanded by the ruthless Colonel Saito. In an attempt to reduce them to pure slave labor, as the Germans were also doing in Europe, Saito plans to force the soldiers and their officers to build a bridge that had to be completed as quickly as possible as it was vital to military strategy. Nicholson indignantly refuses to allow his officers be used for hard labor under enemy orders, invoking conventions governing the treatment of prisoners of war.

The British colonel's proud and stubborn resistance cannot be bent by even the most inhumane treatment and torture. (The film clearly takes ample license in contrasting the cruelty and baseness of the Japanese against pristine British civility.)

Having won the first round, Nicholson receives a proposal of collaboration from his jailer, who has been forced to change his strategy in the face of his adversary's mettle: a request on equal terms. Unable to refuse as a matter of pride and confident that he can ask anything of his men because of the moral example he has set for them, Nicholson fully devotes himself to building the bridge on the River Kwai. The agreement is that he and his officers will direct operations.

Cast: ALEC GUINNESS /
SESSUE HAYAKAWA / WILLIAM HOLDEN /
JACK HAWKINS / GEOFFREY HORNE

1. 2. Alec Guinness is the English colonel, Nicholson, rigid with respect to his own purely pathetic concern for uniformity and stability of hierarchies even in the humiliating conditions of prison. Confrontations with his Japanese peer, Saito, commander of the prison yard, run along the plotline of competition motivated by the Englishman to the paradox of wanting to demonstrate the superiority of his British expertise in construction of a bridge that would be used by enemy forces.

3. 4. William Holden is the American officer who would follow the Allied commander's orders to blow up the famous bridge whose construction cost unspeakable physical hardship for the prisoners, treated like slaves by their Japanese jailors, and motivated by Nicholson's proud and patriotic sense of discipline.

Yet this engenders a striking contradiction. Nicholson is convinced that he is performing a proudly patriotic deed, upholding the honor and dignity of His Majesty's soldiers, without realizing that, in reality, he is collaborating with the enemy.

In the end, however, this paradox is destined to explode tragically when a British patrol commanded by an American officer (William Holden), one of Nicholson's prison mates who has managed to escape, carries out the higher orders to blow up the famous bridge in order to prevent the enemy from using it. The British colonel opposes this action and is so blinded by his smug self-satisfaction over giving his enemy what, in his mind, is a lesson in morality, organization and engineering that he is ultimately blown up with his own creation. The film's dynamics arouse a powerful sense of awe. Likewise, the issue of the conduct and code of ethics to be followed by captives who are forced to compete with each other is fascinating, as the prisoners demonstrate their strength, yet must also acknowledge their adversary and the fairness of the competition itself.

Other films that address this issue also come to mind. One of the most notable is Tony Richardson's *The Loneliness of the Long Distance Runner*, a typical example of British cinema's "Angry Young Man" genre of the early 1960s. In this film, the leading character is convinced to lead the team at his reformatory in a cross-country race against boys from an exclusive boarding school, only to refuse to win the race when he is just a few feet from the finish line. Another example is John Huston's *Escape to Victory*, in which a soccer team of Allied prisoners (and all-star team with Stallone and Pelé) refuse to obey an order by the Resistance to exploit the opportunity of the match to escape, preferring to stay on the field to fight the team of their German torturers.

Screenwriters Carl Foreman and Michael Wilson were not credited in the titles because at the time (1957) they were still blacklisted as a result of Senator McCarthy's campaign against suspected Communist sympathizers in Hollywood. The only name that appears is that of Pierre Boulle, the French author of the novel on which the film is based. *The Bridge on the River Kwai* won seven Academy Awards, including Best Original Score, with the famous whistled "Colonel Bogey March."

The Great War (*La Grande Guerra*) is the supreme celebration of the spirit of Italian comedy. It was an enormous success among Italian audiences and critics (winning the *Leone d'oro* at the Venice Film Festival, making it the first comedy to win such a prestigious award), but it also gained widespread international renown. It is the film that best conveys the encounter between the dramatic subjects and social sensitivity distinctive of Neorealism and the ironically irreverent approach that was the hallmark of director Mario Monicelli, screenwriters Agenore Incrocci and Furio Scarpelli, and actors Vittorio Gassman and Alberto Sordi. With the exception of *Big Deal on Madonna Street* and, to a certain extent, Totò's performance in *Cops and Robbers* and *Totò and Carolina*, *The Great War* was the most daring such combination until then, and it marked the first time that anyone had probed such a sensitive page in Italian history.

It is important to note that in 1959, when the film was made at the actual Italian-Austrian front, where the bloodiest trench warfare of World War I had been waged, the generation that had experienced the war was still alive. As a result, there were still eyewitnesses to many of the events portrayed in the film. Above all, however, there was still the widespread conviction that the subject was sacred and thus untouchable, not only among right-wingers, still influenced by Fascist rhetoric, but also those of the Left. From the very outset, all of this sparked a massive controversy that pitted even the most progressive intellectuals against the film.

Sordi and Gassman respectively played the Roman infantryman Oreste Jacovacci and the Milanese infantryman Giovanni Busacca. The two meet as army recruits and promptly focus on their regional differences, criticizing each other throughout the story. Above all, however, they join forces to avoid work and shirk all responsibility, showing a penchant for opportunism, cowardice and escapism.

Indeed, this is precisely what made the film so shocking. How could anyone dare to depict the hallowed figures of soldiers and their self-sacrifice in such a comical and grotesque light? Even more shocking was the fact that this portrayal was paralleled by the representation of war as a futile and perverse bloodbath; the depiction of the irresponsibility, superficiality, incompetence and vanity of military leaders; and the crudely realistic comparison of officers and men as emblematic of class conflicts that prevailed over patriotic sentiment.

Alongside the vivid portrayal of a large cast of minor characters (notably the prostitute Costantina, played by Silvana Mangano), however, it is the film's dramatic turn that has made it a timeless masterpiece.

1959
THE GREAT WAR

Director: **MARIO MONICELLI**

Cast: **ALBERTO SORDI / VITTORIO GASSMAN**

Convinced that they will never actually see any combat, the two somehow end up behind enemy lines and are arrested by the Austrians. When they are interrogated, they are ready to reveal the little they know about the construction of a strategically important bridge. But the offensive arrogance of the Austrian officer and his disdain for Italians brings out a sense of pride and an instinctively heroic reaction in the two men. "I'm not telling you a thing, you bastard!" is Gassman's unforgettable line as he is dragged in front of a firing squad. Even Sordi, who professes his cowardice until the very end, face his own execution with dignity and honor. No one would ever know that the Italian advance resumed thanks also to the small contribution made by these two "loafers."

The film's third screenwriter, Luciano Vincenzoni, was inspired by Guy de Maupassant's short story "Two Friends" (set during the Franco-Prussian War of 1870). However, the film also draws on other literary works, such as Emilio Lussu's novel *A Year on the Plateau*, the bible of democratic interventionism. Nevertheless, it is telling that Lussu, an anti-Fascist political leader, wanted nothing to do with the film and contemptuously rejected the financial offers that were made to him. There is a famous photograph that was taken after the film won the award at the Venice Film Festival. It shows Incrocci, Scarpelli, Monicelli, producer Dino De Laurentiis (also Mangano's husband), Sordi and Gassman. This picture is the very icon of the triumph of Italian cinema.

1. 2. 3. Oreste Jacovacci (Alberto Sordi) and Giovanni Busacca (Vittorio Gassman) are the two idle and cowardly infantrymen who do everything to get out of their duties and escape the dangers of the war front, also finding a way (Busacca-Gassman) to court the beautiful prostitute Costantina (Silvana Mangano). But in the end, by chance or through an authentic and conscientious reawakening of questionable dignity, they redeem themselves, behaving like heroes when faced with a platoon of Austrian soldiers. Busacca responds disrespectfully to the enemy officer who interrogates and insults him, implying the cowardice of all the Italians with, "I'm not telling you anything, shitface."

BEN-HUR

Director: WILLIAM WYLER

Cast: CHARLTON HESTON / STEPHEN BOYD / JACK HAWKINS /
HUGH GRIFFITH / HAYA HARAREET / MARTHA SCOTT

Made in Rome's Cinecittà studios, *Ben-Hur* is the iconic and most spectacular work in the history of what came to be known as "Hollywood on the Tiber." In effect, in the 1950s the studios welcomed an influx of American productions, attracted by the fame of Italian workers as well as lower costs. A similar trend can be seen today with the transfer of film production to the former Soviet bloc countries.

Ben-Hur was also the first film to win 11 Oscars (out of 12 nominations), a record that remained unbeaten for nearly 4 decades, until *Titanic*. The box-office response broke records that it still holds today based on adjusted parameters.

This was the third screen version of Lew Wallace's novel by the same title. The first was made in 1907 and the second in 1926; William Wyler, who worked on the 1926 version as an assistant, would go on to make the third one in 1959.

The famous chariot race, a marvel by expert and daring stuntmen, remains a legendary scene.

The setting is Palestine during the Roman Empire. The new governor is accompanied by Messala (Stephen Boyd, one of the many heart-throbs of the era), who heads the legions and is responsible for quelling any uprisings by the conquered population. The noble and wealthy Jewish merchant, Judah Ben-Hur (Charlton Heston), clashes with his friend Messala after he defends his fellow countrymen. In response, Messala imprisons the mother and sister of his former friend and enslaves him as an oarsman on Roman galleys. Ben-Hur has his first encounter with Jesus, who comforts him when he oppressed and abused along with other slaves. When the ship on which he is enslaved is involved in a battle, Ben-Hur saves the life of the Roman consul Quintus Arrius (Jack Hawkins), who as a reward brings him to Rome to have him compete in chariot races, in which Ben-Hur becomes a popular figure.

Emancipated by his benefactor, Ben-Hur returns to his homeland to look for his mother and sister, as he has lost all trace of them. Along the way, he encounters Balthasar, one of the Magi, who tells him about the Messiah. Then he meets the sheik Ilderim (Hugh Griffith), who asks him to take part in an important race that will be held in Jerusalem. Ben-Hur agrees, knowing that Messala will also participate.

Already a famous star in the epic film genre after *The Ten Commandments,* here's Charlton Heston maneuvering the chariot in the famous race, the most spectacular attraction in this film.

192 - Already a rich noble Jewish merchant, Ben-Hur is reduced to slavery by Messala, once his former friend and now head of the centurions who has joined forces with the new Roman governor of Palestine. Oppressed and thirsty, Ben-Hur receives comfort from Jesus, whom he encounters for the first time.

193 - Forced to row with other slaves on a Roman ship, Ben-Hur would achieve redemption in a sign of recognition from the Roman consul, Quintas Arrius, when he saves his life.

In the most spectacular scene of the film, the hero wins this fight to the death, killing his rival. Before he dies, however, Messala tells him where to find his mother and sister. The two women, who have leprosy, have been abandoned and live in seclusion. Heedless of the danger of contracting the disease, Ben-Hur goes to them and, with them, watches Christ's Calvary. When Jesus dies on the cross, the two women are cured.

Several Italian directors assisted Wyler, such as Mario Soldati, who was already famous, and the unknown Sergio Leone. Enormous and spectacular productions such as this one always used several units, and the secondary ones were often responsible for filming the crowd scenes.

According to industry anecdotes, Kirk Douglas wanted the leading role, whereas the director wanted to cast him as Messala, a part the star indignantly turned down.

194 and 195 - This is the fatal challenge between Ben-Hur and Messala in the great chariot race arena where the hero will reign victorious. Finally able to return to his homeland, he finds that Messala has imprisoned his mother and sister. Reduced to near death by leprosy, the two women would be miraculously cured just after Jesus dies on the cross.

196-197 - A phenomenon of the proverbial ability of the Italian cinematographic workforce, the very complex set for *Ben-Hur* was created at Cinecittà. Other camera crews with Italian directors, such as the then lesser-known Sergio Leone, worked alongside director, William Wyler, particularly for the impressive crowd scenes. ▼

[USA] Genre: COMEDY

SOME LIKE
IT HOT

Director: BILLY WILDER

Cast: MARILYN MONROE / JACK LEMMON / TONY CURTIS / JOE E. BROWN

Some Like It Hot may be America's most famous comedy, and it is unquestionably Billy Wilder's best known. Moving from the romantic/sentimental sub-genre of *Sabrina* to farce and slapstick, Wilder struck a chord with this film and shocked conformists by playing on sexual allusions and ambiguity.

It is set in America during the Prohibition – the year is 1929 – and specifically in Chicago, the city that was the heart of organized crime during this period. After the police raid the nightclub where the musicians Jerry and Joe (Jack Lemmon and Tony Curtis), respectively the double-bass player and the saxophonist, are working, the two become inadvertent witnesses of the St. Valentine's Day Massacre.

On February 14, 1929 Al Capone murdered the rival gang headed by the Irishman Bugs Moran in order to give the Italian Mafia undisputed control over the city and its illicit trade, particularly bootleg whiskey. (The notorious Italian gangster, who was never caught for his countless string of serious crimes, was finally arrested for tax evasion.)

The film is full of real and historical references, as well as allusions to the great gangster movies that had previously probed these topics (albeit not from a humorous angle): from Mervin Le Roy's *Little Caesar* to William Wellman's *The Public Enemy* and Howard Hawks' *Scarface*.

The two musicians – unemployed and on the run – manage to get hired by an all-girl band heading to a gig in Miami, presenting themselves disguised as Daphne (Lemmon) and Josephine (Curtis). One of the band members is the irresistible Sugar Kane (Marilyn Monroe), a ukulele-player who is dangerously attracted to alcohol, and whom they meet during the train ride to Florida. The two men vie for her attention but cannot unmask themselves, as this would be too dangerous, particularly when it turns out that their pursuers, who work for the fearsome killer Spats Colombo (George Raft, an actor who, in real life, was known for his Mafia connections), happen to be at their hotel.

In the meantime, Joe – unable to accept the fact that he cannot reveal his true identity to Sugar – disguises himself as the bored millionaire Junior and exploits the finances of a real millionaire. In turn, the millionaire, Osgood Fielding III (Joe E. Brown), has fallen madly in love with Jerry, who is still disguised as Daphne.

Here are the saxophonist, Joe alias Josephine (Tony Curtis), and the bass player, Jerry alias Daphne (Jack Lemmon). ▶

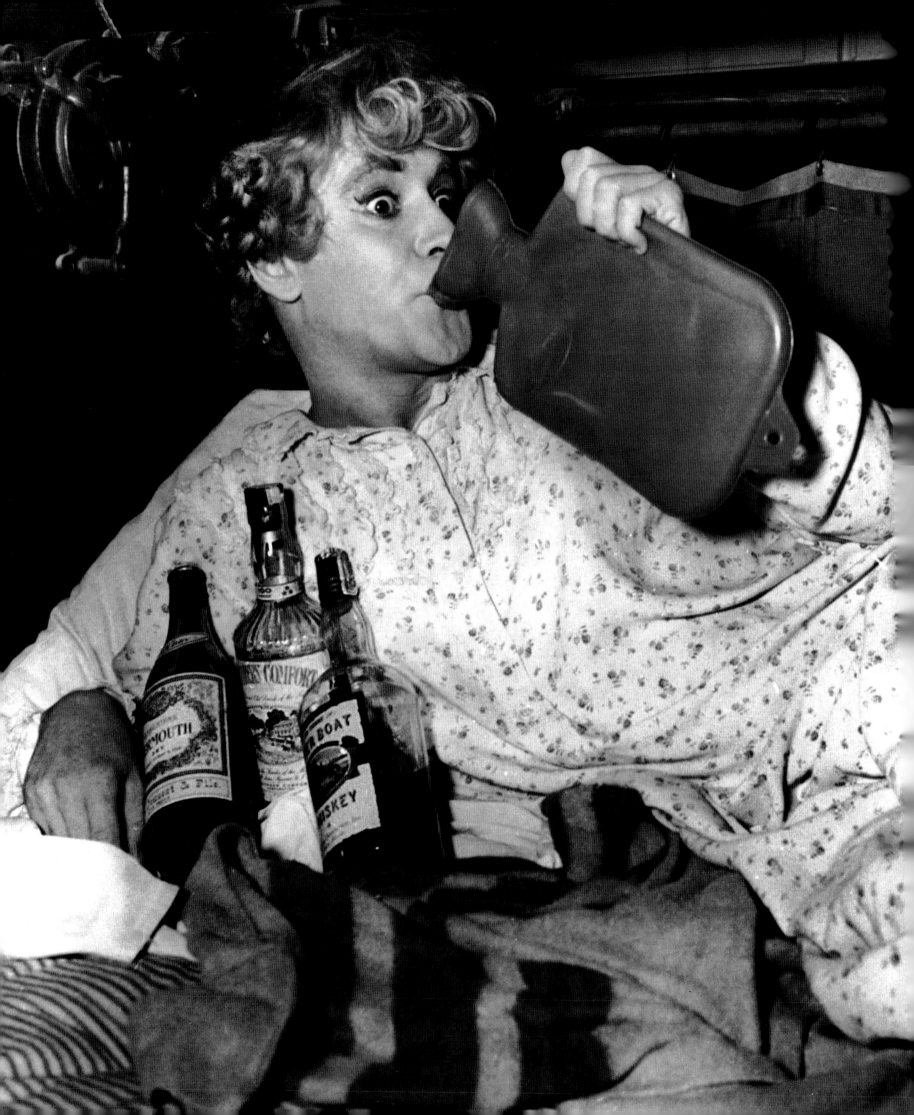

1. 2. Hunted by Chicago gangsters, the two musicians masquerading as women and camouflaging themselves among members of a female band, travel by train from Miami, meet the irresistible Sugar (Marilyn Monroe), and both fall in love with her, but can't reveal themselves and date her openly.

202 and 203 - Joe-Josephine (Curtis) does not resist temptation and, upon arrival at his destination where the two men come across their relentless pursuers, he assumes yet another identity, that of the dandy billionaire, Junior, so he can finally devote himself to courting the splendid Sugar. However, a real billionaire does exist and falls for Daphne, that is, Jerry. When Daphne finally reveals her real identity of Jerry, the billionaire is not disappointed but delivers the famous and outrageous line, "Nobody's perfect."

Everything culminates with the madcap escape of all four characters. When Jerry finally reveals his true identity, the millionaire tries to prove that he can "adapt," uttering the immortal line "Nobody's perfect!"

For Marilyn, who was at the height of her fame (*Some Like It Hot* was released in 1959), this marked her third-to-last completed film (it was followed by *Let's Make Love* and *The Misfits*). She charmed moviegoers with her dreamy sensuality and captivated audiences when she sang "I Wanna Be Loved by You."

At the same time, enchantment and exasperation were probably the two opposite reactions that she aroused in the director who had to work with her, if we are to believe the gossip about his anger over her inability to learn her lines. He had already worked with her in *The Seven Year Itch* and was supposedly planning to cast her in *The Apartment* and *Irma la Douce*, but both of these roles were instead played by Shirley MacLaine. In the first case Marilyn had another commitment, whereas for the latter, by the time filming started she was already dead.

1 ⌃

1959

[USA] Genre: **MELODRAMA**

A SUMMER PLACE

Director: DELMER DAVES

Cast: **RICHARD EGAN / DOROTHY MCGUIRE / SANDRA DEE /**

ARTHUR KENNEDY / TROY DONAHUE / CONSTANCE FORD

A Summer Place, made toward the end of the conformist 1950s, is highly symbolic of a break with the past, striking a blow at securities and prejudices alike, and heralding a new era and a different way of life. It is a classic example of a work that reflects a moment – the term "epochal" would be an overstatement – despite the fact that the film, unquestionably well crafted, falls short in terms of artistic merit.

Bart and Sylvia (Dorothy McGuire) live with their teenage son Johnny (Troy Donahue) on Pine Island, where they run a hotel. One day Ken Jorgenson (Richard Egan), a millionaire businessman, brings his wife Helen and their daughter Molly (Sandra Dee) to see the place where he once spent his summer vacations. While the two young people immediately fall in love, the adults are unable to get along. As they observe their respective children together one rainy afternoon, Ken and Sylvia nostalgically reflect on their youth, when they too had been lovers and Sylvia's mother had been against their relationship. However, they are seen by the night watchman, who tells Helen about their encounters.

1. 2. 3. For a short time only, the very young Sandra Dee becomes a minor yet great star with her role as Molly. She meets Johnny at the beach and falls in love with him. In the backdrop of adolescent love that also stimulates the love of their parents, we find out that his mother (Dorothy McGuire) and her father (Richard Egan) were lovers in their youth, were separated by their parents, both created unhappy families, and are now reuniting as love grows between their son and daughter.

In the meantime, the teenagers go out for a boat ride but are stranded and are forced to spend the night together until help arrives. At the end of the vacation, Molly goes off to an exclusive college in Boston, but Johnny is sent to Virginia. Since both Molly and Johnny are resentful of their parents, Ken and Sylvia – who have divorced their respective spouses and gotten married in the meantime – decide to invite them to spend the summer at their beach house. During the summer, Molly and Johnny realize that they are truly in love.

At the time, audiences were indignant over *A Summer Place* because sex – both premarital and extramarital – was clearly suggested. The film is effectively a denunciation of hypocrisy and bigotry, and although it may seem mild today it was shocking at the time. Couched in a melodramatic form that was more in keeping with the Hollywood standards of the era, it focused on sin and outcomes that were scandalous for a puritanical and sanctimonious society. Nevertheless, the film was enormous popular, particularly with female moviegoers.

Director Delmer Daves was previously known mainly for his Westerns, such as *3:10 to Yuma* starring Glenn Ford, but this famous and prophetic film ushered in an era that focused on the anxieties of the transition from adolescence to adulthood. In this work, based on Sloan Wilson's novel by the same name, he effectively paints a picture that emphasizes the various elements involved: the landscape, nature and the sea, color and photography, and music, with a score by Max Steiner. And, above all, the cast. Teenager Sandra Dee, who had just filmed another melodrama emblematic of the era with Troy Donohue (Douglas Sirk's *Imitation of Life*, starring Lana Turner), became a powerful but fleeting image of the new star system that burst onto the scene in the late 1950s and early 1960s. In fact, she inspired one of the songs in the musical *Grease* as well as a biographical film (*Beyond the Sea*, 2004), but her career as an actress would be short-lived.

Few films can be described as "epochal," but *La Dolce Vita* is one of them. Even today, nearly half a century after it was made, it is astonishing to discover the miracle of a work that, while the outcome of an extremely subjective and imaginative viewpoint that distorts reality, has nevertheless become the most accurate and faithful chronicle of a particular moment in Italian history and 20th-century society. The paparazzi, the glamour of Via Veneto and the very term *dolce vita* (the sweet life), with its implications of high society and ephemeral, reckless frivolity that became universally understood and shared paradigms, were magnified and emphasized – if not literally invented – by the ingenious mind of Federico Fellini. Paradoxically, despite the fact that *La Dolce Vita* was effectively a dream, reverie or hallucination, it ultimately proved to be one of the most accurate documents of the times.

The film does not have a true story or linear plot. Everything revolves around the character of Marcello Rubini (Marcello Mastroianni), a society reporter and gossip columnist who mirrors not only the vices and superficiality of the world he haunts, but also – albeit in a confused and unconscious way – the disquiet of modern intellects facing the skeptical, secularized and complex Western society of the late 1950s.

During his diurnal and nocturnal adventures in Rome, he comes across a host of situations and other figures. We meet them through Rubini's eyes – Fellini's eyes – for a viewpoint that is, in turn, disenchanted, curious, enthralled and childish. We see his encounter with Sylvia (Anita Ekberg), the capricious but fun-loving movie star, and his arguments with his lover Emma (Yvonne Furneaux). We watch his fascination with religious fanaticism, which is the outcome of an allegedly miraculous apparition in the Roman countryside, and observe an aristocratic party that reflects a decaying – if not already disintegrated – world. We follow his meeting at the house of Steiner (Alain Cuny), the intellectual who holds enormous sway over Marcello. Though outwardly serene and happy with his family, Steiner is instead destined for suicide. There is also his encounter with Paola (Valeria Ciangottini), the young girl who symbolizes purity and nostalgia for lost simplicity.

Certain scenes are etched in our minds: the statue of Christ suspended from a helicopter at the beginning of the film, the party at the noble castle, the enigmatic ending with the beached sea monster and Marcello who is unable to understand Paola's words. But above all, there is the scene with Sylvia and Marcello in the Trevi Fountain, which became a worldwide icon.

1960
LA DOLCE VITA

Director: **FEDERICO FELLINI**

Cast: **MARCELLO MASTROIANNI / ANITA EKBERG /
YVONNE FURNEAUX / ALAIN CUNY / VALERIA CIANGOTTINI**

Here is Anita Ekberg cavorting in the Trevi Fountain as the symbol of the Dolce Vita.

1. 2. 3. 4. Via Veneto, its large cafes, the comings and goings of real or wannabe stars and the paparazzi following them. Federico Fellini describes all this, even in large part created and invented by him, entrusting his Marcello Rubini (Marcello Mastroianni) with the task of embodying a new social, human, intellectual, and moral figure. The gossip columnist, simultaneously a witness to that era and active participant as protagonist, is involved and immersed in parties and nocturnal detours. In that hodgepodge of psychological motivations stemming from as much the permanent modernization of society as the illusion of such, the fleeting sensual pleasure of a moment made from nothing, expectations and cynicism, are critically examined and abandoned to trend, to the vital surge and profound disintegration of values.

Made in 1959 (mainly at the Cinecittà Studios in Rome, where a replica of Via Veneto was built), the movie was released at the beginning of 1960 and became an overnight sensation. Although it was immediately considered a major event, it also raised enormous controversies among the press and sparked a public outcry. At the Milan première, the director was showered with insults. The scandal was even discussed by the Italian Parliament, but attempts to have it censored failed, thanks in part to authoritative "protection" by several enlightened members of the Church who defended Fellini and protected the film.

La Dolce Vita also elevated Mastroianni to stardom, despite the fact that the film producer wanted to cast an internationally renowned actor: Paul Newman. (The troubled relations between Fellini and the producer Angelo Rizzoli, a media and movie magnate, represent a legend within the legend.) Something similar happened to Vittorio De Sica, who stood up to those who wanted Cary Grant to star in *Ladri di Biciclette* (*The Bicycle Thief*), and history has clearly proved these two great directors right. For his script, Fellini turned to Pier Paolo Pasolini, although the writer is not listed in the credits. Adriano Celentano, who went on to become a major Italian pop star, was also featured in one scene.

Piero Gherardi received an Academy Award for Costume Design and the movie won the Palme d'Or at the 1960 Cannes Film Festival.

What had not occurred in France following World War II came about in the late 1950s, when the country was at war with Algeria. The *Nouvelle Vague* or New Wave movement did for France's prestige what Neorealism and Rossellini, Amidei, De Sica, Zavattini, Visconti and De Santis had done for Italy, and it marked an extraordinary lesson for world cinema. It brought about formal, expressive and linguistic renewal that was fully integrated with the expectation of great ideal, civic, moral and human renewal. It was the idea of "new" cinema, but combined with a new concept of living, thinking, and acting emotionally and politically. In short, it represented the idea of complete change.

Jean-Luc Godard, François Truffaut, Claude Chabrol, Jacques Rivette and Eric Rohmer, the daring, aggressive, fiercely polemical and violently uncompromising critics who had once written for the film magazine *Cahiers du cinéma*, were the soul of this movement. These authors made the transition from discussing films to making them and the works in which they applied their theories to the creative practice were released at the end of the decade: Truffaut's *The 400 Blows*, Chabrol's *Les cousins*, and *Hiroshima, Mon Amour*, by kindred spirit Alain Resnais (all three films were made in 1959). And, naturally, there was *Breathless* (*À bout de souffle*), made by the 30-year-old Godard in 1960.

Thanks to his debut film, Godard became the reference model of the New Wave, embodying its aesthetic-ethical manifesto. Directly or indirectly, the film conditioned all of French cinema, which was rebelling (often pettily) against "le cinéma du papa," and it had enormous worldwide influence on young and ambitiously innovative directors in the 1960s but also later, from the Italian Bernardo Bertolucci to the Brazilian Glauber Rocha, the Czech Milos Forman and the Pole Jerzy Skolimowski. Unlike Truffaut, Chabrol, Louis Malle and others, who later made films "for the audience," albeit each with his own unmistakable style, Godard alone would remain rigorously and haughtily loyal to his unbending youthful ideals, marking the most radical endpoint of the aesthetics preached by the movement. If anything, he embarked on a reverse path, going from his first work, which was still "narrative," to ideological cinema and then onto "essay cinema,"

Breathless is actually a buildup of situations and ambitions. It contains an enormous legacy of the references that Godard and his companions had avidly absorbed as critics. It contains a love for classic American cinema and, above all, the *noir* genre. At the same time, it is an example of the kind of freedom that, initially theorized but now implemented, overturned the rules and traditions of language, acting, directing, lighting, editing and, above all, narrative structure.

1960

[FRANCE]   Genre: DRAMA

BREATHLESS

Director: **JEAN-LUC GODARD**

Cast: **JEAN-PAUL BELMONDO / JEAN SEBERG**

1. 2. 3. Michel lies on the cobblestones, struck dead after a futile escape and Pat, who was in love with him but not committed to having faith in a man who was so untrustworthy, cries over him. Jean Paul Belmondo and Jean Seberg in the first film by Jean Luc Godard, the guiding light in the *Nouvelle Vague* (French New Wave), the theoretical and artistic leader of a movement that, harshly renouncing their French forefathers and ostentatiously adopting predecessors of their choosing, revolutionized world cinema created between the Fifties and Sixties.

Michel (Jean Paul Belmondo) is a thief who, following a heist in Marseille, steals a car (the first in a long string thefts throughout the film). On his way to Paris, he foolishly kills a motorcycle policeman who has stopped him for speeding. Michel wanders around Paris – which is explored extensively by the fast-moving and nervous eye of the camera – as he makes plans to return to Italy, where he had worked at Rome's Cinecittà studios. He runs into a girlfriend, meets an accomplice who owes him money, stays in a hotel room and skips out without paying for it, takes taxis, also without paying, steals cars, and skims the newspapers reporting the murder and fingering him as the killer on the loose. And then he finally runs into the enchanting Patricia (Jean Seberg), an American student who makes her living by selling *The Herald Tribune* on the street and dreams of becoming a journalist. The two previously had an affair, but it is not over yet. (Is Patricia pregnant? Is the baby his?)

Permanently on the lam and increasingly restless, Michel wants to leave with her, but the girl decides to turns him in for his own good and tells him what she is doing. <0} Michel makes little effort to escape and, in the final unforgettable scene, he staggers down the entire length of a Paris street before collapsing to the ground, shot by a pursuer who thought he was armed. In the final image, the camera lingers on Patricia's face as she looks into the lens and then turns away.

In addition to its plot, it is the film's array of idiosyncrasies and the details of its atmosphere that have made it a legend. We see Michel, imitated by Patricia, who pulls three consecutive faces and then runs his thumb over his lips; Michel with his Borsalino hat and a cigarette rolled in *papier mais* perpetually glued to his lips; Patricia with her short blonde coif, striped top and pleated skirt. The dynamics between the two characters and the backdrop of the city unquestionably influenced Bertolucci and *Last Tango in Paris*, but it is also likely that this model of two tormented souls who are tied to each other by the precarious thrill of a moment may also have inspired the allegedly scandalous *9? Weeks*, although in the latter film the rapport is distorted and transformed into a purely commercial commodity.

The American remake of *Breathless* (1983), directed by Jim McBride and starring Richard Gere, is a poor copy of the original.

[ITALY/FRANCE]   Genre: DRAMA / WAR

TWO WOMEN

Director: VITTORIO DE SICA
Cast: SOPHIA LOREN / JEAN-PAUL BELMONDO / ELEONORA BROWN

Two Women (*La Ciociara*), the film version of the novel by the same name that Alberto Moravia published three years earlier (1957), reunited director Vittorio De Sica and screenwriter Cesare Zavattini, the team that made Italian Neorealism world famous in the postwar period. However, while it proposes themes and atmospheres that the movement had fueled a decade earlier, it offers them in a style targeting the masses.

The source was a successful novel by Italy's leading writer (although the film adaptation downplays the book's bitter impact) and one of Italian top stars played the leading role in the film. Although she was just 26, Sophia Loren, who had already worked in Hollywood, was cast in the seemingly improbable role of a mother, but it brought her enormous fame and international stardom. It also won her the first Oscar ever awarded to an actress for a non-English-speaking role.

Anna Magnani had originally been asked to play Cesira: 52 years old at the time the film was made, she was 26 years older than Loren, who was instead to play Cesira's daughter Rosetta. However, Magnani turned down the part, which thus went to Loren. It is interesting to note that Loren later played the same role in Dino Risi's television remake in 1989, nearly 30 years later.

The film tells the story of Cesira, a young Roman widow with a 13-year-old daughter. During the German occupation and the Allied bombing of Rome, she decides to leave her small shop in the hands of one of her husband's friends, and she takes Rosetta to her hometown in Ciociaria, south of the capital. Here Cesira meets another refugee, a young Communist intellectual working with the Resistance movement (Michele, played by Jean-Paul Belmondo). A difficult but promising relationship blossoms between the two, only to be brutally interrupted when the Germans arrest the young man.

When things appear to settle down, Cesira decides to return to Rome using any means of transportation she can find given the emergency situation. Yet just when it seems that the two are out of danger, tragedy strikes. On their way home, mother and daughter are raped by a group of Moroccan soldiers. Most of the French units that fought in the area and took part in the long Battle of Monte Cassino were composed of colonial soldiers from the Maghreb region of North Africa.

Cesira's despairs over her daughter, who is so traumatized that it seems she will not recover. They also find out that Michele has been killed and, in a certain sense, learning about the death of this man, to whom they were both attached, gives them the will to start living again.

Conceived by Moravia as a metaphorical part representing the whole, the rape scene signifies the annihilation of a population and a nation, but this is not the case in the film. Indeed, history remains in the background and the film instead focuses on the intimate drama of motherhood and of dishonored womanhood.

Unquestionably powerful and compelling, the film was above all an opportunity to show international audiences what could be expected of Italy and its top star, despite the fact that Loren's appeal was powerfully – and courageously – downplayed by the unkempt look required by the part.

In 1961, night had already fallen when the news of Loren's Academy Award reached Italy. When television reporter Lello Bersani got to the house where she was living with producer Carlo Ponti, the actress opened the door in her bathrobe. However, since the two were not married yet, the interview was never aired.

This is Cesira and her daughter, Rosetta, after the girl endures violence, leaving a desperate mother and a devastated daughter. Sophia Loren interpreted the role of Rosetta while Anna Magnani played the role of Cesira. This is a sensational example of how a change in the plan can produce "unprecedented" results. Though difficult to believe, there is something so perfect about a film that wasn't completely designed in advance.

In the endless list of films by Alfred Hitchcock, *Psycho* (1960) was the director's biggest commercial success, though not his master-piece. It seems that the reference model for the character of Norman Bates (Anthony Perkins) was the Wisconsin serial killer Ed Gein, and the details in his biography and those of his macabre crimes largely coincide with those recounted in the film. In any event, the film was based on a novel by Robert Bloch.

A secretary, Marion Crane, has stolen $40,000 from her office and left the city. Looking for a secluded place to stay, she stops at the gloomy motel run by a shy and introverted young man who tells her that he lives with his oppressive old mother. Although we never see her, we can hear her voice (a demonstration of Hitchcock's ability to manipulate emotions without paying too much attention to verisimil-itude).

Marion is stabbed to death as she takes a shower. The private detective (Martin Balsam) hired by Marion's sister and fiancé, con-cerned over the girl's disappearance, tracks down the motel and is also killed. In the end, the other two will be the ones to discover the truth, narrowly escaping the same fate. When Norman murders, he is disguised as a woman. In fact, he is convinced that he is actually his mother, whom he had killed years before.

The film is a marvel of perfection, pure entertainment whose main goal is a taste for storytelling. At the same time, however, it is al-so a psychoanalytical study – although this is not its intent – that, tellingly, has been analyzed extensively by scholars and specialists. The killer embodies all the characteristics of the immature and unaware male, oppressed by an authoritarian mother figure and lacking a fa-ther figure. The killer hates women, whom he is unable to possess except by killing them, and the woman he hates the most is his own mother, whom he has eliminated. As a result, however, he is crushed by his sense of guilt, which leads him to assume her appearance and identity. Indeed, it is a classic study without actually being one, as it is first and foremost pure spectacle for its own sake.

1960
PSYCHO

Director: ALFRED HITCHCOCK

Cast: ANTHONY PERKINS / JANET LEIGH / VERA MILES

Marion (Janet Leigh) in the key scene of the film: murder in the shower.

▲ 1

Although the famous shower scene lasted barely 40 seconds, it required an extremely elaborate procedure, with no less than seven days of filming and more than 70 different camera angles. A double stood in for Janet Leigh. The structure of the scene followed the extremely detailed storyboard created by Hitchcock's close assistant, Saul Bass. A successful graphic artist and designer, Bass created many iconic title sequences, including several for Hitchcock's films. Bernard Herrmann's score, which the director initially did not want, was fundamental to the success of the film and helped create its intense atmosphere.

Psycho and its crude violence made an enormous impression on audiences, who loved the film. Once again, the director demonstrated his exceptional ability to create extremely popular films while also being an innovator. The first sensational innovation of Psycho is the fact that the leading actress dies early in the first half of the film. Nevertheless, with this scene Hitchcock – always extremely respectful of laws, rules and social conventions – also lashed out against censors and the "moral" self-censorship that still prevailed in Hollywood.

Perkins, who subsequently became a slave to his famous character, also starred in the three sequels made respectively in 1983, 1986 and 1990. In 1998 Gus van Sant directed a color remake (Hitchcock was adamant that his film be made in black-and-white). Apart from a few retouches due to the chronological adaptation of the plot, the remake is virtually identical to the original, further confirming that Psycho is truly a cult film.

▲ 2

▲ 3

1. 2. 3. Anthony Perkins is Norman Bates but is also the figure in women's clothing, that of his dead mother, his alter ego who kills. He has personality that is split between the motel he manages and the macabre house behind the motel where he lives. Expert technique (the shower scene), bold narrative (the protagonist disappears and is murdered in the first half of the film), in-depth human analysis, and abundance of elements make common knowledge of psychoanalytical interpretations without ever renouncing the central objective of creating a show for everyone. This is the inimitable "touch" of Alfred Hitchcock.

1960

[USA] Genre: **WESTERN**   Director: **JOHN STURGES**

THE MAGNIFICENT SEVEN

Cast: **ELI WALLACH / YUL BRYNNER / STEVE MCQUEEN /**

HORST BUCHHOLZ / CHARLES BRONSON / JAMES COBURN / BRAD DEXTER / ROBERT VAUGHN

Six years following Akira Kurosawa's masterpiece *Seven Samurai* (1954), its Americanized remake was released, with a Western atmosphere, setting and clothing (1960). It was declaredly a remake, unlike *A Fistful of Dollars*, made a short time later by Sergio Leone, who was inspired by Kurosawa's work (*Yojimbo*, released in English as *The Bodyguard*) but infringed its copyrights. Kurosawa took Leone to court and won the lawsuit, receiving royalties from the distribution of the film – which would prove to be one of the most exceptional examples of a low-budget film that became a blockbuster – in Japan, South Korea and Taiwan.

The structure of *The Magnificent Seven* is exactly the same as the original adapted as a Western.

There is a poor village – the setting is the US-Mexican border – that is regularly visited and sacked by a gang of bandits headed by Calvera (Eli Wallach, who would later play a "bad guy" in Leone's *The Good, the Bad and the Ugly*). Exasperated but also aware that they cannot fight this injustice alone, the farmers send one of their representatives to the city to hire gunmen to protect and defend them, and to drive Calvera and his thugs away forever.

The preparation, presentation of the characters and recruitment of the seven form the most enjoyable part of the film. The process starts with the

218 - Eli Wallach is Calvera, the leader of the bad guys, the band of men that terrorize and starve a village of poor workers.

219 - Yul Brynner is the defender of the weak along with the other "magnificent" six: Steve McQueen, Horst Buchholz, Charles Bronson, Robert Vaughn, Brad Dexter, and James Coburn.

meeting between Chris (Yul Brynner, dressed in black and with his trademark bald pate), the future leader, and the laconic and scornful Vin (Steve McQueen). Together, the two demonstrate their courage and unconventional wisdom to the villagers - enthralled at the spectacle - by agreeing to lead the funeral cart transporting the body of an Indian to the cemetery. Thus, they face the armed opposition of half the town, which does not want to bury a nonwhite person. After this display, the two accept the peasants' proposal. It soon becomes clear that they have not accepted it as hired guns but out of pride as free men who refuse to tolerate oppression and as a tacit rebellion against injustice. They start to seek other men and decide that they need seven, forming the "magnificent" group.

There is the young boy (the debuting actor Horst Buchholz) who hangs around Chris without ever being taken seriously; in the end he will be accepted as part of a group. There is the man who has been working as a lumberjack because he is broke (Charles Bronson). There is the taciturn one who is quick with a knife (James Coburn). There is Chris's old friend, the engaging fatalist (Brad Dexter). Lastly, there is the edgy ladies' man who someone is out to kill (Robert Vaughn).

on comedy, it is time for the most epic part, which is underscored by Elmer Bernstein's famous theme music. The seven continue their mission out of a sense of honor, and certainly not for money, as they will earn nothing. They will victoriously complete their mission, but four of them will not survive. Of the remaining three, Chris and Vin set out for new adventures, but the boy, who is a half-breed, decides to settle in the village because he has fallen in love with a girl. Considered one of the last Westerns of the classic cycle - the films by Leone and Peckinpah were made a short time later, followed by the anti-Western wave "on the Indians' side" - this enormously popular film is marked above all by its study of the individual characters, most of whom lifted directly from the original Japanese model. Nevertheless, the director took some freedom and there were several variations and adaptations to the already established Western genre. One example can be seen in the dynamics between the group leader (Brynner), his right-hand man (McQueen) and the inexperienced but bold and generous boy (Buchholz). Howard Hawks presented the latter type of character in a very similar way in *Rio Bravo*. *The Magnificent Seven* launched its actors to stardom, starting with Steve McQueen who, three years later (1963), would be

1. This was a great personal affirmation for Steve McQueen for whom *The Magnificent Seven* was a launch pad.

2. Eli Wallach would be the "ugly" in *The Good, the Bad, and the Ugly*, directed by Sergio Leone.

The 1961 film written by screenwriter George Axelrod, directed by Blake Edwards and starring Audrey Hepburn bears little resemblance to the novella by the same name that, two years earlier, had consecrated the fame of its eccentric author, Truman Capote.

In the novella, the undisputed charm of the leading character, Holly Golightly, is constrained, suffocated and damaged. It is corrupted by sadness – an underlying sense of despair – that never allows her to escape her fate as an actress *manqué* who sells herself and throws her life away. Holly is a kept woman who adores jewelry from Tiffany's and aspires to affluence that will erase the specter of a bad childhood (Marilyn Monroe – who would have been truer to life in this role – was supposed to play Holly, but the sophisticated and elegant Hepburn was cast instead). She crosses paths with an aspiring novelist – in turn a gigolo – who is also throwing his life away. In short, they both offer sex in exchange for money. But love and the promise of the happy life that the two could have had are not destined to be.

Edwards, the great director of light-hearted and modern sophisticated comedy, seemingly toned down this angle with a relatively scathing and satirical approach, but his film never probes the sense of aimlessness that distinguished the original characters. The film avoids Holly's excesses, starting with her debauchery. And it alters the finale, opting for a happy ending. The charm and style of the up-and-coming star are overwhelmed by the sentimental and comical overtones that sterilize Holly's lifestyle, turning her into a young bohemian alone with her innocently extravagant cat. All the figures around her, starting with George Peppard, the bland "boy next door" of the 1960s, are attractive and winsome, and they override the bitter sense of unchangeable and hopeless destiny that characterizes the novella.

Truman Capote, about whom two films were made just a year apart (Bennett Miller's *Capote* in 2005 and Douglas McGrath's *Infamous* in 2006), was the most famous American writer of the second half of the 20th century. Like his contemporary Andy Warhol, he was an icon of the culture and art of the age of mass communications, consumerism and advertising.

1961

BREAKFAST AT TIFFANY'S

Director: BLAKE EDWARDS

Cast: AUDREY HEPBURN / GEORGE PEPPARD

224 and 225 - Audrey Hepburn is the perfect interpreter of the character created by Truman Capote (her partner, George Peppard, is a bit less than perfect), now leaving behind only a slight impish patina, a trace of her style in that era without all of the bitterness of that period.

Despite the great power and character he demonstrated in reacting to and emerging from a completely loveless childhood, and his brilliant and astonishingly precocious talent, what has remained in our collective memory is his outer persona as a latter-day Oscar Wilde. He was known as an effeminate and eccentric gossip, an exhibitionist who was extreme in all things, a man absorbed by his voguish social life and a trendsetter. He was the darling of New York's and California's most exclusive journalism, film, theater and literary circles, and was called upon by politicians and jet-setters. In fact, until the publication of his controversial masterpiece *In Cold Blood*, he was at the height of his career. In the last 20 years of his life, however, he became more and more isolated for going against the powerful lobbies that had glorified him in the first place.

Henry Mancini's "Moon River" won an Academy Award for Best Original Song.

This is the film version, co-directed by Robert Wise (for the acting parts but not the music and dance sequences) and rewritten by Ernest Lehman, of a musical that was a huge Broadway hit in 1957. The play was written by Arthur Laurents, with music by Leonard Bernstein and lyrics by Stephen Sondheim. Jerome Robbins produced, directed and choreographed the play, and United Artists brought Wise in for the film version, which was made four years later.

West Side Story overturns all the schemata and customs of both stage and screen musicals due to its aggressive style, sophisticated quality, and the harsh drama of the subject, replete with references to social and racial conflicts. It marked a reversal of the convention that this genre should be lighthearted and noncommittal.

The action takes place in the street – mainly in Manhattan's Upper West Side – and most of it was filmed on location, an enormous innovation in a genre that was always the highest celebration of artifice. Two rival gangs face each other, the Jets, composed white Americans of Jewish, Italian and Polish extraction, and the Sharks, Puerto Ricans who have recently immigrated to the country. The main characters are Riff (Russ Tamblyn), who heads the Jets, and his best friend Tony (Richard Beymer), who has just found an honest job at the neighborhood bar and wants to put an end to the "war" between the two gangs, particularly after he falls in love with a Puerto Rican girl. Playing opposite them are Bernardo (George Chakiris), leader of the Sharks, his sister Maria (Natalie Wood), with whom Tony falls in love, Bernardo's girlfriend Anita (Rita Moreno), and Bernardo's friend Chino (Jose de Vega), who is Maria's boyfriend.

The plot clearly reveals that this is a modern interpretation of Shakespeare's *Romeo and Juliet*. After several skirmishes in the streets and a dance attended by both gangs, it is time for the "council of war" in order to decide when and where the rumble will be held. Everyone agrees that it must not be a brawl, but a "fair" bare-handed fight between two members selected by the respective gangs. Tony comes on the scene, as he has promised Maria that he will do everything he can to prevent the fight, but when Bernardo stabs Riff, Tony kills him. The situation degenerates, but Tony and Mary still love each other in spite of everything, and despite opposition reflecting the era's views about sex and women. The two decide to run away together with Anita's help, but Tony cannot avoid a showdown with Chino, who kills him. In the wake of all the bloodshed, Maria finally manages to bring peace between the two gangs.

1961
WEST SIDE STORY

Directors: JEROME ROBBINS / ROBERT WISE
Cast: GEORGE CHAKIRIS / NATALIE WOOD /
RUSS TAMBLYN / RITA MORENO / RICHARD BEYMER

Natalie Wood is Maria, the Puerto Rican girl who, like in *Romeo and Juliet*, falls in love with Tony (Richard Beymer) from the rival gang, the Jets.

1. 2. In the theater before being on screen, West Side Story, with Leonard Bernstein's music and Jerome Robbins' choreography, revolutionized the style of the musical. "Non-escapist" content violently confronts social and racial themes when two factions are in opposition, both belonging to the most dispossessed group in society.

3. Film shots done between the New York's 68th and 110th streets were considered innovative elements at that time.

229 - Here's the challenge between Bernardo (George Chakiris, at right), head of the Sharks, a Puerto Rican gang, and Tony, who is the best friend of the rival gang's leader as well as boyfriend of Bernardo's sister, Maria.

It is significant to note that this message of alarm, pessimism and disquiet toward the opportunities of integration, coexistence and the American dream emerged in a historical moment – the early Sixties – marked by the myth of renewal of the Kennedy years. It is also important to note that the policeman in the film sides with the Americans against the Puerto Ricans, considered hopeless "natural" delinquents.

Much of the film's power comes from the choreography and the songs; "Maria" and "America" are still famous today. (Natalie Wood was dubbed for the singing sequences). *West Side Story* won an astonishing 10 Academy Awards, not only for its technical excellence but also for Best Picture and Best Director. Its elegant "vintage" main titles were designed by Saul Bass.

The film opens with Humbert Humbert (James Mason) entering the house of Clare Quilty (Peter Sellers) and killing him. We then see a flashback to four years earlier. Humbert, a European professor and translator, has been given a position in Ohio and looks for summer accommodation in Ramsdale. He finds a room at the house of Charlotte Haze (Shelley Winters), a lonely widow who lives with her daughter Lolita (Sue Lyon), an arrogant and presumptuous but stunning teenager. Humbert falls in love with the girl at first sight, whereas Charlotte feels attracted to him.

One morning Charlotte leaves a letter on Humbert's desk, confessing her feelings for him and asking him to leave if he does not feel anything for her. Humbert, who is willing to do anything to be close to Lolita, marries her. When Charlotte realizes Humbert's attraction for Lolita, she sends the girl away to a summer camp. Humbert goes so far as to plot Charlotte's murder, but his plans become unnecessary because, after discovering his secret diary declaring his infatuation with Lolita and his repulsion for her, Charlotte runs outside, where she is hit by a car and killed.

Finally free to show his feelings, Humbert goes to pick up Lolita but doesn't tell the girl that her mother is dead. During the trip, they stop at a hotel, where Humbert has a discussion with the sinister Quilty, who had stayed with the two women before him – and also fell in love with Lolita. We see Humbert enter the room he shares with Lolita but he gets into another bed. The following morning – did something happen during the night? – they continue on their journey. In the car Humbert is finally forced to tell Lolita that her mother is dead. Nevertheless, they decide not to return to Ramsdale but to move to Beardsley together, ostensibly as stepfather and stepdaughter. But Humbert soon becomes jealous, even forbidding her from participating in rehearsals for a school play.

Quilty again gets involved, convincing Humbert to let her go. During the play, however, Humbert finds out that Lolita has been skipping her piano lessons. The two argue and Humbert convinces her to agree to move again. Someone follows them when they move, however, and they are also forced to stop because Lolita needs to be hospitalized.

When Humbert goes to pick her up a few days later, she is gone and the nurses explain that "her uncle" has already come to get her. Humbert hears nothing further from Lolita until, years later, he gets a letter from her asking for money. Humbert travels to meet her, only to discover that she is married and pregnant. She explains Quilty, with whom she had had a relationship, followed them and then picked her up at the hospital. After running away with Quilty, she left him when he told her he planned to take "artistic photographs" of her. And this brings us back to the beginning and the settling of scores.

1962
LOLITA

Director: STANLEY KUBRICK

**CAST: JAMES MASON / SUE LYON /
PETER SELLERS / SHELLEY WINTERS**

▶ Sue Lyon is Lolita, archetypal symbol of the strength of seduction performed through a mixture of innocence and perversion.

1 ▲

"My sin, my soul." With these words, Humbert describes his possessive and morbid attraction for the teenaged Lolita in the novel that brought its author, Vladimir Nabokov, widespread notoriety. Rejected by numerous publishers, the book was released first in France in 1955 and in the United States three years later. Its raciness does not stem from explicit words or images, however, but from what it evokes and leaves to the imagination regarding the unspeakable, blind love of an older man for a young and provocative girl. The name Lolita was destined to become iconic. Nabokov, who worked actively on the project that Kubrick had cultivated for some time, wrote the screenplay but was unhappy with the result. Adrian Lyne, a director specializing in erotica, filmed a dismal remake in 1997.

2 ▲

3 ▲

4 ▼

1. 2. 3. Utterly taken with the adolescent Dolores/Lolita, James Mason's character, Professor Humbert Humbert created by Nabokov and adapted for film by Kubrick, echoes the infatuation of Professor Rath/Unrat for Lola Lola in *The Blue Angel* – the novel by Heinrich Mann and the film by Joseph von Sternberg film.

4. Shelley Winters is Charlotte, Lolita's mother.

1962

[FRANCE] Genre: DRAMA

JULES AND JIM

Director: FRANÇOIS TRUFFAUT

Cast:
OSKAR WERNER /
HENRI SERRE /
JEANNE MOREAU

The setting is the Montparnasse district of Paris in 1910. Two students, the Austrian Jules (Oskar Werner) and the Frenchman Jim (Henri Serre) become best friends, united by their love for art and literature. However, a girl comes between them: Catherine (Jeanne Moreau), whose enigmatic smile they think resembles that of a statue that has sparked their imagination. Catherine becomes the third vertex of an inseparable triangle of love and friendship. Both men find her attractive and she loves them both, but in the end she decides to marry Jules.

The Great War (1914–18) breaks out and the two friends are separated as they fight on opposite fronts. Following the war, however, Jules and Catherine – who have gotten married in the meantime – invite Jim to stay with them at their house in the Alps, where they live with their daughter. Here Jim becomes Catherine's lover and, despite the obvious problems, this does not ruin his friendship with Jules or the feelings that unite the three. During an outing in which Catherine is behind the wheel, an accident leaves her and Jim dead, and Jules is left to mourn them.

Alongside Jean-Luc Godard, François Truffaut was one of the most symbolic and representative figures of the New Wave. *Jules and Jim* (*Jules et Jim*) was his third feature-length film, following *The 400 Blows*, in which his alter ego Antoine Doinel was created, and *Shoot the Pianist*.

The film was the adaptation of a debut novel published in 1953 by the 76-year-old Henri-Pierre Roché, whose work also inspired Truffaut's *Two English Girls*, and it is striking that the 32-year-old champion of renewal and the forceful rejection of "le cinéma du papa" should have been

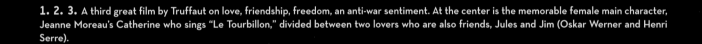

1. 2. 3. A third great film by Truffaut on love, friendship, freedom, an anti-war sentiment. At the center is the memorable female main character, Jeanne Moreau's Catherine who sings "Le Tourbillon," divided between two lovers who are also friends, Jules and Jim (Oskar Werner and Henri Serre).

inspired by a senile novel of love and death. It is even more striking that he should imbue it with the young and rebellious spirit of the New Wave within a romantic period plot, demonstrating that this could be done despite the common prejudice that stories should be set in modern times. The sense of freedom conveyed by *Jules and Jim* (accompanied by a sense of poignant sadness that would become Truffaut's hallmark, even when it was combined with irony or subtle but unmistakable eroticism) hit home so powerfully that, at the time, the film was considered scandalous. Its formula was destined to become a fixed reference for any story revolving around a *ménage à trois*, to the point that it became a cliché: a situation *à la Jules et Jim*.

The sensitive Italian critic Alberto Farassino, one of the leading experts on the New Wave, aptly noted that *Jules and Jim* was not merely the archetype of a love triangle and a paean to freedom and uninhibitedness, but also a story in which war, art, friendship, solidarity and even death are the grounds for measuring behavior and the values of beauty, passion and nonconformism. It also reflects the young director's ability to evoke freshness and lightness.

Along with Godard's *Breathless*, it is a manifesto of the vibrant season that, in the name of a boundless passion for cinema, eliminated all certainty and radically upended the approach to filmmaking. Unfortunately, this passion also fueled much ambiguity, ultimately creating "monsters" in some cases by generating the illusion that the misconstrued role of *auteur* could replace not only technique, experience and professionalism, but also the most essential thing: talent.

Moreau, whose roles in Louis Malle's films *Elevator to the Gallows* and *The Lovers* and Michelangelo Antonioni's *The Night* had already made her a legend of provocative sensuality in the late 1950s and early 1960s, became an icon of the new femininity, famed for her artful masculine garb and her unforgettable throaty voice crooning the words "la femme fatale qui me fut fatale" from Boris Bassiak's song "Le tourbillon."

Who was Thomas Edward Lawrence (1888–1935)? He was an illegitimate Welsh boy who managed to study and gain entry into upper-class circles thanks to influential protection. But he was also an archaeologist, an enthusiast of the Middle East and an expert on the Arab culture; a British officer and member of His Majesty's Secret Service; a legendary military leader according to one version, and a publicity-seeking braggart and extremely ambiguous figure in many ways – including his sexuality – according to others. In any event, he remained a fascinating enigma up to his early death in a motorcycle crash, although here as well some suspect that it was not accidental.

Sent to the Middle East with the rank of lieutenant-colonel during World War I, Lawrence made every attempt to establish contact with nationalist Arabian princes in order to incite the population against the dying Ottoman rule of the Central Empires of Germany and Austria. He very effectively adopted guerrilla techniques. During the peace talks of 1919, however, when it became evident that the victors, France and England, had no intention of keeping the promises they had made to the Arab nation, working instead to pave the way for colonial division (Lebanon and Syria in the French sphere of influence; Palestine, Transjordan and Iraq in Britain's), he shared the Arabs' disappointment and discontent, resigning his commission and isolating himself.

Clearly, this is the stuff of legend and the tale of a great figure, and this is what David Lean's film achieves, sublimely merging the British director's classic tastes and pace with the spectacular and epic exploitation of the richest technical and production resources. Uncoincidentally, Steven Spielberg is a great admirer of the film. In 1989 Lean reedited the film, lengthening the already impressive initial version to 212 minutes.

The singular charisma of the lead actor, Peter O'Toole, who was not well known to audiences at the time, contributed greatly to its success and the enormous popularity of *Lawrence of Arabia* made him a superstar.

O'Toole effectively and credibly embodied the magnetism, ambiguous charm and chiaroscuro personality of a figure who, emerging from nowhere only to vanish once more into obscurity, became the legendary inciter of an entire population composed mainly of nomads, galvanizing them with his almost fanatical behavior and gaining their hard-to-earn trust.

1962
LAWRENCE OF ARABIA

Director: DAVID LEAN

Cast: PETER O'TOOLE / ANTHONY QUINN / ALEC GUINNESS / OMAR SHARIF

▶ The not yet famous Irish actor, Peter O'Toole, is Lieutenant-Colonel T. E. Lawrence, is already becoming a legend with his Lawrence of Arabia.

The roles of his Arab counterparts, princes and Bedouin fighters were played by well-known and outstanding actors such as Anthony Quinn and Alec Guinness (although they look somewhat ridiculous in their makeup and costumes) and the up-and-coming star Omar Sharif, who would be cast in Lean's film *Doctor Zhivago* three years later.

Lawrence of Arabia won seven Academy Awards, including Best Picture, Best Director and Best Music. Its sumptuous photography and art direction were also recognized. Through the luxurious impact of widescreen technology, the aura of the desert effectively plays a leading role in the film, which is considered one of the most popular of the 1960s and of the entire history of cinema. Above all, it is an example of the enormous sense of expectation and satisfaction that could be generated by this medium. Lean's epics *Lawrence of Arabia* and, shortly thereafter, *Doctor Zhivago* – like the nascent phenomenon of the James Bond series and Sergio Leone's Westerns – are probably the last witnesses of a ritual that television and other viewing mediums would ultimately deprive of its uniqueness.

▲1   ▲2

1. 2. Peter O'Toole's interpretation endows the enigmatic character with neurotic and narcissistic traits that amplify his dark charm. Somewhere between historic and fictionalized reality, the figure of Lawrence exercised an important role in the Middle East during the First World War and immediately thereafter, those years that after the fall of the Ottoman Empire determined the region's future development.

3. 4. Lawrence of Arabia made every effort to stir the Arab princes (Omar Sharif and Anthony Quinn in the photos) toward revolt against Turkish rule by playing on their nationalistic aspirations.

1963

THE PINK PANTHER

Director: BLAKE EDWARDS

Cast: PETER SELLERS / CLAUDIA CARDINALE / DAVID NIVEN / CAPUCINE / ROBERT WAGNER

The Pink Panther was the first film in a blockbuster series, although the second film, entitled *A Shot in the Dark* and made the same year, is even more delightful.

Claudia Cardinale plays Princess Dala (Indian?), who has inherited the largest and most valuable diamond in the world, known as the Pink Panther because of a flaw that resembles a panther. David Niven is Sir Charles Lytton, the gentleman thief known as The Phantom, who plans to steal the fabulous jewel. Peter Sellers is the bumbling French police inspector Jacques Clouseau. Capucine plays his wife, who is the secret lover and accomplice of Sir Charles. Robert Wagner plays George Lytton, the nephew of Sir Charles who emulates him not only in the "profession" but also in his uncle's flamboyant playboy lifestyle. The film is set almost entirely in Italy, in Rome and Cortina d'Ampezzo.

In the film's countless comical situations on the snow, at the hotel, and at parties and receptions, Clouseau always shows intuition and experience but constantly fails to find the jewel. In the end, the efforts made by all those involved – including the diamond's owner, who is enamored of Sir Charles – converge to prove, paradoxically, that the guilty party is none other than the inspector, who is discovered in the courtroom with the diamond in his pocket. Initially bewildered, in his immense stupidity Clouseau feels flattered. He is unable to resist the temptation to boast about an escapade, although he was not involved, and is taken away in handcuffs by two Italian policemen who can barely conceal their admiration.

Two of the key ingredients to the film's success are Henry Mancini famous theme and the animated character of the Pink Panther, designed by Fritz Freeling. Originally created for the main titles, the character was later featured in animated shorts.

Nevertheless, the tone and style of the film also played an enormous part. The combination of two different traditions respectively embodied by Sellers and Niven – the immediate and catastrophic effects of farcical slapstick comedy versus the witty and sophisticated comedy of the established genre of romantic thrillers – produces a delightful and extremely successful monument to escapism and light entertainment.

Here, Peter Sellers gives life for the first time to Inspector Clouseau of the French police force, distinguishing him as a slow and bumbling detective. ▶

1. The same year when she plays in The Leopard, Visconti's film of Tommaso di Lamepdusa's novel *Il Gattopardo*, and *8* by Fellini, Claudia Cardinale is pictured here in her finest as the Indian princess, owner of the very valuable diamond called the "pink panther."

2. Capucine plays Clouseau's beautiful wife and David Niven is the terribly attractive thieving gentleman, Sir Litton who, with Madame Clouseau's complicity, has set his sights on this jewel of inestimable value.

3. Here's a failure of epic proportions for the worst policeman in France.

▲ 2   ▲ 3

Although not originally intended as the leading character of the series, Clouseau – and Sellers, of course – would become central to the second adventure. In this case, however, despite the disasters he leaves in his wake and his ineptness, the inspector is victorious. The sequel also spawned two other important characters: Cato (Burt Kwouk), Clouseau's mute manservant and martial arts instructor, and He Inspector Dreyfus (Herbert Lom), Clouseau's boss and sworn enemy, who hates his ineptitude and pays the price for it.

After *A Shot in the Dark*, the saga would continue with five other episodes released between the mid-1970s and the early 1980s, all of which directed by Blake Edwards and starring Peter Sellers. Four others were also made: the 1968 film with Alan Arkin as the inspector (*Inspector Clouseau*), the 1983 film by Edwards but without Sellers (*The Curse of the Pink Panther*), *Son of the Pink Panther* by Edwards with Roberto Benigni (1993) and a new version of *The Pink Panther*, starring Steve Martin and released in 2006.

With 8½ not only did Fellini create what many consider his masterpiece, but he also managed to base this masterpiece on a lack of inspiration: a true paradox.

In the early 1960s Federico Fellini, who was barely 40 years old, had already won two Academy Awards (for *The Road* and *Nights of Cabiria*), made *La Dolce Vita* and become a legend. With the exception of some of the old masters who were still alive and a mere handful of active directors of the same caliber (Kurosawa, Bergman and Kubrick, who was powerfully emerging on the film scene), he was the most famous director in the world.

Countless legends arose around Fellini, encouraged by his own taste for narration, his delight in inventing everything and offering each new person before him different and fascinating versions of the same event, and his irrepressible fancifulness. In this case, the legend goes that Fellini had cultivated an idea but it was so vague and elusive that he could not come up with a title. Consequently, he used a number: 8½, because the film was preceded by 7 feature films and a short segment – hence "half" – entitled *Le tentazioni del dottor Antonio*, which was part of *Boccaccio '70*. Again according to legend, when it was time to start shooting, nothing remained of this vague idea. It had simply vanished, throwing the director into a panic. As he was preparing himself to confess his predicament to producer Angelo Rizzoli, who would certainly not have taken the news lightly, Fellini was distracted by the workmen at Cinecittà, who invited him to the birthday party of one of the stagehands, and suddenly he had a flash of inspiration. The film would accurately recount his situation: the dismay of a director who no longer knows what to narrate.

Regardless of how things may have gone, it is evident that only a genius like Fellini could have pulled this off. And only extraordinary artistic sensitivity could have distilled such a sublime and incisive reflection on art, creativity and cinema, for this is what the film became. It is timeless and, despite an endless string of imitations (Truffaut's *Day for Night* also shows the process of filmmaking), it is completely matchless and ultimately became an archetype.

Marcello Mastroianni (Guido) is Fellini's alter ego on an even more explicit level than in *La Dolce Vita*. His wandering in search of a creative solution that will allow him to complete the film he is making is interwoven with thousands of existential doubts, above all with the unfinished business he has with the women in his life: Claudia (Claudia Cardinale; this film marks the first time in her career that she was not dubbed), Luisa (Anouk Aimée, his wife), Carla (Sandra Milo, his buxom lover), Rossella (Rossella Falk) and others. His examination of his entire emotional and interior existence (diary? psychoanalysis? stream of conscience?), the jumbled accumulation of emotions, dreams and memories, transforms his "director's block" into a burst of creativity.

1963

8½

Director: FEDERICO FELLINI

Cast: MARCELLO MASTROIANNI / CLAUDIA CARDINALE / ANOUK AIMÉE / SANDRA MILO / ROSSELLA FALK

1. 2. Marcello/Guido is the alter ego of Federico. Everything about him is Fellini, his hat, glasses, and scarf. What is surprising about this great film is the contrast between the explosive disorder and the perfectly resolved conclusion. From confusion and loss of inspiration, a masterpiece is born. Grappling with what to say and express, Federico Fellini creates a milestone work throughout the history of film. The real snag is that he created too many artificial imitations, which unfortunately lacked his typical genius.

248 - Sandra Milo is Carla, the sweet and considerate lover, shapely and welcoming. Guido imagines being in a thermal spa where all of his women come to visit him and where, in dreamlike suspension, his whole life passes before his eyes. ▲

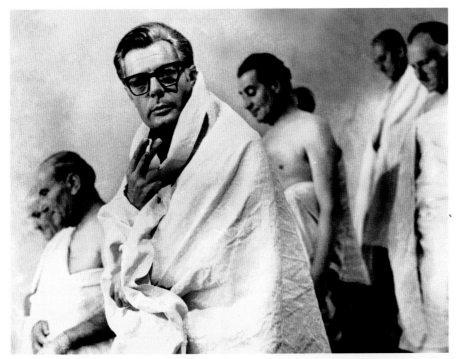

249 - Guido/Fellini, at center, pursues the wild Saraghina (Edra Gale), one of the many female apparitions and one side of the versatile female nature invented by the director and embodied by the actresses that take part in the film: Anouk Aimée (Luisa, his wife), Sandra Milo (Carla, his lover), Claudia Cardinale (Claudia, actress), Rossella Falk, Barbara Steele, Caterina Boratto, and Giuditta Rissone (Guido's mother). Below, the whole cast of characters in white. Fellini actually shot an alternate ending to the final amusement park scene that became famous and is very well known. Here is the entire cast in white, gathered inside a railway-train dining car.

The famous carousel of the closing scene represents the idea of a turning point that allows Guido to find the key to completing his film. Filled with the great fundamental motifs of art, imagination and Fellinian obsession – from the circus to the Church, sexual initiation, and the affectionate but somewhat sinister memory of his family and provincial past – 8½ is a beacon for a generation that burst onto the international film scene in the 1960s, a decade full of innovative ambitions.

The finale we see today was actually filmed as a trailer, and there was supposed to be a different scene, a railroad car in which all the characters, dressed in white, were assembled. The segment with this scene mysterious vanished and what is even more disconcerting is the fact that nearly all those who were there erased it from their memories. This mystery led to a fascinating documentary, "The Lost Ending," by Mario Sesti.

In this major undertaking, Fellini was assisted by Ennio Flaiano, Tullio Pinelli and Brunello Rondi (screenwriters); Gianni Di Venanzo, who can be credited with the stunning black-and-white photography; art director and costumer designer Piero Gherardi; and Nino Rota, who wrote the most often-cited and celebrated music – including the final march – in the history of cinema. The film won two Academy Awards in 1964: Best Costumes and Best Foreign Language Film, the third of the five Oscars awarded to Fellini in his career. The latter category had been created specifically for the first Oscar awarded to Fellini in 1957 for *The Road*.

This may be the only case in which a film has improved and ennobled the novel that inspired it, establishing a uniquely attuned rapport and transforming into images a story that seemed to have been written with a film in mind. Giuseppe Tomasi di Lampedusa's novel *Il Gattopardo* (*The Leopard*) was a literary sensation. A nobleman from an illustrious aristocratic Sicilian family, Tomasi started writing the novel in 1954, when he was 58 years old, and finished it in 1956, but he died in 1957 and never saw it published. The manuscript was turned down by Einaudi and Mondadori, two of Italy's top publishers. The book was published in 1958 by the new and unconventional firm of Feltrinelli (*The Leopard* and *Doctor Zhivago* are two of its all-time bestsellers). In 1959 the book won the prestigious Strega Prize and in 1963 Luchino Visconti made it into a film.

Tomasi was inspired by the history of his family and his great-grandfather, represented by the character of Don Fabrizio, Prince of Salina. The most important works of Sicilian *verismo* of the late 19th century are clearly reflected in the novel, most notably Federico De Roberto's *The Viceroys*. However, the titles of "historical novel" and "sweeping tableau" that have generously been applied to *The Leopard* do little to put it on a par with verist literature. In essence, the novel does not rival the depth of its predecessors in examining the stagnancy of Sicilian society, nor its opportunism, transformism and hypocrisy in welcoming the new Piedmontese "masters" and the ideals of the Risorgimento, and in acknowledging the decline of the nobility and the rise of the new bourgeoisie.

However, Visconti was up to the challenge and plunged in with the fluency of a descendent from a very important aristocratic family, bringing to bear the insight of one who can fully identify with the feelings of the prince of Salina because they were part of his own upbringing. Although Don Fabrizio was a skeptical bystander to the historical process underway, he nevertheless understood it, encouraging the marriage between his nephew Tancredi – a Garibaldian more out of convenience than conviction – and the beautiful Angelica Sedara, a member of the new and emerging class. Tancredi's philosophy is summed up in his famous line, "If we want things to stay as they are, things will have to change." The prince's behavior mirrored Visconti's own personal contradictions: the reckless coexistence within him of an aristocracy that longed for other styles, other worlds and other times, and a sophisticated 20th-century intellectual. Indeed, he was a "committed" Communist intellectual nicknamed "the Red Count." The film was the outcome of enormous production efforts (it was produced by Goffredo Lombardo's Titanus) and the director's legendary and obsessive perfectionism. Visconti assembled an exceptional team, such as screenwriter Suso Cecchi D'Amico, composer Nino Rota, production designer Mario Garbuglia, film editor Mario Serandrei, director of photography Giuseppe Rotunno and costume designer Piero Tosi.

1963
THE LEOPARD

Director: **LUCHINO VISCONTI**

Cast: **BURT LANCASTER / CLAUDIA CARDINALE / ALAIN DELON / PAOLO STOPPA / RINA MORELLI / ROMOLO VALLI**

Burt Lancaster is Prince Fabrizio Salina who delivered the famous line: "For things to stay the same, everything must change."

The prince is curiously attracted to beautiful Angelica. He is aware of how the sun is setting on his own social class as well as of the relentless ascent of the emerging social class embodied by Angelica in her purity as a flawless jewel.

1

2

3

The choice of the cast was brilliant but daring. Perhaps only an aesthete such as Visconti could have come up with a combination as perfect as the duo of Claudia Cardinale (Angelica) and Alain Delon (Tancredi). The other roles were played with magnificent authority by Paolo Stoppa, Rina Morelli and Romolo Valli, all of whom brought with them great experience in theater, as did Visconti himself. But the true revelation was Burt Lancaster as the main character. What now appears as the obvious choice – who else could possibly have played Don Fabrizio? – was a shocking and hotly disputed decision at the time. The American star's personality was light-years away from that character and his culture. It was a magical encounter, however, and Visconti molded the actor – who, in turn, allowed him to do so – to achieve perfection. The highlight of the film, portraying the swansong of a different world, is the magnificent ballroom scene, which reveals the essence of the feelings shared by the prince and Visconti. The film won the Palme d'Or at the Cannes Film Festival.

1. Here, the prince hunts with Don Ciccio (Serge Reggiani).

2. The prince with his nephew, Tancredi (Alain Delon) and the splendid Angelica (Claudia Cardinale), daughter of the nouveau riche Don Calogero Sedàra.

3. The prince with Angelica during the ball, the most famous and symbolic scene in the film. Naturally, he is not immune to nostalgia for his diminishing social status but at the same time contemptuous in recognizing opportunism and transformation that he first "politically" encourages but in his own way also despises.

1964

[ITALY / SPAIN / GERMANY] Genre: **WESTERN**

A FISTFUL OF DOLLARS

Director: SERGIO LEONE

Cast: CLINT EASTWOOD / GIAN MARIA VOLONTÉ / MARIANNE KOCH

According to a well-known anecdote, Sergio Leone came up with the plot for his film after seeing Akira Kurosawa's *Yojimbo* and, indeed, with the exception of Leone's setting in the American West, the two are practically identical. This led to a lawsuit for plagiarism that was won by Kurosawa, who received compensation for damages in the form of royalties from the distribution of *A Fistful of Dollars* (*Per un pugno di dollari*) in Japan, Taiwan and South Korea. Nevertheless, this more unsavory aspect does nothing to detract from the universal recognition of the Italian director's genius.

Leone, who followed in the family tradition (using the pseudonym Roberto Roberti, his father had made silent films, also directing Francesca Bertini, Italy's leading silent-film star), worked in the film industry even as a child when, in the postwar period he also appeared in *The Bicycle Thief*. During the 1950s, he worked on sweeping historical epics made at the Cinecittà Studios in Rome, such as *Quo Vadis?*, *Ben-Hur* and *Sodom and Gomorrah*, which were American productions, and the Italian production of *The Last Days of Pompeii*. He debuted as a director with *The Colossus of Rhodes*.

Nevertheless, he can fully be credited with inventing the "spaghetti Western", although there had also been previous German adaptations of this iconic Hollywood genre. But Leone did not coin this narrow-minded and parodistic term. Indeed, given his extremely proud and almost megalomaniac personality, he never even acknowledged the existence of such a genre, nor that any other directors or films could rival his own invention and distinctive style.

1. 3. Clint Eastwood of *High Plains Drifter* in this first chapter of the future "Dollars Trilogy," was an unknown actor in American TV movies (the *Rawhide* series recalled by *The Blues Brothers* with Dan Aykroyd and John Belushi in 1980) in 1964.

2. Gian Maria Volontè was already an important actor in the theater but unknown in film. Playing the evil and immoral Ramón of the Rojo family, this actor launched his career on the silver screen where he continued to play leading roles for the next three decades.

4. The final duel: the Stranger provokes Ramón reminding him of his own words that to kill a man, you must aim at his heart, enjoying his adversary's surprise and anger each time he gets back up uninjured after Ramón shoots. In fact, the Stranger is energized as he had surreptitiously donned chest armor, hidden beneath his poncho.

The film was the first part of what would become known as the "dollar trilogy" – the other two are *For a Few Dollars More* and *The Good, the Bad and the Ugly* – and was dominated by the laconic character played by a little-known American television actor, Clint Eastwood. *A Fistful of Dollars* burst onto the scene in 1964, breaking all the rules of classic Westerns. There is no heroism, honor or male camaraderie, which are replaced by violence, betrayal and greed. The "Man with No Name" who becomes involved in a duel to the death between two families, the Rojos and the Baxters, is a cynical bounty hunter and acts purely out of self-interest. These moral – or amoral – dynamics are conveyed through a style that seems to contradict all the grammatical and syntactical rules of cinema, employing the exaggerated dilation of timing, obsessive insistence on details, and the accentuation of deeds and actions through repetitive music.

The themes for this film and the ones that followed were composed by Ennio Morricone, who became world famous as a result. In effect, the score contributed enormously to the film's international success. A phenomenon, the film was widely imitated in the 1960s and became a source

of inspiration – and, indeed, a cult – for directors from the generations that followed (including Tarantino).

Fearing that audiences would not easily embrace such blatant adulteration of what was probably their favorite film genre and clearly not expecting the film to become a runaway success, the distribution system used Americanized pseudonyms for everyone involved in the film, starting with the director himself. Leone was billed as Bob Robertson (a tribute to his father), Morricone as Dan Savio and Gian Maria Volonté (the sadistic Ramón Rojo) as Johnny Wels.

The poncho donned by Eastwood and the unlit half-smoked cigar that was always clenched between his teeth became famous, as did the scene in which he is captured and tortured by the Rojos after they discover that he has been double-crossing them. And his strategy against Ramón in the final showdown has become legendary. The Man with No Name is wearing a sheet of steel like a bulletproof vest under his poncho and, knowing his adversary's obsession for aiming straight at the heart, cockily provokes him with the words,

< Aim for the heart, Ramón! >

1964

GOLDFINGER

1▲   2▲

We are talking about one of the greatest mass phenomena in the entire history of cinema, due not only to its worldwide popularity but also its extraordinary commercial success.

Goldfinger is the third film – widely considered the best and most memorable – in saga that has endured for 45 years and beaten all records, totaling 24 films (the 25th is already in the works). It is also the third of the seven starring Scottish actor Sean Connery. The first five with Connery, which were also the first five in this enormously successful series, were filmed one after the other from 1962 to 1967. Connery's sixth film (1971) came on the heels of a one-time appearance by George Lazenby as James Bond, and his seventh – considered apocryphal because it was not produced by the Saltzmann-Broccoli team – came 12 years after the preceding film.

However, Ian Fleming's novels about the brilliant British secret agent 007 (the "00" indicates his "license to kill"), which inspired the film series, were published in a different order.

Of the books written and published between 1953 and the author's death in 1964, *From Russia With Love, Dr. No, Goldfinger, Thunderball* and *You Only Live Twice,* were respectively the second, first, third, fourth and fifth films in the initial cycle starring Connery, but they were the fifth, sixth, seventh, ninth and thirteenth in order of publication. Fleming's character was largely autobiographical, as the author had worked for Britain's Naval Intelligence.

In *Goldfinger,* Bond must deal with an unscrupulous tycoon, Auric Goldfinger (played by Gert Fröbe), who has decided to attack Fort Knox, the

2. Captured by the compulsive liar, Goldfinger (Gert Froebe) who intends to launch an attack on Fort Knox and its gold deposits, James Bond is subjected to torture with a laser.

3. 007 must also clash with the merciless Oddjob, Goldfinger's bodyguard whose knife-like brimmed bowler hat is a deadly weapon.

3 ▲   4 ▲

U.S. gold supply. By making the world's largest gold deposit radioactive, Goldfinger plans to contaminate the world market for this precious metal, thus greatly increasing the value of his own gold reserves. Bond naturally manages to halt his plans after countless adventures, the last of which is a race against time to defuse the deadly atom bomb. His implacable enemy's fearsome manservant, the colossal Korean Oddjob, gives Bond a run for his money, using his steel-rimmed bowler hat as a knife to try to neutralize the secret agent. In the meantime, the fascinating Pussy Galore, Goldfinger's personal pilot, ultimately ends up on Bond's side.

The enormous success of the adventures of James Bond is due to a concoction of elements, only a small part of which is faithful to the original novels. By casting Sean Connery as the first Bond, followed by his most important successors, Roger Moore and Pierce Brosnan, the screen adaptation gives this character brilliant charisma. James Bond is a lady's man with savoir faire, a man who loves luxury. His encounters with women are an important part of his life, and the "Bond Girls" play a key role in his different adventures (although these characters were almost never played by prominent actresses). Likewise, his choice of champagne – strictly vintage Dom Perignon – is important, as is proper preparation of his dry martini: shaken, not stirred.

Several minor but key characters return in *Goldfinger*: his boss M, his secretary Miss Moneypenny, with whom Bond never ceases to flirt, and Q, responsible for showing Bond the latest technological discoveries before giving him the gadgets he needs for his newest mission. *Goldfinger* marked the first appearance of the famous modified Aston Martin. However, his biggest enemy is not featured: the head of the notorious secret organization SPECTRE.

1964

[USA]   Genre: **MUSICAL / COMEDY**

MARY POPPINS

Director: ROBERT STEVENSON

The legend of *Mary Poppins,* which – according to several sources – has been seen by 200 million people around the world since it was released in 1964, is tied above all the songs that were sung onscreen by Julie Andrews in the lead role. The most famous are "Supercalifragilisticexpialidocious," "A Spoonful of Sugar" and "Chim Chim Cher-ee." In fact, the five Academy Awards it won in 1965 include the Oscars for Best Original Music Score and Best Song.

It was also Walt Disney's biggest non-cartoon hit ever, although 17 minutes of the film feature "humans" and cartoons side by side.

The film is set in the late 19th century. The Banks family loses its nanny and, therefore, Mr. Banks publishes an ad to find a new one. As the candidates line up for the job, the two lively Banks children "call in" the magical Mary Poppins, who flies down to their house with her umbrella. Interviewed by the head of the family (although she reverse their roles and effectively interviews him), Mary states – and again, she is the one who decides – that she will stay with them for a one-week trial.

Needless to say, the week will prove to be memorable and adventurous. The new and very special nanny will turn the life of the Banks family upside

**Cast: JULIE ANDREWS /
DICK VAN DYKE / DAVID TOMLINSON /
GLYNIS JOHNS / KAREN DOTRICE / MATTHEW GARBER**

1. 2. 3. 4. In the middle of the Sixties, *Mary Poppins* marked Walt Disney's most successful non-animated feature ever and Julie Andrews' (wife of director, Blake Edwards) great personal success as the actress that gave voice and life to the magical governess. In this fantasy/musical comedy, Andrews performed some songs that became very famous, beginning with "Supercalifragilisticexpialidocious."

down, but she will also solve a number of problems, entertain the children and teach their parents about how to live. And after this lesson in the philosophy of life, she will return whence she came.

It is rumored that other actresses were considered for the role of Mary Poppins, but Julie Andrews would prove to be the perfect choice, as she could do anything: dance, sing, whistle and offer a self-assured, brilliant and lighthearted performance. She is the nanny that every child has always dreamed of having.

After the attempt of the following year to repeat the Disney formula with *The Sound of Music,* the English actress, who had come to Broadway in the 1950s to star in *My Fair Lady* (although Audrey Hepburn was later cast as Eliza Doolittle in the film version), also worked with Alfred Hitchcock in *Torn Curtain.* However, her best opportunities were alongside her second husband, Blake Edwards, particularly with *Victor/Victoria* in 1982.

The film was based on a series of novels by P.L. Travers. *Mary Poppins* received 13 Academy Award nominations and won 5 Oscars, including the one for Best Actress, awarded to Julie Andrews. Like all Disney masterpieces, it is a timeless classic that appeals to audiences of all ages.

DOCTOR ZHIVAGO

Director: DAVID LEAN

Cast: OMAR SHARIF / JULIE CHRISTIE / GERALDINE CHAPLIN /
ROD STEIGER / ALEC GUINNESS / RALPH RICHARDSON

The third of the great epic films by the British director David Lean (following *The Bridge on the River Kwai* and *Lawrence of Arabia*), it is the 1965 adaptation of a monumental novel that had sparked an enormous international scandal only a few years earlier. The film was produced by Carlo Ponti, Sophia Loren's husband.

Boris Pasternak had conceived it as an accusation against the Soviet regime and Stalinism – unlike the film adaptation, which maintained the novel's historical and political setting but transformed it above all into poignant love story – and was unable to publish the book in his own country (it was circulated underground). Due to political pressure, he was forced to turn down the Nobel Prize awarded to him in 1958.

An Italian publisher, Giangiacomo Feltrinelli, played a key role in circulating the novel internationally, first publishing it in 1957 (and clashing with the leaders of the Italian Communist Party, with whom he sympathized) and turning it into an overnight bestseller.

The leading character of the story is the poet and doctor Yuri Andreevich Zhivago who, while at the front during World War I, falls in love with Lara, a nurse. When the October Revolution breaks out in 1917, Zhivago, an anti-Bolshevist, flees to a village in the Ural Mountains with his wife Tonya and his son. Here he meets Lara again and the two become lovers.

They are separated by the civil war (the doctor is arrested by the "Reds," while his family flees the country), only to be reunited by these events and then separated once again. Zhivago ultimately saves Lara – who also bears him a son – but has a heart attack, dying in poverty and solitude. The film's most memorable and heart-wrenching scene shows him falling down in the street as he pursues Lara. After years of silence between the two, he sees her from a tram and desperately tries to get her attention but fails, dying on the sidewalk as she walks on unaware.

The film, which is more than three hours long, won five Academy Awards, including an award for the famous "Lara's Theme" (by Maurice Jarre, who went on to sell an enormous number of records), and it became at least famous as *Gone With the Wind*. The combination of an unhappy love story and melodramatic musical accompaniment deeply moved millions and millions of viewers, but the film's fundamental historical and political implications completely escaped the average filmgoer, rapt in its poignant sentimental contrasts. In turn, the novel (which was underrated) and the film were received diffidently by more sensitive audiences, who viewed the film "from the left" and, blinded by ideological conditioning, branded it as anti-Soviet and anti-Communist propaganda. While it was indeed anti-Communist, it was no mean achievement nevertheless.

The English actress (born in imperial India in 1941) Julie Christie, until this time was known only in her home country and to audiences of "experimental" film. In this she was a muse for the young movement toward "Free Cinema," from *Billy Liar* to *Darling*. Christie took a leap forward in her career playing the role of Lara.

262 and 263 - The Egyptian actor, Omar Sharif who had already been in the cast of a previous epic film by the English directo David Lean *(Lawrence of Arabia)*, interprets the role of the poetic Dr. Zhivago. Married to Tonia (Geraldine Chaplin), he is in love with the Red Cross nurse, Lara who he meets during the First World War. Their love would be swept away by events that shook up the entire world with the Soviet Bolshevik Revolution in October 1917. Censured in his homeland, the scandalous novel by Boris Pasternak would first be published in Italy by Feltrinelli, inaugurating Pasternak's career as a sensational bestselling author.

The film made the Egyptian actor Omar Sharif a major international star, despite his unexceptional expressive qualities, and turned his stunning costar, Julie Christie, into a diva, a status that, as the muse of rebellious English cinema the early 1970s, she had not achieved yet. The film adaptation and screenplay were written by the great English playwright Robert Bolt, who won an Academy Award. An Oscar was also awarded for its dazzling cinematography, with its sweeping scenarios and crowd scenes.

This was an epic production that, naturally, could not be filmed where the story was set and was thus made in Canada, Finland and Spain. The rest of the cast, composed mainly of British actors, was also famous: Geraldine Chaplin, Rod Steiger, Alec Guinness and Ralph Richardson.

Dr. Zhivago is a typical example of a film that is unremarkable from an artistic standpoint, but is memorable as a phenomenon and for its popular appeal.

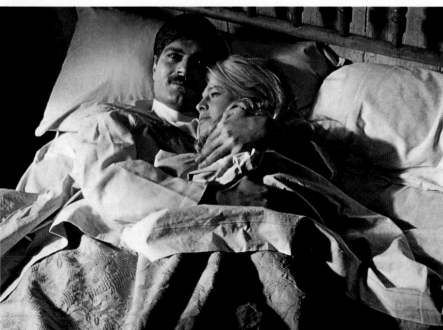

1966

[FRANCE] Genre: ROMANCE

1△

A MAN AND A WOMAN

Director: CLAUDE LELOUCH

Cast: ANOUK AIMÉE / JEAN-LOUIS TRINTIGNANT

A Man and a Woman (Un homme et une femme) by Claude Lelouch (1966) is one of the most striking examples of the divide between public acclaim – audiences everywhere loved this mawkish love story – and almost unanimously negative critiques, which went entirely unheeded by moviegoers.

Anne (Anouk Aimée), who works as a script supervisor for a film company, has just lost her husband, a stuntman who was killed in an accident on the set. Jean-Louis (Jean-Louis Trintignant) is a race-car driver and has also recently been widowed, as his wife committed suicide. They meet in Deauville, where their children attend the same school. On the way home, she misses the train and he offers her a ride. They are immediately attracted to each other and, thanks to their trips to Deauville, they continue to meet. Yet she feels guilty toward the memory of her dead husband.

1. 2. 3. Jean-Louis Trintignant had already done many films with director, Roger Vadim, in particular, "…*And God Created Woman*, launching Brigitte Bardot's image, but perhaps is more famous for films shot in Italy, like Il sorpasso ("The Easy Life") alongside Vittorio Gassman and it is ironic that as passionate about racing as he claimed to be in his role in *Un homme et une femme* (A Man and a Woman), the young Trintignant was himself the accident victim of a daredevil driver. Anouk Aimée's fame is also more closely linked with Italian cinema than that of her own country of France as she was one of Fellini's muses in two of his masterpieces made at Rimini, *La dolce vita* and *81/2*, But, it was French Claude Lelouch, with his unmistakable and soft enveloping style, who made the French actors two international stars.

After their last trip home, her by train and him by car, Anne and Jean-Louis meet again at the station and embrace. The film does not tell us what happens to them, but leaves the audience with the hope that love will triumph.

During a period in which French cinema was breaking with tradition, an era of tension, ideological battles, protests and provocation in the name of style, Lelouch outstripped the entire generation of the New Wave – his own generation – in popularity. In fact, in May 1968 he was alongside Jean-Luc Godard at the forefront of the protests that interrupted the Cannes Film Festival. Yet Lelouch can be termed the inventor of the aesthetics of advertising.

The fawning air of his glossy, cloying cinema was harshly criticized by the close-knit front of "committed" intellectuals. Nevertheless, these critics never gave sufficient credit to his admirable self-confidence with this medium and his extraordinary ability to exploit it to tell love stories and deftly manipulate the audience's sentiments like a juggler: pure professionalism. The icing on the cake is the musical theme by Francis Lai, which was hugely popular. Enchanted, the Cannes Film Festival awarded him the Palme d'Or and the following year the film won an Oscar as Best Foreign Language Film. Interestingly, it was a low-budget film that was made in a very short time.

Guess Who's Coming to Dinner? is a classic American comedy, with its toned-down message against racism and its feel-good optimism.

Spencer Tracy is a liberal journalist from San Francisco, the cradle of the American Left during the 1960s. He and his wife Katharine Hepburn form the classic good-looking liberal and open-minded middle-class couple. However, when their daughter (Katharine Houghton) comes home with an African-American (Sidney Poitier) she met on vacation and plans to marry, numerous contradictions begin to emerge, despite the fact that her fiancé is an elegant, well-to-do and successful doctor who lives in wealthy Switzerland.

The interplay of situations, dialogues and one-liners that the deftly written screenplay orchestrates with enormous skill – and that the two superb stars, Tracy and Hepburn, handle beautifully – reveals the subtle (and pandering) irony of a film that blends critical and self-critical impulse, and a hypocritical and contradictory sentiment that was the target of criticism, albeit with a smile and enormous restraint. This mix was precisely the reason the film was a runaway success. The film, which made people feel good and – to use a modern term – politically correct, gained widespread approval. At the same time, it avoided any exaggeration, as the subject touched a raw nerve in the American culture and mentality, and it skirted the issue for the average filmgoer, who was still sensitive to this heated debate.

In fact, intolerance and racial violence were probed far more profoundly by other films that were made during the same period and were likewise part of the Hollywood mainstream, such as Arthur Penn's *The Chase*, with Marlon Brando, and Norman Jewison's *In the Heat of the Night*.

With his personal success in 1967, starring in two hit films during the same year, *Guess Who's Coming to Dinner?* and *In the Heat of the Night*, Sidney Poitier – who, 40 years old at the time, had a solid career behind him and had already won an Oscar – emerged as Hollywood's first great African-American star. The next one, equally important, would not arrive until 2002 with the Oscar won by Denzel Washington.

1967

GUESS WHO'S COMING TO DINNER?

Director:　**STANLEY KRAMER**

Cast:　**SPENCER TRACY / KATHARINE HEPBURN / SIDNEY POITIER / KATHARINE HOUGHTON**

Spencer Tracy would be dead just a few days after final work on this film.

268 - Spencer Tracy and Katharine Hepburn form the attractive older yet progressive middle-aged couple in San Francisco. Their liberal and open-minded thinking do not hinder them, yet the daughter's (Katharine Houghton) announcement shakes their safe world. The girl is to marry a brilliant young doctor with the same social status but the brilliant young doctor is black (Sidney Poitier). The lively dialogue that ensues can be comedic but does not obstruct the film, on the contrary, it has its place in a light and popular genre that becomes much deeper and proves to be quite effective as a vehicle for discussion of racial themes that are still current today and even more dramatic when recalling the U.S. in the Sixties. Not so much time has passed since the assassination of Malcolm X. And, the year after this film was released, Martin Luther King himself would be assassinated.

With his interpretation, Sidney Poitier confirms himself as the first great Black star graduating from the Hollywood system and achieving universal recognition.

Spencer Tracy, who had a profound emotional and professional rapport with Katharine Hepburn (although, a devout Catholic, he never divorced his wife), died only a few days after filming was completed. She won an Oscar, but it was Tracy who truly deserved one.

The title became proverbial and the situation that was staged is now a classic. For example, *Shrek 2* offers a fanciful parody of this theme.

1▲

1967
[UK / USA] Genre: ACTION / WAR

THE DIRTY DOZEN

Director: ROBERT ALDRICH

Cast: LEE MARVIN / ERNEST BORGNINE / ROBERT RYAN / JOHN CASSAVETES / CHARLES BRONSON / TELLY SAVALAS / DONALD SUTHERLAND /
JIM BROWN / RICHARD JAECKEL / GEORGE KENNEDY / TRINI LÓPEZ / RALPH MEEKER / CLINT WALKER / ROBERT WEBBER / TOM BUSBY

Like other war masterpieces, such as Stanley Kubrick's *Full Metal Jacket*, the best part of Robert Aldrich's *The Dirty Dozen* is in the first half of the
150-minute-long film. In other words, it is the part about preparing and training the human flotsam of 12 men assembled by Major John Reisman (Lee
Marvin) to go on what is probably a suicide mission in exchange for the promise of redemption.

The major himself is disliked by the upper echelons because he is considered the rudest and most undisciplined officer in the United States Army.
At the beginning of the film he is called in by the US command base in England. He has been summoned by Major General Worden (Ernest Borgnine),
who defends him and always stays on his side, against the dapper and rule-abiding head of the paratroops Colonel Everett Dasher Breed (Robert Ryan),
Major Reisman's sworn enemy, with an "indecent" proposal. The story is set on the eve of the Allied invasion of Normandy in 1944, and the men have
been called upon to carry out an unconventional mission: destroy one of the Germans' bases in France, situated in a luxurious château.

1. Led by the rough and tough Major Lee Marvin, John Cassavetes (first from left), Donald Sutherland (fourth), Charles Bronson (seventh), and Telly Savalas (last) were also a part of the notorious *Dirty Dozen*.

2. Following orders to complete a probable suicide mission beyond German enemy lines, "the most ill-mannered and undisciplined officer in the United States Army," Major Lee Marvin turned to a group of soldiers punished for varied serious offenses. The terms were that, if they succeeded, whoever survived would be pardoned.

3. Disguised as German soldiers and officers, the men on an impossible mission would successfully penetrate the castle where enemy command was headquartered and sabotage it. Losses would be extremely high but the courageous mission would be completed.

The top brass makes it clear that the Army will deny any involvement in the top-secret assignment, as its implementation and, above all, the way the "volunteers" are recruited are destined to remain unknown, particularly if anything goes wrong. In short, the mission will never receive official support or visibility. The major is given carte blanche to assemble troops chosen from men convicted for serious crimes and sentenced to capital punishment or life terms by the military court. The major recruits his 12 low-lifes from a prison camp. They are men without hope, men who couldn't care less about hierarchies, their country or the war. Nevertheless, at the risk of turning them all against him, the major manages to instill in them the spirit and solidarity of a team, which are indispensable for undertaking such a dangerous mission.

As noted, however, the most interesting and successful part of the film – which also blends different tones ranging from the most violent to lighthearted camaraderie to almost comic scenes – is the one preceding the actual mission. Naturally, the men's actions are heroic and only the

major and one of the soldiers will survive. In the end, when the survivors receive the visits and hypocritical congratulations of some of the officers who had scorned them and done everything possible to make them fail, the men cannot conceal their bitterness and anger.

The most powerful and stimulating aspect of the film, an aspect that the sheer noise of war films usually conceals, is its indirect reflection on the amoral brutality of war. What this commando of convicts does, ultimately earning the plaudits of the upper echelon, is worst than the terrible crimes for which they had been sentenced. In essence, they redeem themselves – at least in the eyes of the law and the nation – by carrying out ethically deplorable actions. The outstanding cast includes John Cassavetes, Charles Bronson, Telly Savalas and Donald Sutherland, each of whom has a well-delineated personality, as was the fashion in the great "team" films of the period, from *The Longest Day* to *Judgment at Nuremberg*, *The Great Escape* and *The Magnificent Seven*.

BELLE DE JOUR

Director: LUIS BUÑUEL

Cast: CATHERINE DENEUVE / JEAN SOREL / MICHEL PICCOLI / GENEVIÈVE PAGE / PIERRE CLÉMENTI

Belle de Jour opens with a dreamlike scene: a carriage driven by two uniformed coachman take a newlywed couple down the avenue of a park. However, what seems to be an idyllic scene is rapidly transformed into a game of violent sex, in which Séverine is abused by her husband and raped by the drivers.

Séverine Sérizy (Catherine Deneuve) is a beautiful upper-class Parisian. She has been married for a year to the young doctor Pierre (Jean Sorel), who is very involved in his work. She is unable to be intimate with him because, as suggested in a rapid flashback, an older man tried to seduce her when she was a girl and this has left her frigid.

Séverine feels guilty towards her husband, who has been so willing to wait for her. Her sense of guilt is transformed into dreams in which her erotic fantasies take the form of penance.

To celebrate their first wedding anniversary, the couple goes to the mountains for a vacation with two friends. Husson (Michel Piccoli) is a ladies man, the exact opposite of Pierre, and he upsets Séverine by making passes at her. Yet at the same time, she is mesmerized by his words and goes to one of the brothels he mentions, the house of Madame Anais (Geneviève Page). From this moment on Séverine becomes Belle de Jour, the most sought-after woman in the brothel, but she is available only for daytime appointments. Here she discovers men's most unmentionable desires, which are transformed into her sexual initiation (the masochistic gynecologist who pretends he is a butler is unforgettable). The woman finally seems to have found her own equilibrium: as Belle de Jour she is humiliated daily by the anonymous men she encounters in her bed. As a result, her guilt vanishes and Séverine becomes calmer and more open towards Pierre, who is unaware of her secret life.

This scandalous lifestyle starts to become part of her dreams, in which she is no longer abused or disgraced by her husband, but is used by strangers to play a part in a mournful ritual. She even begins to fantasize about her libertine friend Husson. In short, something is changing. The fragile balance she has achieved is finally tipped when Marcel (Pierre Clémenti), a gangster with *maudit* charm, enters the brothel and falls in love with her. Pierre senses her aloofness and begins to suspect that she is cheating on him, but she reassures him that she has never felt so close to him. Yet things are precipitating. While he is out for a walk, Pierre inexplicably stops to look at a wheelchair, as if it were a bad omen. Séverine decides to stop working at the brothel, not only to escape from Marcel's obsession, but also because she has been discovered by Husson, who has humiliated her and made her feel the burden of her immoral behavior.

She goes home, planning to remedy things. Marcel has followed her, however, and breaks into her living room, acting like a jilted lover and threatening to tell her husband everything. She manages to get rid of him but, sick with jealousy, he waits for Pierre by their house and shoots him; he is killed as he tries to escape.

Catherine Deneuve is Séverine, the middle-class woman that lives out her erotic adventures somewhere between a dream world and reality.

Dissatisfied in the relationship with her husband, Pierre (Jean Sorel), Séverine imagines sadomasochistic scenes of being tied up and helpless, of enduring violence. Under the name of Belle de Jour, the blond and elegant middle-class woman frequents a brothel where she becomes the main attraction.

The doctor survives, but cannot speak or hear and is forced to live in wheelchair. Séverine takes care of him like an attentive nurse, in an atmosphere similar to that of the opening scene. Everything seems to have settled down for Séverine when Husson arrives and reveals her secret to his friend, convinced that he can help Pierre stop feeling indebted to his wife. After a moment of powerless desperation, the woman finally accepts her faults and transforms tragic reality into a beautiful fairytale, in which her husband – healthy again – promises that they will return to the mountains and the happiness of the previous year.

Luis Buñuel was nearly 70 years old when he made this film (he was born in Calanda, Aragon, on February 22, 1900), but this work reconfirms his modernity. After being exiled from Spain, he lived in France, the United States and Mexico, and his multifaceted artistic life was constellated by brilliant chapters (his two masterpieces, *Viridiana* and *The Exterminating Angel* were made in the early Sixties).

In *Belle de Jour* he presents his customary array of concepts:<0} his dispute with the middle classes, his obsession with sexual themes and fierce anti-Catholicism, the dreaminess of the old surrealist and the countless recesses of sadomasochism. Like many of his films, *Belle de Jour* was censured as a scandalous work, because it naturally probed subjects with religious overtones. Panned at the Cannes Film Festival, it won the Leone d'oro in Venice. It was his biggest commercial success until *The Discreet Charm of the Bourgeoisie* (1972). *Belle de Jour* was based on a 1928 novel by Joseph Kessel; the screenplay was written by Jean-Claude Carrière.

1. 2. 3. This is Catherine Deneuve with her lover, Marcel (Pierre Clementi at center), and with her husband, Pierre (Jean Sorel below). His first in color, Luis Bunuel directed this film at the age of 67. Demonstrating a modern sensibility, he created a piece that would give him immense public approval tainted with scandalous uproar. Mindful of his own surrealistic youth, he infects this film with a dreamlike and realistic quality. Séverine is the expression of middle-class ambiguity over a backdrop of Eros and desire measured against the vices of the social class to which she belongs. This was a great affirmation for the French actress who would become the supreme symbol of a distant and deceptively indifferent feminine sensuality (in somewhat the same way as Hitchcock liked Grace Kelly), still seeming to hide infinite promises of perversion. The Cannes Film Festival's refusal of this film remains in the record as an advantage to the Venetian Film Festival that would award the Spanish master the Golden Lion for best film.

1

2

3

1967

THE GRADUATE

Director: MIKE NICHOLS

Cast: DUSTIN HOFFMAN / ANNE BANCROFT / KATHARINE ROSS

If any movie can be defined as a "cult film," it is *The Graduate*, and a number of elements have helped establish its iconic status. These details have been etched in the minds of the past three generations, starting with that of the young moviegoers who saw *The Graduate* when it was first released in the mid-1960s.

There is the close-up of Mrs. Robinson's fabulous legs as she puts on her stockings while Benjamin, hands in his pockets, looks on. Then there is the red Alfa Romeo Duetto convertible (the first model designed with the round tail) that Benjamin receives as a gift from his parents and that – with the top down and the wind in his hair – he drives up and down the roads of California. And, naturally, there is the final scene, in which Benjamin arrives at the last minute (after running out of gas) at the church where Elaine is getting married and starts to pound desperately on the enormous window overlooking the nave, packed with wedding guests, and cries out her name. Above all, there is the soundtrack by Simon & Garfunkel, and particularly the songs "Mrs. Robinson" and "The Sounds of Silence."

Benjamin Braddock is going on 21 and has just come home to his parents' opulent California home after graduating from college. All around him, family and friends attend party after party in his honor and pester him with advice and questions about his future. Apathetic and unmotivated, however, he feels that he does not belong to the adult world. He would rather keep to himself and has no idea about what to do. The attractive Mrs. Robinson, the dissatisfied alcoholic wife of his father's partner, provokes him by appearing to him naked after finding a pretext to be alone with him. She then seduces him in a hotel room, where they meet secretly several times. Following his initial embarrassment and then enthusiasm, Benjamin becomes growingly disgusted by the relationship, which has merely underscored his existential drift and made him cynical.

The turning point comes when Elaine, the Robinsons' daughter, comes home on vacation. His parents, along with the unaware Mr. Robinson, urge him to meet and – hopefully – woo her, but Mrs. Robinson vehemently warns him against it. Benjamin feels trapped and his first date with the girl is a disaster. The two barely get past their initial awkwardness – they realize that they like each other – when the revelation of Benjamin's affair with her mother upsets Elaine so much that she indignantly refuses to see him again. At this point, however, Benjamin has finally found his purpose in life and looks ahead to the future: nothing will stop him. He ultimately "kidnaps" Elaine, dressed in her bridal gown, during a wedding that the Robinsons have rapidly arranged and the two leave on a bus headed toward a future of rebellion and happiness.

This is one of the most remembered film scenes throughout the Sixties. The recent graduate, Benjamin, looks at Mrs. Robinson as he takes his socks off.

278 - The young man, Benjamin (Dustin Hoffman), pursues a clandestine relationship with the mature and attractive Mrs. Robinson (Ann Bancroft). This scene is taken from one of his encounters with the woman in a hotel.

279 [LEFT] - Benjamin, who meets Elaine Robinson (Katharine Ross) and falls in love with her, talking to her after she's uncovered the truth in the angry and hostile expressions of her mother who is already the boy's lover.

279 [RIGHT] - In the very famous final scene, Benjamin bursts into the church where Elaine's hasty wedding is being celebrated, taking the girl away with him, to the appalled expressions of onlookers.

The Graduate, which was released in the United States in 1967, preceded and accompanied an era of youthful rebellion, becoming its first cinematographic manifesto. Although it is moderately unconventional in style, the film is actually a rather bland portrait of the generation gap that "defiant" American cinema had already largely explored with Marlon Brando and James Dean. Tellingly, it never even touched the period's hottest issue: the Vietnam War. Rather, it offered a few Bohemian views of the campus at Berkeley and sketched out the domestic dynamics of Benjamin's indifference toward conventional adult values.

It is interesting to note that the thirty-year-old Dustin Hoffman (who launched his career with this film) was actually just six years younger than the "mature" Anne Bancroft. Katharine Ross, the actress who played Elaine, enjoyed a brief period of stardom with her role in *Butch Cassidy and the Sundance Kid*. The actor and comedy writer Buck Henry, who co-authored the screenplay, appears in a minor but unforgettable role as the hotel concierge.

The film received seven Oscar nominations and Mike Nichols won the Academy Award for Best Director. Although the score did not win any awards, it has gone down in history as one of the most successful soundtracks in history.

1▲ 2▲

1967

[USA] Genre: DRAMA

IN THE HEAT OF THE NIGHT

Director: NORMAN JEWISON
Cast: SIDNEY POITIER / ROD STEIGER / WARREN OATES

Greatly overrated by the Academy of Motion Picture Arts and Sciences – it won five Oscars, including Best Motion Picture – *In the Heat of the Night* is nevertheless a compelling social thriller and a trenchant social accusation against racial prejudice.

Traveling south to visit his mother, Philadelphia detective Virgil Tibbs (Sidney Poitiers) passes through the small railway station of Sparta, Mississippi, on the very night a murder is committed. An industrialist who had been planning to build a factory that would employ a large number of people, but also disturbed the town's old ruling class, is found dead.

Tibbs is forced to make the bitterly unpleasant acquaintance of the local police chief Bill Gillespie (Rod Steiger) and his right-hand man Sam Wood (Warren Oates). Without knowing that Tibbs is a cop who also happens to be far more qualified than they are, the two arrest him. Backed by public opinion, they are smugly pleased that they can accuse an African-American and quickly close their investigation. Once his identity is revealed – the two unembarrassed policemen have no intention of apologizing over their mistake – Tibbs is forced to stay on to solve the case, as the victim's widow, who trusts him, has asked him to help.

3▲ **4▲**

1. 2. 3. 4. Having moved to the North, Philadelphia Detective Virgil Tibbs (Sidney Poitier) meets with racial prejudice from the local chief of police (Rod Steiger) of a backward city in Mississippi when he returns on a visit to the segregated corner of the South where he had been born. This film was re-launched in the same year as *Guess Who's Coming to Dinner*, but with undertones that were decidedly different and much less appealing, a huge issue that in those years had to be well thought out and innovative to capture a demographic cross-section of American audiences. A typical balancing act for a Hollywood film released at that time, it did not renounce unpleasant things and portrayed a heartwarming finale as the two adversaries take their leave from each other having learned mutual respect, or rather the white man learned to respect the black man.

The middle scenes constantly underscore the belligerent, closed-minded and backward mentality of the community and a police force that does not serve the law but those in power. They contrast the moral and professional rectitude shown by Tibbs, who dares to fight the master of the city, an elderly Southern gentleman who challenges him, while Tibbs continues to fight back. Nevertheless, the film revolves chiefly around the duel between the African-American detective and the white police chief. A reluctant Gillespie will finally be forced to acknowledge his colleague's worth and shake his hand as a sign of respect and friendship.

Poitier also starred in *Guess Who's Coming to Dinner?*, released the same year, but *In the Heat of the Night* consecrated him as the first African-American movie star in the history of Hollywood. At the same time, however, the film is principally a backdrop for the dramatic skills of Rod Steiger (Academy Award for Best Actor), who captures every instant and every aspect of the film, using all means to garner attention and demonstrate his character's arrogance and vulgarity: from the way

he wears his Ray-Bans to how he chews gum. Poitier also played Tibbs in two sequels. A film from the previous year, Arthur Penn's *The Chase*, did not gain the same recognition, although it certainly deserved it at least as much as *In the Heat of the Night*. Penn's film did not have an African-American hero – it starred Marlon Brando who, unlike Rod Steiger, played an isolated and courageous sheriff in another small town, this time in Texas, paralleling the role played by Gary Cooper in *High Noon* – nor did it focus on racial issues. Nevertheless, it offered a mirror image of prejudice and the blind violence that it can spark. It vigorously pointed a finger at the division of society into two unequal categories of people, and the irresponsible ease with which consciences can be appeased by sacrificing a scapegoat. These two films were very close in terms of timing and were also quite similar in intent. Their different fates are a clear reminder of the fact that, although the Academy Awards often mirror contemporary life and prevalent taste, they can also be wrong.

Quincy Jones composed the score.

In the city of Verona, the Capulets and Montagues are rivals, but during a dance held at the Capulet palace, Romeo Montague (Leonard Whiting) declares his love for Juliet Capulet (Olivia Hussey). The young people know nothing about their respective identities, but even when they find out this does not stop them. Assisted by Friar Laurence, they marry in secret. Unfortunately, however, their families are against their relationship and the war between them flares up again, due also to the fact that Juliet is already betrothed to a nobleman, Paris. One of Romeo's most determined opponents is Juliet's cousin Tybalt, who provokes him. Romeo refuses to accept his challenge to a duel and the price for his decision proves to be the life of his dear friend Mercutio, who is killed by Tybalt. Now Romeo has no choice but to avenge his friend's death and, in turn, kill Tybalt. As a result, he is punished by the Prince and banished from the city, leaving after a night of love with Juliet. In turn, in order to avoid her arranged marriage to Paris, Juliet accepts the advice of Friar Laurence, who gives her a potion that makes her appear to be dead. This trick will allow her to escape with Romeo. However, Romeo – in exile – is misinformed. Believing her to be dead, he goes to her side and poisons himself. When Juliet awakens, she finds Romeo's lifeless body and, in turn, stabs herself. It is only when the families stand before the bodies of the two young people that they finally reconcile under the prince's stern gaze.

For Franco Zeffirelli, a pupil of Luchino Visconti and a multifaceted artist who has worked not only in cinema but above all in musical theatre, *Romeo and Juliet* represents his interpretation of the 1968 uprisings. There is nothing paradoxical about this. In that year of youthful rebellion, this transposition of Shakespeare's tragedy, written four centuries earlier, fully reflected the spirit of the times through the youth of the two main characters. In fact, the film is completely faithful to Shakespeare's play, in which the two lovers from Verona were just teenagers. Their love is interpreted as a courageous rebellion against social conventions. Filmed in English with an almost entirely English-speaking cast, an unusual move for an Italian director at the time, this film – like all of Zeffirelli's films – strived to reach a vast international market, fully succeeding in this intent. The uproar over the very chaste seminude scene of the two young people in bed was ridiculous.

Costume design by Danilo Donati, music by Nino Rota, photography by Pasqualino De Santis, screenplay by Zeffirelli with Franco Brusati and Masolino D'Amico. The film received four Academy Award nominations in 1969 (including Best Picture and Best Director) and won two Oscars (Best Costume Design and Best Cinematography)

1968
ROMEO AND JULIET

Director: FRANCO ZEFFIRELLI

Cast: LEONARD WHITING / OLIVIA HUSSEY /
MILO O'SHEA / BRUCE ROBINSON / MICHAEL YORK / JOHN MCENERY

The very young Olivia Hussey is Juliet, in a to-the-word respect of Shakespeare's text, which indicates that the two lovers in Verona should be adolescents.

284 - Here are Olivia Hussey and
Leonard Whiting. Zeffirelli delivers
a screen presentation of the most
famous love story of all time that
is fully in tune with the sensibility
of the era when the film was shot.
Fresh interpretations of the lead roles
transcend what is fundamentally
nothing more than the rebellion
of a girl and boy against prejudice,
an element that is simultaneously a
victim, violent promoter, and recurring
impetus in a society of adults
symbolized by the rival families of
the Montagues and Capulets.

This is the heart-wrenching conclusion known to everyone, one that cannot knows yet rescue the characters from inevitable tragedy. Juliet surrenders to death after reawakening from her artificially induced sleep that made Romeo believe her dead and led him to take his own life.

The 1968 film that, like its four sequels, was inspired by Pierre Boulle's novel *La planète des singes* marked a turning point in the science-fiction genre, although not to the same extent as the coeval 2001: *A Space Odyssey* by the genius Stanley Kubrick.

The American astronaut Taylor (Charlton Heston), hibernated with his colleagues, is in a spaceship that falls to an unknown planet in the year 3978. As they explore this uncharted territory they encounter a group of humans who have regressed to a primitive state. When they are attacked by gorillas, they discover that the planet is ruled by apes that are far more evolved than humans. The apes are divided into three categories: warriors (gorillas), politicians (orangutans) and scientists (chimpanzees). During the attack, Taylor is hit in the neck and is thus unable to speak. He is captured and locked up with another prisoner named Nova (Linda Harrison). When his jailers discover that Taylor was unable to speak solely because of his injury and is thus different from the human tribe they have conquered, whose members have no spoken language, they become very interested in his case. Although two scientists, Cornelius and Zira, take his side and would like to help him escape, another scientist, Zaius, clashes with Taylor and wants him lobotomized, as already done to one of the other astronauts.

Taylor gradually discovers that the intelligent apes have replaced and conquered a previous human civilization that was very advanced. However, the most traumatic revelation comes in the last scene, when he discovers the partially buried Statue of Liberty. At this point it finally dawns on him that he is not on a remote and unknown planet but that his spaceship has returned to Earth after a journey to the future, and that humans destroyed their own civilization through nuclear war. The film ends with Taylor cursing the human race for the evilness that led to its own destruction.

1968
PLANET OF THE APES

Director: FRANKLIN J. SCHAFFNER

**Cast: CHARLTON HESTON / RODDY MCDOWALL / KIM HUNTER /
MAURICE EVANS / JAMES WHITMORE / JAMES DALY / LINDA HARRISON**

▶ After the enormous fame he achieved in the Fifties from two Biblical epics, *The Ten Commandments* and *Ben-Hur*, Charlton Heston plays astronaut Taylor.

▲1

Planet of the Apes is a philosophical, political and sociological apologue that deftly and expressively combines adventure, pacifism and apocalyptic pessimism in one of the first experiments with a genre that interprets the present through projection into the distant future, a genre destined to become very popular.

The film diverges significantly from the book. First of all, the French hero becomes American in the film and the apes speak the astronauts' language. Most importantly, however, in the book the planet of the apes is not Earth, as the main character instead discovers in the last scene of the film.

In any case, Planet of the Apes was one of the many films – including Kubrick's masterpiece 2001: A Space Odyssey – that in some way interpreted the spirit and atmosphere of 1968. It is ironic that Charlton Heston, the star of The Ten Commandments and Ben-Hur, who was known for his pro-gun position, was chosen for the leading role in a film about pacifism.

John Chambers won an honorary Academy Award for outstanding makeup achievement, as he used makeup rather than masks for the actors who played the apes: Roddy McDowall (Cornelius), Kim Hunter (Zira) and Maurice Evans (Zaius).

Four sequels were released between 1969 and 1973. The film also inspired a television series and an animated series, respectively in 1972 and 1975. Tim Burton's remake dates to 2001.

▲ 2

▲ 3

1. 2. 3. Astronauts on an exploratory mission make an emergency landing on an unknown planet. Their trip has also been a journey through time. The humans inhabiting the planet are slaves to evolved apes that speak the same language as the astronauts. Enduring relentless struggle against the cruel and unyielding Dr. Zaius, Taylor has two ape scientists as allies, Zira and Cornelius.

This film is a precursor to the trend using science fiction as an interpretation of the present and near future. Also innovative in its makeup techniques, the apes don't wear masks and cosmetic products are applied directly onto the faces of actors. Locations included settings within national parks in Utah and Arizona. This was the first of a successful series of films inspired by the novels from Frenchman, Pierre Boulle.

291 - In his flight from the persecution of Zaius, Taylor would reach a remote zone where he would discover the remains of human civilization starting with the Statue of Liberty – and he realize that he's really on Earth, after the destruction of the human race.

[USA]   Genre: **ACTION**

BULLITT

Director: PETER YATES

Cast: STEVE MCQUEEN / JACQUELINE BISSET / ROBERT VAUGHN / JAMES HAGAN

Bullitt is one of those films that, for some mysterious reason (in other words, regardless of their limited qualities), marked an era, a style and a trend. In this case, much of the film's cachet can be attributed to the main character and, above all, to the appeal of the actor who played him, Steve McQueen.

Frank Bullitt is a lieutenant on the homicide squad of the San Francisco Police Department. He's a tough guy, a man who does things his own way and bridles at rules and regulations. A politician gives him a confidential assignment to guard a mobster scheduled to testify against the Mafia. However, Bullitt is unable to protect the man, who is killed by a couple of hit men. At this point, Bullitt hides the corpse and pretends that the man is still alive, taking the case into his own hands and going after the killers. He discovers that the dead man is not who he thought he was (the film is based on the novel *Mute Witness*). Risking his own life, the maverick detective finally discovers the truth.

The film's appeal can be attributed to several closely connected aspects, starting with cars. McQueen (like James Dean and Paul Newman) was a passionate, expert and daredevil driver in real life and refused to use a stuntman for the most dangerous scenes. The film is also famed for its breakneck chase scenes. McQueen drove a Ford Mustang that became a legend, although – despite all his efforts – he never managed to add it to his enor-

1. The Frank Bullitt character played by Steve McQueen.

2. 3. 4. Petty politician Chalmers (Robert Vaughn, already a cast mate of McQueen's in *The Magnificent Seven*) assigns to Lieutenant Bullitt of the San Francisco homicide unit the surveillance of a Mafia star witness. Memorable aspects earning film fame are the energetic chase scene up and down San Francisco's hilly streets and Jacqueline Bisset, McQueen's superb partner.

mous private collection of cars and motorcycles. And there are the hilly streets of San Francisco, which served as the backdrop for the movie's most memorable chase sequence. The film's breathtaking pace rightly won Frank P. Keller an Academy Award for Best Film Editing.

Born in the Midwest, McQueen was abandoned by his father when he was a child. He spent time in reform school, joined the Marines and subsequently studied at the Actors Studio. He was married three times (his second wife was Ali MacGraw, famous for her role in *Love Story* and his costar in *The Getaway*). He was a man who loved to live dangerously and his life story effectively weaves the legend of a wild rebel. During his short life (though not at short as that of his contemporary, James Dean; McQueen was born in 1930 and died in 1980) he was one of the key figures in the American movie industry of the 1960s and 1970s, and at a certain point he was the world's highest-paid actor.

McQueen had been noticed in *The Magnificent Seven* and attained stardom thanks to another film by the same director, John Sturges: *The Great Escape*, in which he rode a motorcycle. He often costarred with the most beautiful actresses of the era, such as Jacqueline Bisset in *Bullitt*, Faye Dunaway in *The Thomas Crown Affair*, also filmed in 1968, and Ali MacGraw in *The Getaway* (1972), directed by Sam Peckinpah. McQueen played one of his most memorable roles – the one that effectively defined his image – in another Peckinpah film, also released in 1972. *Junior Bonner* showcases the harsh but emotional nostalgia – probably shared by both the actor and the director – for a fast-paced, taciturn man's world that, despite all its action and violence, is loyal and courageous.

Indeed, McQueen's appeal was due largely to his physical presence and his sporty way of dressing, shrewdly blending a seemingly scruffy look with well-chosen trendy items such as turtleneck sweaters. His charm lay in the contrast between angelic good looks and a roguish air, and between his pale, delicate features – blue eyes and blond hair – and his irresistible manliness.

1968

2001:
A SPACE ODYSSEY

Director: STANLEY KUBRICK

Cast: KEIR DULLEA / GARY LOCKWOOD / WILLIAM SYLVESTER /
DANIEL RICHTER / LEONARD ROSSITER / DOUGLAS RAIN

What is the most memorable part of *2001: A Space Odyssey*? The ape-man wielding the bone as the film opens? The spaceship gliding through the cosmos to the notes of "The Blue Danube"? Or the voice of the computer HAL 9000? The most famous science-fiction film in the history of cinema is still a legend today. More importantly, it is disconcerting proof of the visionary intelligence of its author. Indeed, although it was written several years earlier, this masterpiece was released in 1968: a year before the first Moon landing. It continues to be a legend despite its exploitation on television, a screen that is completely unsuitable for a work created for the "splendor of 70 mm" (the panoramic format), and despite the competition of later technological advances in the area of special effects.

The repeated appearance of an enigmatic black monolith is the leitmotif of a journey in space and time.

Africa, millions of years ago: initially astonished by the appearance of the monolith, several ape-men subsequently learn to use objects as weapons, kill animals to survive and slay each other to affirm their power.

Millions of years later, the year 2001: a monolith has been discovered on a lunar base, buried there in ancient times. The scientist responsible for investigating it interprets the angle of light that strikes the monolith as a signal, an indication that he must look towards the planet Jupiter.

Two astronauts, Bowman and Poole, and three scientists in cryogenic hibernation are on mission to Jupiter aboard the spaceship Discovery, guided by the intelligent computer HAL 9000, which can not only speak but can also play – and win – chess games. Its artificial intelligence is more sophisticated and evolved than that of man, and it knows far more than its travel companions. However, HAL is torn between the order not to reveal the true goal of their mission and the duty to collaborate with them, for which it has been programmed.

HAL solves this interior conflict by deciding to neutralize the humans, but one of them – Bowman – survives and gains the upper hand, deactivating the computer. Nevertheless, HAL manages to inform the astronaut of the true objective of their mission: investigating the area indicated by the signal from the monolith found on the Moon.

When they reach Jupiter, Bowman finds a third monolith. The power of the conditioning to which he is subjected catapults him into another dimension. Bowman sees himself in a lavishly decorated 18th-century room, and watches himself age rapidly to decrepitude, dying at the monolith's fourth appearance, only to be reincarnated as a fetus floating in space.

Respected today as an absolute classic, the film did not garner widespread public approval when released. To the contrary, it was considered pretentious, obscure, too long, a sleeper, or simply boring.

296 - A very evocative opening dialogue occurs at daybreak when a group of apes now nearly evolved to a human state discover a black monolith emitting a high-pitched hiss in the middle of a desert landscape. One of the apes becomes aware that it is a bone, the tibia pulled from a skeleton lying at its feet, and could be transformed into an offensive and defensive tool, that is, a weapon. The euphoric gesture of throwing the tibia bone into the air concludes the prologue, from the tibia to the spaceship in flight, and from the past to the distant future (2001 was still quite distant in 1968).

Using three stories written in 1948–50 by science-fiction author Arthur C. Clarke as his starting point, Stanley Kubrick worked with his inspirer to create something completely new: so new, in fact, that Clarke later published a novel with the same name as the film.

A boundlessly ambitious work, 2001 investigates topics that we would term "sensitive" today: man's natural destiny – dominating others? – through the altered conditions of space and time; the morality, immorality or amorality of science and its resources; the interaction of man and artificial intelligence. All of this starts with an event that has divided human history into a before and an after: the atom bomb.

Is the film a philosophical essay in the form of a science-fiction adventure? Although he left viewers free to draw their own conclusions, Kubrick himself advised them to understand his work as an emotional rather than a rational undertaking, a visual rather than a logical experience, and the desire and attempt to penetrate and explore the territory of the unconscious.

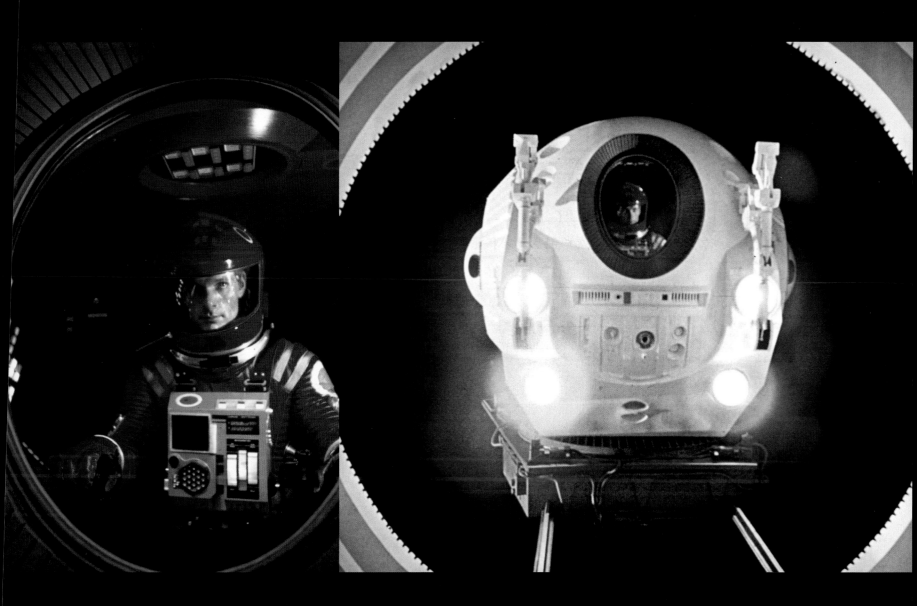

297 - Cosmonaut David Bowman (Keir Dullea), sent on a mission to Jupiter along with his partner, Frank Poole, seeking to uncover the mystery of the reappearing monolith, survives an onboard conflict that sparks between the two men and the "intelligent" computer, HAL 9000, neutralizes Frank. Between David and Hal, however, the latter would succumb. Man triumphs over the machine.

298 and 299 - The computer "dead," David finds himself tossed into a vortex of blinding light before landing within the bright silent cocoon of a room completely furnished in the rococo style. Here, we see him grow old and die to then be born again as a fetus after the last appearance of the black monolith in infinite space.

As would be the case three years later with *A Clockwork Orange*, the score played a key expressive and emotional role, in this case with works by Ligeti and Khachaturian, and Johann and Richard Strauss, notably "The Blue Danube" and "Thus Sprach Zarathustra."

Following Kubrick's death, Steven Spielberg "inherited" one of his projects, completing the film *A.I.* (artificial intelligence) based on the master's indications. In reality, however, he brought a very different slant to the project.

2001: A Space Odyssey received only one Academy Award, for Douglas Trumbull's special effects.

Rosemary's Baby, inspired by Ira Levin's novel by the same name, was released in 1968 and marked Roman Polanski's American film debut. The director was born in Paris in 1933 to a Polish Jewish family that decided to return to Poland in the late 1930s and faced anti-Semitic persecution. As a child, Roman experienced the horror of the Cracow Ghetto, and his parents were sent to Nazi concentration camps, his mother dying at Auschwitz and his father barely surviving at Mauthausen.

Alongside his contemporary Jerzy Skolimowski, Polanski became one of the leading voices in the worldwide renewal of cinema in the early 1960s, but after his first feature-length film, *Knife in the Water*, he emigrated to the West. Working in France and England, he made *Repulsion*, *Cul-de-sac* and *The Fearless Vampire Killers, or Pardon Me but Your Teeth Are in My Neck*. And, immediately after this, he made *Rosemary's Baby* in the United States.

Young newlyweds Rosemary (Mia Farrow) and Guy (John Cassavetes) decide to look for an apartment in New York. Guy, a struggling actor who works in theater and television advertising, is waiting for his big chance. They rent a large apartment in an extravagant old building with a rather gloomy and sinister air. They happily start their new life, but are troubled by a vague sense of disquiet when they hear strange stories about what has happened in the building in the past, seemingly confirmed by the mysterious suicide of a neighbor they had just met. Welcomed and looked after by a wealthy, eccentric and somewhat meddlesome elderly couple, Rosemary and Guy decide that the time has come to start a family and have what they hope will be the first of many children.

Through a series of ambiguous and mysterious signs that build up throughout Rosemary's difficult pregnancy, it slowly dawns on moviegoers – who see the appearance of a beast on the night the baby was seemingly conceived, in a cross between nightmare and reality – and, finally, Rosemary herself that something incredible and monstrous has happened. Rosemary turns out to be the victim of a satanic cult and is carrying the devil's child – with the approval of her husband, a latter-day Faust who agreed to the deal in exchange for a successful career. Rosemary makes every attempt to rebel and is horrified by the sight of the monstrous creature in the black-veiled cradle, but in the last scene she accepts the baby – after all, it is her son – and begins to rock him.

Mia Farrow is Rosemary Woodhouse who, with her actor husband Guy (John Cassavetes), goes to live in a large gloomy Manhattan apartment building (the Dakota, the same building in front of which John Lennon was later slain).

1968
ROSEMARY'S BABY

Director: **ROMAN POLANSKI**

Cast: **MIA FARROW / JOHN CASSAVETES**

Apparently thoughtful and considerate of his pregnant wife but minimizing Rosemary's concerns about the mysterious behavior of the old married Castevet couple in a neighboring apartment, Guy has in reality sold his future child to a satanic sect in exchange for the success he so craves.

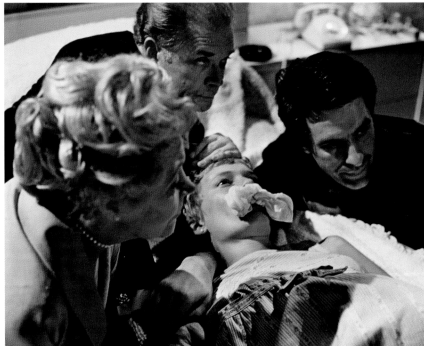

Rose Baby is considered one of the masterpieces of this brilliant director and is effectively a personal and highly original interpretation of Hitchcock's influential works. The Dakota, a large apartment building, which later became infamous as the place where John Lennon was murdered, was used for the exterior shots.

Before casting Mia Farrow (who became divorced from her husband Frank Sinatra during filming) and the director John Cassavetes, Polanski considered other stars, notably Jane Fonda (who was working on *Barbarella*) and Robert Redford. At the time the film was made, Polanski was already married to the model and actress Sharon Tate, who starred in *The Fearless Vampire Killers* and is also cameoed here in a party scene. On the night of August 8, 1969 members of Charles Manson's satanic sect brutally murdered Tate, who was eight months pregnant at the time, and several friends and guests. Her husband had been on his way to California to join her.

Considering the horrible murder and terrible coincidences, in retrospect it becomes hard not to think of *Rosemary's Baby* as a cursed film full of dark omens because of its patently sacrilegious content. In a certain sense Rosemary's character ultimately represents the diametrical opposite of the Virgin Mary. The entire chain of events left a terrible mark on the director's already tragic life.

303 - Neighbor, Mrs. Castevet "takes care" of Rosemary and still her husband mystifies the future mother in his relationships with other disciples of the sect. For Polanski, this film would be a premonition of what was to come. The following year, members of the satanic cult led by Charles Manson would savagely murder his wife, Sharon Tate, in her eighth month of pregnancy.

EASY RIDER

Director: DENNIS HOPPER

Cast: DENNIS HOPPER / PETER FONDA / JACK NICHOLSON / LUKE ASKEW / KAREN BLACK

The soundtrack includes pieces by
**Bob Dylan,
the Byrds,
and Jimi Hendrix,**
symbolizing the soundtrack for an era and more than just one generation.

Easy Rider is the manifesto of a generation. Youth, living on the road, drugs and rock music are the key elements behind the sentiments of freedom, alienation and rebellion against the word of adults. This mindset, which had already been represented extensively by the music, cinema and, above all, the literature of the Beat Generation of the postwar period, was relaunched during the student uprisings and youth movements of the Sixties against the Vietnam War. The only difference was that it was no longer the legacy of artistic elites and the intelligentsia, and instead became part of the general culture through the hippie and pacifist movements. Like *Rebel Without a Cause*, which launched the legend of James Dean, the film now seems quite outdated and disjointed, but at the time it was rightly and understandably considered shocking and even revolutionary.

One of the forerunners of independent production, *Easy Rider* originated from the encounter of different creative ideas, and little does it matter if the director was Dennis Hopper (who was also in *Rebel Without a Cause*), that the screenplay was written by Peter Fonda (son of the great Henry Fonda and Jane's brother) or that Jack Nicholson was officially present only as an actor playing a secondary but unforgettable role. *Easy Rider* is the outcome of a diffuse atmosphere and collective creativity.

Time has given us the distance we need in order to focus on the fact that, underlying the protest and rejection of a way of life in the name of an alternative culture and morality, there is a powerful sense of identification with the most classic legends of the American nation.

Dennis Hopper at left, Peter Fonda at right in the lead, and Jack Nicholson are the three main characters in Easy Rider, a small independent film that quickly became the manifesto for a generation and a movement.

The two leading characters, one of whom (Fonda) calls himself Captain America, like the comic-book superhero, decide to set out on their motorbikes ("choppers," the custom-built motorcycles with high handlebars that were in vogue at the time). They embark on a metaphorical journey in search of a new frontier, reflecting the aspiration to reestablish the myth of America's origins. Although they travel south rather than west, their contemporary sensitivity seemingly draws them closer to the Native Americans than to the pioneers.

After selling some drugs – and, naturally, the film focuses on the different categories of drugs: cocaine is bourgeois, whereas marijuana and LSD are part of the counterculture – Billy and Wyatt (a.k.a. Captain America) head to New Orleans for Mardi Gras. The film records their travels and encounters, including their psychedelic trip on LSD. The journey ends tragically in their murder, which in 1969, when the film was made, echoed the recent assassinations – the Kennedy brothers, Martin Luther King and Malcolm X – that had violently stopped those who strived for progress.

Ideologically confused, esthetically sloppy, pretentious and, in short, full of defects, the film nevertheless maintains its full power above and beyond its inherent qualities – and this would not be the first time in the history of cinema – as the symbol of a historical transition, mentality and attitude.

The Cannes Film Festival acknowledged its significance by giving it an award as best first film. The music, including songs by Bob Dylan, the Byrds and Jimi Hendrix, became the soundtrack of an era and of several generations.

A leading figure in the brief, intense but ephemeral "angry" season of England's Free Cinema, director John Schlesinger successfully debuted in Hollywood with *Midnight Cowboy* in the late 1960s. Throughout the following decade, he would make several exceptional films: from *Sunday Bloody Sunday*, focusing on the subject of homosexuality, to *Marathon Man*, an extraordinary variation on the theme of fear against a historical and political background. The latter starred Dustin Hoffman as a young Jewish man who is an amateur runner and becomes the victim of a Nazi dentist and war criminal (Laurence Olivier).

It is extraordinary that a place can be seen, photographed and narrated in so many different ways. The New York of *Midnight Cowboy* has none of the warm idealization that Woody Allen would make so memorable. It is a city filled with desperate solitudes, like those of Joe and Rico.

Joe (Jon Voight, the father of Angelina Jolie) is a young Texan who, in the first scene, abandons his hometown and restaurant job without looking back. He packs his few possessions in an extravagant two-tone suitcase, proudly dons his best cowboy duds and boards a bus for New York. He thinks he is extraordinarily handsome and decides to try his luck is a gigolo.

His naïve, simple and even obtuse optimism is contradicted by flashbacks that, like a bad dream, reveal a childhood and adolescence full of traumas that have warped his perception of sex: a blend of fear and of macho aggressiveness.

His impact with the Big Apple is terrible, at once ridiculous and desperate. When he meets Rico in the worst of circumstances, however, the two forge a mutual anchor of solidarity even as they painfully and unstoppably commence their downward spiral.

Rico (Dustin Hoffman) is a crippled Italian-American, a human wreck who ekes out a living at the edge of the rich metropolis by pulling minor scams. He offers his new friend a place to stay in his miserable room in a tumbledown building. When Joe's original plan fails, he has no choice but to work as a male prostitute, but he also manages to make his friend's dream of moving to Florida come true – or almost.

Joe gets the money they need for the trip by attacking and robbing a man who had picked him up. The two board a bus but at sunrise, as they approach Miami, Rico dies in Joe's arms.

1969
MIDNIGHT COWBOY

Director: JOHN SCHLESINGER

Cast: DUSTIN HOFFMAN / JON VOIGHT

▶ Jon Voight is the country boy who arrives in New York convinced he would make his fortune as a gigolo and Dustin Hoffman interprets the underprivileged character, Rico.

308 - Frail and disabled, Rico also attempts to cheat the naïve young Texan, but the two would end up becoming friends anyway.

309 - John Schlesinger's film portrays a harsh, rejecting, and inhospitable New York. The two parables of desperation embodied by Joe (who ends up giving in to the most degrading sort of male prostitution) and Rico (it's difficult to forget the terrible squalor of his hovel) diverge on different paths, still leaving a small glimmer of human solidarity. Joe would accompany Rico, at death's door, to fulfill his lifelong dream of seeing Florida.

This melodrama, full of bathos, now seems quite dated, but at the time it was shocking enough to be rated X. It was also considered an insulting desecration of the American myth of success. Hoffman's breakthrough role had come two years earlier with *The Graduate* and he would go on to consolidate a dazzling career, paralleling that of an entire generation of new actors (Robert Redford, Jack Nicholson, Al Pacino), with Arthur Penn's *Little Big Man*. The film also launched Voight's career, which culminated with an Academy Award for *Coming Home* (1979), one of three films released during that period - along with *Apocalypse Now* and *The Deer Hunter* - that took an unflinching look at the collective trauma of the Vietnam War.

Midnight Cowboy won three Oscars, including the coveted award for Best Picture, and the theme song "Everybody's Talkin'" became a classic.

1970

[USA]   Genre: DRAMA / ROMANCE

LOVE STORY

Director: ARTHUR HILLER

Cast: ALI MACGRAW / RYAN O'NEAL

"Love means never having to say you're sorry." One of the things that made Love Story so famous was this saying, which Jennifer teaches Oliver at the beginning of their romance and Oliver repeats to his father after Jenny's death.

In reality, the film directed by Arthur Hiller (written by Erich Segal) is far more subdued and less of a tearjerker than its reputation would lead us to believe. In the end, it is just one of the many representations of the spirit of 1968.

At an Ivy League school, a talented young hockey champion and aspiring lawyer is forced to deal with an illustrious, wealthy but intrusive family, doing everything possible to conceal his background so that he can get ahead on his own merit. We are talking about Oliver Barrett. The other leading character is a working-class Catholic girl with an Italian last name who is studying music, loves Bach and Mozart, and has plenty of talent: Jennifer Cavalleri. When the two meet, they are immediately attracted to each other. She teases him about being a daddy's boy and he reacts with pride and anger, but her comment hits the mark. And they promptly fall in love and get married. She gives up a prestigious scholarship to go study in Paris, while he tries to make ends meet on his own and, without any help from his cold and very demanding father (Ray Milland), he finishes his studies and starts a career.

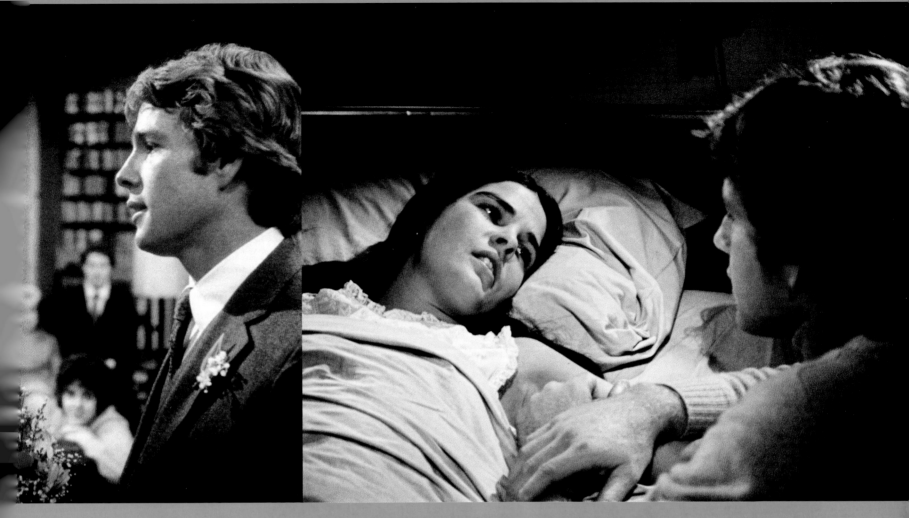

1. 2. 3. Ryan O'Neal and Ali MacGraw are Oliver and Jennifer. He is from an illustrious and wealthy family, burning bridges to make his own way in life based on his own merit. She is from a poor but strong-willed family. In the competitive setting of a prestigious university, the two young people fall in love and marry but an unfortunate fate awaits her, Jennifer becomes ill and dies. This post-'68 "cult classic" was objectionable to the more serious youth of that time and not just for a tearjerker. Rebellious in its own way, it still has a message in favor of the self-determination of young people who can liberate themselves from pressures of social class. All things considered, it still jives with the spirit of those times.

The two desperately want a child, but terrible news awaits them: Jennifer is dying of leukemia at the age of just 25.

Oliver, who has broken all ties with his family, refusing to invite them to his wedding and keeping them out of his new life (despite Jenny's selfless attempts to get him to reconcile with them), goes to his father to ask him for money. But he lies to his him, telling the elder Barrett that he needs the money because he has gotten another girl pregnant. To no avail, because Jenny soon dies in Oliver's arms after getting him to promise that he will try to make a new life for himself. And after making her father, a baker she always called Phil rather than Dad, to be strong so that he can help Oliver.

The two Barretts meet at the hospital entrance. Oliver's father has learned the truth and come to his son's aid, but this gesture is not enough to wipe out the problems of the past and the two do not embrace.

Erich Segal wrote his bestseller *a posteriori*, i.e., after writing the screenplay for the film, which was one of Paramount's biggest blockbusters. Francis Lai's score was an enormous hit and went on to win an Academy Award.

The film, which left a profound mark on the early 1970s, captured the mood of the young generation of the era – albeit couched in a love story – through Jenny's proud and independent character, and Oliver's rebellion against his wealthy family. This role launched Ryan O'Neal to Hollywood stardom, although he was already known to TV audiences, and he would subsequently be cast in *Paper Moon* by Peter Bogdanovich and *Barry Lyndon* by Stanley Kubrick. Ali MacGraw, who also became famous thanks to this film, later met Steve McQueen on the set of *The Getaway* and was married to him from 1973 to 1978.

The setting is the 1950s and the Korean War, but an endless array of details and allusions tells us that Robert Altman's 1970 film is actually about Vietnam.

The acronym MASH means Mobile Army Surgical Hospital and the disorderly company of medical officers working there includes "Hawkeye" Pierce, "Trapper John" McIntyre and "Duke" Forrest. They know their job and are good at it, but they also form the most anarchical, insolent and rebellious company in the United States Army. Their uniforms are a disaster – as are their quarters – and they get drunk, play mean practical jokes and flirt with all the pretty nurses. Above all, they pitilessly poke fun at their hypocritical and self-righteous colleague Major Frank Burns (Robert Duvall) and the new head nurse (Sally Kellerman), who sympathizes with him in denouncing the company's lack of discipline and outrageous behavior – but also spends time with him after hours. In fact, she earns the moniker of "Hot Lips" after the two are surprised in a passionate sexual encounter and their moans are sadistically broadcast to the whole camp over the loudspeaker system, to the great embarrassment of the friendly chaplain "Dago Red," who struggles with the fact that he actually finds it funny.

Altman's film, which perfectly reflected the feelings of the younger generation and America's peace movements of the 1960s, became an emblem of protest. However, it was also inspired by the mildly irreverent and ironic sentiment that was part of the background and identity of the hippie gen-

Cast: DONALD SUTHERLAND /

ELLIOT GOULD / TOM SKERRITT / ROBERT DUVALL /

SALLY KELLERMAN / ROGER BOWEN / GARY BURGHOFF /

RENE AUBERJENOIS / FRED WILLIAMSON

Donald Sutherland and Elliott Gould (first photo, on the left and right respectively) are "Hawkeye" Pierce and "Trapper" McIntyre, two doctors and officers heading a "Mobile Army Surgical Hospital" (M.A.S.H.), which acts as a surgical unit camp during the Korean War and gets into all sorts of mischief, but really without ever rejecting their duties as doctors and soldiers, just accomplishing them more creatively.

3. 4. Their victims are particularly head nurse "Hot Lips" (Sally Kellerman at right, while descending from the helicopter upon arrival at camp, she inadvertently shows her legs) and Major Burns (Robert Duvall), both offended by the non-conformist behavior of the two doctors and their accomplices in all sorts of high jinks.

2 ▾   3 ▾   4 ▾

eration. War, death and blood are far away yet also nearby. Humor is pushed to the confines of absurdity, as the wounded and the dead alike are constantly the butt of seemingly cynical and insensitive jokes. However, when the sanctimonious Major Burns attacks a young assistant, blaming him for the death of a wounded soldier who did not receive proper treatment through the major's own fault, his jokester colleagues – who never take anything seriously – change their stance and punish him harshly.

The film has a very loose narrative structure. Its many-voiced and intentionally chaotic atmosphere is also reflected on an acoustical level through the continuous and deliberate overlap of voices, banter and noise. The service messages, all of which unrelated and contradictory, that are announced over the camp's public-address system effectively form the common thread in the film's episodic structure.

M*A*S*H won widespread recognition that, while well deserved, was probably also conditioned by the climate of the era. It received the *Palme d'Or* at the Cannes Film Festival and Ring Lardner, Jr., who was one of the Hollywood Ten blacklisted during the McCarthy era, won an Oscar for his screenplay.

The film launched two new "anti-stars" who came to represent the "New" Hollywood: Donald Sutherland (Pierce) and Elliott Gould (McIntyre). It also inspired the hit television series that ran from 1972 to 1983.

1▲

DIRTY HARRY

Director: DON SIEGEL

Cast: CLINT EASTWOOD / HARRY GUARDINO /
RENI SANTONI / JOHN VERNON / ANDY ROBINSON

Harry Callahan, a San Francisco policeman known as Dirty Harry because of the ruthless methods he uses with criminals and his highly personal approach to rules and regulations, must confront the madman Scorpio. (The criminal was inspired by the killer who terrorized California in the late 1960s, a figure who was the subject of David Fincher's film *Zodiac* [2007], which references *Dirty Harry*.) Scorpio shoots his victims from rooftops and is effectively blackmailing the mayor. After thrilling shooting and chase scenes, the detective manages to capture the killer, but the criminal is released for lack of evidence. Obstructed by the law and paralyzed by Scorpio's astuteness, Callahan decides to take justice into his own hands, killing the murderer and throwing away his badge.

Made famous by Clint Eastwood's extraordinary performance, Inspector Callahan is the quintessential tough guy, and to certain extent he evokes the historic character, the "Man with No Name" from Sergio Leone's "dollar trilogy," that made Eastwood an international star. He rarely puts down his legendary .44 Magnum, and always has a ready line. When his chief asks, "Have you been following that man?" he replies, "Yeah, I've been following him on my own time. And anybody can tell I didn't do that to him . . . . cause he looks too damn good."

1. 2. 3. In a San Francisco that is different from that of Bullitt (the two police characters are diverse but both undisciplined lone wolves), a hardened detective nicknamed "Dirty Harry" takes on a personal crusade against the underworld, and in particular against the killer Scorpio, making up for the sluggish, superficial, cowardly, and dysfunctional judicial system.

Callahan also conceals a sad and mysterious past in which he lost his wife.

The fast pace of the film, which made detective films popular again, did not penalize the technical side, which is particularly well done. Don Siegel shows a fascinating San Francisco, making the most of the city's visual impact with exceptional overhead shots that enhance the narrative role of the chase scenes. The film was an enormous hit and generated four sequels: the equally successful *Magnum Force* (1973, directed by Ted Post; screenplay by John Milius and Michael Cimino), *The Enforcer* (1976, by James Fargo), *Sudden Impact* (1983, directed by Eastwood) and *The Dead Pool* (1988, by Buddy Van Horn).

William Friedkin's film *The French Connection*, starring Gene Hackman, was made the same year and it largely shares its importance as a work that breaks with the tradition of noir cinema and detective films. Both films reflect the spirit that, several years later, would be brought to caricatural extremes with Michael Winner's successful *Death Wish* saga, starring Charles Bronson. When the film was released, the character of Dirty Harry was viewed as the exaltation of an individualist ideology, spawning forced interpretations of its "message" and the accusation of being overtly fascist.

Alexander DeLarge, or Alex (Malcolm McDowell), is a juvenile delinquent from London who loves two things: "ultraviolence" and the music of Beethoven, whom he refers to affectionately as "Ludwig van." With the gang of friends he has influenced (Pete, Georgie and Dim), he organizes nightly punitive expeditions. They dress in extravagant white outfits, black boots and a top hat or derby, wear eye make-up and lipstick, and always carry sticks and chains. The boys refer to themselves as "droogs" and speak an elaborate and sophisticated argot, some of which they have invented themselves ("gulliver" means brain) and part of which is derived from Russian: ("droogs" means friends). Before every outing they stop at the Korova Milk Bar to drink "milk +": milk laced with mescaline, which they are convinced gives them strength and predisposes them to ultraviolence.

Under a bridge they terrorize and beat an alcoholic vagrant. In an abandoned theater they attack a rival gang that was raping a girl. And after a mad chase in a stolen car, with the pretext of needing help they break into an author's luxurious country home, destroying, humiliating, raping and beating its owners. On their subsequent raid, however, when Alex alone enters the villa of an eccentric contemporary art collector and purportedly the manager of a diet clinic, his rebellious droogs abandon him to his fate when he kills the woman with an enormous white phallic sculpture.

Arrested and sentenced to 14 years in prison for murder, Alex has not changed nor is he repentant, but when the Interior Minister comes to visit the prisoners, he promptly offers himself as a guinea pig for the Ludovico technique. With his eyes held open and under the effect of powerful drugs, Alex is forced to watch scenes of violence and rape over and over again on a screen, accompanied by the notes of his beloved Beethoven. As a result, he develops a negative response toward both. By depriving socially dangerous subjects of all willpower and the ability to choose (brainwashing), the government assures everyone that it has found a way to rehabilitate delinquents and empty overcrowded jails. In short, the state can finally solve the problem of crime.

When he is released from prison, Alex is rejected by his parents, who have rented his room to a boarder. He is tortured and derided by his old friends, who have become policemen. Lastly, when he happens to stop for help at the house of the author who, after the attack, has been widowed and is in a wheelchair, he is drawn into a trap. Pretending not to recognize him, the writer calls members of the opposition, who try to force Alex to commit suicide by jumping from a window. This will allow them to demonstrate that the Ludovico technique is a failure and, at the same time, the writer will get his revenge. Nevertheless, Alex survives his leap and ends up in the hospital surrounded by loving attention. He is visited by the Minister, who is worried about the upcoming election and his low popularity rating, and the two reach a new agreement. Alex returns to his beloved ultraviolence, but in this case he is serving the "right side": the side in power

1971
A CLOCKWORK ORANGE

Director: STANLEY KUBRICK

Cast: MALCOLM MCDOWELL / PATRICK MAGEE / MICHAEL BATES / WARREN CLARKE

Alex (Malcolm McDowell) is the charismatic "drug lord" of a gang addicted to a cult of "ultra violence."

Here are Alex, Pete, Georgie, and Dim during a night mission when they attack a vagrant under a London bridge.

When the film was released it was considered to be so scandalous and shocking that severe restrictions were placed on it. In many countries it was banned to minors and could not be aired on television. Kubrick elaborated his metaphor, or philosophical fable, based on the pessimistic forecast of a near future in which the repression of instincts and the exercise of violence will go arm in arm with a barbaric society, echoing the Platonic allegory of the "myth of the cavern" (the "conditioning" of which Alex is a victim). In staging the film's savage brutality, Kubrick relied on sophisticated and refined elements to create a powerful contrast. One of the most important is music: Beethoven (particularly the *Ninth Symphony*, but also the *Ode to Joy*) and Rossini (*William Tell Overture* and *The Thieving Magpie*), as well as "Singin' in the Rain," which Alex croons in the first scene at the writer's house and, in the second scene, whistles in the bathtub after he has seemingly been welcomed in friendship. It seems that McDowell improvised by singing this song during the filming and the director liked the effect.

The other element has to do with the set. Alex's family home, the bar where the droogs drink "milk+", the writer's house and the "clinic" of the woman Alex murders are decorated in a flashy pop-art style in terms of colors, objects and artwork.

The film was based on Anthony Burgess's 1962 novel *A Clockwork Orange*.

Bizarrely masked, the "druggies" break into a mansion and torture the couple living there. For its pure, gratuitous, and esthetic treatment (gang members use polished language that is musical and affected), this film reigns supreme.

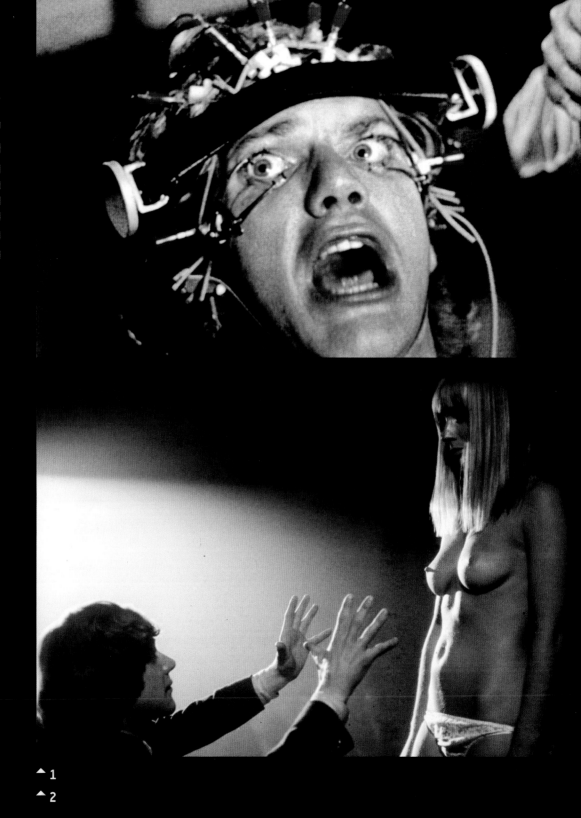

▲ 1
▲ 2

1. 2. Alex ends up being caught, tried, sentenced, and subjected to psychological treatment. He would reenter society without being cured, still ready to put himself back in service to underworld powers.

Based on the 1966 musical also called *Cabaret*, inspired by the 1951 film *I Am a Camera* that, in turn, was influenced by Christopher Isherwood's novel *Goodbye to Berlin* (1939), this masterpiece by American dancer, choreographer, actor and director Bob Fosse is a completely original work, despite these precedents and references.

Living in a cheap apartment in Berlin in 1931, the American singer Sally Bowles (Liza Minnelli) leads a wild life, performing at the Kit Kat nightclub and accepting the gallant company of well-to-do men. She meets the Briton Brian Roberts (Michael York), who has moved there to study German and thus needs a room and a place where he can give English lessons to support himself. The two immediately become friends, a rapport accelerated by Sally's impulsiveness (effectively a reaction to the fact that her family abandoned her). Her bubbly nature completely overwhelms the extremely reserved Brian. In addition to being shy, Brian is unsure about his sexual orientation. When Sally seduces him and he pulls away, making her suspect that he may be gay, he justifies himself by saying that he has been to bed with three women in his life, but that the relationships always failed. Nevertheless, he adds that, although he does not fancy men, his sex life is lackluster. The two eventually become lovers, but when Max, a wealthy young German aristocrat (Helmut Griem) appears on the scene, both Sally and Brian are destined to be charmed – and then abandoned by him.

The news that Sally is pregnant restores their serenity and the desire to plan a future together in Cambridge, but when she decides to have an abortion the two leave each other for good. One of the reasons is the fact that, while they are leading their bohemian life in Berlin, momentous events are occurring around them and are destined to affect everyone's future. The Nazi Party is gaining ground thanks to the scornful yet complicit consensus of the wealthy, who are convinced that Hitler will eliminate "subversives" – Communists – but that then it will be easy to get rid of him too. This aspect is an important part of the parallel story of another friend of the couple, the pleasure-seeking Fritz. He has concealed his Jewish background and courted Natalia, the daughter of a Jewish banker. Although he is cynically after her money, he ends up falling in love with her. When it gradually becomes clear that being Jewish in Germany is enormous risky and that marrying a Jewish woman – rich as she might be – is no longer an appealing or advantageous prospect, he courageously decides to marry her anyway.

1972
CABARET

Director: **BOB FOSSE**

Cast: **LIZA MINNELLI /**

MICHAEL YORK / JOEL GREY / HELMUT GRIEM

Minnelli is Sally Bowles, an American girl who performs in a Berlin nightclub in 1931.

The plot unfolds in a deft and fluid alternation of music and choreography, revolving around Sally as well as the Master of Ceremonies at the cabaret, played by Joel Grey. The structure makes the film a rather unusual musical that successfully conveys the flavor and atmosphere of this era, examining the decline of the fragile Weimar Republic. For example, there is a wonderful scene outside the nightclub when, at a rural beerhouse, a young uniformed Nazi begins to sing an anthem and all the young people fanatically join. Using a few effective yet unmannered brushstrokes, the film illustrates the spirit of the era as well as its artistic tension and libertine mood, particularly on a sexual level. It is a world that is coming to an end, but not because it can simplistically be branded as corrupt or debauched. Indeed, true depravity was around the corner.

Cabaret was a runaway success and earned eight Academy Awards, including Best Director, and the well-deserved Oscars for Best Actress and Best Supporting Actor (Grey). Every film that is considered a legend has attained this status because particular details have remained etched in people's memories. In this case, they are the scenes in which Minnelli sings "Life is a Cabaret" and duets with Grey in "Money, Money."

"**Money Money...**"

324 and 325 - With her well-matched partner (Joel Grey), she is brilliant and confident on stage but fickle, insecure, and unpredictable in her life outside the limelight. Sally sings about love and looks without ever finding it. A precious jewel for its stage sets, choreography, costuming, and music, the film also has something more to offer. It breaks from the fragile democratic Germany of Weimar to disclose that the apparent decadence in those days was in reality an exercise in freedom, and that the real decline would take place shortly thereafter.

1972

THE GODFATHER

Director: FRANCIS FORD COPPOLA

Cast: MARLON BRANDO / AL PACINO / ROBERT DUVALL /
JAMES CAAN / DIANE KEATON / TALIA SHIRE / STERLING HAYDEN

The Godfather is set in New York, immediately after World War II. The film begins with the wedding of Connie (Talia Shire), the daughter of Don Vito Corleone (Marlon Brando), and Carlo Rizzi. It is a long Italian-style celebration in which the audience is introduced to the entire family. We meet Tom (Robert Duvall), Don Vito's informally adopted son, and two of his sons destined to succeed him, Sonny (James Caan) and Michael (Al Pacino), who is in the army. We also meet Kay (Diane Keaton), Michael's fiancée, a pretty American girl who has no idea about Italian-American customs. It is a day in which anyone can ask for and receive the Godfather's help. The singer, Johnny, asks for a favor and Vito promises that he will get him cast in a film. All it takes is the Godfather's promise – "I'll take care of it" – and everything goes as planned, as Johnny soon finds out. But one day Vito decides that does not want to support the drug trade run by Sollozzo, who works for the Tattaglia family, and a feud begins. Luca Brasi, Vito's right-hand man, is killed and then an attempt is made on Vito's own life. At this point Michael, who lives away from the family and, by nature, is far removed from Mafia affairs, decides to come home to take care of the family business. At the hospital he saves his father's life after another attempt, telling his intubated father that he is no longer alone. His father's only response is a tear.

Michael is about to receive his baptism by fire. He gets his revenge against a corrupt policeman, Captain McCluskey (Sterling Hayden), who tried to kill his father in the hospital and punched Michael, by killing both McCluskey and the mobster Sollozzo. As result, he is forced to hide out in Sicily while the family feud continues in America, with Sonny representing the Corleones despite the fact that Vito has come home. In Sicily Michael falls in love with Apollonia and marries her, forgetting about Kay. But when Sonny is killed in an ambush organized by his brother-in-law Carlo and Apollonia is murdered in front of Michael, he decides to leave again.

When he returns to the United States he finds that Vito has established a truce after Sonny's death, but it is during this truce that Michael is appointed to be Vito's successor. He also asks Kay to marry him.

The strategy changes: Michael looks for new advisers and spends time listening to Vito, who dies peacefully. In the end, he puts his father's advice into practice. Everything happens during the baptism of Connie and Carlo's son, as Michael's trusted men take revenge on the enemies of the Corleone family during the long ceremony. Immediate after the baptism, Carlo himself will be killed for his part in the ambush that took Sonny's life. In her grief, Connie blames her brother for shedding so much blood – including that of the brother-in-law whose son he had agreed to baptize, even though he had already decided to kill the man. Kay, who witnesses the scene between the two siblings, begins to wonder about her husband's innocence, a doubt that remains despite Michael's claims to the contrary. After hearing him deny any responsibility, we – and Kay – watch as men come to pay their respects by kissing his hand: Michael is the new Godfather.

Marlon Brando is Don Vito Corleone, the powerful and ruthless mafia boss and family head who at the drop of a hat will either favor someone or order his death.

329 [TOP] - Don Vito Corleone presides over a meeting of "friends."

329 [BOTTOM] - Don Vito receives gifts and is paid respect while granting protection on the day of his daughter's wedding, surrounded by his sons and henchmen, Tom (Robert Duvall) and Sonny (James Caan, at center of the photo), his adopted and natural sons respectively, and his youngest son, Michael (Al Pacino). Destined to succeed him, Michael barely faces forward, looking around and dissociating from family affairs.

After *The Godfather* (1972), Coppola directed the other two films in the trilogy (1974 and 1990). The first part of the second film is a prequel in which we meet the future Don Vito (Robert De Niro), who is still living in his Sicilian hometown of Corleone. When he immigrates to New York, his real surname - Andolini - becomes Corleone. The other half of this film is a sequel that shows the Corleone family up to the end of the late Fifties, with a long digression that sees Michael (Al Pacino) overseeing the Mafia business in Cuba before Castro's rise to power. In the closing scenes, Kay finally leaves her husband. The third film is set in the late 70s and new characters appear: Mary (Sofia Coppola) and Vincent (Andy Garcia), respectively Michael's daughter and nephew.

Inspired by Mario Puzo's bestseller (1969), all three films were written by the author of the book.

Beneath the façade of Don Vito's daughter Connie's (Talia Shire) lavish ritual of matrimony, thousands of strings are pulled, moving silently and discretely to weave alliances, hand out favors, and declare war.

The Godfather was released the same year as Bernardo Bertolucci's *Last Tango in Paris*, bringing Brando's fame to new heights, as these were two of his most memorable roles. Coppola would later offer him his last major role, in *Apocalypse Now*, after which Brando's career declined into a lackluster finale. To achieve the effect of a jutting jaw, the actor used a prosthesis, initially achieved simply by putting cotton in his mouth and subsequently done in a more sophisticated manner.

Nino Rota's score was an enormous success and the film won three Academy Awards: Best Picture, Best Adapted Screenplay and Best Actor. As a protest in favor of Native Americans, however, Brando turned down his Oscar.

330 - Michael (with Don Vito in the photo) would end up renouncing his love for Kay (Diane Keaton), outside of the mafia world, and accepting his own family destiny. An attempt on his father's life and a settling of the scores between families would convince him, and the violent death of his brother, Sonny, would reinforce his choice. After the death of the patriarch, he would be the new godfather.

331 - Don Vito Corleone dies in the yard at his home while his small nephew plays.

The Sting brought back the duo that, four years earlier, had been such a success in *Butch Cassidy and the Sundance Kid*. It was made by the same director, George Roy Hill, who also made the anti-militaristic *Slaughterhouse Five* (1972), based on Kurt Vonnegut's novel, between the two films.

The Sting takes up the playful and cockily irresponsible air that characterized the feats of the two outlaws in the previous film.

The first film examined the lives of two figures from the history of American crime, Butch Cassidy (Paul Newman) and Sundance Kid (Robert Redford). The famous robbers were part of the generation after that of Billy the Kid and Jesse James, whose gang was known as the Wild Bunch (although Sam Peckinpah's 1969 Western by the same name never actually refers to them). Butch and Sundance supposedly died in Bolivia in 1908. Some sustain that they killed each other when they realized that they had been surrounded by the implacable pursuers from the Pinkerton National Detective Agency but others, such as Bruce Chatwin in his book *In Patagonia*, have maintained that, in reality, they two actually lived until the 1930s.

However, *The Sting* is a fictional story set in the Depression, around 1930, and it has the same refined style as its forerunner.

Johnny Hooker (Redford) is a small-time con man. After unwittingly biting off more than he can chew by cheating a violent gangster, Johnny manages to avoid being the target of revenge, but his elderly friend and accomplice Luther, who was planning to retire after the last job, pays the price instead. At this point Johnny, who has also gotten into trouble with the sleazy corrupt cop Snyder (Charles Durning), turns to Henry Gondorff (Newman), a cardsharp and high-class con man who is laying low, to convince him to come up with a plan that will avenge the murder of their mutual friend.

They finagle the underworld boss Doyle Lonnegan (Robert Shaw, one of the "bad guys" in *From Russia With Love*), a tough character who lets nothing stop him, with a poker game organized aboard a deluxe train. Their plan is to convince Lonnegan that Hooker is willing to work for him and give him inside information so he can win through a large off-track betting agency run by Gondorff. In reality, it is a scam that has been set up overnight, bringing in all of Hooker's friends: the very best con artists.

1973
THE STING

Director: GEORGE ROY HILL

Cast: PAUL NEWMAN / ROBERT REDFORD /
CHARLES DURNING / ROBERT SHAW

► An elegant Paul Newman plays a clever swindler during the Great Depression.

1. Robert Redford is Johnny Hooker, mediocre cheat who has committed the careless mistake of arranging a fraud to the detriment of a dangerous big shot, and what's more, it also gets in the way of a corrupt policeman's interests. All of that causes the vengeful death of one of his dear friends and that of Gondorff. He allows himself be lured back in to hatch a plan for the sting of the century to the detriment of the boss, Doyle Lonnegan.

2. Paul Newman is Henry Gondorff, high-class card shark and conman of the first degree, taking a break at the moment.

The effect of Gondorff's constant mispronunciation of Lonnegan's name during the poker game, which infuriates the formidable gangster, is one of the most hilarious moments in the film.

The mechanism of this sting against Lonnegan is extremely intricate yet is presented so fluidly that there is never any suspicion that something is amiss. In short, with its sleight of hand the film manages to con the audience as well, particularly in the tragic faux finale when the FBI bursts in, followed by shootouts and arrests. Yet this immediately proves to be the ultimate mark of the con men's genius.

The film revives the infallible dynamics between the two leading characters, creating a man's world in which women, as in the case of *Butch Cassidy and the Sundance Kid*, are essentially a decorative presence, a world of romanticized outlaws whose criminal activities are ultimately a sign of rebellion and even justice. Nevertheless, another element behind the runaway success of this film, which garnered seven Academy Awards, was Scott Joplin's ragtime music and, in particular, the theme of "The Entertainer."

336 - In order to frame Lonnegan (Robert Shaw), conmen Newman and Redford resort to their cumulative store of imagination and friendships. They unite the best and, with exclusive use of the "sting," create a fake horserace-betting hall.

337 - *The Sting* is one of the most successful and brilliant American films of the Sixties, re-launching the same pair with the same disenchanted light banter, tested four years before in *Butch Cassidy and the Sundance Kid*.

1973

AMERICAN GRAFFITI

Director: GEORGE LUCAS

Cast: RICHARD DREYFUSS / RON HOWARD / PAUL LE MAT /

CHARLES MARTIN SMITH / HARRISON FORD

"Where were you in '62?" is the subtitle of the film that 29-year-old George Lucas, a graduate of the University of Southern California School of Cinematic Arts, intended to use as the springboard for his epic *Star Wars* project. Instead, however, it became the manifesto of a generation and a cult movie.

American Graffiti recounts the night in which four former classmates are about to go their separate ways and face the tests of life after graduating from high school and finishing their summer vacation. Each one has a different personality.

Curt (Richard Dreyfuss) is unsure about going away to college. He is confused and talks to one of his teachers, confessing that he does not feel like a fighter. He plays an impromptu thug with the gang of "The Pharaohs" and falls in love with a blonde he sees driving by in a white Thunderbird.

Steve (Ron Howard) instead says that he wants to continue his studies. He is extremely ambitious and plans to leave their small town to fulfill his dreams. Although he fights with his girlfriend Laurie, the two are madly in love with each other.

Good-looking John (Paul Le Mat) is the idol of the group and drives around in an eclectic souped-up yellow deuce coupe. John beats his rival Bob (Harrison Ford) in a classic race down the highway, which culminates in an accident but without taking the tragic turn of *Rebel Without a Cause*. The proverbial stud who carries a pack of Camels rolled up in the sleeve of his T-shirt, like Marlon Brando and James Dean, John ends up spending the evening with a young girl who never leaves his side. He does not have enough money to go to college and works as a mechanic.

Terry "The Toad" (Charles Martin Smith) is the nerd of the group, an acned complex-ridden boy who has more money than his friends. He has no plans to leave town and, thanks to the fact that Steve has let him borrow his beautiful Chevy, on that fateful night he finally meets a girl.

The night portrayed in the film is an endless sequence of comings and goings, with the young people meeting each other at drugstores, fast-food joints, drive-ins and a school dance before they finally say goodbye to each other. Above all, however, it is marked by their constant cruising the streets of the small town to the endless beat of the songs of the era by big names such as the Platters, the Beach Boys and Elvis Presley, performers that John disdains because, in his opinion, they have watered-down rock and roll.

All of this comes together to make that night the quintessential eve of a new era: the end of a way of life and the beginning of something new and unknown.

It's the summer of '62 in the American countryside. Four high school buddies get ready to receive their diplomas with one leaving for college, another for Vietnam, and the other two remaining at home. Four lives at the cusp of adulthood are seen in a microcosm that has something for everyone (in the image at left, you can see Richard Dreyfuss as Curt).

341 [TOP] - The film that made George Lucas famous is an in-depth sampling of America in the Fifties with muscle cars driven only for a few feet, carefree drive-ins with fast food, and a pack of Camels wrapped in the T-shirt sleeve.

341 [CENTER AND BOTTOM] - Ron Howard (at center, right) is Steve, and seems to be the most ambitious. On the other hand, Charles Martin Smith (below) is Terry, the nerd of the group. In reality, none of their destinies would validate their foundations. John would die young in a car accident, Terry in Vietnam, Steve would never leave their hometown and would have a family, and Curt would leave to become a writer.

Everything works beautifully and the interplay of events is simple but perfect. Lucas evokes all the icons and symbols of the young and still-innocent American epic, of the counterculture of the 1950s that timidly opposed provincial conformism but was tamed by the media, Hollywood, discographic interests and rising consumerism. The film also showcases the myth of independent radio stations, embodied here by Wolfman Jack. Everything has the optimistic slant of the Kennedy years.

Interestingly, it was Lucas who invented the formula of end titles announcing the fate of his young people, a concept that was subsequently imitated widely. John dies shortly thereafter in a car accident. Bumbling Terry is killed in Vietnam. Steve, seemingly the most ambitious, goes to the airport the following morning merely to say goodbye to those who are leaving, whereas he stays behind and gets married. According to the caption, he becomes an insurance agent in Modesto (uncoincidentally Lucas' birthplace). The only one to leave is the hesitant and introspective Curt, who later becomes a writer.

Off the screen, at least three of the actors went on to become major stars, most notably Dreyfuss, Howard, who starred in the television series "Happy Days," and Harrison Ford, who played a marginal role in *American Graffiti*. Francis Ford Coppola, a friend, peer and a classmate of George Lucas, produced the film. The generation that would revolutionize Hollywood and cinema was launched with this film.

THE EXORCIST

Director: **WILLIAM FRIEDKIN**

Cast: **ELLEN BURSTYN / LINDA BLAIR / MAX VON SYDOW / JASON MILLER**

The Exorcist has arrived, an old and taciturn priest and archaeologist, Father Merrin, played by the great Bergman actor, Max von Sydow.

Chris is desperate in the face of their impotence and failure, compounded by the escalation of unusual behavior that has made her daughter completely unrecognizable. Above all, she is alarmed by the death of her friend the director, because she is the only one who grasps the fact that her daughter was the cause, as the girl has also exercised her demonic violence and superhuman force against her own mother. In the meantime, a fourth key figure emerges: police inspector Kinderman, played by Lee J. Cobb.

At this point, Chris turns to extreme measures. Although she declares that she is an atheist, she seeks Father Karras, not for his abilities as a psychiatrist but as a priest. She asks him to exorcise her daughter, as she is now convinced that the girl is possessed.

Skeptical and reluctant, Karras agrees to submit her request to his superiors. In turn, they call in Father Merrin, who reappears in the film at this point as an expert exorcist. Thus, we have come full circle: Father Merrin, the unearthed figurine, the demon that possesses Regan. The extremely violent ritual is performed, during which the heart of the old exorcist gives out. In turn, the young priest's moral strength is about to give in when he hears the possessed child speak with his mother's voice, reproving him for having abandoned her. In an extreme effort, Karras orders the demon to leave the child and take him instead, and as soon as the demon enters his body he kills himself by leaping from the window. Exorcised and without any recollection of what happened to her, Regan leaves the city with her mother.

The film was cut when it was first released, but the full version came out in 2000. Two sequels were made in 1977 and 1990, as well as a prequel in 2004. According to urban legend, countless serious accidents occurred on the set of *The Exorcist*.

344 and 345 - The Assyrian idol appears here when Father Merrin finds a small statuette representing this "demon," which initiates the curse, that is, the possession of little Regan's (Linda Blair, in the last photo, disfigured by the demon living inside her) body and soul, from which only Father Merrin's and younger Father Karras' sacrifice would finally successfully free her.

[USA] Genre: **THRILLER / HORROR**

JAWS

Director: STEVEN SPIELBERG   Cast: ROY SCHEIDER / ROBERT SHAW / RICHARD DREYFUSS / LORRAINE GARY

In the mid-1970s Steven Spielberg was little-known director who was less than 30 years old (he had made *Duel* and *The Sugarland Express*). With *Jaws*, the young and extraordinarily talented director began his triumphant rise to success. Released in the summer of 1975, *Jaws* overturned the industry's traditional platform for launching and distributing films, inaugurating a new concept based on huge promotional investments and nationwide simultaneous premieres at numerous theaters. Based on a book by Peter Benchley, in turn inspired by a real event that took place off the coast of New Jersey in 1916, the film is set in the small Atlantic tourist resort of Amity Island. It revolves around four main characters: local police chief Martin Brody (Roy Scheider), a former New York policeman who moved to the island with his family years earlier; Mayor Larry Vaughn (Murray Hamilton, the actor who played Mr. Robinson in *The Graduate*); oceanographer Matt Hooper (Richard Dreyfuss, who would work with Spielberg again in *Close Encounters of the Third Kind*); the shark hunter Quint (Robert Shaw, the bad guy hoodwinked in *The Sting*).The charming and sleepy resort is shocked by the mysterious death of a girl who had gone skinny-dipping after a nighttime beach party, followed by the death of a little boy on a rubber mattress, a fisherman attacked on his boat and, lastly, a swimmer in broad daylight. The small community, led by the local government and the mayor, is unwilling to admit that these people were killed by an enormous shark. The Fourth of July is approaching – the height of the summer season – and everyone is afraid that a shark warning could harm the island's tourism-based economy. Brody understands the gravity of the situation but is initially influenced by the town's interests and lets himself be intimidated by the mayor, who also happens to be his employer. Following the first incident, the mayor forces Brody to sign the report of the medical examiner,

1. 2. 3. Despite great differences, three of the heroes, or rather antiheroes, unite in coalition to defeat the sea monster that has spread panic throughout the peaceful seaside city on the east coast and to overcome the serious underestimation of emergency on the part of local and colluding petty politicians whose financial interests risk a negative effect on the tourist season. Richard Dreyfuss is the pacifist oceanographer that knows what he's doing despite giving the opposite impression. The head of the small police station, Roy Scheider, is all dignity even when initially under the thumb of someone who prefers to keep him quiet. And the whale-hunter, Robert Shaw, is rough around the edges hiding his humanity beneath the surface.

who changed his initial opinion on the mayor's instructions, saying that the girl was not torn apart by a shark but by a boat propeller. In the meantime, however, Brody has called Hooper to the island and the expert, who immediately hits it off with the policeman, has no doubts whatsoever about the cause of death. Together they secretly autopsy the shark that was captured by amateur hunters, who are after the bounty offered by the mother of the second victim, the little boy. The animal's stomach does not contain any human remains. Therefore, not only are the two positive that the cause of the emergency is an enormous sea predator, but also that the killer shark is still out there. At this point Quint, an abrasive professional shark hunter, comes to town and announces that the $3000 bounty is not enough. He wants $10,000 to get rid of the monster. This ends the first part of the film and opens the second, with a division between the two halves that is almost too abrupt. The men convince Quint not to set out alone, as he would have preferred, and he agrees to allow Brody and Hooper onto his boat, the *Orca*. Nevertheless, he is wary of both men: Brody because he represents the law (the police chief wants to call in the Coast Guard), coupled with the fact that he has little experience at sea, and Hooper because Quint is convinced that the scientist is a "daddy's boy" with book smarts but no practical knowledge. As they prepare for a fight to the death that evokes the epic of Ahab and *Moby Dick*, the three men gradually get to know each other. Quint's famous monologue gives us an idea of his hatred of sharks, as he recalls his terrible experience following a shipwreck during World War II. In the end, however, Quint is devoured by the shark and the hesitant and even-tempered police chief will prove to be the victor. As the boat starts to sink as a result of the enormous beast's increasingly daring and ferocious attacks, Brody manages to throw an oxygen tank into its gaping mouth and then shoots the tank, blowing up the shark. Hooper, who had the guts to descend into the water inside a cage in an attempt to shoot the monster with a poisonous spear, is thought to be dead, but – as opposed to the original version of the script – he emerges unscathed. Clinging to a buoy, the two men return to shore. The "Hitchcockian" music was composed by John Williams, who wrote many of the scores for Spielberg's later works.

One Flew Over the Cuckoo's Nest is set in an Oregon mental hospital. Thirty-eight-year-old Randle McMurphy (Jack Nicholson, who was approximately the same age as the character he played) has been sent to the institution due to his rebellious behavior in prison, where he is serving time following five convictioms for assault and statutory rape. Upon his arrival, the director asks him why he thinks he's been sent there. McMurphy responds by wondering aloud if it is because he likes to brawl and have sex. The director informs he that is there for observation, in order to determine if his unruliness in prison is the sign of a disturbed mind or if it simply means that McMurphy is a slacker, a man who enjoys provoking people: a man who inveterately balks at authority and the rules of any penitentiary system. In short, the first scenes clearly delineate the situation, painting a clear-eyed picture of the mental institution without making it seem worse than it is, and without glossing over the negative sides of McMurphy's personality. While he is indeed violent and an idler, he is certainly not "crazy" and is unquestionably a man in full possession of his obviously brilliant mental faculties.

McMurphy immediately bridles against the rules and begins his battle against them. Discipline is embodied by an unbending nurse, Mildred Ratched (Louise Fletcher) who, in her humiliating brutality, is probably convinced that she is simply doing her duty. McMurphy immediately befriends "Chief" Bromden (Will Sampson), an enormous American Indian who – as we will discover much later – is feigning to be deaf and unable to speak, and pretends to comply with his therapy but actually spits out his medication.

McMurphy wreaks havoc in the daily group sessions run by Ratched, asking her to change the hours and allow them to watch baseball games on TV. Ratched allows the group to vote and when McMurphy is defeated, he stands in front of the dark television screen and improvises a fake news report, inspiring courage in the other patients who, intimidated by the iron-fisted nurse, had previously been too afraid to follow his lead. He heads an innocent group outing aboard the institute's bus, planning to pick up his complaisant girlfriend and steal a boat to go fishing. He also organizes an impromptu casino and, in a poker game, wins the only thing that patients can bet: cigarettes. Consequently, when one of the patients explodes during a group therapy session, protesting against the fact that Ratched has rationed their cigarettes, McMurphy loses his temper and is harshly silenced by a male nurse.

This incident leads to his first serious punishment. He is transferred to the ward for the most serious and aggressive patients and undergoes electroshock treatment.

1975
ONE FLEW OVER THE CUCKOO'S NEST

Director: MILOS FORMAN

Cast: JACK NICHOLSON / LOUISE FLETCHER / WILLIAM REDFIELD / BRAD DOURIF / WILL SAMPSON / DANNY DEVITO / SCATMAN CROTHERS / CHRISTOPHER LLOYD

▶ Jack Nicholson is the "erratic one," Randle McMurphy..

When he is sent back to his ward, he pretends that he has been lobotomized, but as soon as he throws off his mask, the others are elated to discover that he has not changed. Indeed, his fellow patients show that, thanks to him, they have regained a desire for independence, dignity and freedom. However, when he is dealt a harsh psychological blow by the same nurse who had beaten him, who cruelly tells him that he will never leave the institution, McMurphy decides that it is time to try to escape to nearby Canada with the Chief. McMurphy calls his girlfriend, who arrives with another girl and an ample supply of alcohol, and he bribes the night nurse to open a window so that he can enjoy a farewell party with his new friends. Just as the two fugitives are about to leave, touched by the shyness of young Billy (Brad Dourif), who has been reduced to stuttering helplessness by his overbearing mother, of whom Nurse Ratched is effectively a doppelganger, McMurphy encourages one of the women to seduce him. Tired and drunk, the entire group ends up falling asleep.

The following morning, when the nursing staff finds all the evidence of the party held the night before, Ratched humiliates Billy so badly that he disowns McMurphy and then commits suicide. Infuriated, McMurphy tries to strangle the nurse and is taken off to be lobotomized – for real this time – but his extended absence leads the other patients to believe that he has escaped. The Chief is the one who finally sets McMurphy free. Horrified by the idea of leaving his friend in a vegetative state, the giant goes to his bed one night and suffocates him with a pillow. The chief then hoists the heavy marble washbasin that, at the beginning, he had bet McMurphy he could rip up from the floor, throws it through a window and escapes.

1. 2. 3. McMurphy would succumb when confronted with the psychiatric institution, embodied in the authoritarian style of the head nurse, Mildred Ratched. Many of the actors who were McMurphy/Nicholson's companions in misadventure were not yet famous but destined for important careers. Among them was Danny DeVito (photograph 3, at center, from behind).

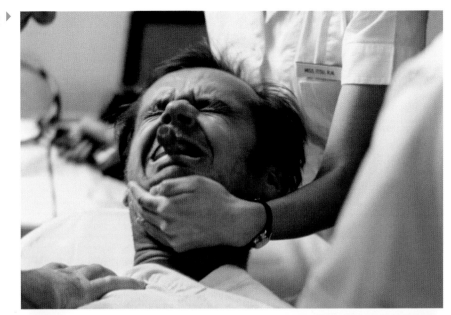

The film is a masterpiece that eloquently expresses the spirit of an era. The Czech director Milos Forman, who fled his country after the Prague Spring and the ensuing repression, made the film based on a 1962 novel in which Ken Kesey recounted his experience working in a psychiatric ward, where he witnessed treatments such as those shown in the film. In 1963 the novel was made into a stage production that starred Kirk Douglas, who later obtained the adaptation rights and planned to produce and star in the film. Several years later, he turned the project over to his son Michael who, after considering other actors for the role of McMurphy (including Marlon Brando), chose Nicholson. Fletcher – an unknown at the time – was cast after more famous actresses such as Ann Bancroft turned it down. The title comes from a nursery rhyme: "One flew east, one flew west, and one flew over the cuckoo's nest." In this case, "cuckoo" is a metaphor for madness, and thus flying over the cuckoo's nest means going mad. The film boasts a formidable cast, with actors who would go on to become famous, notably Danny DeVito, Vincent Schiavelli and Christopher Lloyd, who later played "Doc" in *Back to the Future*.

One Flew Over the Cuckoo's Nest won all five major Academy Awards (Best Picture, Best Director, Best Actor and Actress – Nicholson and Fletcher – and Best Screenplay), a record that Frank Capra's *It Happened One Night* had held for 40 years and would not repeated until 15 years later by *The Silence of the Lambs*.

The film is an exceptional moral tale on the violent prejudice that represses antiauthoritarianism and the desire for freedom, considering them signs of social deviance. These themes were also examined in *Billy's Gang* by John Schlesinger (1963) and *Cool Hand Luke* (1967), starring Paul Newman, two splendid metaphors that were the harbingers of the libertarian movements that exploded in the late 1960s and inspired this enormously influential film.

4. The giant Bromden (Will Sampson, in the photograph he's playing basketball with McMurphy/Nicholson), the Native American who pretends to be a deaf-mute as a sign of lack of engagement and protest against the institution, would be the one collecting an inheritance from McMurphy and escaping the mental hospital after helping him to die.

NASHVILLE

Director: ROBERT ALTMAN

**Cast: NED BEATTY / RONEE BLAKLEY /
KEITH CARRADINE / GERALDINE CHAPLIN /
SCOTT GLENN / SHELLEY DUVALL / LILY TOMLIN**

Numerous storylines are interwoven in the five-day festival that takes place in Nashville, Tennessee, the home of country music. Singers, music fans and ordinary people who aspire to be singers, local and national politicians, and flunkies from the musical and political arenas cross paths in *Nashville*. Their stories unfold against the backdrop of the presidential campaign of Hal Philip Walker, a demagogue who rails against problems such as the surfeit of lawyers in Congress and is determined to exploit the popularity of the event.

We see the local organizer of Walker's campaign (Ned Beatty) and his wife (Lily Tomlin), a singer who lovingly takes care of their two deaf children and is having an affair with one of the stars of the festival (Keith Carradine). There is the tone-deaf waitress, Sueleen (Gwen Welles), who hopes to break into the music business but ends up performing a seamy striptease. We meet Albuquerque (Barbara Harris), who hopes to become famous and has been followed to Nashville by her husband, who instead wants her to settle down. She will get her unexpected moment of glory in the final scene. There is also the girl who, on the pretext of visiting her elderly aunt and uncle, is sucked into the extravaganza and flirts brazenly with every man she meets (Shelley Duvall). Geraldine Chaplin plays a meddlesome BBC journalist. Another character is the soldier (Scott Glenn) who idolizes the capricious star Barbara Jean (Ronee Blakley). We meet Barbara Jean's friends/rivals Connie White (Karen Black), who replaces her when she has nervous breakdowns, and Haven Hamilton (Henry Gibson), who accompanies her to the stage when she is back to normal. There is also an eccentric fellow (Jeff Goldblum) who rides a chopper, the motorcycle that was made famous by *Easy Rider*. We also meet Walker's opportunistic and scheming henchman (Michael Murphy). The cast is joined by a myriad of minor characters, each of whom has a distinctive personality.

Indeed, the group as a whole plays the leading role and, in effect, this masterpiece of the 1970s is a tableau in the purest Altman style. The seemingly complete lack of structure and the disorderly accumulation of the work's boundless material – with frequent overlays of sound – are instead resolved brilliantly through extremely fluid editing.

In the end, however, music is the true star. The film's most famous songs are "For the sake of the children" and "Two hundred years," sung by Henry Gibson, "My Idaho Home," sung by Ronee Blakley, "I'm Easy," written and sung by Keith Carradine – the song won the film's only Oscar – and Barbara Harris' rousing second performance of "It Don't Worry Me," also written by Carradine (who

1. 2. Of the main characters in the musical marathon in this great film, one playing a stereotyped womanizer yet also an extraordinary American is Keith Carradine, and the other is Ronee Blakley who interprets the unpredictable country western star, Barbara Jean.

3. It is really Keith Carradine that sings the two tunes in the film that have remained the most famous: "I'm Easy" and "It Don't Worry Me."

sings the first version). During the grand finale of the festival and under the banners of Walker's presidential campaign, a spectator surrealistically assassinates superstar Barbara Jean during her performance in front of Nashville's monstrous neoclassical Parthenon. Hamilton, who is also wounded, shouts into the microphone, "Y'all take it easy now. This isn't Dallas. It's Nashville. This is Nashville. You show 'em what we're made of. They can't do this here to us in Nashville. OK, everybody, sing. Come on somebody, sing. You sing!" And so petite blonde Albuquerque, who had been crouching in a corner until then, takes the stage and starts to sing "It don't worry me," timidly at first but then with growing confidence until the whole crowd joins in.

Indeed, between the lines the other star of the film – alongside music – is America at the threshold of the bicentennial of the Declaration of Independence and the film showcases the very spirit of the nation: the spirit of the era. Altman grasps all of this but never offers his own slant. He simply aligns and observes things in the course of what, to an undiscerning viewer, may appear to be a very long and anonymous documentary, but is actually one of the most important films of its era.

The character of Travis Bickle in *Taxi Driver* not only represented the consecration of Robert De Niro, who had already worked with Martin Scorsese in *Mean Streets* and Francis Ford Coppola in *The Godfather Part II*, but it also proved to be one of the most iconic of the 1970s.

Travis is an ex-Marine (despite the fact that the film was made in the mid-1970s, the Vietnam War is never mentioned, although at one point Travis says that he was discharged in 1973). He lives in New York and, in his own way, battles loneliness, chronic insomnia and his mounting disgust toward the world around him, which seems to be adrift and in the throes of terrible moral decline.

Two important characteristics must be noted regarding this character. First of all, his point of view and sentiments are almost never expressed verbally. He uses very few words and the ones he does use are very mundane, posing a sharp contrast to the sudden violence of his actions. Secondly, the film never puts the audience in a position to understand whether or not his behavior is that of a madman, deviant and misfit.

Rootless and isolated, Travis spends his free time at seedy porno theaters and drives a cab on the night shift, from 6 p.m. until 6 a.m. He has no education, no points of reference, and is so inept that he ends up frightening the few people with whom he interacts. Nevertheless, he becomes interested in a woman, Betsy (Cybill Shepherd), who is working on the presidential campaign of Senator Charles Palantine. Initially somewhat wary of his eccentric behavior and perhaps also the evident social and cultural gap between them, she then becomes intrigued by Travis and agrees to go out with him. However, when he takes her to see a porno film, she walks out, horrified, and refuses to have anything else to do with him.

In the meantime, in his nocturnal wanderings across town, Travis runs into the child prostitute Iris – played by Jodie Foster, who was little more than a girl herself when the film was made – on two different occasions. The first time, the girl, probably on drugs, climbs into his cab and begs him to drive off, but Travis is so shocked that her pimp manages to catch up with them and drag her away. He encounters her again when she is walking down the street with another girl and decides to follow her, hoping to catch her attention. Finally, he actively seeks her.

1976
TAXI DRIVER

Director: MARTIN SCORSESE

Cast: ROBERT DE NIRO / JODIE FOSTER /
CYBILL SHEPHERD / HARVEY KEITEL

Robert De Niro is Travis Bickle, former marine, solitary taxi driver who, driving around the streets of New York, gets to know the story of child prostitute, Iris (Jodie Foster), for whom he decides to be champion.

In the meantime, he slowly reaches the decision to react against a world that has rejected him and in which he feels that hypocrisy and immorality have triumphed, and as a result he buys 4 guns on the black market. He starts to work out and practice target shooting, and – alone in his rundown apartment – he works on his self-esteem, admiring his own strength and even imagining things. The film's most memorable moment is the scene in which Travis simulates his own response to imaginary provocation, standing in front of a mirror and incessantly repeating the phrase "You talkin' to me?" with a defiant yet questioning air. His first action occurs virtually by chance when he cold-bloodedly shoots a robber in a drugstore. His second step involves his plan to shoot Senator Palantine, but he clumsily gets discovered by the politician's bodyguards and barely manages to escape. In the end, Travis focuses on his mission to "liberate" Iris. He initially pretends to be a customer and, after negotiating with her pimp "Sport" (Harvey Keitel), he goes off with the girl and gives her a fatherly lecture. He subsequently meets her outside and then bursts into the brothel where she works, where he shoots Sport – who shoots him back – and then kills the bouncer and the girl's customer. Travis turns one of the guns on himself, but there are no bullets left in the chamber. Wounded and bloody, he sits down to wait for the police.

1. 2. 3. This is the transformation in the parable of Travis. Disappointed by everything and everyone, he decides to strengthen his body, to arm himself, and to shave his head to take on the appearance of a warrior.

4. The finale is remarkable and after carrying out a massacre in Iris' bordello, Travis attempts to take his own life but does not succeed.

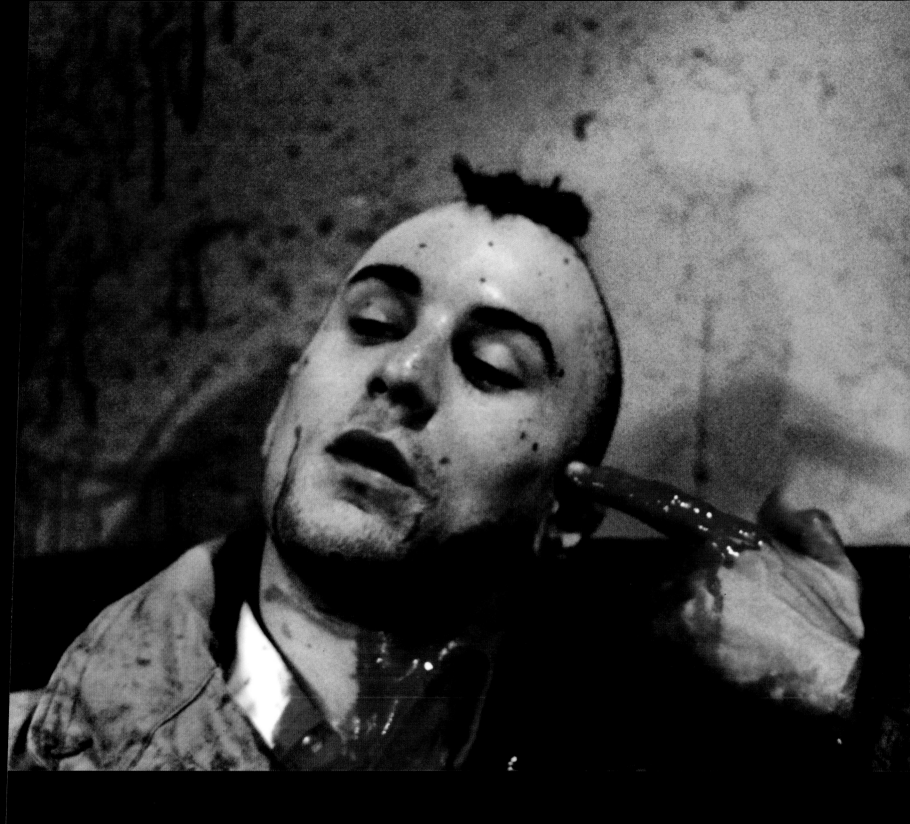

Epilogue: Travis has recovered and is praised as a hero by the newspapers as well as the letter he's reading. It is from Iris's parents, who thank him for saving their daughter, who has returned to her home and the life of a normal adolescent. Back in his taxi, Travis picks up Betsy, who now seems to look at him differently. This time, however, it is Travis – serene and self-confident – who rejects her.

The film is a shocking apologue whose meaning is intentionally ambiguous. Can we truly say that Travis Bickle is an entirely positive – or negative – person? Has Travis been "cured" of his ills? Or, to take things a step further, is it possible that the final scenes are not even real but are pure fantasy? Indeed, it is this sense of ambiguity – of the character and the scenes – that makes *Taxi Driver* so troubling.

The film established Scorsese as a major figure in the film industry, thanks also to the fact that it won the Palme d'Or at the Cannes Film Festival. The director was assisted by two important figures: screenwriter Paul Schrader, and Bernard Herrmann, who wrote the music. Herrmann, who had composed the scores for Hitchcock's films, died before *Taxi Driver* was released.

Genre:
DRAMA / ROMANCE

1976

ROCKY

Director: JOHN G. AVILDSEN

Cast: SYLVESTER STALLONE / TALIA SHIRE / BURGESS MEREDITH / CARL WEATHERS / BURT YOUNG

The story takes place in the winter of 1975/76. Rocky Balboa, who has dubbed himself the Italian Stallion, is a 30-year-old boxer who has never achieved fame or success. He lives in a run-down one-room apartment in a lower-class Philadelphia neighborhood and goes to the gym run by Mickey (Burgess Meredith), a cantankerous old trainer who has never had confidence in him. To earn money, Rocky works as a debt collector for a smalltime local boss, although when he is ordered to break the thumbs of a man who is behind in his payments he cannot bring himself to do it. Whenever he has the chance, he visits a pet shop where Adrian (Talia Shire, the sister of Francis Ford Coppola), works as a clerk. Shy, quiet and badly dressed, the bespectacled Adrian worries about becoming an old maid. Rocky is so smitten with her that he buys two turtles and pretends to like animals, but he finds himself facing a wall of silence. Although he is nice to everyone, Rocky has just one friend. Paulie, Adrian's brother, works at a slaughterhouse and drinks too much. He constantly complains about his bad luck and often loses his temper. In short, he's not the most reliable friend. Given his background, Rocky is headed for a life of failure but he never loses heart. And yet something unexpected bursts into his life and changes his narrow horizons.

Apollo Creed, the World Heavyweight Champion, is preparing for a long-awaited match to celebrate the bicentennial of the American Declaration of Independence. However, his opponent has been injured and must pull out of the match. The advertising and media stakes are too high to cancel the event, and a replacement must be found immediately. Although Apollo Creed is an outstanding boxer, he is above all a money machine, an administrator of his own image. The match that is being prepared is thus merely a carnival benefiting his sponsors, advertisers and everyone who stands to gain by what is intended to be a showcase for politicians and entertainment celebrities. Surrounded by his staff, Apollo looks through a catalog and notices Rocky Balboa, who is unknown but has an interesting moniker. The "Italian Stallion" against the African-American champion, a nobody from the slums against the super-

2 ▲

3 ▲

1. 3. Rocky Balboa (Sylvester Stallone) fights the world heavyweight champion, Apollo Creed. It's an arranged bout. Rocky is a boxer on the periphery, getting older without ever having made his name and Creed is just a clown who needs to perform for the media. However, he's stronger than Rocky and beats him, but not without shedding some tears and blood up to the last round. For Rocky, it's a great moral victory.

2. Sustaining Rocky is his love for Adriana (Talia Shire) who would become his wife.

champion kindly offering him the chance of a lifetime: Apollo likes the sound of it. And, naturally, he is convinced that everything will be a spectacular and demagogic display. That Rocky will immediately be KO'd and that showmanship – as well as Apollo's enormous superiority, victory and glory – will be guaranteed. Astonished, Rocky agrees because he realizes that it is an enormous opportunity, but the start of his training is less than encouraging. He is out of shape. Nevertheless, while he is painfully out of breath the first time he reaches the top of the steps of the Philadelphia Library, the second time he dashes up the staircase in an instant. This is one of the film's most famous scenes, with its iconic music theme in the background.

The momentous night arrives and Rocky's goal is not to win but to stay in the ring. And Rocky keeps going, reaching the 15th and final round. Apollo wins the title, but his reputation has been destroyed. As a reward for his own personal triumph, Rocky only want to hug his Adrian and, worse for wear but happy, he shouts her name from the ring.

Created by and tailor-made for Stallone, who was a little-known actor at the time, *Rocky* was a low-budget film that became so legendary it spawned five sequels. Its author/star created one of the world's most powerful movie icons and, six years later, he would create another one with Rambo. The spirit of the character and the tone of the film are clearly delineated. Despite the fact that Rocky Balboa's background is desolate and depressing, Stallone recounts this aspect subtly, with a sense of understanding that borders on tenderness. At the same time, he never censures its negative sides, such as the neighborhood thugs with whom Rocky always stops for a chat at the street corner, and the smalltime Mafia boss who exploits him but comes to his aid when Rocky needs him. Both his friend Paulie and his trainer Mickey are ill-natured losers who back Rocky only when he looks like a winner, but they represent the sole friendship that Rocky can allow himself. Adrian's sadness and frustration are difficult to handle and seem insurmountable, but Rocky never loses the desire to give her a sense of lighthearted optimism, confidence and happiness. All of these elements form a viewpoint that is very worldly wise: knowing but not cynical, aware that poverty and marginalization do not create solidarity, and full of empathy.

Rocky received 10 Academy award nominations and won 3 Oscars.

[JAPAN / FRANCE]   Genre: DRAMA / ROMANCE

Nagisa Oshima's *In the Realm of the Senses* (1976), based on a true story that occurred in 1936 and about which another Japanese film (*A Woman Called Sada Abe*) had been made a year earlier, was one of the most sensational films of the 1970s. The director was one of Japan's leading representatives of the youthful avant-garde that, led by the Parisian New Wave, revolutionized cinematographic language around the world in the late 1950s and early 1960s. Consequently, Oshima surprised audiences when he made this film, which was labeled as pornographic and thus was either shown in porno theaters or was heavily cut.

The film unquestionably contains very explicit – and real – sex scenes as well as extremely graphic male and female nude shots. At the same time, however, their ritual, obsessive and repetitive staging, figuratively inspired by period Japanese prints and ideologically influenced by the works of Bataille and Sade, is not conveyed as a voyeuristic invitation, nor do they satisfy the expectation of erotic entertainment. Instead, they produce a sense of repulsion, pain and anguish.

Without being given any historical or social context, we are introduced to the young Sada, who has been hired as a servant in the home (inn? bordello?) of a wealthy man (or pimp?), Kichizo. Sada is the object of the "special" attentions of another girl in the house, whom she turns down, and at this point we are privy to the encounter – and immediate attraction – between her and master of the house. That very evening the two begin their exploration of pleasure. Their sexual encounters are methodical and incessant, and to prevent Kichi's wife from becoming suspicious about their numerous encounters, Sada pretends that she is offering him musical entertainment. However, Sada spies on Kichi while he is making love to his wife and imagines killing the woman out of jealousy.

In this possessive crescendo, the two leave the city and stage a fake wedding, after which they make love while several geishas watch them. The geishas then join them while a dancer entertains the group. This is a moment in the film that, while imitating the topos of hard porn, removes all realism and carnality from the scene, presenting it as an abstract pictorial composition in which the bodies do not act but are posed.

On the way home Sada cannot resist making love again outdoors, this time while an old woman approvingly observes them. Sada leaves her lover momentarily to meet an elderly professor for money and she tries masochistic practices with him; the man is initially reluctant but then titillated.

1976

IN THE REALM OF THE SENSES

Director: NAGISA OSHIMA

Cast: EIKO MATSUDA / TATSUYA FUJI / AOI NAKAJIMA / YASUKO MATSUI / MEIKA SERI

In the Realm of the Senses portrays the escalation of a sexually obsessed relationship.

The intensity of her insatiable passion for Kichi continues to grow. In front of witnesses, the two try new games probing the relationship between food and sex. She feeds him food she holds between her legs, while he forces her to place an egg inside her to "hatch" so that he can eat it. The woman also becomes increasingly aggressive and makes Kichi swear that he will no longer touch his wife. But Kichi breaks his word and Sada, who saw them together, threatens him with a knife when they meet again. We are in the final phase and her lethal compulsion begins to emerge. At first it is the girl who asks the man to strangle her while he penetrates her, so that her pleasure is even more intense, and then they trade places. Despite the fact that Kichi feels involved with her, he maintains a playful and skeptical attitude toward their relationship. After yet another game of voyeurism and exhibitionism imposed by Sada – she forces him to couple with an elderly maid – the woman raises the stakes, becoming increasingly extreme and demanding. She wants to play their erotic game of asphyxiation again. Exhausted, Kichi allows her to do what she wants, but Sada brings their game to its deadly conclusion. She then emasculates the dead man, uses his blood to write their names on her chest and places his severed member inside her. An off-screen voice, which informs us that what we have just seen is a true story, then tells us that the woman was arrested in this state a short time later.

362 and 363 - Her name is Sada and he is Kichi. They experiment with everything, falling gradually into a downward self-destructive spiral. To the end, it proves to be the "perfect" twist of fate between love and death. This film from Japanese director, Nagisa Oshima, was billed as pornographic, created an enormous scandal, and was censured.

SATURDAY NIGHT FEVER

Director: JOHN BADHAM

Cast: JOHN TRAVOLTA / KAREN LYNN GORNEY

Saturday Night Fever launched the film career of John Travolta, who had been noticed by director John Badham in the musical *Grease*, which he later turned into a film version starring Travolta. Although it turned the actor into the sex symbol of the late 1970s, to a certain extent it also ruined his career. Travolta subsequently turned down the leading roles in *American Gigolo* and *An Officer And A Gentleman*, which made Richard Gere a star, and with the sole exception of *Look Who's Talking* (1989, followed by two sequels), Travolta's explosive fame as a film and fashion icon was followed by a long period of oblivion. In fact, it was not until many years later that Quentin Tarantino offered him a second chance and a second skin: that of the killer Vincent Vega in *Pulp Fiction* (1994).

In this film, Tony Manero is a young Italian-American from a working-class family in Brooklyn; his brother is a priest. He works at a local store and is optimistic and popular, but has no faith in his abilities. His family has pinned all its hopes on his brother, only to be bitterly disappointed when Frank decides to leave the priesthood. His brother is the only one to tell Tony that he must never take the road other people expect him to, nor should he deny who he is. The important thing is to understand what he wants and pursue his goal.

Weekends, when he let himself go on disco dance floors, represent Tony's sole entertainment and chance for self-fulfillment. A dance fanatic, he is the best on the floor and has all the girls at his feet. But Tony is seeking himself and has a hard time sharing the macho attitudes and rituals of his group of friends, one of whom – the weakest one in the group – is destined to lose his life because of a dangerous stunt on the Verrazano-Narrows Bridge. Tony seems to find the right path through his relationship – both on and off the dance floor – with a girl who lives in Manhattan, works as a secretary at an entertainment agency, has her own apartment and puts on airs by talking about Eric Clapton, Cat Stevens, Laurence Olivier and Franco Zeffirelli: illustrious unknowns to the coarse but more vital Tony.

In reality, the entire plot is purely an intermezzo for the music scenes and dance numbers. Travolta-Manero became an icon of the 1970s with his glitzy demeanor: puffy hair, gold chains around his neck, a white suit with black vest and a dark shirt open to show his hairy chest, and bellbottom trousers. His upraised finger was one of the film's most iconic gestures.

The film shocked audiences because of the coarse and direct language of its leading players. Touted as a cultural cross section, in reality the film was simply a pretext to showcase the songs of the Bee Gees (notably "Stayin' Alive," which became the title of the sequel, and "Night Fever") and the choreography. The life of marginalized young people is a latter-day parody of *Rebel Without a Cause*, with the addition of drugs, violence and more explicit sex. Likewise, the rivalry with the equally alienated Puerto Ricans is a pale reflection of *West Side Story*.

Stallone-Rocky and Al Pacino are presented as role models through the posters in Tony's room.

The phenomenal John Travolta creates Tony Manero's character. A boy from Brooklyn, an Italian-American from a humble working-class family, a sales clerk in a neighborhood general store, finds his moment of glory on the stage of Saturday night dance floors when, wearing his tight white suit, he becomes the main attraction in the disco, moving his body to the rhythms of the Bee Gees.

STAR WARS
[A New Hope]
Episode IV

Director: GEORGE LUCAS

Cast: MARK HAMILL / CARRIE FISHER / ALEC GUINNESS / HARRISON FORD

"A long time ago, in a galaxy far, far away" is the tagline that, along with John Williams' score and the three-dimensional aura of outer space, crossed slowly and majestically by monumental spaceship-cities, has been repeated at the beginning of each film since 1977, relaunching the enormous success of this epic.

The young George Lucas, who had graduated with a degree in film, conceived of this saga in the early 1970s and approached Universal Studios. However, the film studio agreed to produce only one of his two projects, *American Graffiti*, which was the least demanding, expensive and risky of the two.

In Lucas' mind, *Star Wars* was to be a colossal nine-chapter saga. Given the fact that when he finally managed to make his first film he was unsure that he would ultimately make them all, he decided to start with the central part, or in other words, chapters 4, 5 and 6, and then continue with the rest. In the wake of the extraordinary success of the first *Star Wars* film, he soon made the next two chapters (not as the director in these cases, but as writer and producer) and approximately 20 years later he continued with the second trilogy, which was the prequel of the first. The idea of a third trilogy, the sequel of the first and comprising chapters 7, 8 and 9, has been sidelined in the meantime.

The setting and characters are presented in the first film. Fighting against the widespread and pervasive power of the forces of evil and the Death Star, its murderous weapon, a small group of resistance fighters – the Rebel Alliance – attempts to revolt in the name of good and the liberation of the Galaxy. It relies on the Force, which opposes the Dark Lord or Evil, and represents intuition, instinct, and the quest for harmony and balance over reason and technology.

They are Princess Leia Organa (Carrie Fisher); the young warrior Luke Skywalker (Mark Hamill), who is still unaware of his own resources and mission, and above all is unaware of a destiny that will pit him against his own father, Anakin Skywalker, a noble Jedi Knight who has fallen to the dark side as Darth Vader; and the aging Jedi Master Obi-Wan Kenobi (Alec Guinness), the holder of knowledge and secrets. Lastly, there is Han Solo (Harrison Ford) with his ramshackle spacecraft Millennium Falcon. He is seemingly a mercenary, a base and cynical adventurer, but his growing feelings for Princess Leia (contrasted by her relationship with Luke, initially ambiguous until they discover that they are brother and sister) and his heartfelt and impulsive espousal of justice turn him into a diehard fighter against evil. The small patrol also has non-humans: the philosopher Yoda (who does not appear until the second film, the fifth chapter of the saga), with his convoluted speech pattern, fuzzy Chewbacca, and the odd couple of robots R2-D2 and C-3PO.

Alec Guinness is Obi-Wan Kenobi, Jedi Master and old friend of Anakin Skywalker before he goes to the Dark Side with the name of Darth Vader. ▶

1. 4. Onboard the Millennium Falcon, the ramshackle spaceship piloted by only apparently cynical Hans Solo (Harrison Ford) and furry Chewbacca. With them, is the young intended hero, Luke Skywalker, and the old master.

2. Completing the group of "good guys," are the two squabbling robots, R2-D2 and C-3PO, as well as Princess Leia.

3. This is the duel between the Force of good, Obi-Wan Kenobi and that of the bad Darth Vader, the black knight with no face.

Star Wars and the saga that followed not only relaunched the science-fiction genre, but also created a new mythology based on the sweeping recognition of well-established popular genres. These films effectively revived Westerns, tales of chivalry, fantasy and adventure stories (there are numerous visual references, such as the tall robot that resembles the figures from Fritz Lang's *Metropolis*). There is a sentimental and romantic side, coupled with a powerful sense of humor and comedy.

Although the personal adventures of Lucas and his friend Spielberg are closely entwined, Lucas' saga is closer to *Indiana Jones* than it is to *Close Encounters of the Third Kind* (released the same year as the first *Star Wars* film) and other Spielberg works about extraterrestrials. Tellingly, Harrison Ford was the testimonial of both *Indiana Jones* and *Star Wars*. Like *Star Wars*, the adventures of the archaeologist are rooted in mass culture and literature, comic books (notably "Flash Gordon") and a childlike vision that separates good and evil, under the banner of clear-cut Manichaean optimism, but with the ironic touch noted here. And this holds true for both characters played by Ford.

1

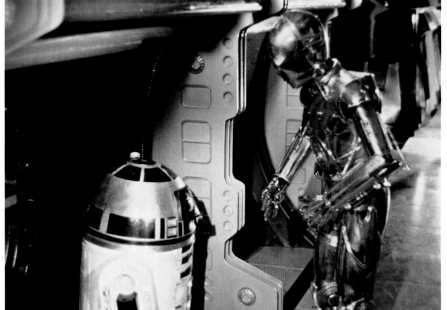
2

3

4

This project would give Lucas great power and prestige and influence subsequent creative, publishing and production decisions (the film was immediately followed by *Alien* and *Blade Runner*) as well as merchandising (e.g., the lightsaber). It also established the preeminence of the Industrial Light & Magic company on the new frontier of special effects and was exploited by every genre including video games, virtually becoming a caricature of itself.

In 1997, the 20th anniversary of the release of the first film, a new special edition presented the first trilogy with a series of corrections of the effects that the technology of the time had not rendered perfectly and with which Lucas was unhappy.This is a spectacle marked by enormous ambition that, despite its sophisticated and industrial execution, exalts imagination rather than technology.

It is significant that *Star Wars* has been listed in the National Film Registry as part of the national cultural heritage safeguarded by the Library of Congress.

370-371 - Hans Solo, Luke Skywalker and Princess Leia temporarily form a sort of love triangle until any ambiguity is swept away by the discovery that Leia and Luke are sister and brother. *Star Wars*, the first part of a saga that thus far is composed of six parts where in reality the second trilogy chronologically precedes the first, signals a historical turning point in this story of adventure and science fiction, and one of the most popular eras in film.

Close Encounters of the Third Kind, which was released the same year as the first *Star Wars* episode, marked a turning point in the history of cinema. Released in 1977, when Steven Spielberg was 31 years old, it was a fundamental step in the invention of a modern fairy-tale and fantasy. At the same time, it also marks the triumph of what came to be known as the "New Hollywood" – represented by figures such as Spielberg, Lucas, Scorsese, Coppola and De Palma – that successfully emerged in the early 1970s.

Rather than developing a linear and coherent plot, the film uses a sequence, the accumulation and interweaving of signals on two fronts. First of all, there is the French scientist Claude Lacombe, who is cooperating with American scientific and military authorities in an attempt to interpret several mysterious apparitions: a squadron of fighter planes lost in Mexico during World War II, a ship in the middle of the Gobi Desert in Mongolia, and other enigmatic manifestations in India. François Truffaut plays the scientist and his presence in the cast of Spielberg's film unquestionably has enormous symbolic value, effectively passing the baton in the name of a cinematic style full of emotion and close to the hearts of virtually all audiences.

The parallel story revolves around two ordinary citizens from small towns where UFOs have been sighted and in which there have been uncontrollable events such as sudden blackouts or, inversely, excess power (toys and appliances that mysteriously start working on their own). Both of these characters are "touched" by unexplainable and irresistible forms of attraction towards the unknown.

Jillian (Melinda Dillon) lives alone with her young son Barry who, to his mother's despair, trustingly follows an unknown being and vanishes, swallowed up by a dazzling light. Roy (Richard Dreyfuss) is an electrical lineman who, bewildering his wife and three children, is increasingly captivated by these events, not on a physical level like Barry, but emotionally and mentally. These events seem to torment him and he feels compelled to understand what is happening within himself and outside. Roy and Barry are the chosen. However, there are many others like them around the country, in the present but also from the past, as the film's powerful last scene reveals.

The two stories gradually converge, and Roy and Jillian are inevitably united in their quest. Lacombe concentrates all his efforts to perfect a nonverbal language that is based on musical notes in order to decipher the luminous signals coming from these unknown beings and communicate with the life forms that he is convinced they must contain. At the same time, Roy is obsessed by a vertical form. He has no idea what or where it is, but for some reason he knows it exists and that he must find it.

1977

CLOSE ENCOUNTERS OF THE THIRD KIND

Director: STEVEN SPIELBERG

Cast: RICHARD DREYFUSS / FRANCOIS TRUFFAUT

Richard Dreyfuss plays Roy, one of the protagonists that entwines the destinies of other characters in the film.

He behaves as if he were increasingly "possessed" and attempts to re-create it with anything at hand, from garbage to the mashed potatoes his wife serves at dinner. Young Barry and – as we will discover – many others have received the same signals.

The "form" exists and it is a mountain in Wyoming. The characters converge there, for this is where the "close encounter" will occur. The government tries to discourage people from coming by announcing that the area is contaminated. In reality, they have sprayed it with innocuous gas and the livestock, which appear to be dead, are merely asleep. Nevertheless, the authorities are unable to stop Roy and Jillian. In the end, the authorities – led by Lacombe – will have to give in and rely on Roy's special gift. When the enormous spaceship descends and opens, following an exchange of musical and luminous signals, there is a blinding beam of light from its interior and dozens of soldiers, thought to be killed or missing in action more than 30 years earlier, emerge unchanged. Little Barry, who had also been abducted, runs from the spaceship into his mother's arms. Lastly, the extraterrestrials emerge. After Roy goes aboard to depart with them, Lacombe and the being who seems to be the captain of the spaceship exchange a peaceful and friendly signal with their hands, successfully testing the scientist's method to convert sound and light impulses. *Close Encounters of the Third Kind* is a watershed in the science-fiction genre. It breaks away from a tradition that flourished above all in the 1950s and the Cold War, which paralleled the "alien" invasion with the imminent and propagandized thread of Communism. Indeed, in this film extraterrestrials are friendly for the first time. Friendship and the exchange of knowledge are possible and their diversity is not antithetical to peace. It is in this aspect that we can see Spielberg's unmistakable mark: anti-ideological, but also anti-intellectual and childlike. The film boasts exceptional names, from photographer Vilmos Zsigmond to Douglas Trumbull, who created the special effects, and Carlo Rambaldi, who designed the characters of the extraterrestrials.

374 and 375 – Each one individually follows his or her own convictions or intuition, his or her own instincts as Roy, the French scientist Claude Lacombe (Truffaut), little Barry with his mother, Gillian, finally all converge on the large platform where the Close Encounter with extraterrestrials takes place. For the first time in the history of science fiction film, aliens are not represented as a threat to humankind but as an opportunity for knowledge.

The night before they ship out to Vietnam, three friends – Michael (Robert De Niro), Nick (Christopher Walken) and Steven (John Savage) – hold a euphoric but ingenuous celebration to say goodbye to the small but close-knit community of Russian immigrants in the polluted and squalid industrial town in Pennsylvania where the three work at a steel factory. The boisterous festivities revolve around Steven's marriage.

The long introductory part of *The Deer Hunter* also highlights two important elements. The first one involves Linda (Meryl Streep) and the girl's confused feelings for Michael – the two are mutually attracted but are unable to say so – and Nick, to whom she is engaged. Nevertheless, this ambiguity does not affect the bond between the two friends, whose intensity is silently expressed through their common passion for mountain landscapes and hunting. The second aspect involves the latter aspect, deer hunting. Following the party and before their departure, Michael expresses and puts into practice his inviolable principle and ethics as a hunter: "one shot." If it misses, there is no second chance and the prey wins. (In this case, the shot is on target, but during the second hunting trip, after the men return from Vietnam, it is off the mark.) This concept is a metaphor for fighting honestly and fairly, and the segment serves as a bridge for the second part of the film, into which the audience is catapulted with unprecedented violence.

In the infernal confusion of an incomprehensible reality, we find that the three young men are prisoners of war, captured by a furiously cruel and inhuman enemy. Locked in a cage plunged in the muddy waters of a rat-infested river, one by one they are taken to the riverside, where a Vietcong officer, surrounded by his men, beats, provokes and humiliates the prisoners, forcing them to play Russian roulette while his men lay their bets. Terror breaks Steven, but Michael holds out and begs Nick to do the same. Taking advantage of the moment in which one of the two is holding the gun to play Russian roulette, they overpower their jailers and manage to escape. However, only Nick is rescued by a helicopter that manages to skim the waters of the river, but is then forced to abandon enemy territory. The other two also try to hold on, but fall. Michael picks up his friend, who was seriously injured by his fall from the flying helicopter, and carries him to a safe zone, where he hands Steven over to a patrol of South Vietnamese allies.

Cut. Time has elapsed and the three have been separated from each other. For only a moment, and without being able to reach him and talk to him, just before flying home Michael catches sight of Nick one evening in Saigon, a city depicted as a dark and revolting labyrinth of perdition. Nick has become involved with a shady French wheeler-dealer who, amidst bloody corpses, organizes illegal bets on the macabre game of Russian roulette.

1978

THE DEER HUNTER

Director: MICHAEL CIMINO

Cast: ROBERT DE NIRO /

JOHN SAVAGE / CHRISTOPHER WALKEN /

MERYL STREEP / JOHN CAZALE

The image and symbol of the film by Michael Cimino is that of Russian roulette.

378 and 379 - Michael (Robert De Niro), Nick (Christopher Walken, first at left with the pool cue), and Steven (John Savage, photograph below, between his "wife" and De Niro) are three friends that, on the day following Steven's wedding, leave the smoky city in Pennsylvania where all three are factory workers in order to enter combat in Vietnam after one last witty remark about deer hunting, "one shot."

Upon his return, everyone welcomes Michael warmly, especially Linda, but he is not the same person and feels removed from everything. He discovers that Steven has also come and finally tracks him down in a VA hospital. Steven has lost both legs and one arm, and refuses to home. He tells Michael that someone continues to send him large amounts of money from Vietnam. Michael realizes who it is and, just before the fall of Saigon, he returns to look for Nick. He discovers a man who has been destroyed in body and soul, an automaton and a mere shadow of his former self. Nick does not even recognize Michael (or pretends not to recognize him) and scornfully turns him away, spitting into his face. A drug addict who does nothing but play Russian roulette – he is a champion at it and has become rich as a result – his sole mission is to send money to the friend who suffered the worst fate of the three. Desperate, Michael instinctively does the only thing that can convince Nick's specter that he must believe in his friendship and come home with him. He challenges him. As it turns out, however, his friend goes first and, after smiling at Michael, shoots himself in the head.

Made the same year as Hal Ashby's *Coming Home*, a year before *Apocalypse Now*, eight years before *Platoon* and nine before Stanley Kubrick's masterpiece *Full Metal Jacket*, Michael Cimino's film depicts the nightmare of Vietnam with harrowing realism. *The Deer Hunter* won five Academy Awards, including Best Picture and Best Supporting Actor (Walken). However, no recognition went to the great Vilmos Zsigmond, who visually expressed not only the Vietnamese setting, but also the American environment and the idea of the antihero, coupled with a sense of repugnance, depression and wasted lives.

1. 2. 3. Without mincing words, Vietnam is hell. The attack is violent. We rejoin our main characters as they endure imprisonment by the North Vietnamese. At the mercy of cruel jailers, they undergo treatment that irreparably destroys their mental and emotional balance. It is during their imprisonment that they are forced to "play" Russian roulette. They succeed in finding a way out and all three escape but then they scatter, each man pursuing his own destiny.

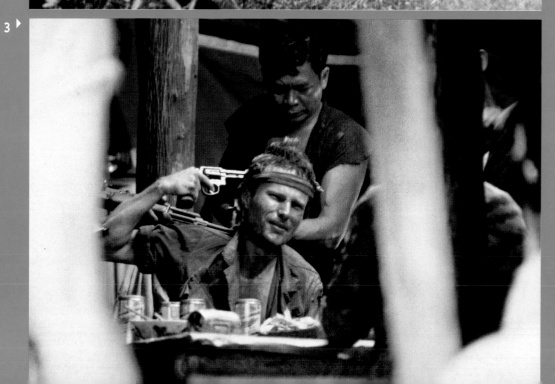

Michael (De Niro) succeeds in returning home uninjured as a decorated soldier. He sees Nick one last time just after they escape, in the bowels of a Saigon "Sodom," wasting away and covered with sores. However, he loses track of Steven that he'd sent, seriously wounded, to the South Vietnamese allies,

Steven (Savage) has also returned home disabled and lives in a rehab institution for war veterans.

Nick (Walken) remains in Saigon, enduring hardship and earning a lot of money with Russian roulette. ▲

< Steven's gettin' married in a couple of hours. We're talkin' about huntin' the last time before the army. The whole thing, it's crazy. I'll tell ya one thing. If I found out my life had to end up in the mountains, I'd be all right. But it has to be in your mind. What? One shot? Two is pussy. I don't think about one shot that much anymore, Mike. You have to think about one shot. One shot is what it's all about. A deer has to be taken with one shot.>

GREASE

Director: RANDAL KLEISER

Cast: JOHN TRAVOLTA / OLIVIA NEWTON JOHN / STOCKARD CHANNING / JEFF CONAWAY / MICHAEL TUCCI

In the wake of the runaway success of *Saturday Night Fever,* John Travolta was cast in the film version of the musical Grease by Jim Jacobs and Warren Casey.

The film, set in 1958, opens with Danny Zuco (Travolta), who meets an Australian girl, Sandy Olsson (Olivia Newton-John), at the beach during summer vacation. The two fall in love, but at the end of the summer they say goodbye to each other because Sandy must return to Australia.

However, her family has a change of plans and does not leave after all. As a result, Sandy is enrolled at Rydell High School, which Danny also attends although at first neither one is aware of the fact that they are at the same school. Sandy is befriended by a group of girls who call themselves The Pink Ladies, headed by Betty Rizzo (Stockard Channing), and she tells them about her summer romance, revealing the boy's name. The girls, who obviously know Danny very well, laugh at their new friend's ingenuity and decide to have the two meet again, slyly bringing Sandy over to Danny's gang, the T-Birds.

Caught off-guard, Danny is embarrassed in front of his friends and, pretending that he is not in love with her, brushes her off. Deeply hurt, Sandy runs off in tears. Danny tries to win her back, but the workings of the two groups – both the boys and the girls – makes everything more difficult.

Danny takes Sandy to the school dance contest, which will be aired on national television. The two seem favored to win until Danny's ex-girlfriend and dance partner Cha-Cha Di Gregorio, arrives on the scene. Backed by the T-Birds and determined to win the dance competition, she takes Sandy's place. Naturally, Sandy feels betrayed and angrily leaves the dance.

Once again, Danny tries to win her back and takes her to a drive-in movie. He tells Sandy he wants her to be his girl and give her his ring, but then immediately tries to kiss her. Offended, she pulls back and leaves again.

The next day, Danny's friend Kenickie, a member of the T-Birds, is supposed to compete in a car race against the rival gang, the Scorpions, but a mishap puts him out of the running. Therefore, Danny steps in for him and wins the race as Sandy looks on. Still in love with him, she decides to ask her new friends to help transform her from a shy and naive Australian student into the kind of girl who would be right for Danny.

For the festivities on the last day of school, Sandy – far more self-confident and aggressive – sidles up to Danny with her new look and he is completely besotted.

John Travolta and Olivia Newton John are the dancing couple in Grease, among rival cliques and emotional skirmishes.

1. 2. 3. 4. It's 1958 and everything says it, from the greased-back hair to the cars, clothing, and optimism of the times. Vacations, school, parties, flirtations and revenge, juvenile and fickle games in the spirit of feminine or masculine cliques, press on new, more adult, emotions. But, all of this is pure decoration, a garnish to the conventional and innocuous parade of musical numbers with singing and dancing. With previous theatrical success, the musical film version of Grease takes second place after the innovation of *West Side Story*.

1 ▼

4 ▼

5 ▼

5. *Grease* is a confirmation of John Travolta's great personal success. Success that nevertheless, after the extraordinary flash of *Saturday Night Fever* and this film, would endure a long idle period. It would be Quentin Tarantino that offered the actor another chance and another artistic life by calling upon him to play the gangster, Vincent Vega, in *Pulp Fiction*.

Grease is a lighthearted version of the time-honored story of rival gangs and their meddlesome actions that come between two young lovers. In this case, the story also features music and songs, notably *Hopelessly Devoted to You* and *You're the One That I Want*, written by John Farrar. Thanks above all to these songs and the already successful figure of Travolta as a dancer, the film set a trend and while some of the variations on this theme are seasonal and generational, Grease is a timeless classic.

The scope and ambition of Francis Ford Coppola's film *Apocalypse Now* (1979) stem from the astonishing duration of the filming (in the Philippines), dotted by drama and incidents such as Martin Sheen's heart attack, as well as the epic length of the first version – 150 minutes – and, even more so, of the second version of 2001, which restored some of the cuts for a length of 200 minutes. The filmmaker also encountered countless financial, medical, climatic and interpersonal difficulties, effectively experiencing the descent into hell he recounted in the film.

Inspired by Joseph Conrad's novella "Heart of Darkness," an adventure that, in turn, is a sweeping metaphor exploring the darkest and most recondite reaches of the human soul. The film takes place soon after the end of the first war ever lost by the United States (1975). Coppola penetrates the horror of the Vietnam experience: "My film is not a movie; it's not about Vietnam. It *is* Vietnam."

The setting: Saigon in the mid-1960s. Intelligence officer Willard (Sheen) is sent into the jungle on a delicate mission. He must track down Colonel Kurtz (Marlon Brando), a deserter who has gone into Cambodia, taking with him a personal army he is using to continue a personal and extremely violent war. Willard's order is to "terminate his command" or, in other words, kill Kurtz. Willard's journey along a river "that snaked through the war like a main circuit cable" in search of the hideout used by Kurtz, who represents this fatal Landing Zone, marks his descent into the "heart of darkness" of a hostile setting and climate, a collective psychosis that forces everyone to be either victim or killer, in a monstrous deformation of human sentiments and reactions, and the complete loss of self among all those who happened to be there.

When he arrives he finds Kurtz, who is living in the rotting shadows of the tropical rainforest, surrounded by men who have lost all their humanity and adore him like a god/dictator who can ask anything of them – and dispose of them as he desires. But what Kurtz wants from Willard is the very thing that Willard has been sent to accomplish. He wants to die because he knows that self-sacrifice is the only way for him to escape a condition – a personal existential abyss, above and beyond his culpability in the eyes of the law and military justice – from which there is no return. He is embodies the barbarization of patriotic sentiment, transformed into the pure exercise of violence and abuse of power, and of a civilization that considered itself superior but had never fallen so low before. This is what Willard will do in the end, and it is a gesture that represents his own catharsis amidst the general collapse.

1979
APOCALYPSE NOW

Director: FRANCIS FORD COPPOLA

**Cast: MARLON BRANDO / MARTIN SHEEN /
ROBER DUVALL / DENNIS HOPPER / HARRISON FORD**

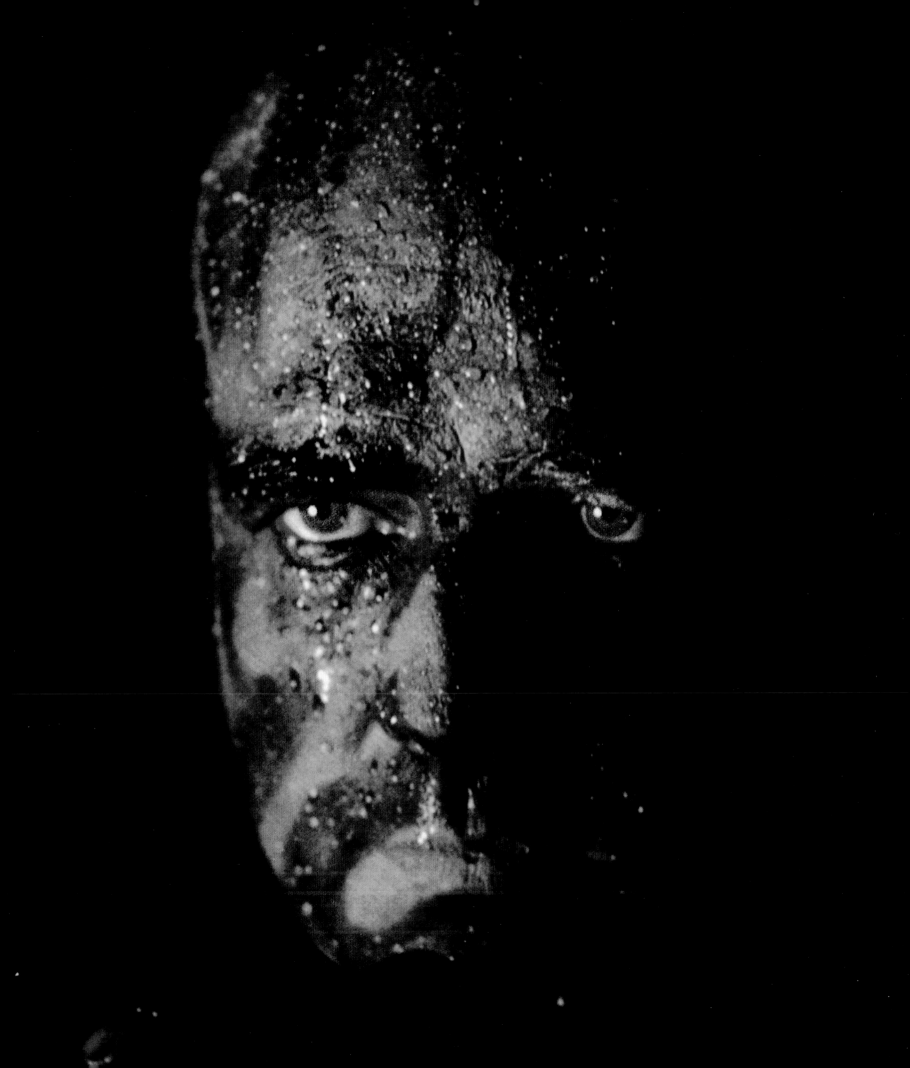

This sweeping delirium – on both a visual level (Vittorio Storaro won an Academy Award for Cinematography) and an audio one ("The End" by The Doors) – palpably discomfited viewers and conveyed an almost intolerable sense of disquiet. There are unforgettable moments, such as the scenes of Willard's preparations to leave and his encounter with the cavalry battalion headed by Lieutenant Colonel Kilgore (Rober Duvall), who leads his helicopter unit's napalm bombing to the sound of Wagner's "Ride of the Valkyries." We also see the impact of Willard's encounter with Kurtz in his hellish lair: the genius of evil, the trapped animal, the beast lost in his rants of "purifying" omnipotence, which we merely glimpse in characteristics such as his shaved head and his mad gaze. In the role of Kurtz, Marlon Brando created the last giant in his gallery of monumental figures, subsequently entering into an inexorable decline. Brando had recently finished *Last Tango in Paris* and *The Godfather*, the latter also with Coppola (for which he received his second Oscar, which he turned down out of solidarity for Native Americans). At the time *Apocalypse Now* was made, he was 55 years old.

1. 2. 3. 4. Colonel Kilgore, played by Robert Duvall (below, with the guitar) leads his air force unit in spraying napalm over the jungle from their helicopters, accompanied by the Wagner-esque soundtrack of "The Cavalcade of Valkyries."
About his experience of deeply penetrating the horror and hollowness of war, director Coppola said: "my film is not ABOUT Vietnam, my film IS Vietnam.

Shortly before *Apocalypse Now* was completed, Michael Cimino had released *The Deerhunter*, which was equally shocking but did not have the same impressive complexity as Coppola's masterpiece. In any event, the two films ushered in a new way of interpreting America's most traumatic episode until 9/11. Screenwriter John Milius worked on the film with Coppola; the cast included Dennis Hopper and Harrison Ford. The film won the Palme d'Or at the 1979 Cannes Film Festival and two Academy Awards in 1980, one for Best Cinematography and the other for Best Sound. In a historical scandal, the film was excluded from the most sought-after categories and that year the tearjerker *Kramer vs. Kramer* garnered awards for Best Picture, Best Director and Best Actor (Dustin Hoffman). Coppola's masterpiece did not even receive a nomination in the latter category. Although it is difficult to deny that the Academy Awards often accurately reflect current trends, there have also been the egregious oversights. *Apocalypse Now* will go down in history; *Kramer vs. Kramer* will not.

392 and 393 - Martin Sheen is Captain Willard, charged by the Secret Service to discover Kurtz's hiding place after he's escaped every attempt at capture, and to "put an end to his command," to neutralize him. Succeeding in his efforts at reaching the "heart of darkness" and driving out the demon that in reality still waits for him, Coppola's film is a second adaptation of the novel by Conrad. However, his journey to the crux of confusion and loss of consciousness deeply involves him, forcing him to see with his own eyes, the hasty cruelty of which Kurtz's insanity and delirium are only an extreme manifestation, and just the tip of the iceberg.

"You think you're God!" – the answer to which is "I gotta model myself after someone" – is just one of the many memorable lines from Woody Allen's masterpiece *Manhattan* (1979).

Isaac Davis (Allen) is a rather successful television comedy writer, but he detests what he does and the compromises demanded by show business, despite the fact that it has brought fame and wealth. He would like to express his artistic ambitions (or pipe dreams?) by penning a book that he never actually writes, although he talks about it constantly.

His wife (Meryl Streep) has left him for another woman and – to Isaac's enormous chagrin – she is writing a book about their failed marriage, accusing him of trying to run her and her girlfriend over with his car after discovering that she had betrayed him.

He starts seeing Tracy (Mariel Hemingway), but she is 25 years younger than he is and although he accepts the beauty and affection at the girl offers him, he urges her to live her own life with men of her own age.

He also falls in love with Mary (Diane Keaton), a pseudo-intellectual and typical sophisticated and neurotic New York snob. In turn, she is secretly involved with her best friend Yale (Michael Murphy), who is happily married.

Torn between these two loves, after Mary decides to break up with him to resume her difficult relationship with Yale, Isaac runs after Tracy, who is leaving for London on a scholarship, begging her to give it up and stay with him. Although she is determined to leave, she asks him to wait for her for six months. After so much superficiality cloaked in complexity, after so many words devoid of emotion, this is a simple, clear and authentic message from which Isaac, who has now discarded his insincere paternal role, has a great deal to learn.

The film is a summa of the style, world and humor of Woody Allen, but it is above all a paean and an unreserved declaration of love and esteem to New York. The city is painted as an ideal dream rather than reality, staged with the affectionate care of a marvelous black-and-white photograph, and set to the music of George Gershwin. It an ideal, a place of the heart.

1979

MANHATTAN

Director: WOODY ALLEN

Cast: WOODY ALLEN /

MERYL STREEP /

MARIEL HEMINGWAY /

DIANE KEATON /

MICHAEL MURPHY

This image is the film in a nutshell, encapsulating the New Yorkese poetry of its creator.

396 and 397 - The TV comedy writer, Isaac Davis, focusing on all of the ticks of the intellectual Jew embodied by Woody Allen, is divided between self-pity, narcissism, and three women: the ex-wife, Meryl Streep, the very young Mariel Hemingway, and the sophisticated woman, Diane Keaton.

This humorous self-caricature takes a look at the Jewish/New York culture, replete with psychoanalytical aspects, guilt complexes, impossible relationship between men and women, and castrated or obsessively heightened sexuality. Through Allen and thanks to him, these elements become the founding motifs of the modern concept of the comedy film, and Allen adds a number of references that revolve around his obsession with cinema. One of the most delightful is his dialogue about Ingmar Bergman. He also cites Groucho Marx as one of his reasons for living, and in one of his dialogues there is a reference to Fellini. This sophisticated concept of comedy smugly examines the neuroses and substantial immaturity of the characters, poking fun at their pretentious and vacuous mania for ostentation and tastes that are seemingly sophisticated and unconventional, but are actually faddish and conformist.

This portrait emphasizes Allen's inimitable merits, special touch, irresistible charm and keen intelligence. Indeed, virtually everything that he describes and recounts would be insufferable without him, starting with the plethora of lexical quirks that have long been the bane of anyone attempting to translate his dialogues into other languages.

In the late 1970s Allen (who was 44 at the time) had already filmed his ambitious *Interiors* as well as the blockbuster *Annie Hall* (four Academy Awards) and the comic exploits of *Take the Money and Run*, *Bananas* and *Play It Again, Sam*, and had enjoyed a long career as a humorous author and scriptwriter. The 1970s were also marked by his personal and artistic relationship with the actress Diane Keaton; he did not become involved with Mia Farrow until 1980.

In space no one can hear you scream" is the tagline that, in 1979, presented the second film in the great career of Ridley Scott, made two years after his first feature film, *The Duellists*. The slogan perfectly conveys the overwhelming sense of terror that characterizes the entire film. *Alien* is a legend of horror fantasy, a genre rooted in the low-budget American films of the 1950s, although it seems that the film *Planet of the Vampires*, by the Italian director Mario Bava, also influenced Scott's film. In any event, Scott elevated the genre's quality and technical aspects to the highest levels.

In the film, the interstellar commercial spaceship *Nostromo* is forced to land on the moon of an unknown planet that has sent a mysterious request for help. The three crew members who go to investigate find a derelict spaceship full of what seem to be alien eggs. When one of them suddenly bursts open, an organism emerges and attaches itself to the face of Kane (John Hurt). His colleagues take him back to the *Nostromo*, but have no idea how to save him. The man is in a coma and the alien, which releases a corrosive substance when attacked, seems to have no intention of letting go. However, at a certain point the organism dies and releases Kane. This is merely the prelude to one of the film's most celebrated and extraordinary scenes. As his companions celebrate his return to health, Kane dies suddenly when a creature, the "daughter" of the alien that had attacked him, bursts from his abdomen.

This is the beginning of a desperate race. The six survivors make every effort to eliminate the intruder but fail, and the alien starts to exterminate them one by one. As if the monster's terrible hostility were not enough, the crew's efforts are impeded by the spaceship's Science Officer Ash (Ian Holm), who proves to be an android in the service of the mysterious company that owns a spaceship. Ash is mesmerized by the superior power and adaptability of the horrible creature, which he defines as "a survivor, unclouded by conscience, remorse, or delusions of morality."

Ripley (Sigourney Weaver) will ultimately be the only one left, vanquishing the deadly extraterrestrial by hurling it from the shuttle in which it has hidden, and thus condemning it to death in outer space.

1979
ALIEN

Director: RIDLEY SCOTT

Cast: SIGOURNEY WEAVER / TOM SKERRITT / BOLAJI BADEJO

JOHN HURT / VERONICA CARTWRIGHT / HARRY DEAN / STANTON / IAN HOLM / YAPHET KOTTO

400 and 401 - Harry Dean Stanton is face to face with the Alien, created by the Italian wizard of special effects, Carlo Rambaldi who won the Oscar in that category in 1980.

Alien is a masterpiece of science fiction, but without the exaggerated use of special effects now seen in this genre, which became extremely popular and had made *Star Wars* a legendary success two years earlier. Much of the credit goes to Hans Ruedi Giger and Carlo Rambaldi, who made *Alien* a benchmark in this genre. Their special effects won them an Academy Award in 1980.

The film was a box-office hit – its budget was $11 million, but it took in $103 million – and it spawned three sequels made by important directors (*Aliens* by James Cameron, 1986; *Alien?* by David Fincher, 1992; *Alien: Resurrection* by Jean-Pierre Jeunet, 1997), as well as two far inferior prequels (*Alien vs. Predator* by Paul W.S. Anderson, 2004, and *Aliens vs Predator: Requiem* by Colin and Greg Strause, 2007).

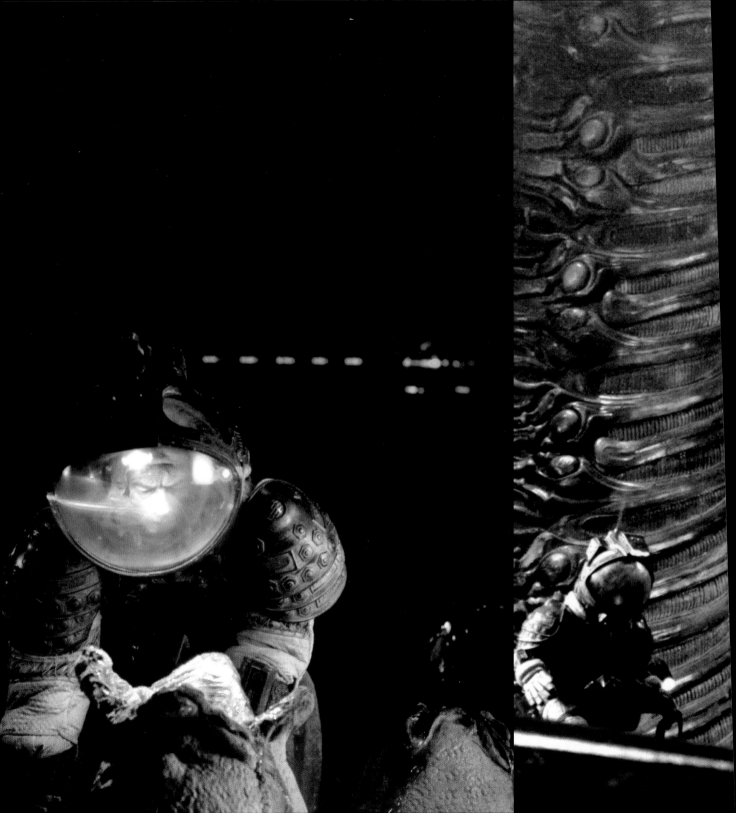

402 and 403 - *Alien* is, along with *Blade Runner*, a masterpiece by director, Ridley Scott. This film marks a historical moment in reinvention of the science fiction/horror film genre. It owes a debt to all preceding Fifties films of that genre when this type of storyline was nevertheless ostentatiously subjected to legal action as the ideological cause of the Cold War.

405 - The enormous success of the film would lead to three sequels of remarkable quality and two "prequels," all the work of different directors.

THE BLUES BROTHERS

Director: JOHN LANDIS

Cast: JOHN BELUSHI / DAN AYKROYD / JAMES BROWN / CAB CALLOWAY / RAY CHARLES / ARETHA FRANKLIN / CARRIE FISHER

The Blues Brothers is the quintessential "cult film" of the 1980s. The dark clothes, glasses and hats of the two siblings, Jake and Ellwood, their Bluesmobile, their constant repetition that they are on a "mission from God" and all the other elements of the film – from the "Illinois Nazis" to the Mystery Woman who follows them everywhere, appears suddenly and attacks them – helped create a minor myth that started from virtually nothing and has continued to grow over the past three decades. In fact, the film that John Landis made with John Belushi (who did all the stunts without a double) and Dan Aykroyd (who co-wrote the script) did not initially do very well in the United States, where it was considered not only a box-office flop but also a bad comedy. In this sense, it paralleled the trend – and particularly the grassroots popularity – of *The Rocky Horror Picture Show* in the 1970s, although it is not as unconventional.

In the film, Jake is released from prison after serving a sentence for robbery and is handed over to his brother Ellwood, who picks him up in a black-and-white Dodge bought at an auction of old police cars. The two go to visit The Penguin, the very strict nun who raised them at an orphanage that is now about to be closed because it owes back taxes. Determined to come up with the $5000 she needs, the two decide to reunite their old band, the Blues Brothers, for a performance that will allow them to earn the money as quickly as possible.

After visiting the eccentric pastor of a Baptist church who illuminates them about their mission, they set off to find their old friends. This will prove to be difficult because, in the meantime, all of their former colleagues have found honest jobs.

They devastate a supermarket by plowing through it at high speed and go to the shop of an old blind friend, buying the instruments they need on

1980

credit. Lying about their identities and musical specialization, they have a disastrous gig at a typical country-western bar. At a sauna, they convince their old but reluctant manager to support them and, aided by the children from the orphanage, who conduct a door-to-door ad campaign, they finally stage their triumphant concert at the Palace Hotel. With the earnings from their performance, they dash to the tax office and settle the debt just in time, but the entire group is arrested immediately afterwards. In prison, the band performs a rousing version of "Jailhouse Rock."

All of this takes place while countless characters pursue the brothers: the policemen who catch them running a red light and discover that Ellwood's license had been taken away; the Nazi fanatics who are after them because they disturbed a demonstration; the country-western band they replaced through trickery; the Mystery Woman (Carrie Fisher), who turns out to be Jake's ex-girlfriend and is out for revenge because he left her at the altar.

The film is a legend of madcap comedy. It owes a great deal to its fabulous guest stars, famous R&B musicians: Cab Calloway (the nun's assistant, who in the end performs one of the numbers that made his famous at the legendary Cotton Club in the 1930s), Ray Charles (from the music shop), Aretha Franklin (a restaurant owner and the wife of one of the old band members whom the brothers have convinced to join them) and James Brown (the Baptist reverend). Nevertheless, it also owes a great deal to the songs performed by the two leading characters, climaxing in the final performance with "Everybody Needs Somebody To Love."

The outstanding dynamics between Belushi and Aykroyd, as well as the characters they play, were inspired by the hit television show *Saturday Night Live*, which launched a new idea of comedy. Belushi had already worked with Landis in 1978 in *Animal House*, and Landis had also directed Aykroyd in the outstanding comedy, *Trading Places*. The locations, the neighborhoods of Chicago, also play a leading role in the film. The look and style of the Blues Brothers set the pace for an era and would be referenced in many films, from *Men in Black* to Tarantino's *Reservoir Dogs*. The power of the two comedians as a team stems from the contrast between Belushi's sheer size and Aykroyd's unflappable nature.

The Blues Brothers received a lukewarm reception when it was first released in the United States, as it was expected to repeat the failure of *1941*, starring both actors and directed by Steven Spielberg (who played the tax assessor's clerk in *The Blues Brothers*). The film was also criticized for its use of elementary slapstick humor. European audiences instead turned into a cult movie. Rumor had it that, with the exception of a brief scene, Belushi never took off his dark sunglasses because he showed up on the set drunk or on drugs (he died of an overdose in 1982) and thus used them to conceal his blank stare. The Blues Brothers Band continues to perform and record even today.

406 and 407 - Dan Aykroyd is Ellwood and John Belushi is Jack, the Blues Brothers. Over the course of their adventure, they encounter great stars in Black music: Ray Charles (photo at right), Cab Calloway, Aretha Franklin, and James Brown. Not only would their style of comedy and look (dark sunglasses, hats, suits and ties) have many imitators, but the true Blues Brothers Band would have a long life in concerts as well as recordings.

Like all of Stanley Kubrick's films, *The Shining* challenges the spectator as well as the established rules of cinematographic genres, which the brilliant American artist overturned and altered with iconoclastic and innovative impetus.

Eight chapters that differ in length seem to indicate a chronology, but it is called into question by the labyrinthine development of the events.

Jack Torrance (Jack Nicholson) has accepted a seasonal job as the winter caretaker of the enormous Overlook Hotel in the mountains of Colorado. Since the hotel is closed in the winter, Jack is convinced that five months of isolation and concentration, with only his wife Wendy (Shelley Duvall) and their son Danny (Danny Lloyd) for company, will help him overcome writer's block and revive his career.

In the first chapter, we see him going to the hotel for an interview with the manager; in the second he returns with his family and all their luggage to start his new job. During the interview, however, the manager has reluctantly told Jack about a macabre event that occurred years earlier. A previous winter caretaker, Mr. Grady (Philip Stone), who later appears to Jack, went mad and hacked his wife and eight-year-old twin daughters to death. Jack is undaunted by the information, but we are then privy to an enigmatic conversation between little Danny and the head chef, Dick Halloran (Scatman Crothers). Halloran, who inexplicably knows that the boy's family nickname is Doc, questions him to see if the boy is aware that he has paranormal powers, revealing that he too has what he refers to as "shining": the ability to foresee events, receive visions and communicate telepathically. Danny, who is already troubled by the "imaginary friend" who speaks through him and is confusedly convinced that he must face something sinister and obscure, is taken aback by this. But the horrifying visions have already begun, and in particular they involve the twin girls. The boy is also drawn to Room 237, although Halloran warned him never to set foot in it for any reason.

In the following chapters (titled "A Month Later, "Tuesday," "Saturday," "Monday," "Wednesday" and "4 p.m."), we see growing tension as the situation starts to fall apart. Wendy becomes increasingly concerned over her husband's sudden and unwarranted fits of anger and the unexplained bruises on Danny's body. Danny receives more and more signals of impending disaster and falls into a trance. Jack increasingly shows signs that he is becoming unhinged, "meeting" people from the hotel's past, and his aggressiveness gains the upper hand.

1980

THE SHINING

Director: STANLEY KUBRICK

Cast: JACK NICHOLSON / SHELLEY DUVALL / DANNY LLOYD / SCATMAN CROTHERS

Uninspired writer, Jack Torrance (Jack Nicholson) accepts the job of watching over the Overlook Hotel during its winter season closing.

410 - Many strange things happen at the Overlook Hotel where Jack Torrance moves with his wife, Wendy (Shelley Duvall, in the photograph below) and son, Danny, for a few months, in complete isolation. The child is clairvoyant and appears to them as twin girls that were murdered by their father along with their mother in room 237 when he was previous winter watchman at the hotel. Jack's behavior becomes increasingly incomprehensible and aggressive.

Things come to a head when Wendy finds out that Jack has sabotaged the hotel radio as well as the snowmobile (the only way to communicate with the outside world or leave in the event of an emergency). To her horror, she discovers that, over the past months, her husband has filled reams of paper with the very same sentence, written over and over: "All work and no play makes Jack a dull boy."

Called telepathically by Danny, Halloran rushes back to the hotel, but by this time Jack is already hunting down his wife and son, although Wendy manages to defend herself with a baseball bat and a knife. He kills Halloran and chases Danny, who gets away from him by hiding in the tortuous hedge maze, in which Jack is trapped and freezes to death. Wendy and Danny flee on Halloran's snowmobile.

Based on the novel by Stephen King (who was not happy with the adaptation), the film is a concentration of shock, emotional earthquakes and fear, effects that Kubrick achieved in various ways: the deft use of color, editing, the choice of music (including works by Ligeti, Bartok and Penderecki), and the circular and geometric settings. Kubrick also made enormously effective use of the steadicam (operated by the camera's inventor, Garrett Brown), which made it possible to follow the characters' movements at close range.

Just as Kubrick's film *2001: A Space Odyssey* marked a turning point in science-fiction cinema, *The Shining* was a watershed for the horror genre. It holds a unique place among similar works about paranormal or supernatural phenomena, such as Brian De Palma's *Carrie* (also based on a novel by Stephen King). In terms of box-office appeal, it ranks third among horror films, after John Carpenter's *Halloween* and William Friedkin's *The Exorcist*.

Wendy?

Stanley Kubrick took his starting point that became a departure from the novel by Stephen King. As other directors have already done in other genres such as film noir, war and historical fiction, science fiction (*The Killing, Paths of Glory, Spartacus, 2001: Space Odyssey*), as well as in the horror genre, he appropriated general rules and codes to endow the film with its own poetic sensibility.

1980

AMERICAN GIGOLO

Director: PAUL SCHRADER

Cast: RICHARD GERE / LAUREN HUTTON / HECTOR ELIZONDO

American Gigolo is a film that would like to be much more than it actually is or appears to be. The ambition of its author, Paul Schrader (who wrote and directed the entire film, a rarity in the Hollywood system), is to offer a parable.

Julian Kaye (Richard Gere) lives in a luxurious residence in Los Angeles, wears Armani, drives a Mercedes convertible, and haunts exclusive clubs and restaurants. He makes his living – earning plenty of money – by selling himself to wealthy upper-class women. His pander is a seductive blonde named Anne (Nina van Pallandt), but he is tired of the relationship and, aware that he is "the best" on the market, he also works for Leon (Bill Duke), an unscrupulous and abusive pimp. It is Leon who introduces him to the Rheimans, a married couple willing to spend a great deal of money for "special" services, i.e., sadomasochism. Not long after Julian's visit to their house in Palm Springs – and from a later conversation he has with Leon, we learn that he has been invited to return – Mrs. Rheiman is found dead after being tortured and raped. The suspicions of Detective Sunday (Hector Elizondo) fall on Julian, who is unable to furnish an alibi.

In reality, Julian is being framed by Leon, Leon's young lover, Mr. Rheiman and probably also Senator Stratton, who wants to damage him after discovering that Julian has been seeing his wife Michelle (Lauren Hutton).

Michelle is one of the many women from California's upper crust who have turned to Julian for his services, but the two are immediately attracted to each other and want to share much more. When he is sent to jail for accidentally killing Leon after the two get into a fight, Michelle finally reveals that Julian was with her on the night of the murder, providing him with the alibi he needs and saving him.

The word "salvation" is apropos here, as the film is full of ethical implications. Inebriated by easy money and the seductiveness of a life devoted to the pursuit of pleasure, Julian starts out as a man who is losing himself, prey to a sense of omnipotence and superiority. Everything he has done transpires to turn him into a scapegoat and force him to atone for a sin he never committed – although this doubt is planted in everyone's mind, including the audience's. Michelle is the only one who continues to believe in Julian when everyone else has abandoned him. Lastly, the selflessness shown by Michelle, who sacrifices her own social position, reveals the redeeming power of love over a glittering but ephemeral and corrupt way of life, in which Julian is victim rather than tormenter. After all, he truly believes that he is giving something to his clients, who are trapped in arid lives.

Richard Gere's career as a hot leading man and sex symbol took off with the ambiguous character of Julian Kaye.

The Italian critic Paolo Mereghetti cites references to Dostoevsky and the spiritual cinema of Robert Bresson, but we can also add the names of two other influences: the Japanese director Yasujiro Ozu and the Danish director Carl Dreyer, who unquestionably represent Schrader's icons. Schrader – who also wrote the screenplays for Martin Scorsese's *Raging Bull* and *The Last Temptation of Christ*, Peter Weir's *Mosquito Coast* and Brian De Palma's *Obsession* – is certainly no stranger to the themes of Catholicism and of religiosity experienced in a grim and dark manner that revolves around sin. Nevertheless, why Richard Gere gained such enormous appeal through this film as the icon of manliness, the object of desire and the testimonial of a message of new elegance represented by the Armani label remains a mystery. Interestingly, the film's success proved to be fundamental for the Italian designer's ascent to the heights of international fashion.

414 and 415 - Having a keen interest in his body, his own wellbeing and freedom, Julian is on one hand motivated to give in to feelings of love for his client, Michelle (Lauren Hutton). On the other hand, he sees all of his pseudo-values go up in smoke and his conquests end up victim to a machination when he takes the blame for things that aren't his fault, compelling him to look at his lifestyle that, according to director Paul Schrader, is completely self-destructive.

1980

[FRANCE]   Genre: ROMANTIC COMEDY

THE PARTY

Director: CLAUDE PINOTEAU

Cast: SOPHIE MARCEAU / CLAUDE BRASSEUR / BRIGITTE FOSSEY

Vic Berreton (Sophie Marceau) is a pretty 13-year-old Parisian girl with a happy family life. Her witty and fascinating father, François (Claude Brasseur), is a dentist. Her beautiful young mother, Françoise (Brigitte Fossey), is an illustrator and comic-strip writer who is passionate about her work. Vic's dynamic great-grandmother Poupette is a very important part of her life, as the 85-year-old harpist is the young girl's friend and adviser.

The Party (La Boum) opens with Vic's first day of school. From this moment on, Penelope, Vic's uninhibited schoolmate and companion in countless adventures, becomes her best friend. The first "adventure" is a party at the house of one of their classmates. Vic has to convince her mother to give her permission to go, must borrow the right outfit and is determined to win over the boy she likes. However, there is an evident generation gap between parents and daughter. The former, distracted by countless everyday problems, are abrupt with her and, in turn, Vic naturally feels misunderstood.

The night of the party finally arrives, a scene in which some of the young people spend the entire time making out while others listen to rock music on headphones when the DJ plays slow songs. We see the young girl with a squeaky voice, the nerd who takes off his braces and glasses to look more attractive, and those who act as lovers' go-betweens but are unable to keep a secret. The teenage crowd gets worked up when it comes time for each girl to choose the boy with whom she wants to dance.

It is a world that is off-limits to adults. In fact, the owners of the house have hidden out in the kitchen to get something to eat (their son warned them to lay low) and the parents of the guests were not only forced to drop off their children at the end of the block because the young people were ashamed to be seen with them, but they must also wait in the car until the party is over because none of them dare ring the doorbell to interrupt the party. The scene of the phone booth surrounded by dozens of fathers waiting for their children is a classic. When François tries to call the party to tell

416 and 417 - This is the quintessential French coming-of-age film that takes a clever new direction, inaugurating the decade of the Eighties and introducing a new child star in Sophie Marceau. Meanwhile, even Hollywood is arming itself for a younger audience demographic, gambling on similar films that could either be soaring successes or box office bombs.

Vic that it's time to leave, she is in the arms of Mathieu, her new love. The two are dancing to the notes of the film's hit song "Reality," which he lets her hear on his headphones while all the others are dancing to a rock song. They later exchange their first kiss at a movie theater, amidst other couples from their group, one of whom plays a prank by poking a hole in the bottom of a bag of potato chips.

While Vic is experiencing her first romance, her father encounters an old lover to whom he has promised one last night before they go their separate ways. To keep his wife from finding out, he pretends that he has had an accident and has a friend put a fake cast on his leg. But the burden of this absurd lie soon becomes too much for François, who confesses everything to Françoise. The two decide to separate and when they tell Vic, her only concern is that she does not want to spend weekends with her father, because the teen parties are held on Saturday night. Vic can think of nothing but her own love problems – it seems that Mathieu is dating another girl – but the same holds true of her parents. Cheerful Poupette tells her great-granddaughter what to do to make the boy jealous. Vic follows her advice and one night, at a discotheque at which roller skates are required attire, she kisses her father in front of Mathieu, leading him to believe that the man is her lover.

Vic is punished, but her mother and father are still too involved in their own problems to notice that Poupette has accompanied the girl to visit Mathieu at a beach resort north of Paris. In fact, Françoise is now dating Vic's German teacher. Going against her great-grandmother's shrewd advice, Vic throws herself into Mathieu's arms as soon as she sees him, but the romantic getaway proves to be a disappointment.

In the meantime, back in Paris Françoise tells François that she is pregnant, but he ruins the moment by insinuating that he may not be the father. Françoise decides to go to Africa with the German teacher, but then changes her mind and returns to her husband. As always, Vic's life seems to be far removed from her parents' problems. Her sole concern is preparing her 14th birthday party – as the title implies, parties are the film's central theme – during which she meets a new boy and the two dance to the usual song.

The debut of 14-year-old Sophie Marceau, née Sophie Maupu, who was selected among countless auditioning teens, launched a box-office phenomenon that became an international hit. While there is nothing new about the role played by adolescents in films, what is innovative here is the awareness – or perhaps the fortuitous discovery – that the teen generation of the 1980s represented a new set of moviegoers, effectively the movie industry's most appealing and significant audience. A sequel was made two years later with the same cast.

RAIDERS OF THE LOST ARK

Director: **STEVEN SPIELBERG**

Cast: **HARRISON FORD / KAREN ALLEN / PAUL FREEMAN / JOHN RHYS-DAVIES / RONALD LACEY / WOLF KAHLER / DENHOLM ELLIOTT**

Bag slung crosswise over his chest, leather jacket, and fedora is the look of the adventurer, explorer, archaeologist, and occasionally reckless detective of Indiana Jones' fame. Renewal of an old stereotype from Thirties' consumer literature and comic strips is the ace up the sleeve for the creation born from the brilliant and infantile minds, with no contradiction in terms, of Spielberg and Lucas. ▶

Raiders of the Lost Ark is one of those rare films that you never tire of seeing, despite the fact that you know every scene by heart. Indeed, for this very reason, you watch it because you know that, time after time, you'll experience the euphoria of discovery and the childlike enjoyment of the very first time. It is an absolute and magically successful monument to entertainment and pure spectacle.

Thanks to George Lucas and the first two episodes of *Star Wars* (actually the fourth and fifth in the saga), Harrison Ford emerged from a decade of minor roles. But it was with *Raiders of the Lost Ark* that Ford would cross paths with the character destined to bring him worldwide popularity, further confirmed by his role in *Blade Runner*. He was the perfect choice and the perfect actor, not only for the role Indiana Jones but also Hans Solo, as he fully grasped these two-dimensional characters modeled after comic-book heroes.

The setting is Boston University, 1936. The government and the Secret Service assign the archaeologist Jones, nicknamed Indiana, to a delicate mission. It seems that the Nazis have identified the location of the Ark of the Covenant, the sacred container with the tablets of the Ten Commandments that God dictated to Moses. The Third Reich has attributed symbolic and propitiatory meaning to this finding and, as a result, the authorities of the free world have made it a matter of strategic importance and principle to get there first. For Indiana, in turn, it would be a discovery of immense historical and scientific importance. Therefore, he accepts the assignment and leaves, accompanied by his friend Marion (Karen Allen).

The final showdown takes place in Egypt. And, naturally, everything is far more difficult and complicated than expected, with chase scenes, danger and traps set by Indiana's rival, the treacherous Rene Belloq (Paul Freeman).

The film is full of breathtaking scenes and sequences that have become legendary, from the enormous rolling stone ball to the coldness with which Indiana – with an irresistibly comical effect – shoots a sinister fellow threatening him with a scimitar. Indiana's look is iconic: a broad-rimmed hat, a leather jacket, a crop and a knapsack over his shoulder. More than a scientist, he is an adventurer and detective, an athlete, an acrobat, and an indefatigable and savvy fighter with thousands of unexpected resources. The blend that produced this extraordinarily successful icon owes a great deal to pulp iconography and the unique comics of the 1930s, such as the work of the Franco-Belgian design school and the mysteriously exotic setting of the adventures of Tintin. However, the film has an important innovation. It was written so that the female lead would take up the qualities, spirit and style of Katharine Hepburn. Indeed, the film's exotic and adventurous side is accompanied by the brilliance of sophisticated comedy.

The marvelous score composed by John Williams also played a key role in this legend. Although the final result can be credited to the hand of Steven Spielberg, it is appropriate to consider *Indiana Jones*, which was followed by two sequels (a third one is currently being made), as a joint effort on the part of the director, Lucas as the author of the subject and producer of the film (Indiana was his dog's name and the surname of Jones was chosen by Spielberg, who did not like the original idea of Smith), and screenwriter Lawrence Kasdan.

1. 2. 3. 4. 5. 6. Breathless chase scenes, exotic scenarios, dangers lying in wait at every corner, bad guys everywhere, and Harrison Ford at his best, embodying a one-dimensional character who is deprived of psychology and emotion. These are the secrets of an obvious formula of adventure plus spy thriller plus brilliant comedy, but one that would be bet on in the Eighties? Of course, it was so successful that it became a film series.

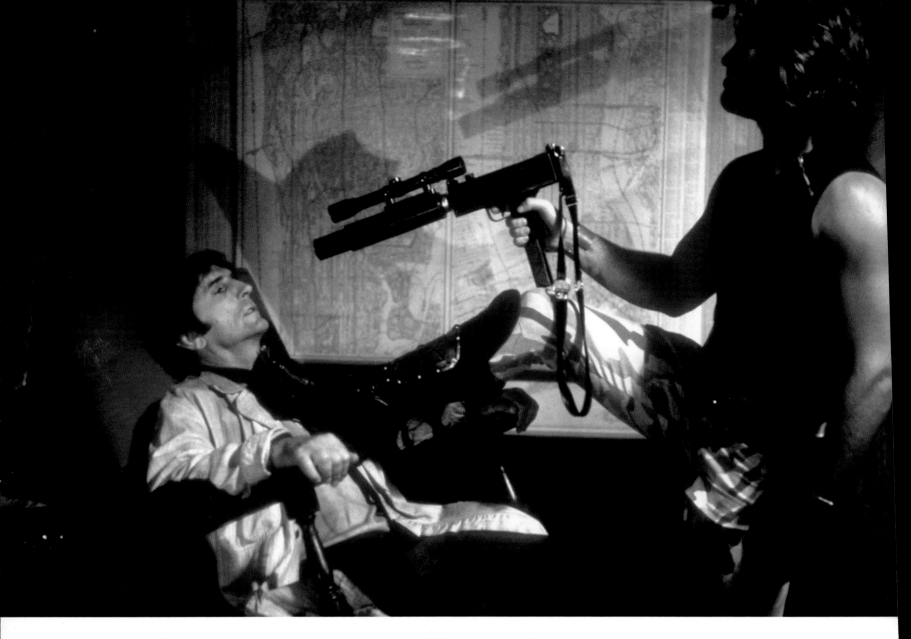

422 - Jena Plissken (Kurt Russell) aims at the double and triple-dealer, Brain (Harry Dean Stanton).

In 1988 crime in the United States rose to such levels that the entire island of Manhattan was transformed into a maximum-security prison. Surrounded by water and impassable walls, its bridges mined and its perimeter guarded by swarms of policemen, all of New York was evacuated and the prisoners abandoned to their own devices. It has become an inferno that no one would ever want to enter and from which it is impossible to escape, a place in which bullying reigns in a regime of barbaric self-determination.

We are now in the year 1997. Air Force One has been hijacked by terrorists, who crash the plane into a skyscraper. The president (Donald Pleasance), who is en route to a critical summit meeting and has a briefcase handcuffed to his wrist containing a cassette with key information on nuclear warfare, survives because he is in an escape pod that is ejected when the plane crashes. When the pod lands, however, it is discovered by the gang of criminals that rules New York, and the president is kidnapped.

Police Commissioner Bob Hauk (Lee Van Cleef) is put in charge of the case and he intercepts a former soldier, "Snake" Plissken (Kurt Russell), who is being transferred to the city/penitentiary to serve time for armed robbery. Knowing that Snake is the only man capable of undertaking such a desperate mission, Hauk assigns him to sneak into the city – in a jet glider that lands on the roof of one of the Twin Towers – to find and rescue the president and his valuable tape. If Plissken is successful, he will be released and pardoned. However, he has just 24 hours to complete his mission and a deadly device has been implanted in him. When the time is up, the substance in his veins will explode, but if he succeeds before the deadline he will be injected with an antidote. Although he is reluctant and suspicious, Plissken agrees and sets out on the mission.

Once he is inside the prison, he is assisted by one of the prisoners, "Cabbie" (Ernest Borgnine), who has recognized and admires him. However, he must get past the sinister and opportunistic inmate "Brain" (Harry Dean Stanton), who has set up his headquarters in the old New York Public Library.

ESCAPE FROM NEW YORK

Genre:
SCIENCE FICTION / ACTION

Director: JOHN CARPENTER

Cast:
KURT RUSSELL /
LEE VAN CLEEF /
ERNEST BORGNINE /
DONALD PLEASENCE /
ISAAC HAYES /
HARRY DEAN STANTON /
ADRIENNE BARBEAU /
SEASON HUBLEY /
TOM ATKINS

1981

423 - Sworn enemy of Jena Plissken is the "Duke" (Isaac Hayes), a gigantic Black man with lots of bling, always in full uniform, and absolute boss of a Manhattan that's been reduced to a maximum-security prison where ironically criminals are left alone.

The battle against the colossal gang leader Duke (Isaac Hayes), who rides in a limousine whose hood is decorated with lavish chandeliers, and his right-hand man, the psychopath Romero, is destined to be deadly. Snake succeeds at the very last minute, following a breathtaking chase scene across the Brooklyn Bridge as he miraculously avoids the mines to save the president, himself and the tape. But not without making a fool of everyone. To avenge the way he was treated – he gets the antidote with just seconds to spare – Plissken switches the original tape with a music cassette that the president then plays at the summit, much to his own embarrassment. Nevertheless, the true "tough guys," Plissken and Police Commissioner Hauk, come to an understanding and may even work together in the future.

With this 1981 film John Carpenter, who was already a favorite among fans of action and horror movies (e.g., *Assault on Precinct 13*) confirmed his model of the catastrophe genre. He would go on to make *The Thing* the following year, as well as the sequel, *Escape from L.A.*, 15 years after the original *Escape from New York*. An enthusiast of B movies who gained an enormous following among fans of this genre, Carpenter made this film, which would gross more than $25 million, with a budget of just $6 million. The character of Plissken, with his eye patch and deadpan one-dimensional comic-book personality, became a model for adventure stories set in an ultra-violent, barbaric and dystopian future. The role turned Kurt Russell's career around and the actor would work with Carpenter again in *Big Trouble in Little China* and the sequel to *Escape from New York*. His antihero is effectively the counterpart to the character of Indiana Jones. Originally created for Clint Eastwood, the role was then offered to Tommy Lee Jones and Charles Bronson, who was passed over because he was too old, before Russell was chosen. Quentin Tarantino, an enormous fan of this film, cites Plissken in *Kill Bill* with the one-eyed character played by Darryl Hannah and the stuntman from *Grindhouse*, played by Russell. However, Carpenter himself referenced notable film names, calling one of his characters Cronenberg and another Romero.

1982

1

Cast: SYLVESTER STALLON / BRIAN DENNEHY / RICHARD CRENNA

John Rambo is a soldier who has just returned from the Vietnam War. After visiting the family of a fellow soldier and discovering that one of his friend died of cancer, Rambo wanders aimlessly, hitchhiking and carrying all his belongings in a sack slung over his shoulder. As soon as he arrives in a mountain town he is singled out an approach by the local sheriff, Will Teasle (Brian Dennehy), who is wary of him and considers him a dangerous drifter. Teasle accompanies him out of town and warns him not to return. But Rambo, who has never uttered a word and cannot understand the policeman's suspiciousness and aggressive attitude, claims his right to circulate freely and return to town to find a place to eat. The reaction is violent. The entire local police force is against Rambo, who gets arrested and mistreated. Police checks revealing that he has received medals for valor carry little weight.

Initially acquiescing to these unmotivated attacks, Rambo subsequently reacts by neutralizing everyone and fleeing to the mountains. An intense manhunt ensues and one of Rambo's most violent pursuers is killed, at which point the State Police and the National Guard are called in. Rambo applies all the guerrilla techniques he learned in Vietnam and what triggers his reaction of self-defense is the memory of the fear and nightmare of his imprisonment in Vietnam.

This deadlock is resolved when Colonel Trautman (Richard Crenna) from the Green Berets, Rambo's superior in Vietnam, is asked to step in. Trautman constantly tries to alert Teasle and his men that a soldier who has been trained in the harshest and most inhuman conditions is invincible. Rambo has been trained to be an indestructible war machine. It is only after a massacre that Rambo finally breaks down in tears in his colonel's arms.

FIRST BLOOD (RAMBO)

Director: TED KOTCHEFF

2 ▲

1. 2. 3. Veteran John Rambo is somewhat crazy because of his ugly experiences in Vietnam but all things considered, still nonviolent until he's provoked by a stupid intolerant country sheriff (here, Brian Dennehy is threatened at knife-point by Rambo after he's lost patience), and while Rambo has done his duty in the Vietnamese jungle, the sheriff has been a draft dodger. After Rocky, Stallone re-launches his career and invents the second great icon in popular film.

3 ▲

The film was inspired by David Morrell's film *First Blood*. Following the worldwide success of *Rocky*, Sylvester Stallone virtually "became" Rambo, actively participating in creating this character (Stallone wrote the screenplay). Like *Rocky*, *First Blood* was a low-budget film without enormous expectations and, as a result, its unexpected success calls for a new interpretation. In reality, Rambo is not a character who is willingly violent and aggressive. If anything, he wants to leave war and violence behind him. Yet he has been molded to do evil and, as a result, when people are cruel to him, all hell breaks loose. He has been forced into a corner by other people's prejudices and small-town mentality, and the obtuse xenophobia of the police.

At the time, the film was viewed as a representation of the rightwing views of the Reagan era and an expression – as opposed to war films that had preceded it, from *Apocalypse Now* to *The Deer Hunter* – of the sen-

timents of veterans who felt they had been given all the blame. Yet they had simply done their duty for their country, and any responsibility for the lost war was instead to be attributed to the lack of public support.

While all of this is part of the spirit of the film, however, there is also something much more subtle. This aspect emerges in Rambo's monologue toward the end of the film, when he breaks down in his colonel's arms. Rambo, clearly a man who has been sorely tested mentally and spiritually, suffers and cannot understand why he has been isolated and sidelined. He cannot comprehend why he must face suspicion, hatred and difficulties in finding a decent job. He refuses to be considered a base assassin, because it is not his fault that he was transformed into a killing machine.

First Blood was an enormous success that spawned three sequels, to the enormous embarrassment of Hollywood in the early 1980s, which never gave the film any recognition.

E.T.
THE EXTRA-TERRESTRIAL

Director: STEVEN SPIELBERG

**Cast: HENRY THOMAS / DEE WALLACE /
ROBERT MACNAUGHTON / PETER COYOTE / DREW BARRYMORE**

E.T. the Extra-Terrestrial was one of the most successful and popular movies of all time. It drew record crowds and was the film industry's biggest financial success, making more money than blockbusters such as *Jaws*, *Close Encounters of the Third Kind* and *Raiders of the Lost Ark* (Spielberg later beat his own record with *Jurassic Park*), subsequently topped by *Titanic*.

The member of a group of aliens who landed on Earth to conduct botanical studies, wrinkly little E.T. is left behind by his colleagues, who flee in their spaceship when the police suddenly arrive. The lost extraterrestrial ends up at the house of a 10-year-old boy named Elliott, who lives with his older brother Michael, his little sister Gertie (Drew Barrymore) and his recently separated mother, Mary. Elliott hides the creature and gets to know him, initially on his own and then sharing him with his siblings – but not his mother.

Between ploys, games, disguises, a new language (sad and anxious to get in touch with his family, E.T. learns to utter the famous phrase "phone home"), the development of extrasensory communication between Elliot and the alien who, while the boy is at school, allows him to "feel" what is happening to his new friend, danger and close calls, the situation is finally discovered by the authorities. There is a general mobilization, as the U.S. Army and scientists take over Elliott's house and quarantine both the boy and E.T., placing them under observation.

In a state of complete interpenetration, both start to die, affected by an unknown malady: an illness of the spirit. <0} With the help of his friends, however, Elliott manages to sneak E.T. away from the government agents and, thanks to the creature's powers, the two take off into the sky on a bicycle – in the film's most iconic scene – to accompany E.T. to the rendezvous he has managed to set up by contacting his spaceship. The final scene is powerful and poignant, as E.T. and Elliot must say goodbye to each other. But before he goes, E.T. points his finger – as long as his slender neck – at Elliott's heart and says, "I'll be right here."

While the secret to the magical success of this film lies in the coexistence of two tones, juxtaposing comedy and children's adventure stories with pathos and melodrama, Spielberg also takes up the cause of peaceful coexistence that he had espoused in *Close Encounters of the Third Kind*. Here, however, it acquires a more sinister air. Children are also "the good guys" in *E.T.* Nevertheless, whereas the adults in *Close Encounters*, embodied by François Truffaut's scientist and the character played by Richard Dreyfuss, are open to dialogue and the friendly desire for knowledge, in this film they represent hostile prejudices.

Naïve and poetic like this one, there are images that remain imprinted in our collective memory as much as they are reiterated, even accompanied by gestures like the disproportionate index finger of E.I. pointing upward to some unknown location in outer space, becoming the soundtracks of an era with "E.T. phone home."

The great optimistic dream is materialized as the reinterpretation of Peter Pan, Spielberg's favorite classic tale (the flying bicycle alludes to the Disney film that was inspired by J.M. Barrie's book and may also be a nod to Zavattini's fable-like *Miracle in Milan*). Yet it is muted by an undercurrent that, on closer inspection, is not all that optimistic after all. The world can be saved by children and their innocence – as long as adults do not interfere.

Spielberg owes a great deal to screenwriter Melissa Mathison (Harrison Ford's second wife), with whom he discussed the project while he was making *Star Wars* (which is also cited in the games played by Elliott and his unusual "friend"). The film's success can also be attributed in part to the marvelous animatronics of Carlo Rambaldi, who created the aliens for *Close Close Encounters of the Third Kind* and also worked on two other hits, *King Kong* and *Alien*.

428 and 429 - The kind little creature makes the acquaintance of all the children in the house, including Elliott who becomes his best earthly friend, and little sister, Gertie (Drew Barrymore). Spielberg reinforces a profitable revolution with *Close Encounters of the Third Kind* then *E.T.* The extraterrestrial, that is, the alien or foreign body, is not a threat but a potential friend.

\<phone home\>

Rambaldi perfected several ideas in order to animate the alien, from completely electronic elements to mechanical solutions in which dwarves were used for the creature's movements. The face of Albert Einstein supposedly inspired the extraterrestrial's expressions. As was the case with *Close Encounters* and *Raiders of the Lost Ark*, the film won Oscars only in technical fields. Spielberg would not gain full recognition as an artist – and this reflects an old but deep-seated prejudice – until his "serious" films, *Schindler's List* and *Saving Private Ryan*.

The 20th-anniversary Special Edition, released in 2002, has added scenes as well as some changes: the policemen no longer hold guns.

1982

BLADE RUNNER

Director: RIDLEY SCOTT

Cast: HARRISON FORD / JOANNA CASSIDY / EDWARD JAMES OLMOS / DARYL HANNAH / RUTGER HAUER / SEAN YOUNG

n addition to being director Ridley Scott's magnum opus – rivaling *Alien* – *Blade Runner* is a masterpiece of science-fiction cinema and one of the world's biggest blockbusters, not only of the 1980s but of all the past few decades.

Inspired by *Do Androids Dream of Electric Sheep?*, a novel by Philip K. Dick, one of the greatest science-fiction writers, the film projects us into a post-nuclear future years ahead of the period in which the film was made and in which the novel was set, but this era is now virtually upon us. Written in 1966 and published in 1968, the novel was initially set in 1992, but later editions changed the time frame to 2021. The film is set in 2019. The action takes place in the dark and degraded megalopolis of Los Angeles, an overpopulated, dangerous and highly polluted place where it always rains and no one ever sees sunlight.

Retired policeman Rick Deckard (Harrison Ford) is called back into the special Blade Runner unit that hunts down "replicants." He must find and "terminate" four Nexus-6 replicants, two males and two females. These robots, which are identical to humans, have escaped from the off-world colonies and are out of control. Their plan is to force the Tyrell Corporation, which designed them, to extend their four-year lifespan. After all, it was to be expected that this evolved generation of robots could conceivably develop emotional capacities and a conscience, ultimately deciding to affirm their will and claim their right to live beyond the planned number of years.

Deckard must find and deal with them one by one: first Zhora (Joanna Cassidy), then Leon (Edward James Olmos), followed by the acrobatic Pris (Daryl Hannah) and, lastly, the toughest one of all, Roy (Rutger Hauer), the group leader and the most evolved of the four replicants. It is during this fight that Roy – who alternates polished and philosophical language with the cold-bloodedness of a killer – utters his famous line: "I've seen things you people wouldn't believe." These words reveal the replicants' unimaginable and unbearable pain. In short, these robots suffer.

Deckard's difficulties are further complicated by his encounter with the beautiful Rachel (Sean Young). Is Rachel a replicant too? She is, but she is different from Roy and the others in her group. She does not know or believe that she is one. In fact, she is convinced that she can feel love and has a memory. And she has fallen in love with Deckard who, initially unwilling to admit it, also loves her.

Is beautiful Rachel (Sean Young) a replicant or isn't she? She is different from the others. Deckard, replicant investigator and hunter, falls in love with her. ▶

‹I think, Sebastian, therefore I am.›

432 - The acrobatic Pris (Daryl Hannah) gives Deckard a run for his money when he's already successfully gotten rid of Zhora and Leon.

433 - Tireless, Deckard travelss throughout the metropolis that was once Los Angeles, now unrecognizable, perpetually dark and dismal, rainy, and very polluted,

Many consider the final scene of the version released in 1982 comfortingly optimistic, as Deckard and Rachel leave Los Angeles for a world that is still luminous and colorful. However, this version is not considered "original" and a new director's cut, which is shorter than the first version, was released in 1991. Sacrificing Deckard's narrating off-screen voice, which distinguished the original version and was enormously effective, it proposes a final scene that is fittingly more nuanced and problematic. The new finale leaves viewers wondering if Deckard himself is a replicant and if the two are a pair of outcasts attempting to affirm their right to love. "Rachel was special. No termination day. I don't know how long we'll live together. Who does?"

The entire visual structure the film, which is so inventive that it is a milestone in the representation of a pessimistic near future, clearly takes up the legacy of Fritz Lang's *Metropolis*, but the leading character's emotional dynamics and moral insight were instead inspired by hard-boiled and noirish fiction. Like Sam Spade and Philip Marlowe, Deckard is a lonely, nauseated hero. Harrison Ford gives this character the poignancy of a dehumanized lack of emotion.

All of the elements in the film are outstanding, from Douglas Trumbull's effects to the score by Vangelis, with the song "One More Kiss, Dear."

The Academy of Motion Picture Arts and Sciences once again demonstrated that it can be as blind in some cases as it can be tapped into current tastes in others. The 1983 Academy Awards ignored *Blade Runner* in favor of Richard Attenborough's saintly portrait of Gandhi.

A new high-definition copy (*The Final Cut*) was released in 2007.

◀ 1

1. *Blade Runner* comes from a novel by Philip Dick, a master of science fiction. After Indiana Jones, Harrison Ford adds another memorable character to his repertoire. Creased and crumpled by life, he interprets his Deckard as a Philip Marlowe tossed into a murky and catastrophic future. Ridley Scott takes stock of *Metropolis*, the silent masterpiece by Fritz Lang, when creating the atmosphere for this film.

▲2

< I've seen things you people wouldn't believe. Attack ships on fire off the shoulder of Orion. I watched C-beams glitter in the dark near the Tannhauser gate. All those moments will be lost in time, like tears in rain. Time to die.>

2. 3. Deckard (Harrison Ford) is here in a final clash with the leader, the most intelligent and toughest of the replicants, Roy (Rutger Hauer, below).   3 ▶

Once Upon a Time in America (C'era una volta in America) is the story of the powerful friendship between Noodles (Robert De Niro) and Max (James Woods), two street urchins who become wealthy and fearful gangsters by joining forces with three other boys. It is the story of a gang accustomed to living with blackmail, theft and violence.

The plot uses an interplay of flashbacks illustrating a true American saga that starts in the 1920s. It also examines the love story between Noodles and Deborah (Jennifer Connelly in the flashbacks, Elizabeth McGovern as an adult), the girl he secretly observes while she practices dancing.

Noodles is instinctive, eager and generous to the point that the first time he kills it is purely out of loyalty and revenge; Max instead seems to be cold, a capable strategist who wants to be the sole gang leader.

Their faith in this friendship strengthens the gang, which continues to expand during Prohibition, trafficking in liquor and pulling off heists. Their undertakings continue even while Noodles is in jail, and after his release he returns to the gang as if nothing had ever happened. Nevertheless, every so often they face the risk that something or someone can break their bond, and Noodles says to Max: "Today they asked us to get rid of Joe. Tomorrow they ask me to get rid of you. Is that okay with you? 'Cause it's not okay with me."

The only thing that can potentially upset the clan's balance is Noodles' love for Deborah, but she chooses the theater over him.

"You're the only person that I have ever ... That I ever cared about. But you'd lock me up and throw away the key, wouldn't you? And the thing is, I probably wouldn't even mind ... So I got to get to where I'm going ... To the top," Deborah confesses to Noodles who, furious that she has rejected him, rapes her.

What changes the clan's game is the end of Prohibition. Max plans a big job now that the bootlegging trade is no longer profitable. It turns out to be too big, however, and in an attempt to save the lives of Max and his other friends, Noodles informs the police.

Noodles is forced to leave, accompanied only by his feelings of guilt for his friends who were killed in the shootout with the police. But in the end he returns: the year is 1968.

Deborah is a well-known actress who has never gotten married, but she does not live alone. Noodles receives a mysterious invitation to a party, where it finally dawns on him that Max was never killed and that he is the man living with Deborah.

1984
ONCE UPON A TIME IN AMERICA

Director: SERGIO LEONE

Cast:　ROBERT DE NIRO / JAMES WOODS / ELIZABETH MCGOVERN /

TREAT WILLIAMS / TUESDAY WELD / JOE PESCI / JAMES HAYDEN /

WILLIAM FORSYTHE / DANNY AIELLO / DARLANNE FLUEGEL / ROBERT HARPER / BURT YOUNG

The New York of Sergio Leone is, like his Wild West, the ideal concept of New York cultivated in the fertile imagination of an admirer.

438 - As children, the protagonists in the story begin their long journey of friendship and animosity.

Max has invited him because he has decided to die and wants Noodles to kill him. To convince him, Max provokes him: "I took away your whole life from you. I've been living in your place. I took everything. I took your money. I took your girl. All I left for you was years of grief over having killed me."

But his words are futile. Noodles refuses. Now he is a man, though old, and Max is merely the ghost of what he had been.

Sergio Leone made this film 16 years after *Once Upon a Time in the West*. Following the initial concept, all the phases – identification of the subject (based on Harry Grey's autobiographical novel), the final screenplay (involving five writers: Leo Benvenuti, Piero De Bernardi, Enrico Medioli, Franco Ferrini and Franco Arcalli) and filming (from June 1982 to April 1983) – took more than 12 years. Nevertheless, this film crowned Leone's career and artistic vision. It is effectively a statement of all his passions and quirks, starting with inordinately long film time. This monument to technical perfectionism is 220 minutes long, although the version released in the United States is much shorter and was heavily cut. It was also his last work. The great director died in 1989 at the age of 60.

1. Street kids in New York during prohibition and gangster period of the Twenties when little Noodles is already falling in love with little Deborah.

2. 3. The story of Noodles (Robert De Niro) and friend and rival, Max (James Woods), would progress and conclude in 1968 when Noodles discovers not just that his friend he believed dead because of him is really alive, but also learns that he has stolen the love of Deborah (Elizabeth McGovern): "I stole your life and lived it in your place." A monumental and very ambitious film, *Once Upon a Time in America* finally brought Leone recognition as a great director and film artist that, despite the enormous popularity of his westerns, he had always been denied.

1984

Cast: ROBERT ENGLUND

A NIGHTMARE ON ELM STREET

Director: WES CRAVEN

Made on a very low budget and in a very short time frame, *A Nightmare on Elm Street* became the top cult movie of the 1980s. Yet its creator, Wes Craven, had to knock on countless doors before he finally found a producer. Nonetheless, it would proved to be a turning point for the horror genre and became one of the longest and most successful serial phenomena of our time. Its enormous success can be attributed to the aura of one of the characters, the ruthless killer Freddy Krueger. Freddy is one of the living dead – and this is no innovation – but in this case he continues to live and perpetuate evil, not in the real world but through the nightmares of his victims, entering their dreams to sow panic, terror and real death. The film can also be credited with the invention of truly horrific makeup, distinguished by a burnt face and extremely long and terrifying blades in the place of nails, all of which made the actor Robert Englund completely unrecognizable.

Let's see what happens in the first adventure of this series. There are two teenage couples: Nancy and Glen (Johnny Depp, in his debut role), and Tina and Rod. Terrible nightmares begin to disturb Tina, who remembers that her dreams are about a monstrous figure wearing a striped sweater and a hat. When she wakes up, however, she discovers that she also has other signs of her dreams: real cuts. She confides this to Nancy, who confesses that she has had the same nightmare. All four young people spend a night together at a sleepover to help calm down the terrified Tina. When everyone

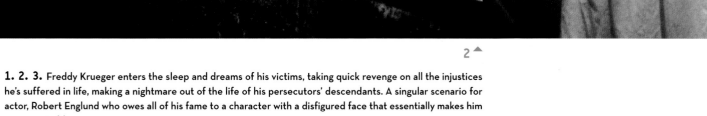

1. 2. 3. Freddy Krueger enters the sleep and dreams of his victims, taking quick revenge on all the injustices he's suffered in life, making a nightmare out of the life of his persecutors' descendants. A singular scenario for actor, Robert Englund who owes all of his fame to a character with a disfigured face that essentially makes him unrecognizable.

wakes up, however, things are even worse: Tina is dead and her boyfriend Rod has been arrested and accused of murder. Now it is Nancy who is pursued by the nightmares. She talks to her mother about it, but finds her reaction suspicious.

In the meantime, Rod is found strangled in his cell. He has seemingly committed suicide, but Nancy refuses to believe it. She is increasingly convinced that the murderer is the man from their shared dreams. After checking into a clinic for sleep therapy – a terrible idea, as she wakes up with cuts, but has also managed to grab the murderer's hat during her dream – Nancy finally forces her mother to confess after the woman recognizes the hat. Her mother tells her about Freddy Kruger, a monster who killed numerous children. When he was caught, the parents of the young victims lynched him and burned him alive. Now he is back, populating the dreams of their progeny and seeking revenge. Nancy and Glen are determined to neutralize Freddy, but the young man falls asleep and thus becomes yet another victim of the dream assassin. Nancy instead manages to fight him. She keeps herself awake, refuses to look at him, convinces herself that he does not exist and forces herself to be unafraid. As a result, he can have no effect on her.

At the end, however, the door remains open to further developments. For example, the third episode tells us that Kruger was the son of a nun who had been raped by a gang of juvenile delinquents. The film was followed by seven sequels made between 1985 and 2003, although Craven directed only one of them. Craven's own story is fascinating. After getting a good education and landing a professorship, he decided to pursue his passion for cinema and began to make porn films. A fan of Bergman, he ultimately ventured into the horror genre, revolutionizing its standards by creating the "splatter and gore" subgenre. The icon of pure excess, Craven also showed a darkly ironic spirit and the ambition to write a moral tale on the American dream transformed into a nightmare.

The leading character in *Back to the Future* is the teenager Marty McFly. He does not have a model family – his father is a subservient failure, his mother is unhappy and out of shape, his sister has no social life, his brother works at a fast-food joint and his uncle has been arrested – nor is he the best student. In fact, at the beginning of the film the school principal hands him yet another tardy note and admonishes him, "And one for you, McFly. I believe that makes four in a row." But he can count on two true friends: the scientist Emmett "Doc" Brown (Christopher Lloyd) and his girlfriend Jennifer. On the night of October 25, 1985 Doc shows him his great discovery: a time machine made by mounting a flux capacitor on a DeLorean. This device is one of the scientist's brilliant inventions, exploiting plutonium and the speed of 88 mph to travel from one date to another. During his demonstration, however, the Libyan terrorists from whom Doc stole the plutonium arrive on the scene. They kill the scientist, but Marty manages to escape in the DeLorean, which reaches 88 mph and thus transports him to the precise moment that his friend had set for the demonstration: November 5, 1955. Here – and this is one of the miracles of cinema – he soon happens to bump into his father, George, who is naturally the pathetic victim of Biff, the bully (later his boss in 1985), and then his mother, Lorraine, who is decidedly more attractive than Marty remembers. Realizing that she is attracted to him, he flees to find Doc, who is 30 years younger.

At first Doc is bewildered and waffles over what to do: "I'm sure that in 1985 plutonium is available in every corner drugstore, but in 1955 it's a little hard to come by!" However, he learns from Marty that a powerful bolt of lightning will strike the city's historic clock tower the following week, so the scientist decides to use his electrical charge to send his friend back to his own era.

Marty then spends a week trying to remedy the damage he has done by meeting his parents (his siblings begin to vanish from a photo he keeps in his wallet). Lorraine has become infatuated with him and, as a result, his parents seem to be anything but a match made in heaven. Coming to her defense after she has several clashes with Biff, Marty appears to be far more courageous and fascinating than his father. Nevertheless, George manages to prove his worth at a school dance, when he knocks Biff out for pestering Lorraine. The two fall in love, the existence of the McFly family in 1985 is safe and Marty can finally dash off for his rendezvous with Doc under the clock tower. When they meet, however, he is unable to warn his friend of the danger that awaits him 30 years later, because the scientist refuses to listen to anything about the future. Consequently, after a series of mishaps – Doc manages to hook up the electrical wire at the last minute – the DeLorean goes back to 1985, at the precise moment in which the terrorists are killing Marty's friend.

1985
BACK TO THE FUTURE

Director: ROBERT ZEMECKIS

Cast: MICHAEL J. FOX / CHRISTOPHER LLOYD / LEA THOMPSON

Michael J. Fox is Marty McFly. Christopher Lloyd is "Doc" and the time machine inventor.

Hanging onto his clock, "Doc" must permit Marty to return to the future after the end of his voyage to the year 1955 when the boy assures himself that his future parents' lives don't take a turn that could compromise their marriage and his birth.

In tears over his body, Marty discovers that Doc is alive and well thanks to a bulletproof vest. The scientist had changed his mind about the future and pieced together Marty's letter, which he had torn up in 1955. After this incredible adventure, the film naturally has a happy ending. The McFly family is happier than ever, his father is a well-known writer, his siblings have a social life and rewarding jobs, and his mother is in wonderful shape, Biff is washing their car and Marty himself as a 4x4 he can use to take his girlfriend to the beach. Everything would be perfect, except that Doc arrives on the scene, back from 2015, and asks Marty if he can borrow his car ...

The film was an enormous hit and spawned two rather successful sequels, the 1989 film, which naturally takes place in 2015, and the 1990 film, set in the Far West. Steven Spielberg produced all the films. Part Four of the story has not been produced due chiefly to the illness of Michael J. Fox, who became a star thanks to the film.

The comical and enthralling screenplay by Robert Zemeckis and Bob Gale is based on nostalgia for the past as well as the fads of the 1980s (Marty is rarely without his skateboard, and he manages to find impromptu models in both 1955 and 2015). The film is also sprinkled with allusions and intriguing details. For example, when Marty plays Johnny B. Goode, a musician calls his cousin, Chuck Berry, to tell him, "You know that new sound you're looking for? Well, listen to this!"

445 - Here is "Doc's" super-tricked-out DeLorean as it starts gaining speed so Marty can return to the year 1985. About to expire, the race against time keeps everyone in suspense.

In 1955, Marty very inconveniently risks everything by making Lorraine, that is, the girl destined to be his future mother, fall in love with him. Before an astonished audience, he even begins playing instruments that hadn't yet been invented.

447 - In the past, Marty meets his future father and mother, George and Lorraine (photo above). And, he has to do it with the town bully, the rough and tough Biff (photo below, behind the steering wheel). But, he succeeds in arranging things in such a way that George, who does not have a reputation for bravery fights with Biff and wins, making himself look better in the eyes of Lorraine.

[USA] Genre: **ACTION / DRAMA**

🏆 TOP GUN

Director: TONY SCOTT

Cast: TOM CRUISE / KELLY MCGILLIS / VAL KILMER / ANTHONY EDWARDS

Time and distance give us greater objectivity in considering the climate and issues of an era and while we can say a great deal and debate the political and ideological significance of *Rambo*, instead *Top Gun* – made a short time later at the height of the Reagan years – is simply a militaristic and reactionary rodomontade with a superman complex. It was an enormous hit with the general public, turning Tom Cruise's Ray-Bans, leather jacket and motorcycle into icons and transforming him into a superstar. But audiences can be wrong.

Lt Pete "Maverick" Mitchell (Cruise) and LTJG Nick "Goose" Bradshaw are daring and experienced young fighter pilots with the U.S. Navy aboard the aircraft carrier USS *Enterprise*. After intercepting two Soviet MiGs (the bad guys, naturally) that have gone off course, as a reward the two pilots are sent to TOPGUN, the United States Navy Fighter Weapons School.

The training staff includes a very attractive astrophysicist codenamed Charlie who dons very civilian garb: tight skirts, stiletto heels and provocative outfits. When Charlie and Maverick discuss MiGs, the sparks fly between the two.

1. 2. 3. 4. Kelly McGillis and Tom Cruise. He is lieutenant pilot, Maverick, and as a reward for his fearless exploits, is sent to Top Gun school for the best in pilot training. She is astrophysicist, Charlie, who would be his instructor. You don't have to be a genius to predict that things will spark between them.
While Tom Cruise would use the film as a stepping-stone to a powerful career, McGillis would reveal herself to be a short-lived star and almost completely end her acting career shortly thereafter.

Between sexual attraction, the mystery surrounding the death of Maverick's father in Vietnam, the rivalry with the school ace "Iceman" (Val Kilmer) – an apt nickname – Maverick becomes increasingly daring as he maneuvers the F-14 Tomcats, ultimately causing the death of his companion and best friend, Goose. Maverick is devastated. Nevertheless, he manages to graduate from TOPGUN with full honors. He is then sent on a secret and highly dangerous emergency mission with his companion and rival Iceman against the dreaded Soviets, and is subsequently glorified as a dauntless hero and flying ace.

A propaganda carnival to bolster military recruitment (after its release there was an upsurge to levels that had not been seen since Pearl Harbor), the film was conceived by the producers of *Flashdance* and *Beverly Hills Cop* and entrusted to a director who an expert in glossy commercials, Tony Scott (the brother of Ridley).

Charlie was played by the actress Kelly McGillis at the height of her short career, which was concentrated entirely in the 1980s. Before *Top Gun* she was cast in the marvelous role of a woman who breaks away from the isolation of the Amish community in Peter Weir's *Witness*, alongside Harrison Ford. McGillis played in several other films, but then essentially disappeared.

Genre: DRAMA / ROMANCE

Cast: KIM BASINGER / MICKEY ROURKE

The film 9½ Weeks can probably be defined as a textbook example of how to create a paradigm and scandal out of nothing. It was a worldwide attraction that broke box-office records and gained extraordinary TV audience shares, although the television version was cut extensively.

Although the notoriety and success of Adrian Lyne's film benefited enormously from its promise of transgressive behavior and sexual perversion, 9½ Weeks can be considered a classic case of much ado about nothing. This was evident from the differences between the titillating trailer launching the film and the film itself, in which there is actually little to see. A scene mingling food (strawberries) and sex in front of a refrigerator is pawned as super-erotic, yet it pales compared to the erotic/culinary message launched 20 years earlier by the forerunner of this genre, Tom Jones.

In any event, hats off to its inventors, who made a fortune with this monument to banality. Most of them are women: Elizabeth Mc-Neil, the author of the original story (supposedly autobiographical) and the two screenwriters, Sarah Kernochan and Patricia Louisianna Knop, who flanked the only male screenwriter, Zalman King (who also produced it and, as a director, specialized in soft porn).

Elizabeth (Kim Basinger) owns an art gallery and John (Mickey Rourke) is a Wall Street broker. This very characterization clearly indicates the intent to construct a glossy image and package a concentrate of clichés revolving around Zeitgeist. In other words, it is about the hedonistic Reagan years, appearance over substance, and the superficial desire for success symbols, wealth, power and satisfaction. And, naturally, sexual satisfaction is the pièce de résistance.

▶ In the middle of the Eighties, Kim Basinger (Elizabeth) preceded Sharon Stone who would be the sex symbol of the next decade.

1986
NINE ½ WEEKS

Director: ADRIAN LYNE
Cast: KIM BASINGER / MICKEY ROURKE

▲1 ▲2

The expensively dressed yuppie with a faux scruffy look meets the beautiful gallery owner in the steamy atmosphere of New York's Chinatown. For 9½ weeks – any longer and Elizabeth would have risked her sanity – he drags her into a passionate vortex of debauchery, with sadomasochistic games of domination and submission, and cheap voyeuristic semidarkness. She finally rebels and leaves him when she meets another man with more constructive prospects. Thus, in the end, there is a moral to the story that is intended as a way to reestablish healthy values: deviation and excess are punished.

The film is famed for the backlit striptease scene in which Elizabeth, dressed in a slip, wriggles her hips to the throaty voice of Joe Cocker singing "You Can Leave Your Hat On." The scene came to be synonymous with eroticism for conventional tastes, a cult object for those willing to settle for second-rate titillation.

The elegance and sophistication of the lighting, settings and atmospheres are undeniable, but they have the clever aura of a fashion shoot or an ad. The film made Basinger, who played a Bond Girl in *Never Say Never*, a major star. Rourke, an overrated young rebel who (involuntarily) parodied James Dean in Coppola's *Rumble Fish*, continues to stay afloat.

▲ 3 ▲ 4

▼ 5

1. 2. 3. 4. 5. Mickey Rourke (John, a broker by trade) spies on her as she strips to the music of Joe Cocker. Unfortunately, striptease linked with this song have been pathetically reproduced many times and with the most awkward imitations. The two do very few other things together besides thinking about and having sex.

1987

[GERMANY / FRANCE] Genre: **DRAMA / ROMANCE**

WINGS OF DESIRE

Director: WIM WENDERS

Cast: BRUNO GANZ / SOLVEIG DOMMARTIN / OTTO SANDER / PETER FALK

Wings of Desire is the story of Damiel (Bruno Ganz) and Cassiel (Otto Sander), two angels in street clothes (although they have wings) who, from above, watch life as it unfolds in black and white. In fact, their pure spirits are not allowed to see color. They watch a myriad of isolated lives in Berlin, a city that must coexist with the Wall for only a short time longer. They observe and listen, and despite the fact that they can hear human thoughts, they are unable to help people and prevent their drama and pain.

Anguished by his impotence and his fate as a powerless witness, Damiel falls in love with Marion (Solveig Dommartin), a beautiful circus trapeze artist on the verge of failure, and out of love for her he renounces immortality. In this, he is advised and assisted by a former angel who had once taken the same step: Peter Falk playing himself, an American actor who has come to Berlin as he has been cast in a film.

Director Wim Wenders returned to his homeland to make a film after spending many years in the United States, where he made *Lightning Over Water* dedicated to the director Nicholas Ray, *Hammet*, a flop produced by Francis Ford Coppola, *The State of Things* (Leone d'Oro at the Venice Film Festival), and *Paris, Texas*, which earned him international accolades heaped and won him the Palme d'Or at the Cannes Film Festival.

454 - The angel, Damiel (Bruno Ganz), is perched on the winged statue of Victory at the top of the column by the same name, one of the symbols of the city of Berlin.

A tenuous concept and a vague subject without a true plot are the underpinnings for the symphony of a metropolis sung by a silent chorus. Only angels – and, with them, the audience – can hear the thoughts of the men and women, old people and children, of Berlin. It is a throng of solitudes pursued in streets and homes, subways and shops: an unhappy, unsatisfied humankind full of resentment and regrets. An invisible wall prevents them from communicating, expressing feelings and living a full life.

A very "poetic" pace, created by Peter Handke's script and the constant allusion to the verses of Rainer Maria Rilke, characterizes yet also detracts from this work, whose sophisticated images have unquestionably given it a place in the European cinematographic imagination of the late 20th century. At the same time, the film is influenced by its anti-narrative and destructured approach, which yields flat and repetitive results that are unable to hold the attention of more demanding viewers.

Of the film's many affections, some of the views of the city are probably the most contrived, although the film was not shot entirely on site and "place" is often evoked and reconstructed. One of the most particular is the Potsdamerplatz, which had not yet been redesigned and revitalized, and was still a broad shapeless clearing, a no-man's-land and boundary close to the Berlin Wall, which was still standing. The most striking character is the sick and elderly Homer (Curt Bois) – and his name is no accident – who wanders around those unrecognizable places and tries to revive his memories of a place that, before the war, had been full of life, the vibrant heart of a big city.

However, the symbol of the film is the gilded statue of Victory that surmounts the Victory Column, the monument that, during the second half of the 19th century, celebrated Prussian grandeur. Hitler later had it moved from its original location to the center of the Tiergarten so that it would be perfectly visible from the long and spectacular promenade opening in front of the Brandenburg Gate. At certain moments in the film the angel Damiel is perched on it (in a close-up, whereas the statue is visible only as a detail, as it is a reconstruction).

Wenders, who after this film completed his previous project for *Until the End of the World*, filmed the sequel to this film, *Faraway, So Close!*, in 1993. The 1998 American remake, *City of Angels*, is set in Los Angeles and stars Meg Ryan and Nicolas Cage.

1. 2. 3. Angels like Damiel and his friend, Cassiel, have the ability to listen to the thoughts and concerns of human beings but unfortunately without any power to intervene, do something, help them, stop them before it's too late. When he encounters the beautiful trapeze artist, Marion (Solveig Dommartin), Damiel decides to give up eternal angelhood, wanting instead to become a man and fall in love.

The Last Emperor is the true story of Puyi, the last ruler of the Chinese Empire (the adult Puyi is played by John Lone). It is the true story of a little boy taken away from his mother, forced to live in the gilded prison of the Forbidden City and crowned emperor at just 3 years of age.

The Emperor of China, the Son of Heaven and the Lord of Ten Thousand Years is honored by everyone but does not know the freedom of playing with friends or the warmth of family.

He soon understands that he is being manipulated by all those in the Forbidden City who want to maintain the status quo. "I'm not allowed to leave the Forbidden City. I want to go out ... I want to see the city of sounds," he confesses to his Scottish tutor, Reginald Johnston (Peter O' Toole).

In the Forbidden City, even a pair of eyeglasses raises a fuss. "An Emperor does not wear spectacles," comment the courtiers, afraid of any novelty, although they later change their minds when Johnston threatens to inform the press that Puyi is virtually a prisoner.

"I think the Emperor is the loneliest boy on earth," the tutor observes, and this loneliness is certainly not filled by the two wives given to the boy emperor. One serves as empress, the other as a second wife, yet Piyu would have been happy with just one. "I want a modern wife ... who speaks English and French, and who can dance the quickstep."

None of his desires are fulfilled, however, and the habit of depending on the will of others brings him to a state in which everything seems to be a blur. He does not realize that the years are passing and that the present and future of China are moving in an opposite direction with respect to life in the Forbidden City.

The Republic lives outside the walls and cannot boast thousands of years of tradition, and its population travel on bicycles and even in cars, no longer using camels and rickshaws. Long accustomed to obeying the mysterious will of those who act in the shadows, Piyu becomes a puppet in the hands of the Japanese invaders when the gates of the Forbidden City are forced open.

Piyu would never take a position of any kind, but he finally examines his life and responsibilities when he is reeducated in prison by the new Communist regime that rose to power in 1949 with Mao's revolution. Realizing his role in the events, he tells the prison director, "I was responsible for everything." And when he is freed, he spends his days working as a gardener at what had once been his palace.

At only three years old, the tiny Pu Yi is crowned emperor yet is a prisoner at the Forbidden City. It is 1909.

1987
THE LAST EMPEROR

Director: BERNARDO BERTOLUCCI

Cast: JOHN LONE / JOAN CHEN / PETER O'TOOLE / RUOCHENG YING / VICTOR WONG

458 - Apparently, the tiny emperor has all of China at his feet. In reality, he has no real power. Royal court ministers and dignitaries are actually the ones who exercise "his" power.

The film, which deftly uses flashbacks spanning the years from 1908 to 1959, ends in 1968 when, at the height of the Cultural Revolution, Puyi sees the prison director dragged off by the Red Guards as a criminal, vanquished by the folly of history and the blind fanaticism of ideology, just as Puyi himself was vanquished. *The Last Emperor* won nine Academy Awards in 1988: Best Picture, Best Director, Best Screenplay, Best Cinematography, Best Film Editing, Best Music, Best Art Direction–Set Decoration, Best Costume Design and Best Sound. It was also an enormous personal triumph for Bernardo Bertolucci, the most famous Italian director after Vittorio De Sica, Roberto Rossellini, Federico Fellini and Sergio Leone. With this masterpiece, the 46-year-old director crowned a career that began very early and had already yielded two extremely ambitious and universally acknowledged and discussed films: *Last Tango in Paris* and *1900*.

The director's great personal success contributed significantly to reviving the international image and credibility of Italian cinema, whose prestige had seriously declined in the previous decade.

Last but not least, it must also be noted that Bertolucci has always conveyed his own poetics in his cosmopolitan approach. Starting with his first success, the powerful adaptation of Alberto Moravia's novel *The Conformist*, the director has always shown great sensitivity toward honorable losers and antiheros crushed by the weight of history.

To the age of 15, the only person with whom Pu Yi has contact to the outside world is his Scottish private tutor, Reginald F. Johnston (Peter O'Toole). ▶

460 - Pu Yi grows up and pursues his education in complete isolation, insulated and ignorant of the sociopolitical spasms jolting his country.

461 - First, the 1911 revolution then the civil war when the Kuomintang opposed Mao Tse-tung communists are only distant
echoes in his cocooned life as the imprisoned de facto emperor, here busy playing with the eunuchs at court.

462 and 463 [TOP] - Pu Yi (seen here as an adult by actor, John Lone) marries twice and, despite everything, successfully embraces non-conformist behavior such as the use of eyeglasses.

463 [BOTTOM] - History violently interrupts his unfortunate life. When the Japanese invade China, he is put in charge of the puppet government created in Manchuria to the North. When at the end of the Second World War Pu Yi goes to confirm the new communist power, abandoned by his Japanese protectors, he is arrested, confined and "re-educated" for fifteen years. After his release, he would return to his kingdom but only as a gardener. Pu Yi would die in the second half of the Sixties in the midst of a cultural revolution.

[USA]   Genre: DRAMA

RAIN MAN

Director: BARRY LEVINSON
Cast: DUSTIN HOFFMAN / TOM CRUISE / VALERIA GOLINO

Charlie Babbitt (Tom Cruise) is a handsome but high-strung luxury sports car dealer and successful businessman. In the opening scenes, we see him at work, checking on the delivery of several gleaming Lamborghinis and breathlessly negotiating their price over the phone. Working with him are his young partner and Charlie's girlfriend Susanna (Valeria Golino) who, after the deal has been settled, leaves with him for a quiet weekend in Palm Springs. Charlie's dark and taciturn personality emerges when he is behind the wheel. He never speaks a word to Susanna for the entire trip and she, in turn, has long been impatient with his moods. Just as Susanna is accusing him of never thinking about her, he receives a phone call that forces them to call off their short vacation Charlie's father has passed away and he must go to the funeral. He reacts coldly to the news, explaining to Susanna that he and his father have not spoken to each other for years.

As soon as they get to his father's luxurious house, the first thing Charlie shows Susanna is a 1949 Buick Roadmaster convertible, the car that caused the rift between father and son so many years ago. Mr. Babbitt never allowed him to drive it and when Charlie borrowed it one day without asking and was stopped by the police, his father left him in jail for two days. After that, Charlie moved out and never spoke to his father again. His mother died when he was still a child and the only memory that Charlie can describe to Susanna involves the "Rain Man," whom he describes as an imaginary childhood friend. When Charlie meets his father's lawyer the next day, he is astonished to learn that the elder Babbitt's entire estate of $3 million will go to an anonymous beneficiary. Charlie has inherited only the Buick and some prize rosebushes. Determined to discover the truth, Charlie and Susanna climb into the shiny convertible and drive to an institution, where they discover his father's secret: Raymond (Dustin Hoffman), the beneficiary of the entire estate. He is the big brother Charlie does not remember, because he was too young when Raymond was brought to the institution. Raymond is an autistic savant with an exceptional memory and mathematical ability, but he is also a man who is completely defenseless and protects himself through series of rituals.

Furious, Charlie tricks him into coming with him so that he can then negotiate to receive half of his inheritance. Susanna is completely against the idea and leaves them alone in a motel, the first in a series during the brothers' long car trip from Cincinnati to Los Angeles. Their journey marks the beginning of a new relationship.

The trip takes approximately a week because Raymond not only refuses to take a plane, having an attack of hysteria at the airport, but he also forces Charlie to get off the main highway and take secondary roads.

Dustin Hoffman and Tom Cruise. Charles Bebbit discovers only after the death of his father with whom he had a very contentious relationship that the "rainman" who he'd put aside as only a vague and false childhood memory actually existed and in reality was his brother, Raymond, affected by autism and endowed with an exceptional memory.

◀ 1

◀ 2

◀ 3

1. 2. 3. Their long journey together across the U.S., based on Charles' absolutely instrumental premise of only wanting to use Raymond to recover the inheritance his father had denied him, becomes instead an opportunity to get to know each other. Charles' upcoming engagement to Susanna (Valeria Golino) would have an important role in this turn of events.

4. Despite Charles' mature decision to live with his brother and take care of him, the brothers would be forced to separate in the end. But when saying goodbye to Charles, Raymond would for the first time establish physical contact on his own by pressing his forehead against his brother's.

In both cases, the reason for his fear lies in accident statistics, which Raymond knows by heart. On state roads, at highway restaurants and in motels, Charlie gradually gets to know his brother. He discovers that when Raymond is nervous, he constantly repeats Abbott and Costello's "Who's on first" sketch, without understanding its humor because he has only read it but never actually seen it. He sees him crazed with fear when he turns on the hot water for a bath and understands that Ray is actually the Rain Man, who was sent to an institution so that he could not hurt his little brother after an episode in which Raymond risked scalding Charlie in the bathtub. As the journey continues, Charlie's initial objective – getting his hands on the inheritance – is replaced by his plan to ask that he be named Ray's guardian. For the first time in his life, Charlie establishes a family relationship.

In the meantime, Charlie's company has gone bankrupt and he has a debt of $80,000, which he plans to settle by exploiting Ray's extraordinary memory to gamble at Las Vegas. It is at the casino that Susanna rejoins the Babbitt Brothers, and it is here that Ray dances for the first time and, in an elevator, Susanna gives him his first kiss.

When they get to Los Angeles, during a meeting to settle his guardianship, the lawyer demonstrates that Raymond is incapable of making decisions. Charlie sadly understands that he must inevitably be separated from his brother, who finally accepts physical contact with Charlie for the first time, resting his head against his brother's when they say goodbye to each other.

Rain Man won the Golden Bear at the Berlin Film Festival and three Academy Awards: Best Picture, Best Director (Barry Levinson) and Best Actor (Dustin Hoffman).

1990

NIKITA

Director: LUC BESSON
Cast: ANNE PARILLAUD / MARC DURET / JEAN-HUGUE ANGLADE / TCHÉKY KARYO

Nikita (Anne Parillaud) is nearly 20 years old and is a juvenile delinquent. She is as ferocious as an animal born in captivity and has never known anything but solitude, violence and despair. Empty inside, she is about to explode.

Nighttime. Like a pack of ravenous beasts, she and three other outcasts wander the streets of Paris looking for drugs. They enter pharmacy and start to tear the place apart, searching for narcotics. All hell breaks loose when the police arrive and a massacre ensues. The rest of the gang is killed and Nikita is the only one who survives. Her cold eyes, lost in the darkness of withdrawal, make her look like a defenseless little girl. A policeman goes to her to help her up, but she shoots him in the neck.

Nikita is given a life sentence and is sent to prison, but something unexpected happens to her. Instead of being locked up in a cell, she is given a fatal injection. She loses consciousness, but instead of dying she wakes up in an all-white room. She thinks she must be in heaven, but she is actually in a place worse than hell.

A man dressed in black enters with a folder in his hand. He is Bob (Tchéky Karyo), a secret agent. The French government has a killer-reeducation program to recover the most ruthless elements from the dregs of society and turn them into perfect war machines. Bob explains to her that she is "officially" dead, but that the government wants to offer her another chance and a new life: an opportunity she cannot refuse.

Over the course of three years, in the basement of the Paris Prefecture a staff of secret agents trains Nikita to become a killer. The girl quickly learns to how to handle weapons and become proficient in the martial arts, but she finds it far harder to look like a woman. Bob treats her with paternal affection. His teachings are the first real education the girl has ever received and they fill the great emptiness she has long felt inside. At the end of the three years, she is ready to return to the real world.

For her 23rd birthday, Bob takes her to dinner at Le Train Bleu, the restaurant at the Gare de Lyon train station. She is very excited and finally feels alive, but Bob quickly douses any hope. They are there because she must kill the man eating at the table next to theirs. Bob gives Nikita her birthday present: a gun. And then he leaves her to her destiny.

Nikita miraculously succeeds in pulling off this difficult mission, proving to Bob and the government that she is truly ready to begin the work for which she was trained. She is given a fake identity and a codename: Joséphine.

In the real world, Nikita has an enormous need for normality. She goes shopping at the supermarket and invites out to dinner the first man who talks to her: the friendly cashier. Marco, attracted by the girl's candor, accepts the invitation, sensing that Nikita needs affection. He finds it touching that she refuses to answer any questions about her past. The two fall in love and move in together in the apartment that Nikita has just rented.

The restaurant massacre. Nikita's baptism by fire (Anne Parillaud) after a long training period, demonstrated that she's the perfect killing machine.

Time goes by and, inevitably, the first phone call arrives for Joséphine. Overwrought, Nikita listens to the instructions and carries them out. The first orders involve innocuous missions and the girl initially feels reassured. But soon she will be forced to kill more and more violently. As result, her happiness is constantly broken up by moments of enormous tension. Minor disagreements crop up between Nikita and her boyfriend, but Marco never stops showering her with patient and understanding love. The unstable balance of her double life is tipped when one of her missions goes wrong and she is forced to flee. She returns to Marco to try to explain to him that she needs to leave immediately, but at that point he has already figured everything out. Heartbroken, he says goodbye to her and Nikita disappears forever.

Director Luc Besson, who was just 31 when he made this film in 1990, had already gained enormous acclaim with *Subway* and *Le grand bleu*. Besson marked a turning point in French cinema in the last two decades of the 20th century, adopting daring and aggressive aesthetics that were enormously popular with audiences. His subsequent films, *Léon* and *The Fifth Element*, would be equally successful. The film inspired a number of imitations (*Codename: Nina* with Bridget Fonda), a television series and a videogame (Resident Evil) with a character resembling Nikita.

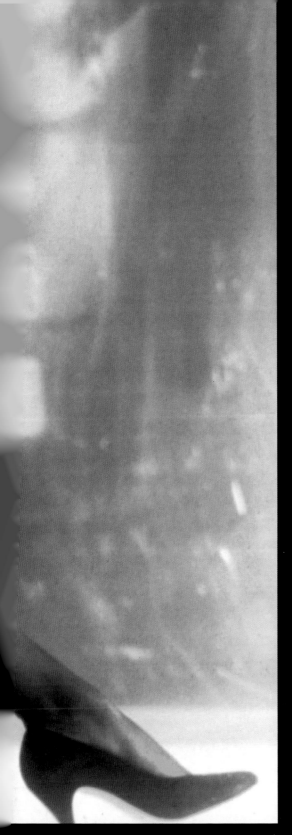

1▲   ▲2
        ▲3

1. 2. 3. Nikita was picked up by the police when she was a 20-year-old druggie and desperate, ready for anything. Arrested and incarcerated, they recruit her for a special secret service training program. Her former identity declared void, Nikita becomes another person and a ruthless killer. Naturally, not everything functions as it should. Nikita experiences feelings and love for the first time, and learns for herself the irreconcilability of the two.

Genre: ROMANTIC COMEDY

PRETTY WOMAN

Director: GARRY MARSHALL

▼ 1

Vivian (Julia Roberts) is a Hollywood prostitute. Edward (Richard Gere) is an unscrupulous tycoon, a vulture who buys failing companies, breaks them up and then resells them for an enormous profit. They meet and he asks her to spend a week with him, for a sum of money that she can't possibly refuse.

Naturally, there are no feelings on his part at first, but rather the cynicism of a man who is used to getting what he wants and then throwing it away when he's done with it. Despite the fact that life should also have made her a cynic, Vivian has an air of ingenuousness, simplicity and freshness, qualities that she has managed to maintain – coupled with an irresistible smile.

Vivian's entry into the great world of luxury (lavish hotels), refined pleasures and culture (he takes her to the opera) is a whirlwind of emotions in which her "training" for the good life in high society is punctuated by thousands of conflicting thoughts. Edward lives well and knows how to treat her like a lady, but he is also capable of making her feel inadequate and reminding her of what she is: a mercenary. Vivian alternates natural elegance with inferiority complexes. One of the keystones of this typical example of the romantic comedy genre (a lackluster heir of the "Lubitsch touch," which Garry Marshall's blockbuster unfortunately lacks) is the delightful minor figure of the discreet and professional concierge who openly sides with the girl, affectionately supporting all her qualities and merits.

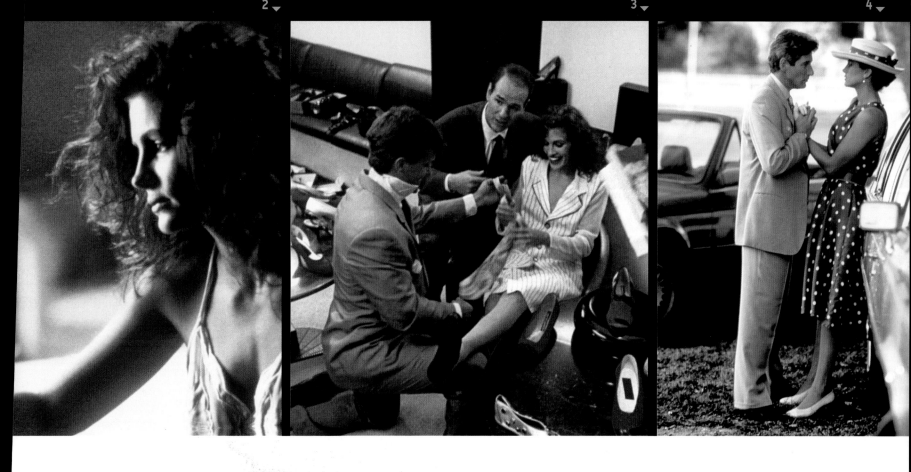

Although the two say goodbye to each other to return to the status quo, Vivian ultimately finds her way into Edward's cold heart – to the notes of Roy Orbison's song "Pretty Woman." With a classic happy ending that could not have had a more fairytale or indulgent air to it, the two get married and live happily ever after.

The revisitation – a pompous euphemism for "copy, blend and paste" – of two myths, Cinderella and Pygmalion, *Pretty Woman* was one of the biggest international box-office hits of all time. It is hard not to be won over by the cloying but irresistible power of the most obvious of fairytales.

The first draft of the script supposedly called for a sad ending, with Vivian back on the street, but this would have been ludicrous considering the promising air of the opening of the film. Several actresses were considered for the role of Vivian, including the Italian Valeria Golino. The role launched the 23-year-old Julia Roberts to superstardom. After a decline that followed his hits of the early 1980s (*American Gigolo, An Officer and a Gentleman*), Richard Gere's career has taken off again.

Genre: COMEDY / FANTASY

Edward Scissorhands is the film that, in 1990, marked the affirmation and consecration of one of the most extraordinary visual talents of contemporary American cinema. It is the film through which Tim Burton – who was just over 30 years old at the time – finally succeeded in fully expressing his highly original sensitivity. Indeed, its very originality was the reason for the director's struggle to gain recognition and be allowed to express himself. Nevertheless, we must also acknowledge that, as influential as the Hollywood system may be on an industrial level, it is equally capable of discovering artistic talents and pulling the most surprising innovations from its hat.

Burton began his career as a Disney animator, but his concept of animated drawing and his idea of a dark fairytale without a happy ending were understandably difficult to accept. A fan of comics and, above all, horror films – his childhood idol was actor Vincent Price, to whom he dedicated his first short film and whom he later cast in *Edward Scissorhands* – Burton made his directorial breakthrough with *Batman* (1989), which has been credited for Burton's highly convincing slant on the main character.

The story and character that Burton invented for *Edward Scissorhands* is a surprising impasto, an intensely personal reinterpretation of various sources of inspiration: *Frankenstein* and *Beauty and the Beast*, but also *Pinocchio*.

On the outskirts of a town distinguished by its immaculate order (exterior) and brilliant, sunny pastel colors (which seem to evoke a setting from the Fifties or Sixties, although many other signals allude to much more recent times), there is an old and sinister-looking mansion that creates a sharp contrast with these surroundings. The owner of the mansion is an inventor with a grim and disquieting air but a heart of gold (Vincent Price) who has created an artificial child he has named Edward (Johnny Depp). The "father" is busy teaching Edward good manners, but dies suddenly before he has the chance to give the machine-boy a pair of hands. Edward thus has enormous and threatening-looking scissors with which – left alone in the secluded mansion – he clumsily tries to survive, often cutting himself.

1990
EDWARD
SCISSORHANDS

Director: TIM BURTON

Cast: JOHNNY DEPP / VINCENT PRICE / WINONA RYDER / DIANNE WIEST / ALAN ARKIN

▶ Johnny Depp is the unhappy, solitary, and defenseless Edward, a manmade boy like Pinocchio yet also somewhat like Frankenstein.

476 - With such good intentions, Edward makes his bizarre scissorhands available to his welcoming friends, including the family of kind cosmetics representative, Peg, by clipping dogs, clipping and shaping hedges.

477 - His eccentric creator and adopted father (Vincent Price) dies without first providing him with a pair of normal hands.

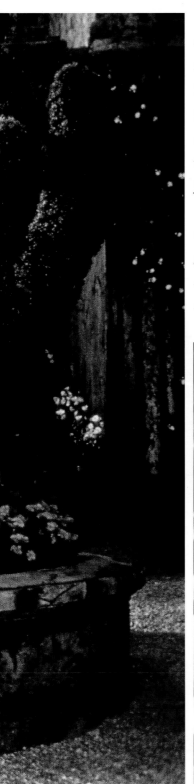

Kindhearted Peg, an Avon Lady, visits the mansion, hoping to sell her products, but finds a frightened Edward, his face covered with scars. The kindly woman selflessly adopts Edward as her son and brings him home, where her husband (the outstanding Alan Arkin), her young son and her teenage daughter Kim (Winona Ryder) are reluctant to accept him but ultimately come to love him. The small community is initially fascinated by Edward and everyone wants him to come help trim their hedges, clip their dogs and create coiffures that look like extravagant sculptures. When the novelty wears off, however, the neighbors begin to ostracize him precisely because of his diversity but, above all, because of his love – initially rejected but then reciprocated – for Kim and his eccentrically clumsy courtship of the girl, which provokes the aggressive and treacherous jealousy of her brawny and obtuse boyfriend Jim.

When the entire town – with the exception of his adoptive family – turns its back on him, Edward hides out in the old mansion. However, he is unable to avoid a showdown with his rival for Kim's love, whom he stabs with his deadly knives in legitimate self-defense. Kim comes to the mansion and, in order to save him from the blind rage of the crowd, she is forced to abandon him, telling everyone that Edward also died in the duel. Indeed, the entire film is the story that Kim, an old woman at this point, recounts to her granddaughter.

This apologue marks the beginning of the extremely close collaboration – and profound friendship – between Burton and Depp, which would continue with *Ed Wood, Sleepy Hollow, Charlie and the Chocolate Factory, Corpse Bride* and *Sweeney Todd: The Demon Barber of Fleet Street*. Tellingly, Depp is considered Burton's alter ego.

1991

[CHINA / HONG KONG / TAIWAN] Genre: DRAMA Director: ZHANG YIMOU

RAISE THE RED LANTERN

Cast: GONG LI / JINGWU MA / JIN SHUYUAN

"I will be a concubine. This is the fate of every woman." With this statement, Songlian, a university student facing financial difficulties after her father's death, agrees to become the fourth wife of Chen, a wealthy man in northern China in the 1920s.

She immediately understands the privileges reserved for Chen's four wives, starting with the profound pleasure of foot massages reserved for the wife with whom Chen will spend the night. She also learns that red lanterns are lit only at the house in which Chen will spend the night.

However, Songlian grasps the other women's hostility from the very outset, as her wedding night is disturbed by the requests of Chen's third wife.

The First Mistress, Yuru, is elderly and wary; the second, Zhiuyun, is smiling but not trustworthy; Meishan, an ex-singer, is the only one who has managed to give Chen a son.

Adding to this climate of mystery and constant hostility is Yan'er, Songlian's personal maid, who does little to conceal her resentment toward her mistress, as she too is having an affair with Chen.

When she enters her maid's room, Songlian discovers proof of the woman's resentment: stolen red lanterns and a doll with Songlian's name written on it, pierced by dozens of pins. The maid confesses to her that this witchcraft was staged with the help of the Third Mistress.

Songlian starts to react instinctively and while she is cutting the hair of the Third Mistress she cuts part of her ear. In order to gain power, she pretends to be pregnant but is soon discovered.

To get revenge against Yan'er, the first to realize that Songlian's pregnancy was fake, the girl reveals her maid's wrongdoings and shows everyone the lanterns the woman stole. As punishment, Yan'er is forced to kneel in the snow for hours and later dies of pneumonia.

Songlian starts to drink out of guilt and one day, while she is drunk, she reveals the secret she has learned about the Third Mistress: Meishan is having an affair with the house physician. As a result, the Third Mistress is punished and killed.

Songlian discovers Meishan's body in the death room, an area in which other women who had broken the rules were killed. Her guilt drives her to insanity. She lights the lanterns in the third house and, with a record player, broadcasts Meishan's voice like that of a ghost.

The red lanterns are lit again with great pomp to celebrate a wedding, as Chen has taken his fifth wife.

By now, however, the fourth mistress wanders through the house, frightened and desperate. The bride is told, "She's our Fourth Mistress, but she has gone out of her mind."

Raise the Red Lanterns is an extraordinary discourse on the immutable and cynical power of tradition, the laws of male power and the internal relations of a world of women forced into submission. Yet everything is unspoken, expressed and recounted through the slow and hieratic repetition of rituals and gestures, and through the power of images, light and the color (red).

The film, which won the Silver Lion at the 1991 Venice Film Festival, faced enormous obstacles in its country of origin, the People's Republic of China, where it was censored. In addition to revealing to international audiences the beauty and talent of Gong Li, who went on to become China's top movie star, *Raise the Red Lanterns* was also the first major success of director Zhang Yimou (40 years old at the time), who – with Chen Kaige – was a leading figure in the so-called Fifth Generation. This was the group whose impressive sequence of awards at the most important international festivals demonstrated that the Chinese movement was the new frontier in the renewal of cinema.

1. 2. 3. 4. Orphan student forced to earn her living in China of the Twenties, Songlian (Gong Li) becomes the fourth wife of the rich Chen. She would get used to the benefits of her social status but would also understand its base, perverted, ruthless, and painful implications. Red lanterns light up in front of the room of the wife Chen selects for the night. This film significantly launched the new Chinese cinema into the limelight of large international film festivals.

Jonathan Demme's *The Silence of the Lambs* is one of the few films that won Academy Awards in all the main categories: Best Picture, Best Director, Best Actor and Actress, and Best Screenplay. The chronology of the films (this is not the only film nor the first) and the novels that inspired the films, written by Thomas Harris, who invented the character of Hannibal Lecter, a psychiatrist and cannibalistic serial killer, is extremely complicated. *The Silence of the Lambs* was published in 1988, whereas Demme's film was made in 1991. It was the second book after *Red Dragon*, also featuring the character of Hannibal Lecter. Michael Mann's *Manhunter* (1986) was made before *The Silence of the Lambs*, which was followed by Ridley Scott's *Hannibal, Red Dragon* – a remake of *Manhunter* – and *Hannibal Lecter*. Nevertheless, the chronological order of the narrated events is completely different with respect to their development in the novels and the five films, of which Demme's is fourth.

The extremely dangerous criminal Hannibal Lecter, who also happens to be a man of extraordinary sensitivity, culture and intelligence, has spent the past eight years in an asylum for the criminally insane headed by Dr. Chilton. The deeds of a new serial killer, who flays his female victims, leads FBI Director Jack Crawford to seek the help of Hannibal Lecter. In order to obtain it, he decides to appoint a young and brilliant recruit, Clarice Starling, who is still in training, to go talk to him.

Lecter knows a great deal about Buffalo Bill, the name the murderer uses. But he also establishes a very direct and demanding relationship with Clarice, exhibiting a magnetic and authoritarian manner that waylays the girl. Although his responses are laconic, cryptic and seemingly elusive, he expects Starling to be completely sincere with him and discuss her life with him. In short, he is the one who asks the questions and she is the one who is expected to answer. Under pressure and profoundly troubled by Lecter's personality but determined to get to the bottom of everything, Clarice discusses her memories and deepest feelings with him. She reveals – and this is the source of the title – her childhood trauma, telling Lecter about the farm where she lived, the lambs that were slaughtered and their heart-wrenching cries that, even today, continue to persecute her. At the same time Clarice, who in return for Lecter's collaboration promises him better prison conditions (he would like a window so that he have natural light, rather than drawing from memory), are circumvented.

1991

THE SILENCE OF THE LAMBS

Director: JONATHAN DEMME

Cast: ANTHONY HOPKINS / JODIE FOSTER / SCOTT GLENN / TED LEVINE

Anthony Hopkins wears his mask as Dr. Hannibal the Cannibal Lecter.

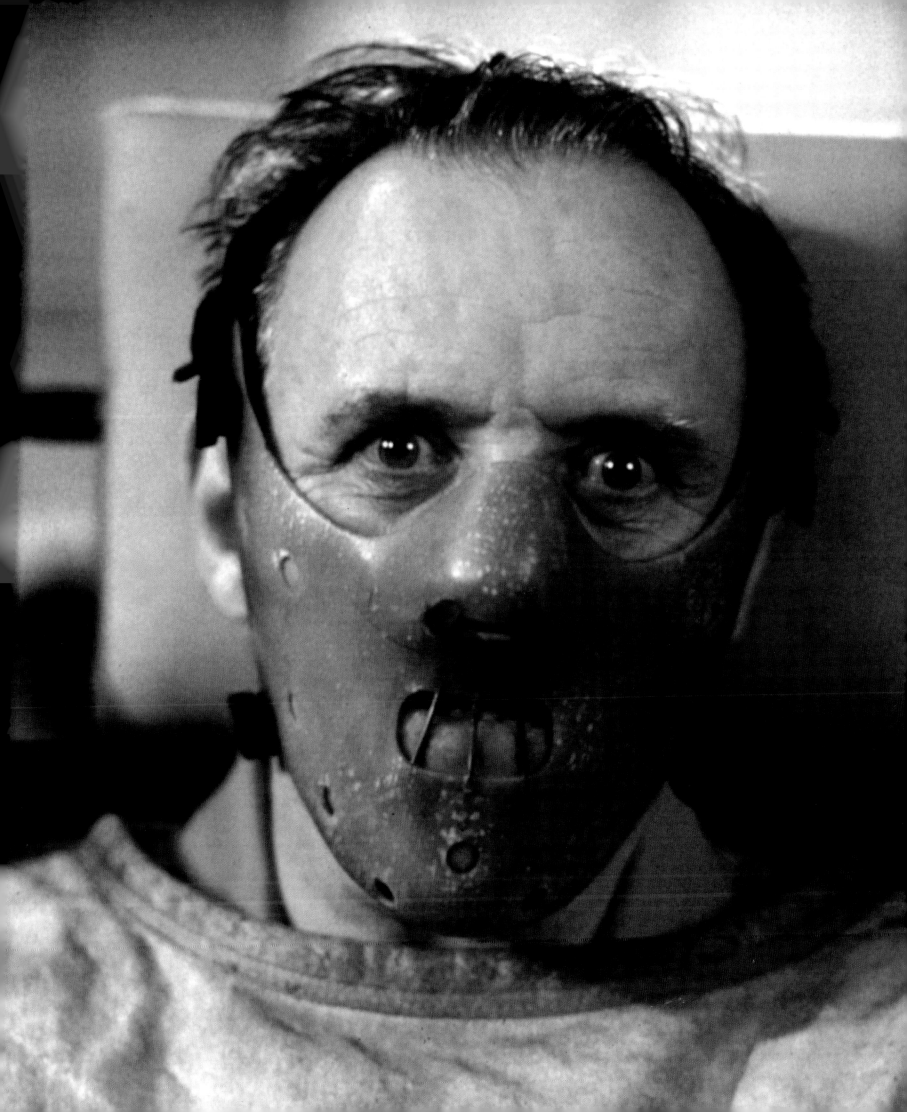

483 - Based on the novels by Thomas Harris inspiring this and other films, a real serial killer was prosecuted for similar types of murders he committed in the 1940s and 1950s. Young female FBI recruit, Clarice Starling (Jodie Foster) takes on the serial killer investigation and the Cannibal establishes a complex, ingratiating, and magnetic relationship with her. Although Dr. Lecter succeeds in making a fool of her even under maximum-security surveillance, he puts the agent in the right state of mind for catching another psychopathic serial killer. Dr. Lecter's character is probably also based on another real murderer who practiced his "art" in the Twenties and Thirties.

In agreement with the senator whose daughter has just been kidnapped and is the new victim of Buffalo Bill, the hated and arrogant Chilton transfers Lecter to another prison, but the prisoner takes advantage of low security measures to murder policemen and escape. In the meantime, Clarice manages to make the most of what Lecter has helped her understand. During her promotion ceremony, she is called to the phone: Lecter is on the other end, announcing that he is "having an old friend for dinner": Chilton.

The soul of the film, whose complex thriller structure has difficulties, gaps and unclear connections that are concealed by the power of the director and the acting, lies in the bond established in the two leading characters. The knowledge and experience of pain forms a bond between them that culminates in mutual respect. Anthony Hopkins' histrionic display is eclipsed by the combination of fragility and energy that Jodie Foster brings to her character.

1991

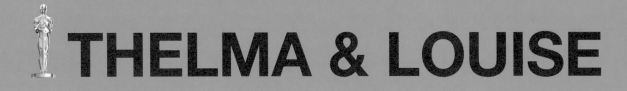

THELMA & LOUISE

Director: RIDLEY SCOTT

Cast: GEENA DAVIS / SUSAN SARANDON

HARVEY KEITEL / MICHAEL MADSEN / BRAD PITT

It is fitting that *Thelma & Louise* should be included in this book, as it is a legendary and epochal film. This paradigmatic work is a hymn to feminism that takes time-tested approaches: escape and adventure on the road. Its contents, new yet not innovative, reflect perfectly recognizable narrative standards.

The setting is a dismal town in Arkansas. Two friends, Thelma and Louise (Geena Davis and Susan Sarandon), decide to enjoy a girls' weekend out of town. Louise, who works as a waitress, is dating Jimmy (Michael Madsen) but is restless because she wants more out of life. Thelma, who is seemingly sweeter and more malleable, is a housewife whose husband neglects her, lies to her and does not appreciate her.

For her, their departure in Louise's fantastic Ford Thunderbird convertible is a true escape, because Thelma has not worked up the courage to tell him that she is leaving for the weekend, an innocent trip for which she should not need to ask permission in the first place. Euphoric and ingenuous, she packs all sorts of things in the car: clothing of all kinds, fishing rods and – almost distractedly – a gun.

Soon after leaving town, they stop at a bar for a drink. It is the kind of dive seen in countless American road movies. They all look alike: smoky and dark, packed with drunken men ready for a brawl and waiting to corner the first woman who comes along. Music is playing and, downing drink after drink, the two women start to dance. Thelma lets herself go and accepts the crude courtship of a local boor, Harlan. When she starts to feel dizzy, he takes her outside – it is dark by this time – and tries to rape her in the parking lot. However, Louise arrives, gun in hand, and shoots him. At this point, their journey is transformed from a carefree weekend to a getaway. It is a journey fraught with both fear and excitement for Louise, who had a bad experience in Texas years before but refuses to talk about it, and for Thelma, who proves to be far readier for adventure than she initially seemed. Convinced that the police would never believe them – after all, everyone at the bar saw Thelma laughing and enjoying herself with Harlan and no one witnessed him harassing her – the two women decide to escape to Mexico. But before they can get there, many of other things are destined to happen.

Jimmy comes to meet them to bring Louise her life savings, they meet a handsome drifter (Brad Pitt) who, after spending the night with Thelma, steals all their money. Thelma robs a store, unaware of the fact that it has a security camera. The two immobilize a highway patrolman and blow up the tanker driven by an obscene trucker. Everything alternates between hilarity and desperation. In the meantime, however, Hal (Harvey Keitel), the detective who is on their trail and is sincerely sympathetic toward them, is gradually closing in. Hal manages to get information from Jimmy when the man gets home, from Thelma's husband, whose phone has been tapped, and from the vagabond thief, who has been arrested. The symbolic showdown takes place against a backdrop that fully represents America as the land of hope and freedom. Thelma and Louise stop their car at the edge of the canyon, while all escape routes have been closed off by dozens of police cars and hundreds of agents with their guns aimed at the two women. They refuse to listen to Hal's plea that they turn themselves in, preferring to hit the accelerator and go over the side of the cliff.

In classic Hollywood style, several high-profile names were considered for the leading roles, from Meryl Streep and Goldie Hawn to Michelle Pfeiffer and Jodie Foster. The sure hand of the wizard of entertainment, Ridley Scott, who had already made *Alien* and *Blade Runner*, is evident in this feminist update of the rebel genre of the Sixties and Seventies, which would become a prototype for later variations on this theme. It won only one Academy award in 1992, for Best Original Screenplay.

Rather than
be captured and
spend the rest of
their lives in jail,
they make a final
choice ...

1. 2. 3. Without much thought, Thelma has also put a pistol in her purse. It is this pistol that starts all the trouble, including an encounter with the unpredictable sweet-talking guy played by Brad Pitt and concluding at the edge of a cliff with the state police force lined up against the two women. Thelma and Louise don't give up. They prefer to end their adventure with a permanent escape, with a radical choice of freedom by driving over the cliff.

[USA / FRANCE] Genre: **THRILLER / DRAMA**

BASIC INSTINCT

Director: PAUL VERHOEVEN

Cast: SHARON STONE / MICHAEL DOUGLAS / GEORGE DZUNDZA / JEANNE TRIPPLEHORN

This mediocre film from the early 1990s is distinguished by its inordinately contorted plot and intentions. A sly attempt to give an erotic twist to the tradition of thrillers and noir movies, it launched Sharon Stone as the incarnation of the new *femme fatale* and the new dark lady. In reality, above all it involved marketing, advertising and image but very little substance, with the exception of the inordinately famous scene in which, during a police interrogation, Stone's character crosses and uncrosses her legs to reveal that she is not wearing any underwear.

Stone plays Catherine Tramell, a psychologist and mystery writer. He is Nick Curran (Michael Douglas), nicknamed "Shooter," the detective who has been assigned to the investigation and is enchanted by Tramell. In between, there is a string of murders – Catherine's rock-star lover, Nick's boss, the female lover of openly bisexual Catherine, Nick's colleague and Beth, a psychoanalyst and Nick's ex-girlfriend (Jean Tripplehorn) – and venomous suspicions.

489 - Designated victim of this later reincarnation of the Forties film noir femme fatale is Detective Nick Curran, interpreted by Michael Douglas.

The top suspect is none other than Tramell herself, whose novels describe crimes of passion – Eros and Thanatos – committed at the end of steamy sex using the same weapon, an ice pick, that killed the rock star in the opening scenes of the film. Nick, however, who has fallen under her spell and wants to take her to bed, instead accuses Beth.

The finale is open-ended and leaves numerous doubts, paving the way for a sequel that would not arrive until 14 years later because Stone, who became a superstar in the meantime, negotiated at length to gain control over the film.

Sharon Stone's career is fascinating. Despite the fact that she never showed any enormous acting talent (possibly with the exception of Martin Scorsese's *Casino*) and became famous rather late (she was 34 when she was cast in *Basic Instinct*), she has successfully emerged as a latter-day diva. Her campaigns to raise awareness on serious social problems, to which she has generously contributed, her personality and unquestionable beauty, repeatedly in the public eye not only in public settings but also through numerous advertising campaigns in which she has been a testimonial, her discreet but open discussion about some of the more dramatic aspects of her personal life – from her illness to her adopted children – and her undeniable charisma have also contributed enormously to her diva status.

Writer Joe Eszterhas received the highest sum ever paid for a Hollywood screenplay.

1992

BATMAN RETURNS

Director: TIM BURTON

Cast: MICHAEL KEATON / DANNY DE VITO / MICHELLE PFEIFFER / CHRISTOPHER WALKEN

There is an initial consideration to make regarding Tim Burton's interpretations of Batman (*Batman*, 1989, and *Batman Returns*, 1992). In addition to being well made, they are fundamental (and rare) examples of the successful transfer of a subject from comics to cinema. In fact, Burton succeeded where many others failed, transforming a comic-book legend into an outstanding version for the big screen. The difference with respect to those who made the same attempt and the handful who succeeded to a certain extent (Richard Donner's *Superman*, 1978, and Sam Raimi's *Spiderman*, 2002) is Tim Burton himself. *Batman* was the director's third feature film, released a year before his blockbuster *Edward Scissorhands*, and it displays the visual power that would make him famous. His imaginative directing beautifully compensates for the weak script. Burton creates a darkly memorable Gotham City, and above all, he brings out all the freshness and brilliance of the characters. Michael Keaton may not be the best actor in history, but he is unquestionably the best Batman/Bruce Wayne cinema has ever seen. He is a man with physical weaknesses, capable of affection and with a sense of humor that none of the other actors were able to convey, not even George Clooney in *Batman & Robin* (1997). Furthermore, Batman is not the all-powerful leading player, and in the two films he must deal with The Joker (an extraordinary Jack Nicholson), Penguin (Danny De Vito) and Catwoman (Michelle Pfeiffer), cruel enemies with intriguing multifaceted personalities. Everything is set in an ambiguous atmosphere that draws the hero himself into the rich theme of diversity explored extensively by Burton. Apart from a few minor elements, the plots of the two films are not closely connected, thus making them viewable as separate films. In the first film Batman must face the mad Joker/Jack Napier, who was disfigured by acid, leaving him with permanent and gruesome grin. This eclectic and ruthless character has taken control of organized crime in Gotham City after killing the mobster Carl Grissom. The criminal initially puts the entire city in danger by contaminating cosmetics thanks to his control over Axis Chemicals, but Batman thwarts his plans. Consequently, The Joker decides to frame him, gaining the population's approval by tossing $20 million to the crowds.

The plot flags somewhat, but is bolstered by the romance between Bruce Wayne and photojournalist Vicki Vale (Kim Basinger) – in whom The Joker is also interested – and by the hero's realization that his enemy is none other than the man who had killed his parents years earlier. Wayne recognizes him when he hears the words that the criminal recites for every murder: "Ever dance with the devil in the pale moonlight?" A battle at the top of the old cathedral of Gotham City, involving Batman, The Joker and Vicki, ends with the murderer's death when Batman throws him over the edge. The end titles are anticipated by the luminous beam of the Bat-Signal projected against the night sky. *Batman* was awarded an Oscar for Best Art Direction-Set Direction in 1990. The sequel, *Batman Returns*, is more varied and has a broader array of characters. The key figure is Max Shreck (Christopher Walken), who is probably the least "celebrated" but also the most evil and best-masked character, posing as a business tycoon who perfectly fits into Gotham society. He tries to kill his secretary Selina Kyle, who miraculously survives with the help of cats and is transformed into the powerful but deranged Catwoman. He is also the one who informs the city about the existence of Penguin, who was abandoned by his parents as a child because he was deformed. Ever since then, he has lived in the sewers with penguins and the Red Triangle Circus Gang, composed of freaks who are now at his service.

1. 2. 3. Michelle Pfeiffer plays the ambiguous character of Catwoman. Selina Kyle is humble and oppressed secretary to treacherous industrialist, Max Shreck who tries to kill her. Selina escapes death with help from cats and becomes Catwoman, liberating her repressed aggression. Bruce falls in love with Selina and Catwoman allies with Batman in the battle against Shreck, yet never giving up her own freedom when she flees at the end of her adventure.

When Mayor Hill and Wayne realize that the tycoon's plans to build a power plant actually conceal his intent to steal energy from the city, Shreck exploits the Penguin for his own benefit by having the "monster" run for mayor. Ultimately, however, Penguin is painted as a public enemy.

Batman must deal with his romantic interest in Selina, the ambiguous attitude of her alter ego, Catwoman, and the shenanigans of Shreck and Penguin. He is never central to the plot, however, serving as the common thread and, ultimately, the avenger. He defeats Penguin, who at this point has lost every shred of sanity, but is unable to prevent Catwoman from carbonizing Shreck. The ruthless tycoon, who had shown love only for his son by sacrificing his life for him, dies alone, while the horrible freak is regaled by his penguin friends. The woman flees the scene and the audience sees her looking up at the Bat-Signal shining in the darkness.

Batman and *Batman Returns* were not the only Batman films and, in fact, one was made in 1966 as a spin-off of the popular TV series. The four that followed were *Batman Forever* and *Batman & Robin* (1995 and 1997, by Joel Schumacher), and *Batman Begins* and *The Dark Knight* (2005 and 2008, by Christopher Nolan).

1. Christopher Walken (at center) is the repugnant Shreck who wants to steal Gotham City's electricity and uses the Penguin by getting him elected as mayor of the city.

2. 3. Tim Burton hadn't yet created his other masterpieces when he directed his first *Batman* in 1989. With both of his *Batman* films, he created one of the most successful screen adaptations of a comic book character.

Below, Catwoman with the hideous Penguin.

Based on the book by Thomas Keneally, which is not an official biography but a work of historical fiction based on real events and people, *Schindler's List* unquestionably fulfills the mission that the Jewish-American director Steven Spielberg had set for himself. In fact, the director did not accept any money for his work. The outcome is one of the most poignant and enthralling films ever made on the Holocaust, the black hole of the 20th century and all of human history. It effectively seems to want to remind the German population – *all* Germans – of the crushing burden of responsibility and guilt that will be difficult to forgive for many years to come.

It is the story of Oskar Schindler (1908–1974). The film – through Liam Neeson's interpretation of this figure – presents him as a self-assured and maverick businessman with a flair for adventure. A brilliant and charming man who loved living in style, Schindler was known for his exceptional s*avoir faire* and diplomatic skills. In fact, one of the merits of the film is that it maintains Schindler's ambiguity until the very end.

He was a German of Moravian descent, i.e., from what was the Sudetenland before the war and then became part of Czechoslovakia, in the area that is now the Czech Republic. The area had been populated by a large German minority that was expelled en masse at the end of the war.

Schindler moved to Cracow, occupied by the Third Reich, with the intention of making easy money. With the complicity of the German authorities, whom he knew how to handle and bribe generously, he took over an old factory and managed to get Jewish labor assigned to him at no cost, thus profiting enormously.

At the same time, however, the city's large Jewish population was being deprived of all rights, enclosed in ghettos and starved, and amid inhuman abuse and massacres many Jews were transferred to concentration camps. Nevertheless, their fate as slave laborers was better than the alternative of certain death. Plying all his negotiating skills and putting his own life at stake, by greasing palms and offering persuasive gratuities Schindler managed to protect "his" Jews throughout the war. By the time the Soviet liberators arrived, he had saved between 1100 and 1300 lives, although his tombstone says 1200.

The tides turned and the impoverished entrepreneur who had gained the confidence of the Nazi Party was forced to bid his "employees" farewell and flee, but in his pocket he carried a letter from them recounting his heroic efforts. He moved to Argentina, returned to Germany in 1958, visited Israel in 1961 and was recognized as "Righteous among the Nations" in 1967. He died in his homeland in 1974, although he was later buried in Jerusalem.

1993
SCHINDLER'S LIST

Director: STEVEN SPIELBERG

Cast: LIAM NEESON / BEN KINGSLEY / RALPH FIENNES / CAROLINE GOODALL / EMBETH DAVIDTZ

▶ Liam Neeson is German industrialist and entrepreneur, Oskar Schindler (1908-1974).

When Nazi defeat was imminent, Schindler assembled all the people he'd saved to say goodbye then made his own escape since, based on Hitler's documented decree, any person officially maintaining a stance against his régime would also be subject to ethnic cleansing.

499 - Protecting hundreds of Jews and spending a lot of money to do so, Schindler accomplished his "mission" as a poor man. A statement from "his" Jewish refugees would exonerate him in the eyes of his liberators.

501 - The pervasion of evil, the cruelest oppression of the defenseless, the brutal crimes, the exaggerated and unjustified abuses of power end with murders in cold blood. Spielberg, as Polanski would later do with *The Pianist*, puts his mark on a film whose vision is not the standard reiteration of history for those too young to be familiar with it or who prefer to forget it.

Spielberg filmed the entire story in grim black-and-white. The only note of color is the red coat of a little girl we see as she attempts to escape at the beginning but is then killed. In the final scene, set in the colored world of today, we see hundreds of men and women, children and old people, from his "list" – such as the actor Ben Kingsley, who plays Itzhak Stern, Schindler's accountant and right-hand man – or their descendents as they file past Oskar's marble grave and set a stone on it.

Schindler's List won seven Oscars in 1994, including Best Picture, Best Director, Best Screenplay (by Steven Zaillian) and Best Supporting Actor, awarded to Ralph Fiennes for his role as the monstrous German officer Amon Göth.

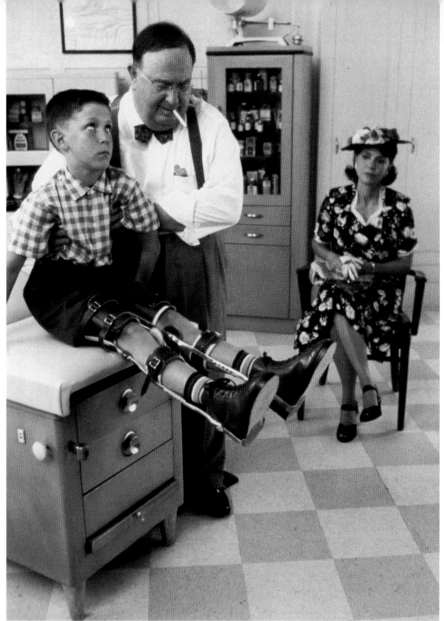

1994

[USA]   Genre: **COMEDY / DRAMA**

FORREST GUMP

Director: **ROBERT ZEMECKIS**

Cast: **TOM HANKS / SALLY FIELD / ROBIN WRIGHT PENN / GARY SINISE / MYKELTI WILLIAMSON**

Thirty years of American life are examined through the eyes of Forrest Gump (Tom Hanks), whom we meet as a boy in the 1950s. Handicapped both physically (his legs) and mentally (his IQ is below average), he is raised in segregationist Alabama by a single mother (Sally Field), who is attentive and protective but not smothering. Forrest has one true love: Jenny (Robin Wright).

The film, directed by Robert Zemeckis, tells his story as a flashback. Seated on bench at the bus stop, Forrest entertains the various people who sit down next to him. Only at the end of the film do we understand that he has gone there to wait for Jenny, who is finally ready to accept his love and marry him before she dies of a terminal illness, leaving him the little boy who - unbeknownst to him - was conceived the only time the two ever slept together.

Forrest goes through life without the aid of intelligence, and it is his kind-hearted generosity that helps him unconsciously and naïvely excel in

502 and 503 - Forrest Gump is a special child who would be a special man. He was born with physical and mental disabilities but receives encouragement from his mother (Sally Field) and friendship from Jenny (Robin Wright) as his two greatest supports. The film uses flashback to tell the whole story that Forrest, seated on a park bench looking for the courage to return to his Jenny, tells to whoever sits next to him with a contagious candor and grace that distinguish him, confirming that he is quite special.

everything. Through sheer willpower, Forrest overcomes his leg problem and learns to run like a gazelle, embarking on an extraordinary undertaking that transforms him into a national icon: he runs across America. Despite his mental handicap, he graduates with top grades thanks to the unexpected talent he demonstrates on the football field. Called to serve in Vietnam, he helps and saves many of his fellow soldiers, notably his lieutenant (Gary Sinise). After hating him for saving his life and forcing him to live as an amputee, Lt Dan finally manages to thank him many years later, because life is precious even if one no longer has legs.

He is also decisive in a diplomatic rapprochement between China and the United States, thanks to his extraordinary performance playing ping-pong as a soldier. Decorated as a hero, he unwittingly becomes a driving force in the historic peace march in front of the White House. Simply to keep a promise he had made to a fellow soldier he didn't manage to save, he becomes a fisherman and a shrimp merchant, and then a millionaire and benefactor.

A latter-day Candide, he takes part in the era's most significant events and meets its most famous figures. He shakes hands with presidents (Kennedy, Nixon and Johnson), triggers the alarm that leads to the Watergate scandal, and meets and inspires Elvis Presley, John Lennon and other stars. Rather than being a satire on the conformism and ignorance of others, he is a tribute to purity of heart, resembling the simple and ignorant gardener played by Peter Sellers in *Being There* (1979).

504 - The life of this modern Candide traverses all the significant American events from the Fifties through the Seventies. Shy, simple, reserved but also loyal and instinctively brave, Forrest becomes a protagonist or even a hero in spite of himself. He saves many of his fellow soldiers in Vietnam. Becoming a ping-pong champion, he assumes a prominent role in the process of détente between the U.S. and People's Republic of China. But, his obsessive thoughts fix on Jenny who boldly enters his experiences uninvited and he regularly pays the consequences. He would like to protect her and can learn to love her.

Forrest goes through all this without ever forgetting his Jenny, finding and losing her again and again, as her life is the antithesis of his. In fact, Forrest would willingly settle for a small and simple world, just as Jenny, whose childhood was ruined by an abusive father, is projected towards the great wide world and its experiences, even the strongest and most painful.

Nothing is omitted from this panorama of the 1960s and 1970s: the protests of the Black Panthers, drugs, and the freest or most dangerous sex. On the surface, Forrest appears to be passive, conservative and devoid of any ambition to influence history, whereas Jenny is dynamic, a person who is willing to take risks and wants to shape her own destiny.

Forrest has learned from his mother's wisdom and constantly repeats the aphorism: "Life is like a box of chocolates. You never know what you're gonna get." At the same time, however, he reacts with dignity to the insults to which life has accustomed him, telling himself, "Stupid is as stupid does." In the end, he proves to be the one who has gone through life and left a mark – unlike Jenny, who devoured, consumed and threw hers away.

The special effects, in which Forrest is inserted alongside historical figures in film clips, are exceptional. Tom Hanks won his second Oscar for this film; he had received his first one just a year earlier for *Philadelphia*. The soundtrack features epochal songs, from "Blowin' in the Wind" to "San Francisco," "Mrs. Robinson" and "California Dreamin'."

Among Forrest's many endeavors, he takes up running and crisscrosses the entire country even though as a child, he could barely walk. Another of his incredible accomplishments, it makes a sort of guru out of Forrest.

Quentin Tarantino is probably the figure who has left the deepest mark on cinema as it enters its second century. Paradoxically, while Tarantino boasts that his job at a video rental store was fundamental to his training, he is actually a sophisticated and highly cultured cineaste. The word "paradoxically" is in order here because, for inspiration, he turns to an imaginary world sketched out by films, books, music and comics that, during its development and growing popularity, was explicitly referred to as a minor consumer medium that laid no claims to being artwork. In adopting this immense wealth of knowledge and manipulating it through his films, anticipating and silencing any possible objection that his is a "recycled" creativity, Tarantino openly dignifies the concept of "stealing," of skillfully borrowing rather than just copying, and transforms it into artistic genius.

The boundless heritage that inspired Tarantino in this film and in all of his works is unknown to most people or, in any event, to those who did not grow up in certain settings. It is a type of production that often settles for circulation on narrow national, regional, generational or even ethnic markets.

We can start with *Pulp Fiction*. In the original sense of the term, it refers to the material used to produce low-quality paper. By extension, it came to be used to define a narrative genre. It was published in episodes in pulp magazines printed on cheap paper and sold for very low prices; their authors were paid by the word. Pulp fiction, which developed between the 1920s to the 1950s but enjoyed its golden age in the 1930s, was distinguished by its garish covers with sexual overtones, and its sensational and violent content, i.e.,, crime stories, Westerns, science fiction, horror and adventures. This type of fiction spawned stories, comic characters and authors who became enormously famous: writers Dashiell Hammett, Raymond Chandler, H.P. Lovecraft, Ray Bradbury, Philip K. Dick, Arthur C. Clarke and Isaac Asimov, as well as characters such as Hopalong Cassidy, Zorro and Tarzan. Before pulp fiction lost ground to comic books (although pulp fiction targeted an adult readership whereas comic books were for a young audience) and then to television, the movies – particularly in the 1940s – relied enormously on pulp for their popular productions and series. Noir and science fiction are the genres that have held out the longest.

1994
PULP FICTION

Director: QUENTIN TARANTINO

Cast: JOHN TRAVOLTA / SAMUEL L. JACKSON / TIM ROTH / HARVEY KEITEL / BRUCE WILLIS / UMA THURMAN / CHRISTOPHER WALKEN / MARIA DE MEDEIROS / ROSANNA ARQUETTE

Uma Thurman as gangster's wife, Mia, is the symbol of Tarantino's film and probably the most insightful figure throughout American film of the Ninetics

This was the terrain in which Tarantino developed his passion for "exploitation." In other words, he was inspired by the types of films that, from the 1960s (i.e., the spaghetti Western) through the 1980s and the rise of videos, exalted all forms of sensational effects. Many of these became cult objects in America and around the world: grind houses and their B movies, Melvin Van Peebles's black exploitation genre, the sex exploitation films of Jesus Franco and Russ Meyer, Joe D'Amato's soft porn, and the splatter or gore subgenre by masters such as Roger Corman and George A. Romero.

All of these elements are essential in order to understand Tarantino's personality, tastes and style.

The circular structure of *Pulp Fiction* – it does not have a linear plot but is a sequence and accumulation of suggestions – involves a host of different situations and characters whose paths are destined to cross. Its stellar cast was the outcome of a series of possible choices and combinations, subsequently rejected, that involved virtually half of Hollywood in the 1990s, and includes Tim Roth and Harvey Keitel, who also starred in Tarantino's previous film *Reservoir Dogs*, Bruce Willis, Christopher Walken, Maria De Medeiros and Rosanna Arquette. Nevertheless, one of the film's two key figures is Uma Thurman, who was destined to become the icon of this film and of Tarantino's works in general. The other is John Travolta, whose twist scene with Thurman has become legendary. *Pulp Fiction* sensationally revived Travolta's career, which had taken a downturn following *Saturday Night Fever*.

The jury of the Cannes Film Festival, chaired by Clint Eastwood, awarded *Pulp Fiction* the Palme d'Or in 1994.

508 - The heavy, Vincent Vega (John Travolta) is charged with showing a good time to boss, Marsellus Wallace's wife and spends a hot evening with her on the dance floor at Jack Rabbit Slim's, doing the twist.

509 [LEFT] - Vincent and Jules (Samuel L. Jackson) in the struggling with settling the score, remember that some will lose and some will rule in the city.

509 [RIGHT] - Awkward robber, Pumpkin (Tim Roth) terrorizes the whole restaurant along with his Honey Bunny.

In *Se7en*, a grisly murderer is inspired by the seven deadly sins. He starts with gluttony, killing an obese man, and then murders a lawyer, writing the word "greed" near the body. The cases are assigned to Detective Somerset (Morgan Freeman), a cultured but cold and lonely policeman who is about to retire. To his chagrin, he is assigned to work with the young, handsome and impulsive Detective Mills (Brad Pitt), who is not nearly as sophisticated, but is determined to move up in the force and is married to the lovely Tracy (Gwyneth Paltrow).

The mission is not destined to be easy. There are no fingerprints, no witnesses and no ties among the victims, whose number continues to grow, following the list of deadly sins: gluttony, greed, sloth, lust, pride, envy and wrath.

In the macabre sequence of the sins that are left, a proud woman, a hardened pederast and a prostitute are slain. Reading the messages left by the murderer, Somerset realizes that they are cultural clues and starts to examine books and libraries, discovering the one used by the criminal. Certain aspects of *Se7en* are reminiscent of the style of the French mystery writer who uses the pseudonym Fred Vargas, particularly in reference to elements from his novel *Have Mercy On Us All* (original title *Pars vite et reviens tard*), although the novel postdates the film.

Mills spares no effort in the investigation and the two detectives establish a mysterious but close bond, despite the fact that they often criticize each other's different views and lifestyles. "You must divorce yourself from your emotions," Somerset advises Mills, who promptly replicates, "I feed off my emotions."

1995

SE7EN

Director: DAVID FINCHER

Cast: MORGAN FREEMAN /
BRAD PITT / GWYNETH PALTROW /
KEVIN SPACEY / R. LEE ERMEY

Brad Pitt and Morgan Freeman are Detectives Mills and Somerset.

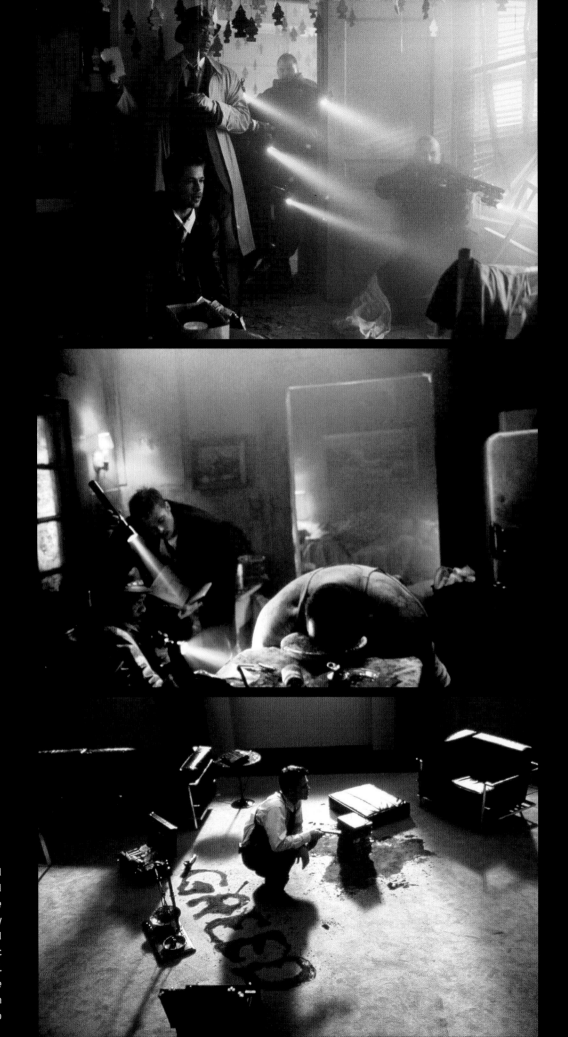

512 - Pitt and Freeman as Detectives Mills and Somerset are as different as night and day and reluctantly share a difficult investigation. The killer draws inspiration from the seven deadly sins to "title" his murders, starting with Greed then advancing to Avarice. Having two different styles, the older detective is more thoughtful and finds it useful to do book research while the younger one is impulsive and prefers acting on instinct and gut reactions. Yet, the partnership works anyway.

The psychopathic murderer (Kevin Spacey) ends up leading Mills down a blind alley, also insinuating his beautiful wife (Gwyneth Paltrow) into the picture who goes along for the ride.

They engage in a gunfight with the murderer, who proves to be a religious psychopath. Just when it seems that Mills is about to be killed, the madman spares his life for an incomprehensible reason that will be revealed later.

Covered in blood and immobile, the killer (Kevin Spacey) appears before the two detectives, posing no resistance but with a very specific plan in mind.

He offers to confess who his last victims are and show the detectives where their bodies can be found. Mills enthusiastically agrees to the appalling pact, involving the last two deadly sins, and Somerset reluctantly goes along.

The tragic epilogue revolves around envy and wrath. Mills is overcome with despair when he discovers that the first of the two "punishments" was dealt to his own wife, while the conclusion – for the last on the list is Mills himself – leaves Somerset an embittered man.

This atypical thriller is highly original and has a rich, distinctive atmosphere.

MISSION: IMPOSSIBLE

Director: BRIAN DE PALMA

Cast: TOM CRUISE / EMMANUELLE BÉART / KRISTIN SCOTT THOMAS /

JON VOIGHT / JEAN RENO / VING RHAMES / VANESSA REDGRAVE

Mission: Impossible, inspired by a celebrated television series created in 1966 (from which the film also inherited the famous theme music by La-lo Schifrin) is a rich mosaic of characters, betrayals and spectacular scenes revolving around the key figure of secret agent Ethan Hunt (Tom Cruise, who also produced the film). It was composed piece by piece by director Brian De Palma and screenwriters David Koepp (*Jurassic Park, Carlito's Way, Spider-Man* and the most recent *Indiana Jones*) and Robert Towne.

The plot is fairly simple. Ethan's team must protect the list that contains the names of all the post-1989 covert agents from the robbery that will take place in Prague. However, the mission proves to be impossible. Everyone but Ethan dies and he discovers that he has been tricked. The entire operation was designed to flush out the mole who was selling information to a weapons trafficker named Max. Ethan, the only one who survived the massacre and thus the prime suspect, decides to ally himself with Max, who turns out to be a woman, in order to steal the list of names and accomplish his personal vendetta.

With the help of two agents who have been dismissed (one of whom played by Jean Reno) and Claire, a member of his team who reveals that she survived the massacre but is also the wife of the group's former mentor Jim Phelps (Jon Voight), Ethan infiltrates CIA headquarters in Langley, Virginia,

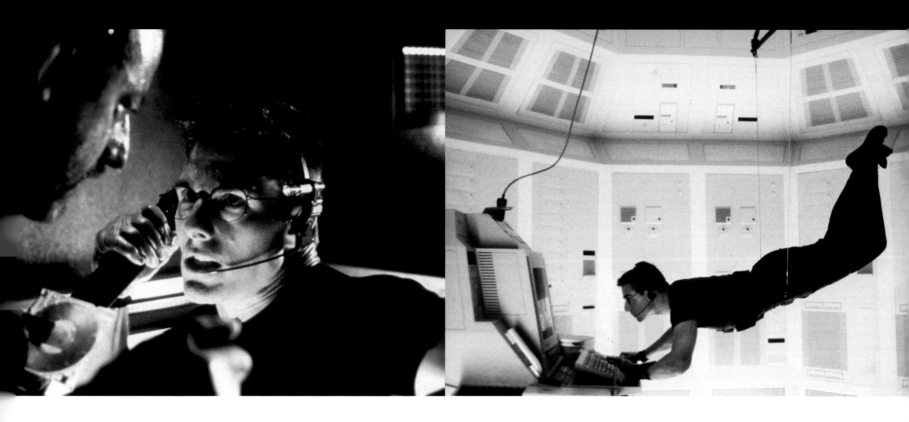

and steals the list. This is one of the film's most celebrated and successful scenes. It is significant that it was Cruise's physical and athletic talent, rather than his acting ability, that made the film so successful.

The last half hour of the film is a sequence of revelations, alliances and deceptions that culminate in the spectacular high-speed battle on top of a train between Ethan and Jim, who turns out to be the one who betrayed the team. Ethan has no other choice but to defeat him, facing a close brush with death and then retiring as a secret agent. Yet the ending is left open. Unsurprisingly, the film was followed by *Mission: Impossible II* (directed by John Woo) and *Mission: Impossible III* (by J.J. Abrams, producer of the television series Lost), respectively in 2000 and 2006. The sequels were on a par with the original, if not better. The first stunning cast included Emmanuelle Béart, Vanessa Redgrave and Kristin Scott Thomas. In the third film the "bad guy" was played by Philip Seymour Hoffman.

The film's pros and cons are evident in the fact that the viewer must weigh suspicion and irritation towards the triviality of this moneymaking extravaganza against devotion to a top-level artist (De Palma) and inevitable admiration for a cult director (Woo).

Life Is Beautiful (*La vita è bella*) is one of the most popular Italian films of all time. When it was first broadcast on Italian television it attracted an audience of more than 16 million viewers. In a certain sense, it would be simplistic to refer to Benigni as an actor or even as a filmmaker. Benigni is something special. And this film is special.

Guido Orefice is a cheerful and optimistic young man who, in a small town in central Italy, would like to open a bookstore but, in the meantime, must settle for working as a waiter at the Grand Hotel. One day he sees Dora, a schoolteacher, and immediately falls in love with her. Despite the fact that she is engaged to the arrogant Rodolfo, Dora responds to Guido's childlike and rambunctious courtship. On the night of her engagement party at the Grand Hotel, Guido bursts in on a white horse and carries off his Princess – his pet name for Dora – who willingly leaves with him. This ends the first part of the fairytale. The year is 1938, Guido is Jewish and Rodolfo is a Fascist party leader.

A few years go by: Guido and Dora are married and have a little boy, Joshua. They have opened their bookstore and are happy. In the meantime, however, racial laws have gone into effect, war has broken out and the Nazis are deporting Jews.

As a result, Guido and Joshua are deported and Dora, who is not Jewish, willingly goes with them. Separated from her, Guido and Joshua experience the same hardships as their fellow prisoners, but Guido manages to invent thousands of different ways to convince the boy, who does not understand the guards' orders, that it is all a game and that the winner will receive a prize.

The war finally comes to an end and the concentration camp is about to be shut down. Guido and the other surviving deportees have been taken away and shot, but little Joshua emerges from the hiding place his father managed to find for him. Reunited with his mother as the Allies are freeing the camp, he thinks that the game is over and that this is the prize.

Negative criticism – albeit quite minor – was leveled at the film, accused of taking a lighthearted approach to such a horrifying subject. Its fairytale air and happy ending (at least in part) were considered inappropriate, misleading, morally wrong and even "negationist." Nevertheless, the film gained widespread and emotional approval comparable to the praise that Charlie Chaplin received for *The Great Dictator*.

▶ Here are the waiter/bookseller, Guido Orefice (Roberto Benigni), his wife the teacher, Dora, who he calls Princess (Nicoletta Braschi) and their little boy, Giosuè (Joshua).

1997
LIFE IS BEAUTIFUL

Director: ROBERTO BENIGNI

Cast: ROBERTO BENIGNI / NICOLETTA BRASCHI / GIORGIO CANTARINI

Life is Beautiful may not be an exemplary demonstration of directorial skill or of how a film should be structured. Nevertheless, it has countless unforgettable moments, such as the scene in which, as the evidence of racism spreads throughout the city and shop windows begin to display signs prohibiting Jews from entering, Guido offers Joshua comically poetic explanation of what is happening. There are also other memorable scenes, such as the ones in the concentration camp when Guido gives his son a highly inventive translation of what the Nazi guards are saying, and when he manages to get a loudspeaker so that Dora can hear his voice. And, naturally, there is the scene at the beginning of the film when Guido, pretending to be a school inspector so that he can meet Dora, gives an impromptu speech satirically extolling the Italian race and its superiority.

518 and 519 - When Guido and his little boy end up in a Nazi camp for Jews, he does the impossible to hide reality from Giosuè by inventing constant stories as explanations, successfully making him believe to the end that it's all a big game.

In addition to Benigni, two other figures contributed decisively to the success of this film, Vincenzo Cerami, who worked with Benigni in creating and writing the film, and Nicola Piovani, who composed the score.

Benigni's emotions and antics were literally uncontainable on the evening of March 21, 1999, when Sophia Loren called him to the stage for his Oscars. *Life Is Beautiful* won Academy Awards for Best Foreign Language Film, Best Original Dramatic Score and Best Actor, an exceptional recognition for a non-English-speaking actor and the most coveted Oscar after that of Best Picture. A year earlier, *Life Is Beautiful* won the Grand Prize of the Jury at the Cannes Film Festival, where the award was given by Martin Scorsese.

[USA]   Genre: ROMANCE / DRAMA

TITANIC

Director: JAMES CAMERON

Cast: KATE WINSLET / LEONARDO DICAPRIO / BILLY ZANE / KATHY BATES

Titanic broke all records, but this giant cannot be considered purely in terms of numbers, because it is also a work of quality. It marks cinema's impressive return to its origins – it had celebrated its first century two years before the film was released – and to the ambition of appealing to the emotions, just as it had done when it was a young art or, rather, part art and part carnival. Regardless of whether one loves or hates it, it is a film that, like two other classic historical melodramas, *Gone With the Wind* and *Doctor Zhivago,* is simply unforgettable.

The film opens with a famous treasure hunter who is looking for a priceless diamond, the Heart of the Ocean, which is thought to be inside the wreck of the *Titanic* at the bottom of the Atlantic. The only clue he finds is a drawing portraying a nude woman with the diamond around her neck. The story is broadcast on television and is seen by Rose Calvert, who is over 100 years old and claims to be the woman in the portrait. She contacts the treasure hunter, who invites her aboard his team's boat in order to hear her story.

A flashback takes us to 1912, the year the *Titanic* was launched. The *Titanic,* the biggest and sturdiest ship ever built, is about to set sail on her maiden voyage from Southampton to New York.

Rose (Kate Winslet), an aristocrat, boards the ship with her authoritarian mother and her fiancé Caledon Hockley, whom she is being forced to marry. She is not in love with him, however, and is so unhappy that she decides to commit suicide by jumping from the stern of the ship. She is saved by Jack Dawson (Leonardo DiCaprio), a penniless young man who is traveling in third class after winning the ticket in a poker game. Jack also happens to be a very talented artist. The two immediately have feelings for each other and start spending time together. Thanks to him, Rose rediscovers the joy of living and when she sees Jack's drawings, she asks him to make a nude drawing of her with the diamond she received as an engagement gift from Caledon. Naturally, Caledon is not about to have someone from third class steal his girl and starts having Rose followed.

But tragedy is about to strike. Due to errors at the command bridge, the *Titanic* collides with an enormous iceberg that rips its hull open and eventually sinks it. The two lovers stay together. In order to save Jack, who was locked up when Caledon accused him of stealing the diamond, Rose refuses to board a lifeboat reserved for aristocrats; the *Titanic* had enough for only half of its passengers and they were reserved for the upper classes. After the ship sinks, Rose and Jack are still alive, but the water is icy and Jack returns the girl's altruistic gesture by having her lie on a piece of wall paneling that is not sturdy enough to bear them both. By the time rescuers arrive, Jack – like all the others – has succumbed to hypothermia. The only one to be saved is Rose, who will cherish the memory of her courageous lover forever.

The scene switches back to modern times. As she stands on the deck of the expedition's ship, the elderly Rose – unnoticed – throws the famous diamond back into the ocean.

Starving artist, Jack Dawson (DiCaprio) who travels in third class, saves the life of heiress, Rose Calvet (Winslet)

1. 2. Rose appreciates Jack's painting talent and has him do her portrait. Her relations with the poor boy are seen badly by her mother and the young man her mother's decided should be her fiancé.

The *Titanic* set sail on April 10, 1912 and sank on the night of April 15. The film's running time is longer than the amount of time it took the ship to sink. The production budget alone came to $200 million, although in inflation-adjusted figures it cost more to make *Cleopatra*, starring Elizabeth Taylor and Richard Burton, in the early 1960s. Despite the fact that it was not an instant hit, it holds the record in terms of box-office receipts, although not the number of viewers, which is a more significant indicator. It garnered 14 Oscar nominations, tying with *All About Eve* (1950), and took home 11 Academy Awards, the same number as *Ben-Hur* (1959).

Everything about this film is spectacular, but the realization of the dream that director James Cameron had cultivated for years is more than a display of wealth and grandeur. By merging various Hollywood stereotypes (epic, a tragic love story, disaster), he also carefully reconstructed one of the most sensational and mysterious events of the 20th century, in which responsibilities and errors, superficiality and vanity, were interwoven with the expression of society's most ruthless class division. The outcome is a sweeping tableau that employs the power and surprise of special effects.

1. 2. 3. 4. Setting sail from Southampton on 10 April 1912, a state of the art ship, the transatlantic Titanic sinks on the night of April 14th. This is historical fact. On the fictional side, Rose gives up her privileged spot on a lifeboat reserved for more well-to-do clientele and remains next to Jack who, finding another spot in a lifeboat by chance, gives his place to her. Rose is the only survivor with regret invading her memory throughout her very long life.

1999

[AUSTRALIA / USA]   Genre: ACTION / SCIENCE FICTION

THE MATRIX

Directors: ANDY AND LARRY WACHOWSKI

Cast: KEANU REEVES /
LAURENCE FISHBURNE /
CARRIE-ANNE MOSS /
HUGO WEAVING /
JOE PANTOLIANO /
GLORIA FOSTER

Thomas Anderson, an employee at a software company who is famous among hackers as Neo, perceives strange occurrences in the world, seemingly "faults" in the system and sensations that are hard to describe. His doubts are confirmed by the revelations of the mysterious Morpheus, who tells him that the planet on which he thinks he lives is actually the Matrix, a program that machines have used for centuries (the film is set well after the 20th century) to imprison and cultivate human race, a source of energy for mechanical conquerors. Only a few thousand human beings are free of the Matrix. Morpheus himself is the commander of the Resistance and the hovercraft *Nebuchadnezzar*, and he believes that Neo is "the One" who is destined to free humans from this bondage.

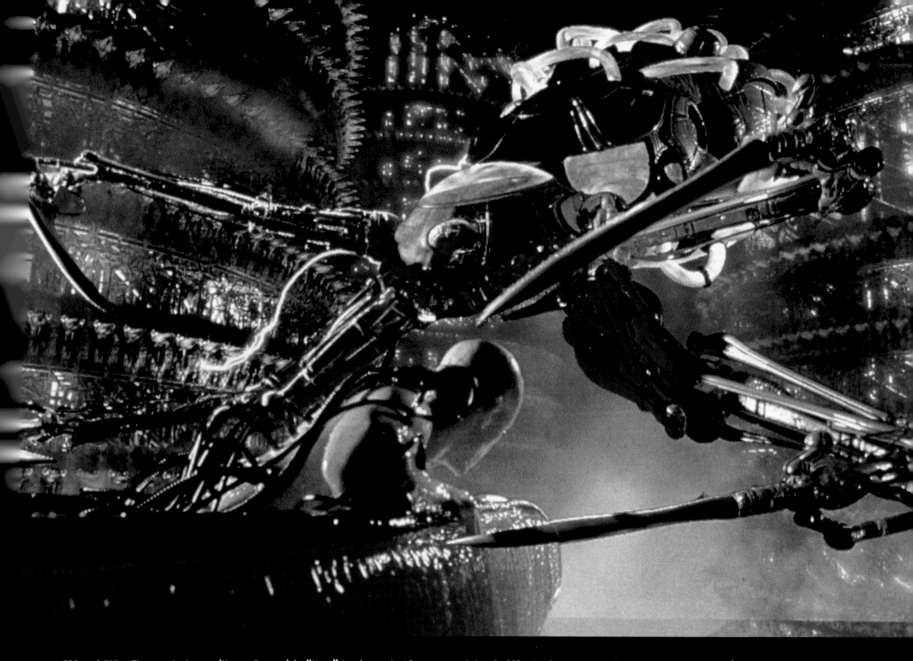

526 and 527 - Thomas Anderson (Keanu Reeves) is "Neo," having a double name and double life. Employed by a software manufacturer, he's also a famous hacker. Trinity's (Carrie-Ann Moss) kiss makes him realize that he's the Chosen One, predestined to save humanity from the slavery to which it's been reduced.

At this point, we see the famous scene of the choice between the Matrix and Reality: "You take the blue pill – the story ends, you wake up in your bed and believe whatever you want to believe. You take the red pill – you stay in Wonderland and I show you how deep the rabbit-hole goes." Neo awakens from the larval state in which he is imprisoned and the audience finally sees the extraordinary visual and special effects that characterize the rest of the film. As the plot develops, Neo proves to have exceptional qualities in opposing and modifying the structure of the Matrix, but until the epic finale the leading characters – and the audience to a lesser extent – continue to wonder whether or not he is the One. Any doubts are settled when he is resurrected from the dead after he is kissed by Trinity, also member of the Resistance, and shows his incredible power as he defeats the Agents of the Matrix.

Yet he has merely won the battle but not the war. This becomes obvious in the two sequels, *The Matrix Reloaded* and *The Matrix Revolutions*, which were released in 2003 but were not nearly as successful.

The film by the Wachowski brothers, Andy and Larry, is an exaggerated mixture of philosophical elements (the reawakening from a false reality clearly alludes to the Platonic allegory of the cave) as well as religious and messianic allusions. If the manifest concept of the One is not sufficiently clear, there are also many nomen-omens: Trinity, Anderson (Son of Man) and Neo, the anagram of One. *The Matrix* also boasts astonishing special effects, such as bullet time, with the famous slow-motion leaps while everything else is shot at normal speed.

The impasto of references and allusions and the abundance of allegorical and metaphorical ambitions also extend to many other elements. For example, the film shows the influence of Buddhism and knowledge of the science-fiction works of Philip K. Dick, and is a tribute to the martial arts and the discipline's screen icon, Bruce Lee. It also shows the perfect integration – enhanced in the two sequels – of the aesthetics of video games. After the first film was released, video games were created containing unseen portions of the film and, in turn, the video games were incorporated in the two sequels.

Keanu Reeves was cast in this role after it was turned down by Ewan McGregor and Leonardo DiCaprio. It won four Academy Awards in 2000: Best Film Editing, Best Visual Effects, Best Sound and Best Sound Editing.

1. 2. 3. 4. 5. Laurence Fishburne is the enigmatic Morpheus, commander of the resistance and the ship, *Nabucodonosor*, and he reveals the truth to Neo. The Earth he knows is in reality the Matrix, a software program that has imprisoned the human race.

3 ▶

▼ 1

▼ 2

4

Several lines from *Gladiator* are etched in our memories.

1]   General Maximus' cry – "At my signal, unleash hell!" – at the beginning of the film, before the battle against the Germanic barbarians.

2]   "My name is Maximus Decimus Meridius, commander of the Armies of the North, General of the Felix Legions, loyal servant to the true emperor, Marcus Aurelius. Father to a murdered son, husband to a murdered wife. And I will have my vengeance, in this life or the next," spoken when he is finally face to face with Commodus in the Colosseum.

3]   "The general who became a slave. The slave who became a gladiator. The gladiator who defied an emperor," uttered by Commodus to provoke him.

The film is set at the end of the reign of Marcus Aurelius, who died in AD 180. After another crushing victory and the defeat of yet another population in the name of Rome, the emperor (Richard Harris) feels that he is close to death and is determined that he must not be succeeded by his dissolute son Commodus (Joaquin Phoenix). He would have preferred to have his daughter Lucilla (Connie Nielsen) take up his legacy but, unfortunately, she is a woman. Consequently, he entrusts the fate of Rome to his valiant general, Maximus (Russell Crowe), who is adored by the legions. When they meet in the ruler's tent after the battle, the two talk like father and son, the kind of son the emperor would have wanted. The elderly ruler gives the young warrior an extremely difficult legacy, sketching out a bitter and worrisome picture of what the great city of Rome has become and of the enormous risks it faces in the future.

What is Rome, and wherein lies its greatness? It is not the geographical extent of its domain, the political class that is in power, or the intrigue of interests and corruption in command. In Maximus' simple wisdom, unconditionally approved by the paternal emperor, Rome means homecoming. Rome is a sentiment, a value and a concept that must be restored to the populace and to its republican institutions.

Unfortunately, before any of these plans can be implemented, Commodus, suspicious and angry over his father's lack of trust, strangles the elderly ruler and crowns himself emperor, ordering that Maximus be put to death. Commodus does not have Maximus' courage or Marcus Aurelius' wisdom, but he is not naïve. In his own way, he is tapped into the feelings of the masses and proves this by reintroducing the circus games that his moralizing father had abolished. This leads to the dilemma that ultimately pits him against the heir his old father would have preferred and the spirit the other man represents. Commodus wants to eliminate the Senate and its power, in a move that today we would call populism. He relies on the fact the population will not realize that it is placing its fate in the hands of a dictator.

2000

GLADIATOR

Director: RIDLEY SCOTT

Cast: RUSSELL CROWE / RICHARD HARRIS /

JOAQUIN PHOENIX / CONNIE NIELSEN / OLIVER REED

Russell Crowe is Maximus Decimus Meridius, the general that became a slave, the slave that became a gladiator, and the gladiator that dared to oppose an emperor.

"My name is Maximus Decimus Meridius, Commander of the armies of the North, General of the Felix Legions, loyal servant to the true emperor, Marcus Aurelius, and father to a murdered son, husband to a murdered wife. I will have my vengeance, in this life or the next."

Maximus, however, escapes execution. He becomes a slave and, bought by Proximo (Oliver Reed), the head of a group of gladiators, he rapidly gains popularity and is called to the most sought-after stage of all: the Colosseum. He gains enormous prestige and finally reveals his true identity to the astonished Commodus, challenging him. Maximus manages to defeat Commodus but, treacherously stabbed in the back, he does not survive. We see his spirit meet those of his wife and son, murdered by Commodus, in Elysium as his body is carried off in triumph, his name acclaimed and glorified by his fellow soldiers and the entire populace.

Ridley Scott's epic film is an anthology of inaccuracies, errors, oversights and distortions of historical truth and verisimilitude. The director himself admits this and openly declares that his intent was never philological and that his only goal was to create spectacular grandeur. He achieved this goal and, catering to more demanding palates, he also managed to convey his thoughts about the anesthetizing effects of spectacle: from the circus of gladiators to television.

Gladiator won five Academy Awards, including Best Actor and Best Visual Effects.

533 - Maximus Decimus Meridius, above, inspects his troupes. At center, the general is in conversation with the old and dying emperor, Marcus Aurelius (Richard Harris) and below with his daughter, Lucilla (Connie Nielsen), sister of the future emperor, Commodus, despotic and cruel because he's weak and indecisive.

1. Commodus (Joaquin Phoenix) holds the power and Rome is apparently at his feet. But Maximus would return and make him pay in full for all his misdeeds.

2. 3. Condemned and a fugitive, reduced to slavery and redeeming himself as a gladiator, here is Maximus fighting in the largest arena In the empire, the Coliseum.

2001
2002
2003

THE LORD OF THE RINGS

Director: **PETER JACKSON**

Cast: **ELIJAH WOOD / VIGGO MORTENSEN / ORLANDO BLOOM / CHRISTOPHER LEE / SEAN ASTIN / IAN MCKELLEN / DOMINIC MONAGHAN / BILLY BOYD / LIV TYLER**

[THE FELLOWSHIP OF THE RING]

[THE TWO TOWERS]

[THE RETURN OF THE KING]

The *Lord of the Rings* trilogy is best understood by analyzing the entire saga. Composed of *The Fellowship of the Ring* (2001), *The Two Towers* (2002) and *The Return of the King* (2003), the film version of J.R.R. Tolkien's monumental fantasy (1955) was a blockbuster that brought worldwide fame to actors Viggo Mortensen (Aragorn), Elijah Wood (Frodo Baggins, the leading character) and Orlando Bloom (Legolas), and director Peter Jackson.

The long, intricate yet powerfully effective and appealing story takes places in the mountains of Middle-earth, represented in the film by the stunning landscapes of New Zealand. Frodo Baggins, a Hobbit, must destroy the extremely danger-threatening Ring of Power to prevent it from falling into the hands of its greedy creator, the Dark Lord Sauron, resurrected in the form of an enormous fiery eye after centuries. Sauron plans to get the ring back to become the undisputed lord of the world. However, Frodo is unable to face Sauron alone and his ally, the cruel wizard Saruman (Christopher Lee, who played Dracula in the late 1950s), needs help. The Fellowship of the Ring is thus established, composed of the wizard Gandalf, the dwarf Gimli, the wanderer Aragorn, the elf Legolas and Boromir, the Steward-prince of Gondor.

Elijah Wood plays the hobbit, Frodo Baggins. ▶

The Fellowship must reach Mount Doom, the only volcano whose lava can destroy the Ring. During their journey, the group breaks up, and its members face epic battles and strange encounters. One of the most famous is Frodo's with Gollum, once a Hobbit but now a pathetic creature obsessed with the Ring and accustomed to a dark and solitary life for centuries. Extraordinary computer graphics were used to transform Gollum into the character symbolizing the saga. The group faces danger and even death (Boromir), until the final confrontation in Mordor, the Land of Shadow, which is the location of Mount Doom and the home of Sauron.

Frodo manages to destroy the Ring, the hordes of evil Orcs are defeated and Good finally triumphs. It would be the perfect ending if it weren't for the fact that the Hobbit, marked forever by the traumatic circumstances that led him to save Middle-earth, decides to abandon his home and loved ones to travel to faraway kingdoms in the company of elves.

541 [TOP] - Wicked Saruman (Christopher Lee, historical "Dracula" of the silver screen) plots with smarmy Grima Wormtongue.

541 [BOTTOM] - Believed dead, Gandalf reappears to the group in the form of the White Wizard. For a moment, the audience is persuaded to believe he's Saruman.

542 - Amazing Viggo Mortensen interprets Aragorn and later becomes known as a great actor in two David Cronenberg films, *A History of Violence* and *Eastern Promises*. He is the most courageous here, therefore the hero of the group. Over the course of the saga, the story of impossible love between him, a human, and the princess of the elves, Arwen the Immortal (played by Liv Tyler) takes on more importance.

1. One of the horrible Orcs in service to Sauron.

2. The elf, Legolas, is the infallible archer of the group. Orlando Bloom's interpretation of this character garnered him great fame, also making him an idol to millions of teenage girls.

Although the sensational popularity of the first two films was not paralleled by unanimous critical recognition (*The Fellowship of the Ring* won four Academy Awards and *The Two Towers* won two, but strictly for technical merits), *The Return of the King* broke box-office records, grossing over $1.1 billion worldwide. It also garnered 11 Oscars, including Best Picture and Best Director, matching the record set by *Ben-Hur* and *Titanic*.

The saga's cinematographic version – and thus not the extended edition – is more than 9 hours long and is a remarkable blend of extraordinary special effects and breathtaking settings. However, diehard Tolkien fans turned up their noses at it, as did many moviegoers, who found that the film's scenic spectacularity detracted from the development of the characters and a perfect rendition of the book. Nevertheless, *The Lord of the Rings* set a majestic precedent in the fantasy and epic genres, and in the history of cinema as a whole.

544 and 555 - In the two photos, we can see Arwen, daughter of the king of the elves, Elrond. She goes against her father's wishes and her own non-human destiny due to her love for Aragorn, becoming his wife at the end of the third film in the trilogy. It is the happy ending after the terrible war against Sauron.

3 ►

4 ►

1. 2. Gandalf is Frodo's guide and mentor, and fundamental character to the story. The first episode's finale leaves us believing he's dead as we see him fall into the abyss. Returning as the White Wizard, he would lead the group to victory.

3. Amazing special effects characterize the trilogy.

4. Under the armor, you can recognize Faramir, brother of Boromir who is mortally wounded at the end of the first episode.

2001
AMÉLIE

Director: JEAN-PIERRE JEUNET

Cast : AUDREY TAUTOU / MATHIEU KASSOVITZ

Audrey Tatou, in the role of the pure and innocent Amélie, the revelation of 2001. ▷

We are in Paris. After losing her mother as a child, Amélie Poulain grows up in a "fabulous" fantasy world, isolated at home due to an alleged heart problem that her father, apprehensive as a doctor but aloof as a parent, is convinced afflicts her. The narrating voice and images tell us about the childhood of Amélie, and then introduce us to her when she is 23, living alone and working as a waitress at a bar in Montmartre. Although she is an adult, she continues to live in a fantasy world, delighting in the small pleasures that it gives her.

The night that Princess Diana dies changes everything for her. In her apartment, Amélie finds a box of toys and memories, hidden by a little boy who had lived there in the 1950s. She looks for him, finds him and returns the "treasure" she has found, unleashing in the boy – now a man – a storm of emotions and the desire to find his own daughter.

From that moment on Amélie tries to improve the lives of as many people as possible, until she finally encounters a mysterious collector of discarded ID photos, a dreamer like her. Amélie falls helplessly in love with him and, finally thinking about her own life, decides to meet him. After an hour of investigations, pursuits and rendezvous, the two finally find each other and kiss tenderly.

Amélie (Le Fabuleux Destin d'Amélie Poulain) boasts outstanding photography, unique digital virtuosity and a marvelous score, but above all the bizarre figures who revolve around Amélie: the fragile painter who copies the same Renoir painting every year, a suicidal fish, a hypochondriac cashier and a mysterious photo-booth technician.

Although the film did not win any Academy Awards, it garnered five nominations in 2002: Best Original Screenplay, Best Cinematogra-

phy, Best Art Direction and Best Sound – in other words, some of the most important categories – as well as Best Foreign Language Film. Enormously popular in France and attracting an audience of 8 million, the film also was also successful on the international market, launching the very French model and look of the young actress Audrey Tatou.

A cinema enthusiast, young amateur filmmaker and the author of award-winning short films, Jean-Pierre Jeunet studied animation techniques and emerged as the director of ads and music videos. His first success, *Delicatessen*, was the outcome of his collaboration with comic-book artist Marc Caro and it revealed a well-defined and distinctive style.

With its unique appeal as a romantic comedy and fairytale with an aestheticizing Baroque taste, *Amélie* exalts a powerful personality, examining the encounter of the imaginary world of animation, graphics, photography, video games, advertising and promotion of the music industry, the poetry of small things and minor sentiments, the memory of French cinema (from Clair to Tati and Truffaut) and more, but also a love for the city of Paris. It is a catalog of tastes and preferences, of love and intimate passions ("*bricolage*" is a recurring definition). The film makes extensive use of the resources of digital technology and entertainment, but to express an anti-consumerism ideology, a poetic option composed of nostalgia, the safe haven of imagination and fantasy, and the childlike choice of a point of view: that of a latter-day Alice/Amélie. Yet it is actually the choice – adult and conscious – of those who react and resist against carnivals and circuses with special effects placed at the service of noise, terror and the forecast of a deteriorated and catastrophic world.

The Spanish director Pedro Almodóvar is one of the artists who made the biggest contribution to bringing innovation and invention to cinema. He is part of the generation that débuted in the 1980s and whose members are now in their 50s and 60s: essentially the generation of Tim Burton, Zhang Yimou, Nanni Moretti, Lars von Trier, Emir Kusturica and Jane Campion.

Talk to Her (Hable con ella), which preceded *Bad Education* and *Volver*, came immediately in the wake of *All About My Mother*, the film that brought international fame to the director and his highly original works, which reflect an utterly personal imaginary universe.

Only a wild and lively imagination could have created a work like this. Two parallel stories converge in the rooms of a hospital specializing in assisting and, if possible, rehabilitating patients in a coma following serious injuries. *Talk to Her* is a puzzle that uses a complicated series of flashbacks and flashforwards.

Benigno (Javier Camara) is a nurse who lived with his mother until her death. An extremely lonely man, he says that he is a virgin and everyone thinks he is a homosexual. From the window of his house he can see the interior of a dance school attended by Alicia (Leonor Watling), a girl with whom he falls hopelessly, possessively and awkwardly in love. In a desperate attempt to get close to her, he sets up an appointment with her father, a psychiatrist. When a car accident leaves Alicia in a coma just a few days after that appointment, the girl is brought to the clinic where Benigno works and he manages to get himself put exclusively in charge of her case. He talks to her constantly and tells her about all the shows he goes to see, describing the ones he liked and the ones that she would have liked.

Marco (Darío Grandinetti) is a freelance travel writer. When he loses the great love of his life, he becomes very fragile and prone to tears. In the meantime, in order to write an article he contacts the matador Lydia (Rosario Flores), who in turn has just ended a relationship. Although she initially turns Marco down, the two eventually become romantically involved. One day Lydia is distracted – we later learn that, unbeknownst to Marco, she has started seeing her old boyfriend again – and is gored by a bull in the ring. She goes into a coma and is brought to the same clinic where Benigno works. Marco, who is unable to talk to Lydia the way Benigno talks to Alicia, soon befriends the nurse.

For both men, everything started four years earlier. The difference is that the beginning of Benigno's "love story" with Alicia essentially coincides with the moment she falls into a coma. For Marco (and Lydia) the accident, the coma and the clinic are instead an endpoint. Benigno believes so strongly in his love that he tells his astonished friend that he plans to marry Alicia. Marco has no such plans and thus decides to leave in order to resume his work.

2002
TALK TO HER

Director: **PEDRO ALMODÓVAR**

Cast: **JAVIER CÁMARA / DARÍO GRANDINETTI / LEONOR WATLING /**
ROSARIO FLORES / MARIOLA FUENTES / GERALDINE CHAPLIN

The two women whose destinies intertwine: the ballerina, Alicia (Leonor Watling) and the matador, Lydia (Rosario Flores).

While he is away, a scandal breaks out. It turns out that Alicia, whose organic functions have been unaffected despite her vegetative state, has stopped menstruating and it promptly becomes clear that she was raped and is now pregnant. It is easy to identify the culprit, Benigno, who remorselessly accepts the consequences. He is fired and sent to jail. When Marco learns about Lydia's death, he calls the hospital and finds out about what happened to Benigno. Although she is indignant and disgusted by what happened, one of Benigno's colleagues nevertheless begs Marco to help his friend, who has been abandoned by everyone. Marco returns and gets permission to see Benigno, who asks him to investigate. He wants to know what happened to Alicia's baby. Marco discovers that the child did not survive, but he also finds out that Alicia is no longer in a coma. However, the lawyer prevents him from telling his friend the latter truth. After bidding his friend Marco an emotional goodbye, Benigno kills himself in prison.

The first time they met, Benigno urged Marco to talk to Lydia, adding, "A woman's brain is a mystery" and explaining that women need to be reminded that they are important to men. In the message he leaves for his friend, before his final gesture – which was not actually a suicide attempt but a way to be near Alicia (whom he believes is still in a coma) and keep her company in the same condition – he writes to Marco: "Wherever they take me, come and see me, and talk to me."

Who but the daring Pedro would have been brazen enough to view a deed as obscene and deplorable as the rape of a comatose woman as a gift of love and life?

Lydia does not survive her coma after being gored in the bullring. On the other hand, Alicia miraculously reemerges.

553 - Geraldine Chaplin is Alicia's dance teacher. Javier Camara is Benigno, the male nurse who takes care of Alicia, cultivating a sudden and intense love for the girl in a coma. Dario Grandinetti is Marco, the journalist wholoves Lydia and, in the clinic where his true love was also a patient, he also becomes a friend to Benigno.

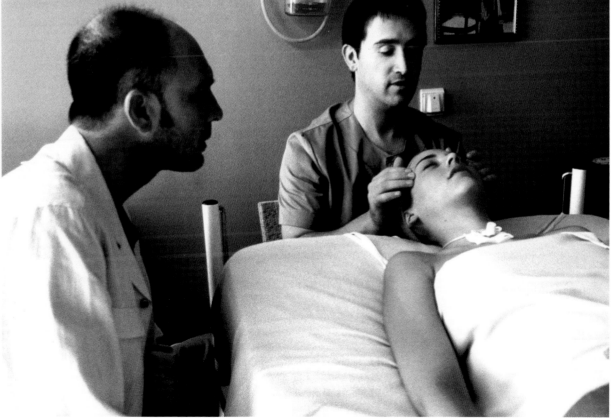

[USA] Genre: **ACTION / THRILLER**

KILL BILL
VOLUMES 1 AND 2

▼1

It may sound simplistic, but nothing could be closer to the truth. When talking about Kill Bill, it is hard to know where to begin.

Quentin Tarantino sketched out the story with Uma Thurman while filming *Pulp Fiction* (in fact, she is listed in the credits for both the subject and the script) and originally conceived of *Kill Bill* as a single film. However, when Miramax objected to its length, rather than shortening it the director suggested releasing it in two parts, one right after the other.

The two "volumes" are respectively divided into five chapters each, plus two prologues – one each – and an epilogue that concludes the second part of the entire story. The order of the chapters is not chronological and the sequence unfolds in an intricate puzzle of flashbacks and flashforwards.

On the day of her wedding rehearsal The Bride, a.k.a. Beatrix Kiddow a.k.a. Black Mamba (Thurman), is attacked by her ex-lover Bill (David Carradine) – despite the fact that she is carrying his child – and the gang of ruthless killers to which she herself once belonged: the Deadly Viper Assassination Squad (DiVAS). Bill has left her to start a new life. The group is composed of Vernita Green (Vivica A. Fox), O-Ren Ishii (Lucy Liu), Elle Driver (Daryl Hannah), Bill's new companion and assistant head, and Budd Gunn (Michael Madsen), Bill's brother. They break into the chapel and a massacre ensues. But The Bride, believed to be dead, instead survives and, after being in a coma for four years, wakes up and commences her relentless vendetta.

Cast: UMA THURMAN / LUCY LIU /

VIVICA A. FOX / DARYL HANNAH / DAVID CARRADINE /

MICHAEL MADSEN / JULIE DREYFUS /

CHIAKI KURIYAMA / SONNY CHIBA

1. 2. 3. Uma Thurman is the Bride, or Beatrix Kiddo, or Black Mamba. She has the superhuman task of confronting the entire gang of ruthless killers commanded by her ex-man, Bill, also code name for the Deadly Viper Assassination Squad whose members are: Vernita Green, O-Ren Ishii, Elle Driver, and Budd Gunn.

One by one, she seeks, finds and kills the members of the gang until the only one left is The Bride's final and main target, Bill himself, whom she slays at the end of the second part. She also finds her daughter, B.B., with whom she finally begins a new life. We leave them together in a motel room, the girl watching cartoons on TV and her mother laughing and crying. She is crying over the fact that she has had to kill Bill, but is laughing because of the side effects of the powerful truth serum that Bill made her take before their final confrontation. Aware of his fate, he probably wanted to bid her farewell with a gift: helping her laugh with her daughter. The final caption reads: "The lioness has rejoined her cub. All is right in the jungle."

Kill Bill provides compulsive proof of Tarantino's maniacal and fetishistic devotion to his passions, which are so concentrated in the film that the list is virtually endless.

The two chapters are gold mines in terms of citations, references, allusions and nods, and the director himself noted that the two films reflect his desire to pay tribute to Oriental films (Part One) and spaghetti Westerns (Part Two).

1. 2. 3. Bill (David Carradine) is in front of the chapel where Beatrix must get married. The missed wedding celebration would be colored with rivers of blood and Beatrix herself endures horrific punishment for leaving Bill and the gang. Believed dead, she reawakens after four years in a coma and from there, she initiates her ruthless vendetta until she settles the score with Bill.

557 - Here she is as the Bride who would be prevented from getting married. She would carry a baby in her womb but would lose it. And, she would become much more merciless than her enemies.

The Chinese and Japanese images of kung fu, Bruce Lee, the martial arts, animation, the themes of violence and revenge, swords, virtuoso acrobatics, the Yakuza and Hong Kong cape-and-sword films occupy the first "heart" of the film and are blended at a dizzying pace. The film's abundant tributes, above all to Sergio Leone and Ennio Morricone, reveal Tarantino's debt to the world of B movies and Italian cinema of the 1960s and 1970s. The third source of references is Tarantino himself. In fact, the film often alludes to the director's previous films. Nonetheless, there are also details that declare his devotion to great masters such as Ridley Scott (*Blade Runner*) and Stanley Kubrick (*A Clockwork Orange*).

Kill Bill boasts a virtually endless gallery of characters, situations, objects and names destined to attract hordes of fans and expressly conceived for them by a filmmaker who, in turn, has the same fanatical and partisan spirit as his enthusiasts.

The film is *The Last Samurai* and the year is 1876. After dishonoring his Army uniform by massacring a defenseless tribe of Native Americans during a punitive expedition ordered by his superior, Captain Nathan Algren (Tom Cruise) allows himself to be exhibited as a hero in order to advertise Winchester rifles, a job he accepts amidst alcohol problems and repressed bitterness. Algren is then recruited by his despised commanding officer, who offers him a large salary as a mercenary to train the inexperienced Imperial Japanese Army, which is fighting against a heroic samurai unwilling to accept modernization: Katsumoto (Ken Watanabe). During their first conflict, Algren's men are defeated by their enemy's fearless soldiers, who use hand-to-hand combat against artillery. After fighting courageously, Algren is taken prisoner but, going against the custom whereby the valiant vanquished soldier is "helped to die" as a sign of respect, the captain's life is spared. He is kept alive and treated with enormous care, because the rebel samurai greatly admires him and avidly reads Algren's journals while the American is recovering from his numerous battle wounds. During ceremonious conversations in which the American (the "barbarian"), who cannot understand these customs, reluctantly takes part, the samurai wants to hear the story of General Custer, under whom Algren once fought: 211 against 2000 Indians. Nevertheless, once the samurai and the American break the ice and earn each other's respect, Algren explains that Custer was no hero, commenting, "He was a murderer who fell in love with his own legend."

Oppressed by nightmares and shame over what he has seen and done in the past, and admiring the harmony and arcane spirituality of this remote corner of the world, Algren becomes one of them. When the village is attacked, he fights to defend Katsumoto and his men. By living with them, he begins to understand their principles of service, discipline and compassion: the destiny and mission of a samurai. The American also understands that two parties are vying for the future of Japan. One is the side that recruited him and influences the "divine" but young and insecure emperor, and now wants to accelerate westernization at any price, including that of forgetting their roots and surrendering to foreign interests. The other side is that of Katsumoto, who is actually a court dignitary and is greatly respected by the emperor. In reality, it is Katsumoto who is defending the honor of the ruler and the nation.

2003

THE LAST SAMURAI

Director: EDWARD ZWICK

Cast: KEN WATANABE / TOM CRUISE /

TIMOTHY SPALL / BILLY CONNOLLY / TONY GOLDWYN / HIROYUKI SANADA / KOYUKI KATO / SHIN KOYAMADA

Tom Cruise is Captain Algren.

After Katsumoto is arrested and then freed by the captain, the samurai face the final battle, a handful of men armed with only swords and arrows battling against two well-organized and trained regiments. But Algren tells Katsumoto the story of the heroes of Thermopylae: "Three hundred brave Greeks held off a Persian army of a million men." After all his men are killed, Katsumoto asks Algren to help him commits seppuku and all the enemy troops bow to the samurai as a sign of respect.

Likewise, the young emperor bows when, before astonished American emissaries and treacherous Japanese dignitaries, the captain comes to present Katsumoto's sword to him. The samurai's last wish as he lay dying was to convey the strength of the samurai to the emperor, in memory of and as a sign of respect towards their ancestors.

Time and again, too many directors have unfortunately thought of themselves as latter-day Sergio Leones, dilating every battle scene into pointless and presumptuously "poetic" excess. If this intriguing and even thrilling tale had been less than 150 minutes long, it could be honored as a stirring albeit arbitrary reinterpretation of American history. It takes up the self-criticism of the Westerns of the early 1970s, which sided with Native Americans (*Soldier Blue, Little Big Man, Jeremiah Johnson* and *A Man Called Horse*). In any event, Cruise is better in this film than Kevin Kost-

561 - Captured by Samurai Katsumoto's (at center) rebels (in reality loyalists, the true enemies are the courtiers sold to the West), Algren is considerately taken care of by the war widow to the man that he's defeated and killed in battle (below). He would learn about dignity, pride, and honor from the samurais, later obtaining an audience with the emperor who would liberate him from his hostage status.

562 and 563 - Finally admitted among Katsumoto's samurais with a grandiose ritual of dress, permitted to wear the armor of the warrior he's killed at the beginning, Algren becomes an honorable samurai warrior, fighting with courage

"Heartbreaking" is the best adjective to describe this masterpiece. The story recounted by Clint Eastwood, director and costar, and screenwriter Paul Haggis is based on a collection of short stories by F. X. Toole.

Frankie (Eastwood) is a crusty ex-boxer turned trainer and manager who has difficulty relating to others. He has an unhappy family life (he is estranged from his daughter) and unresolved religious issues. He and his only friend (Morgan Freeman) run a small and seedy-looking gym. His combination of honesty and pessimism have sidelined him from the world of boxing, and one of his most promising students leaves him to go on to become a champion.

His opportunity for redemption comes in the form of a poor 30-year-old woman, Maggie (Hilary Swank), who loves boxing and is driven by steely resolve. Frankie does everything in his power to discourage her, but must finally give in. He agrees to train her and takes her under his wing, maintaining his inflexible façade. Yet he is gradually touched by a new and regenerating sense of affection.

Maggie's first matches prove the determination of this late bloomer, who promptly beats her adversaries by KO'ing them in the first round. Consequently, Frankie decides to help her move up in her boxing division, but is forced to bribe people and give in to blackmail because, given her reputation, no one is willing to fight against Maggie. Therefore, Maggie fights her key match against the reigning welterweight champion, Billie, who has a widespread reputation for fighting unfairly. When the champion hits Maggie after the bell and sends her sprawling, the girl hits her head and is paralyzed for life. The drama of Maggie's immobility is compounded by heart-wrenching episodes (one of her legs must be amputated) but, once again, she demonstrates her extraordinary fortitude and indomitable spirit. Disappointed by her own family, which proves to be petty and interested only in her money – although she had embarked on this great adventure in order to give them a better life – she asks Frankie to help her die. Frankie initially refuses, but finally slips into the hospital at night to inject her with a fatal dose of adrenaline. It makes no difference that the epilogue seems highly unlikely, because the powerful sentiment that runs through this film is so overwhelmingly compelling.

For the great and monumental work of his creative maturity, Eastwood often turns to the concept of classicism. If by classicism we mean understatement, human nature that is tested by life but not vanquished, attention – not absolving but understanding – to every implication and hidden nuance, then Eastwood's film is surely a classic. All of this clearly emerges in Eastwood's investigation – never overt but relying on sudden aperçus – of the complex relationship that links these two underdogs, respectively in search of a daughter and father figure.

2004
MILLION DOLLAR BABY

Director: CLINT EASTWOOD

**Cast: CLINT EASTWOOD /
HILARY SWANK /
MORGAN FREEMAN**

Maggie (Hilary Swank) comes from a poor and dysfunctional family, but has a will of iron. She wants establish herself as a boxer at any cost.

Winners
are simply
willing to do
what losers
won't.
TAPE OR TRASH IN SPITTOONS.
THAN TWO PER CORNER DURING SPARRING.
BOXEN

Maggie succeeds in convincing the tough Frankie (Eastwood) to train her and look after her along with his friend, Eddie (Freeman), the only one that Frankie has.

It has rightly been said that it would be one-sided to consider it a film about boxing, but it would be equally limiting to term it a manifesto about the pros and cons of euthanasia. These are important elements, but they serve a higher purpose, as there is far more. Frankie's final gesture, which certainly does not claim to be the "right" one, is an act of love for the girl and the life she has lost, the life she grasped and that Frankie help her achieve. Consequently, after a gesture that he would never term as murder, he knows that he bears within him a legacy: the confidence that he instilled in Maggie. This may ultimately help him to deal with his sense of guilt over being an inadequate father and to start over again, seeking within himself his ability to give something to his natural daughter. In his grief, Frank knows that he did the right thing. His gesture reflects the simplicity of a taciturn man who has nevertheless learned to dialogue with himself and plumbed his own soul.

The film's triumph at the Academy Awards could not have been better deserved. *Million Dollar Baby* won the awards for Best Picture, Best Director, Best Actress and Best Supporting Actor (Freeman).

1. 2. 3. 4. A strong will is not enough for Maggie. The fight with the welter-weight champion, remarkable for her crude behavior, leads to a very serious accident paralyzing Maggie for life, non-life rather, one that compassionate Frankie would help her to leave behind. An absolute masterpiece when honoring a story-telling objective that speaks of humanity, speaking to all of us on a more personal level.

**2002
2004
2007**

The BOURNE IDENTITY

Director: DOUG LIMAN

Cast: MATT DAMON /

FRANKA POTENTE / CHRIS COOPER / BRIAN COX / JULIA STILES / CLIVE OWEN / ANTHONY GREEN

The BOURNE SUPREMACY

Director: PAUL GREENGRASS

Cast: MATT DAMON /

FRANKA POTENTE / BRIAN COX / JULIA STILES / KARL URBAN / GABRIEL MANN / JOAN ALLEN

 # The BOURNE ULTIMATUM

Director: PAUL GREENGRASS

Cast: MATT DAMON /

JULIA STILES / DAVID STRATHAIRN / SCOTT GLENN / PADDY CONSIDINE / EDGAR RAMIREZ / ALBERT FINNEY / JOAN ALLEN / DANIEL BRÜHL

The trilogy starring Matt Damon as the ex-CIA agent Jason Bourne is based on three novels by the American writer Robert Ludlum (1927–2001), whose books had already inspired other films such as Sam Peckinpah's last work, *The Osterman Weekend*. The three novels were published respectively in 1980, 1986 and 1990, whereas the three films were made in 2002, 2004 and 2007. The first was directed by Doug Liman, and the other two by Paul Greengrass. The films have the same names as Ludlum's thrillers: *The Bourne Identity*, *The Bourne Supremacy* and *The Bourne Ultimatum*.

All three adventures revolve around a single background event whose details we do not learn until the end, but whose consequences are fundamental in Bourne's life, as are his acrobatic efforts to rid himself of this burden. Bourne was an American secret agent. However, something that happened during his last mission gave him total amnesia and he cannot remember who he is, where he is from, what happened to him or why someone is chasing him. It rapidly becomes clear that his pursuers are none other than his former colleagues and that, since he is alive and free, he is considered dangerous.

At a certain point in this spiral of unconsciousness, persecution and the attempt to defend himself and discover what happened – we are now in the second episode – Marie, the German girl who helped him escape in the first film and became his girlfriend (played by Franka Potente in both films), is killed by Bourne's ruthless pursuers.

Matt Damon in the role of the absent-minded agent, Jason Bourne who is being pursued.

1. 2. 3. 4. This trilogy quintessentially captures the action, rhythm, speed, and movement of its genre. Over the course of the three films, on-location sets are used in Italy, Switzerland, France, India, Germany, the U.S.A., Russia, England, Spain, and Morocco.

The plot becomes even more complex and moves in various directions, and it becomes clear that Bourne is being framed for murder.

This brings us to the final chapter, in which Bourne – doubly motivated because he is out to avenge Marie's death – manages to uncover the mystery, revealing the origins of the entire conspiracy and recovering his identity. He discovers that the CIA placed him in a special program, canceled his identity and memory – his real name is David Webb – and transformed him into a ruthless killer.

After a journey around the world to Italy, Switzerland, France, India, back to Italy, Germany and, in the third episode, Moscow, Paris, Turin, London, Madrid and Tangier, the final confrontation takes place at the organization's headquarters in New York, where everything first started. Absolute evil is embodied by the unflappable Albert Finney. At the end of an astonishing sequence, everyone believes that Bourne has finally been neutralized, but that is not the case.

The countless deaths, but above all the supersonic speed at which the action plays out, made the film a watershed in the adventure and espionage genre. The editing of this film could easily be used as study material for all cinema schools. The incredible amount of information and its extraordinary pace reflect the age of the audience of these films, which cater to spectators accustomed to the speed of ads and video games. By the same token, they are difficult for older audiences, i.e., members of the Bond/Connery generation, who prefer a hedonistic hero romancing a woman or sipping a martini between chase scenes. Regardless, the Bourne trilogy is a spectacle worth taking the time to admire.

2003
2006
2007

PIRATES OF THE CARIBBEAN

[The Curse of the Black Pearl]

[Dead Man's Chest]

[At World's End]

Director: **GORE VERBINSKI**

Cast: **JOHNNY DEPP / ORLANDO BLOOM / KEIRA KNIGHTLEY /**

GEOFFREY RUSH / JACK DAVENPORT / JONATHAN PRYCE / KEVIN MCNALLY / MACKENZIE CROOK / LEE ARENBERG / BILL NIGHY /

TOM HOLLANDER / NAOMIE HARRIS / STELLAN SKARSGÅRD / CHOW YUN-FAT / KEITH RICHARDS (THIRD EPISODE)

Walt Disney Pictures inaugurated the new millennium with an ambitious and pyrotechnical pastiche that revived the glorious film-maker's credentials, merging the exaggeration of the adventure genre with comedy, romance, fantasy and a touch of the supernatural.

Pirates of the Caribbean is ambitious in the sense that it targets a worldwide audience, a goal that was fully achieved and confirmed by the last two chapters of the first trilogy (another trilogy is scheduled to follow).

It is a pastiche in the very postmodern sense of recycling a consolidated tradition of entertainment that caters to children and adults alike – with hefty doses of creative innovation and countless special effects – and is based not only on cinema but also literature, from the exotic adventures of Emilio Salgari to the great Robert Louis Stevenson's *Treasure Island*. In short, it parallels what George Lucas and Steven Spielberg did with the saga of Indiana Jones.

The imaginative characters and, to an even greater extent, Johnny Depp's extraordinary incarnation as the main figure, the extravagant pirate Jack Sparrow, were decisive to the success of the film.

▶ The wonderful Johnny Depp plays eccentric protagonist, Jack Sparrow.

▲ 1

The other players are the fearsome Captain Barbossa (Geoffrey Rush) and the courageous blacksmith Will Turner (Orlando Bloom), the orphan who survives a shipwreck thanks to the English governor of Port Royal (Jonathan Pryce) and falls in love with his daughter, Elizabeth (Keira Knightley). The girl returns his feelings, despite their class differences and the fact that her father has promised her in marriage to Captain Norrington (Jack Davenport).

Eight years earlier, when the governor saved the young Turner from the smoking wreck, Elizabeth, who was with him, picked up a skull medallion and saw a mysterious vessel with black sails leave the scene.

Now, on the day that Norrington has asked for Elizabeth's hand in marriage, Port Royal is in turmoil over the arrival of Sparrow who, following a duel with Turner – the two will then become friends – is captured and sent to jail.

That night, the city is raided by the *Black Pearl*, the black-sailed pirate ship commanded by Barbossa. In order to obtain the medallion, the pirates kidnap Elizabeth and take her aboard their ship. Turner frees Sparrow and convinces him to follow the pirates. He discovers that Sparrow was the captain of

2

1. Jack Sparrow is always accompanied by a series of arms and other, often defective, items. It's also difficult to separate the captain from his hat, or the hat from the captain, as it were.

2. Here is Captain Barbossa of the Black Pearl with his crew of the "damned."

3. Here is one of the spectacular onboard and maritime battle scenes, occurring frequently throughout the film series.

4. The two characters that support Jack Sparrow in his exploits are the beautiful Elizabeth (Keira Knightley) and the courageous William (Orlando Bloom), both men in love with Elizabeth.

3 ▲

4 ▲

the *Black Pearl* and that, following a mutiny led by Barbossa, he was abandoned on a desert island. It also turns out that Turner's father was a pirate and that Sparrow knew him well. The two
commandeer a fast ship and set sail for the island of Tortuga.

In the meantime, Elizabeth discovers that the *Black Pearl*'s crew is composed of the living
dead, whose nature is revealed only in the moonlight, although there had already been a clue:
Barbossa's pirates were untouched by gunfire during the siege of Port Royal. Elizabeth also
learns that the curse befell them after they stole the treasure of the conquistador Hernán
Cortés. The pirates cannot be saved until they return all the coins from the treasure, and there
is only one left: Elizabeth's.

To put an end to the curse, all the pirates must also shed a drop of their blood in the treasure chest. The blood that is missing is that of "Bootstrap" Turner, Will's father, who had rebelled against the mutiny and was punished by being thrown overboard. The blood of one of his relatives would suffice, but Elizabeth – who told the pirates that her name was Turner, believing that she had been kidnapped because she is the governor's daughter – is not related to him and thus cannot serve their purpose. They need Will, who manages to save the woman he loves thanks to the medallion.

There are numerous thrilling *coups de théâtre*, in which Jack seems to be double-crossing everyone, before the curse is finally lifted, making the pirates mortal again and neutralizing them. Will and Elizabeth declare their love, while Sparrow, who had been sentenced to death, is saved and resumes command of the *Black Pearl*, returning to the high seas.

This is the plot of the first chapter. The adventure continues in *Dead Man's Chest* and *At World's End*, by the same director, Gore Verbinski, and the two screenwriters of Shrek, Ted Elliott and Terry Rossio, but the sequels are not as successful.

The inspiration for the saga was Disneyland attraction that is now also featured at all the other Disney theme parks, from Florida to Paris.

578 - Here's a scene from the second episode when Sparrow escapes a tribe of cannibals on the island of Pelegosto.

579 - Will's fate is almost predetermined. Initially hostile towards the pirate life, he discovers he's the son of the famous corsair, Bill "Bootstrap" Turner. Over the course of the saga, he would gradually change his stance, eventually becoming the King of the Pirates.

1. Davy Jones, captain of the Flying Dutchman and his crew of monsters, half men and half sea creatures.

2. In the third film, Teague Sparrow would appear to advise the nine prominent pirates of the Brethren Court, of which Jack Sparrow and Will Turner are a part. Keith Richards makes a cameo as this special character and Jack's father.

3. The two Turners, father ("Bootstrap") and son encounter the character of Bootstrap, only mentioned in the first film then making an appearance in the second episode as a member of Davy Jones' crew of the "damned."

4. The character of Elizabeth Swann would undergo a change over the course of the series, taking her place at her true love, Will's side. As the spoiled and overindulged daughter of the governor of Port Royal, she would eventually make a U-turn and become a courageous piratess.

ACADEMY AWARDS

THE ACADEMY OF MOTION PICTURE ARTS AND SCIENCES IN HOLLYWOOD, THAT IS, A JURY COMPOSED OF THOUSANDS OF FILM PROFESSIONALS AND ARTISTS, INCLUDING ALL PREVIOUS PAST-YEAR WINNERS AND NOMINEES, DETERMINE AND PRESENT THE ACADEMY AWARDS OR THE OSCARS. THE FIRST AWARDS CEREMONY FOR FILMS RELEASED BETWEEN 1927 AND 1928 TOOK PLACE ON 16 MAY 1929. IN 1934 AND THEREAFTER THE AWARDS CEREMONY OCCURRED BETWEEN FEBRUARY AND MARCH, AND FROM 1935 FORWARD, FILMS RELEASED FROM JANUARY 1 TO DECEMBER 31 IN THE PRECEDING YEAR WERE CONSIDERED FOR RECOGNITION. BOB HOPE HOLDS THE RECORD FOR BEING THE MOST FREQUENT PRESENTER AT AN EVENING AWARDS CEREMONY THAT OVER TIME HAS CHANGED LOCATIONS, THE LATEST SITE BEING THE KODAK THEATER. THE MOST IMPORTANT AWARDS CATEGORIES ARE BEST FILM, BEST PERFORMANCE AS AN ACTOR AND ACTRESS IN A LEADING ROLE, AND BEST DIRECTOR. OTHER CATEGORIES HAVE BEEN ADDED OVER THE YEARS, INCLUDING ONE FOR BEST ANIMATED FILM IN 2001. THE OSCAR FOR BEST FOREIGN FILM (IN A LANGUAGE OTHER THAN ENGLISH) HAS A DIFFERENT STORY. ORIGINATING IN 1948 AS A "SPECIAL" AWARD GOING TO *SCIUSCIÀ* (SHOE-SHINE), DIRECTED BY VITTORIO DE SICA, IT EVOLVED IN 1951 INTO AN "HONORARY" AWARD, AND BECAME AN OFFICIAL CATEGORY UNTO ITSELF IN 1957 WHEN FEDERICO FELLINI WON IT IN TWO CONSECUTIVE YEARS FOR *LA STRADA* (THE ROAD) AND *LE NOTTI DI CABIRIA* (NIGHTS OF CABIRIA).

year

1929	*Sunrise: A Song of Two Humans* (aka Sunrise), directed by F. W. Murnau
1930	*The Broadway Melody*, directed by Harry Beaumont
1930	*All Quiet on the Western Front*, directed by Lewis Milestone
1931	*Cimarron*, directed by Wesley Ruggles
1932	*Grand Hotel*, directed by Edmund Goulding
1934	*Cavalcade*, directed by Frank Lloyd
1935	*It Happened One Night*, directed by Frank Capra
1936	*Mutiny on The Bounty*, directed by Frank Lloyd
1937	*The Great Ziegfeld*, directed by Robert Z. Leonard
1938	*The Life of Emile Zola*, directed by William Dieterle
1939	*You Can't Take It With You*, directed by Frank Capra
1940	*Gone With the Wind*, directed by Victor Fleming
1941	*Rebecca*, directed by Alfred Hitchcock
1942	*How Green Was My Valley*, directed by John Ford
1943	*Mrs. Miniver*, directed by William Wyler
1944	*Casablanca*, directed by Michael Curtiz
1945	*Going My Way*, directed by Leo McCarey
1946	*The Lost Weekend*, directed by Billy Wilder
1947	*The Best Years of Our Lives*, directed by William Wyler
1948	*Gentleman's Agreement*, directed by Elia Kazan
1949	*Hamlet*, directed by Laurence Olivier
1950	*All the King's Men*, directed by Robert Rossen
1951	*All About Eve*, directed by Joseph L. Mankiewicz
1952	*An American in Paris*, directed by Vincent Minnelli
1953	*The Greatest Show on Earth*, directed by Cecil B. DeMille
1954	*From Here to Eternity*, directed by Fred Zinnemann
1955	*On the Waterfront*, directed by Elia Kazan
1956	*Marty*, directed by Delbert Mann
1957	*Around the World in Eighty Days*, directed by Michael Anderson
1958	*The Bridge on the River Kwai*, directed by David Lean
1959	*Gigi*, directed by Vincent Minnelli
1960	*Ben-Hur*, directed by William Wyler
1961	*The Apartment*, directed by Billy Wilder
1962	*West Side Story*, directed by Robert Wise and Jerome Robbins

1963	*Lawrence of Arabia*, directed by David Lean
1964	*Tom Jones*, directed by Tony Richardson
1965	*My Fair Lady*, directed by George Cukor
1966	*The Sound of Music*, directed by Robert Wise
1967	*A Man for All Seasons*, directed by Fred Zinnemann
1968	*In the Heat of the Night*, directed by Norman Jewison
1969	*Oliver*, directed by Carol Reed
1970	*Midnight Cowboy*, directed by John Schlesinger
1971	*Patton*, directed by Franklin J. Schaffner
1972	*The French Connection*, directed by William Friedkin
1973	*The Godfather*, directed by Francis Ford Coppola
1974	*The Sting*, directed by George Roy Hill
1975	*The Godfather: Part II*, directed by Francis Ford Coppola
1976	*One Flew Over the Cuckoo's Nest*, directed by Milos Forman
1977	*Rocky*, directed by John G. Avildsen
1978	*Annie Hall*, directed by Woody Allen
1979	*The Deer Hunter*, directed by Michael Cimino
1980	*Kramer vs Kramer*, directed by Robert Benton
1981	*Ordinary People*, directed by Robert Redford
1982	*Chariots of Fire*, directed by Hugh Hudson
1983	*Gandhi*, directed by Richard Attenborough
1984	Terms of Endearment, directed by James L. Brooks
1985	*Amadeus*, directed by Milos Forman
1986	*Out of Africa*, directed by Sydney Pollack
1987	*Platoon*, directed by Oliver Stone
1988	*The Last Emperor*, directed by Bernardo Bertolucci
1989	*Rain Man*, directed by Barry Levinson
1990	*Driving Miss Daisy*, directed by Bruce Beresford
1991	*Dances with Wolves*, directed by Kevin Costner
1992	*The Silence of the Lambs*, directed by Jonathan Demme
1993	*Unforgiven*, directed by Clint Eastwood
1994	*Schindler's List*, directed by Steven Spielberg
1995	*Forrest Gump*, directed by Robert Zemeckis
1996	*Braveheart*, directed by Mel Gibson
1997	*The English Patient*, directed by Anthony Minghella
1998	*Titanic*, directed by James Cameron
1999	*Shakespeare in Love*, directed by John Madden
2000	*American Beauty*, directed by Sam Mendes
2001	*Gladiator*, directed by Ridley Scott
2002	*A Beautiful Mind*, directed by Ron Howard
2003	*Chicago*, directed by Rob Marshall
2004	*The Lord of the Rings: The Return of the King*, directed by Peter Jackson
2005	*Million Dollar Baby*, directed by Clint Eastwood
2006	*Crash*, directed by Paul Haggis
2007	*The Departed*, directed by Martin Scorsese
2008	*No Country for Old Men*, directed by Joel and Ethan Coen

CANNES INTERNATIONAL FILM FESTIVAL

THE CANNES INTERNATIONAL FILM FESTIVAL LAUNCHED ITS FIRST CELEBRATION OF THE CINEMATOGRAPHIC ARTS FROM SEPTEMBER 1ST TO 30TH, 1939, PRESIDED OVER BY THE INVENTOR OF CINEMA HIMSELF, LOUIS LUMIÈRE. AFTER WORLD WAR II, THE FESTIVAL SCHEDULE WAS AT FIRST BIENNIAL; IT OCCURRED IN 1946 (HONORED PREVIOUSLY UNRELEASED FILMS WITH MAJOR WORLDWIDE RELEVANCE) AND IN 1948 AND 1950, BEFORE BECOMING AN ANNUAL EVENT. TODAY, THE CANNES FESTIVAL IS THE SHOWCASE THAT ENJOYS THE MOST MEDIA "COVERAGE" AS WELL AS BEING THE MOST IMPORTANT MARKET FOR FILM INDUSTRY PROFESSIONALS. AS A RESULT CANNES HAS THE MOST LAVISH "CATWALK" OF STARS PARADING DOWN THE STAIRCASE OF THE FESTIVAL PALACE. IN 1968 THE CEREMONY WAS CANCELLED IN SOLIDARITY WITH THE STUDENT MOVEMENT AND INDUSTRY PROFESSIONALS INVOLVED IN THE STRIKE SUCH AS DIRECTORS, LOUIS MALLE, FRANÇOIS TRUFFAUT, JEAN LUC GODARD, CLAUDE LELOUCH, AND ROMAN POLANSKI. THE MOST IMPORTANT AWARD GIVEN BY THE FESTIVAL JURY, MADE UP OF PROMINENT FILM INDUSTRY PERSONALITIES, IS THE *PALME D'OR* (GOLDEN PALM); SINCE 1955, IT HAS REPLACED THE PREVIOUS *GRAND PRIX*.

year

1939	*Union Pacific*, directed by Cecil B. De Mille
1946	*Torment*, directed by Alf Sjöberg
1946	*The Lost Weekend*, directed by Billy Wilder
1946	*Red Meadows*, directed by Bodil Ipsen and Lau Lauritzen
1946	*Neecha Nagar*, directed by Chetan Anand
1946	*Brief Encounter*, directed by David Lean
1946	*María Candelaria* (aka *Portrait of Maria* or *Xochimilco*), directed by Emilio Fernandez
1946	*The Turning Point*, directed by Fridrikh Markovitch Ermler
1946	*La symphonie pastorale* (Pastoral Symphony), directed by Jean Delannoy
1946	*The Last Chance*, directed by Leopold Lintberg
1946	*Muzi bez krídel* (Men Without Wings), directed by Frantisek Cáp
1946	*Open City*, directed by Roberto Rossellini
1947	*The Damned*, directed by René Clément
1947	*Antoine and Antoinette*, directed by Jacques Becker
1947	*Crossfire* (aka *Cradle of Fear*), directed by Edward Dmytryk
1947	*Dumbo*, directed by Ben Sharpsteen and Walt Disney
1947	*Ziegfeld Follies*, directed by various directors
1949	*The Third Man*, directed by Carol Reed
1951	*Miss Julie*, directed by Alf Sjöberg
1951	*Miracle in Milan*, directed by Vittorio De Sica
1952	*Othello*, directed by Orson Welles
1952	*Two Cents Worth of Hope*, directed by Renato Castellani
1953	*The Wages of Fear*, directed by Henri-Georges Clouzot
1954	*Gate of Hell*, directed by Teinosuke Kinugasa
1955	*Marty*, directed by Delbert Mann
1956	*The Silent World*, directed by Jacques-Yves Cousteau and Louis Malle
1957	*Friendly Persuasion*, directed by William Wyler
1958	*The Cranes Are Flying*, directed by Mikheil Kalatozishvili
1959	*Black Orpheus*, directed by Marcel Camus
1960	*La dolce vita* (The Sweet Life), directed by Federico Fellini
1961	*The Long Absence*, directed by Henri Colpi
1961	*Viridiana*, directed by Luis Buñuel
1962	*Keeper of Promises* (aka *Payer of Promises*, *The Given Word*, or *The Promise*), directed by Anselmo Duarte
1963	*The Leopard*, directed by Luchino Visconti
1964	*The Umbrellas of Cherbourg*, directed by Jacques Demy
1965	*The Knack... and How To Get It*, directed by Richard Lester
1966	*A Man and a Woman*, directed by Claude Lelouch
1966	*The Birds, the Bees, and the Italians*, directed by Pietro Germi

1967	Blow-Up, directed by Michelangelo Antonioni
1969	If…, directed by Lindsay Anderson
1970	M*A*S*H, directed by Robert Altman
1971	The Go-Between, directed by Joseph Losey
1972	The Mattei Affair, directed by Francesco Rosi
1972	The Working Class Goes to Heaven (aka Lulu the Tool), directed by Elio Petri
1973	Scarecrow, directed by Jerry Schatzberg
1973	The Hireling, directed by Alan Bridges
1974	The Conversation, directed by Francis Ford Coppola
1975	Chronicle of the Years of Fire, directed by Mohammed Lakhdar-Hamina
1976	Taxi Driver, directed by Martin Scorsese
1977	Father and Master (aka My Father My Master), directed by Paolo & Vittorio Taviani
1978	The Tree of Wooden Clogs, directed by Ermanno Olmi
1979	The Tin Drum, directed by Volker Schlöndorff
1979	Apocalypse Now, directed by Francis Ford Coppola
1980	Kagemusha the Shadow Warrior (aka Shadow Warrior or The Double), directed by Akira Kurosawa
1980	All That Jazz, directed by Bob Fosse
1981	Man of Iron, directed by Andrzej Wajda
1982	Yol (aka The Way), directed by Serif Gören and Yilmaz Güney
1982	Missing, directed by Costa-Gavras
1983	Ballad of Narayama, directed by Shohei Imamura
1984	Paris, Texas, directed by Wim Wenders
1985	When Father Was Away on Business, directed by Emir Kusturica
1986	The Mission, directed by Roland Joffé
1987	Under the Sun of Satan (aka Under Satan's Sun), directed by Maurice Pialat
1988	Pelle the Conqueror, directed by Bille August
1989	Sex, Lies, and Videotape, directed by Steven Soderbergh
1990	Wild At Heart, directed by David Lynch
1991	Barton Fink, directed by Joel & Ethan Coen
1992	The Best Intentions, directed by Bille August
1993	Farewell My Concubine, directed by Kaige Chen
1993	The Piano, directed by Jane Campion
1994	Pulp Fiction, directed by Quentin Tarantino
1995	Underground (aka Once Upon A Time There Was a Country), directed by Emir Kusturica
1996	Secrets & Lies, directed by Mike Leigh
1997	The Eel, directed by Imamura Shohei
1997	A Taste of Cherry (aka Taste of Cherry), directed by Abbas Kiarostami
1998	Eternity and a Day, directed by Theo Angelopoulos
1999	Rosetta, directed by Luc and Jean-Pierre Dardenne
2000	Dancer in the Dark (aka Taps), directed by Lars von Trier
2001	The Son's Room, directed by Nanni Moretti
2002	The Pianist, directed by Roman Polanski
2003	Elephant, directed by Gus van Sant
2004	Fahrenheit 9/11, directed by Michael Moore
2005	The Child, directed by Luc and Jean-Pierre Dardenne
2006	The Wind That Shakes the Barley, directed by Ken Loach
2007	Four Months, Three Weeks and Two Days, directed by Cristian Mungiu
2008	Entre les murs, directed by Laurent Cantet

VENICE INTERNATIONAL FILM FESTIVAL

THE VENICE INTERNATIONAL FILM FESTIVAL IS THE MOTHER OF ALL FILM FESTIVALS AND HAS BEEN RUNNING FOR LONGER THAN ANY OTHER IN THE WORLD. IT OPENED IN 1932 THROUGH THE DETERMINATION OF COUNT GIUSEPPE VOLPI DI MISURATA, WITH THE GOAL OF PROMOTING THE INTERESTS OF LUXURY HOTELS ON THE LIDO, VENICE. IN FACT, THE FIRST FESTIVAL WAS CALLED AN EXPOSITION AND WAS HELD ON THE TERRACE OF THE EXCELSIOR HOTEL; IT TARGETED AUDIENCES IN HIGH SOCIETY AND THE TRIUMPHANT MUSSOLINI RÉGIME. AFTER THE SECOND BIENNIAL IN 1934, IT BECAME AN ANNUAL EVENT FROM 1935. IN 1937, THE *PALAZZO DEL CINEMA* WAS INAUGURATED AS THE OFFICIAL SITE AND IS STILL IN USE TODAY. THERE WERE NO FESTIVALS IN DURING WORLD WAR II, FROM 1939 TO 1945. IN 1968 THE TROUBLED POLITICAL SITUATION LED TO THE CANCELLATION OF THE VENICE FESTIVAL. UNLIKE THE SITUATION AT CANNES, THERE WAS NO RAPID RETURN TO NORMAL; THE FESTIVAL AS NOT REINSTATED UNTIL 1979, AFTER A DIFFICULT DECADE. THE AWARDS WERE RESTORED TO THEIR FORMER GLORY, BUT MANY CHANGES HAVE OCCURRED IN THE LAST QUARTER-CENTURY. THE NAMES OF THE AWARD CHANGED, BUT NOW IS CONFIRMED AS THE *LEONE* (THE LION, THE TRADITIONAL SYMBOL OF THE FORMER REPUBLIC OF VENICE – *LA SERENISSIMA*). AND, DESPITE ITS MORE GENUINELY AND RADICALLY ARTISTIC FOCUS, VENICE HAS ALWAYS ANTICIPATED CANNES IN THE CREATION OF NEW CATEGORIES DESIGNATED FOR WORKS FROM YOUNG FILMMAKERS, ALTERNATING WITH THOSE OF MANY ESTABLISHED DIRECTORS SUCH AS CARLO LIZZANI AND GILLO PONTECORVO. EVERYONE COMES TO VENICE. THE GREATS LIKE KUROSAWA, ROSI, DREYER, AND ANTONIONI MADE NAMES FOR THEMSELVES HERE. VISCONTI'S TWO FAILURES TO WIN THE *LEONE D'ORO* (GOLDEN LION) FOR *SENSO* (LIVIA) AND *ROCCO E I SUOI FRATELLI* (ROCCO AND HIS BROTHERS) IN 1954 AND 1960 ARE ESPECIALLY MEMORABLE; THE FILMS WERE FAVORED TO WIN YET OVERLOOKED AS "MEDIOCRE" AND "FORGETTABLE" FILMS.

year

1934	*Teresa Confalonieri*, Best Italian Film, directed by Guido Brignone
1934	*Man of Aran*, Best Foreign Film, directed by Robert Flaherty
1935	*Casta diva*, Best Italian Film, directed by Carmine Gallone
1935	*Anna Karenina*, Best Foreign Film, directed by Clarence Brown
1936	*White Squadron*, Best Italian Film, directed by Augusto Genina
1936	*The Kaiser of California*, Best Foreign Film, directed by Luis Trenker
1937	*Scipio the African*, Best Italian Film, directed by Carmine Gallone
1937	*Dance of Life* (aka *Dance Program* or *Life Dances On*), Best Foreign Film, directed by Julien Duvivier
1938	*Luciano Serra, Pilot*, Best Italian Film, directed by Goffredo Alessandrini
1938	*Olympia* (aka The Olympiad), Best Foreign Film, directed by Leni Riefenstahl
1939	*Cardinal Messias*, directed by Goffredo Alessandrini
1940	*The Siege of the Alcazar*, Best Italian Film, directed by Augusto Genina
1940	*The Stationmaster*, Best Foreign Film, directed by Gustav Ucicky
1941	*The Iron Crown*, Best Italian Film, directed by Alessandro Blasetti
1941	*Uncle Kruger*, Best Foreign Film, directed by Hans Steinhoff
1942	*Bengasi*, Best Italian Film, directed by Augusto Genina
1942	*The Great King*, Best Foreign Film, directed by Veit Harlan
1946	*The Southerner* (*Hold Autumn in Your Heart*), directed by Jean Renoir
1947	*Siréna*, directed by Karel Stekly
1948	*Hamlet*, directed by Laurence Olivier
1949	*Manon*, directed by Henri-Georges Clouzot
1950	*Justice Is Done* (aka *Let Justice Be Done*), directed by André Cayatte
1951	*Rashomon* (aka *Rasho-Mon* or *In the Woods*), directed by Akira Kurosawa
1952	*Forbidden Games* (aka The Secret Game), directed by René Clément
1954	*Romeo and Juliet*, directed by Renato Castellani

1955	*The Word*, directed by Carl Theodor Dreyer
1957	*The Unvanquished*, directed by Satyajit Ray
1958	*The Rickshaw Man*, directed by Iroshi Inagaki
1959	*The Great War*, directed by Mario Monicelli
1959	*General della Rovere*, directed by Roberto Rossellini
1960	*Tomorrow Is My Turn* (*The Crossing of the Rhine*), directed by André Cayatte
1961	*Last Year at Marienbad*, directed by Alain Resnais
1962	*Family Diary*, directed by Valerio Zurlini
1962	*My Name is Ivan* (aka *The Youngest Spy* or *Ivan's Childood*), directed by Andrej Tarkovskij
1963	*Hands Over the City*, directed by Francesco Rosi
1964	*The Red Desert*, directed by Michelangelo Antonioni
1965	*Sandra of a Thousand Delights*, directed by Luchino Visconti
1966	*The Battle of Algiers*, directed by Gillo Pontecorvo
1967	*Belle de jour* (aka Beauty of the Day), directed by Luis Buñuel
1968	*The Artist in the Circus Dome: Clueless* (aka *Artists Under the Big Top: Perplexed*), directed by Alexander Kluge
1980	*Atlantic City*, directed by Louis Malle
1980	*Gloria*, directed by John Cassavetes
1981	*Marianne and Juliane* (aka The *German Sisters*), directed by Margarethe von Trotta
1982	*The State of Things*, directed by Wim Wenders
1983	*First Name: Carmen*, directed by Jean-Luc Godard
1984	*The Year of the Quiet Sun*, directed by Krzysztof Zanussi
1985	*Vagabond* (aka *Without Roof or Rule*), directed by Agnès Varda
1986	*Summer* (aka *The Green Ray*), directed by Eric Rohmer
1987	*Goodbye, Children*, directed by Louis Malle
1988	*The Legend of the Holy Drinker*, directed by Ermanno Olmi
1989	*Città dolente* (*Beiqing chengshi*), directed by Hou Hsiao-Hsien
1990	*Rosencrantz and Guildenstern Are Dead*, directed by Tom Stoppard
1991	*Close to Eden* (aka *Territory of Love*), directed by Nikita Mikhalkov
1992	*The Story of Qiu Ju* (aka *Qui Ju Goes to Court*), directed by Zhang Yimou
1993	*Short Cuts*, directed by Robert Altman
1993	*Three Colors: Blue* (aka *Blue)*, directed by Krzysztof Kie lowski
1994	*Vive L'Amour*, directed by Tsai Ming-Liang
1994	*Before the Rain*, directed by Milcho Manchevski
1995	*Xich lo*, directed by Tran Anh Hung
1996	*Michael Collins*, directed by Neil Jordan
1997	*Fireworks*, directed by Takeshi Kitano
1998	*The Way We Laughed*, directed by Gianni Amelio
1999	*Not One Less*, directed by Zhang Yimou
2000	*The Circle*, directed by Jafar Panahi
2001	*Monsoon Wedding*, directed by Mira Nair
2002	*The Magdalene Sisters*, directed by Peter Mullan
2003	*The Return*, directed by Andrei Zviagintsev
2004	*Vera Drake*, directed by Mike Leigh
2005	*Brokeback Mountain*, directed by Ang Lee
2006	*Still Life*, directed by Jia Zhang-ke
2007	*Lust, Caution*, directed by Ang Lee

THE BERLIN INTERNATIONAL FILM FESTIVAL (AKA THE BERLINALE)

THE BERLINALE RANKS THIRD IN IMPORTANCE IN THE WORLD'S FILM FESTIVALS. IT HAS BEEN HELD EVERY FEBRUARY SINCE 1951 AND ITS MOST PRE-
STIGIOUS PRIZE IS THE GOLDEN BEAR. UNLIKE CANNES AND UNLIKE VENICE, IT HAS ENJOYED AN UNINTERRUPTED LIFE AND ITS FOUNDER, ALFRED
BAUER, REMAINED IN CHARGE UNTIL 1977. MORITZ DE HADELN TOOK THE HELM FROM 1980 TO 2001. THE DECISION TO CREATE A PRESTIGIOUS ARTI-
STIC AND CULTURAL EVENT IN THE CAPITAL OF THE FORMER THIRD REICH AND TO ESTABLISH A DIALOGUE BETWEEN TWO WORLDS DIVIDED BY THE COLD
WAR HAS HAD ENDURING POLITICAL SIGNIFICANCE. THE FESTIVAL WAS INITIALLY HELD AT A VENUE JUST A SHORT DISTANCE AWAY FROM THE "BOR-
DER" BETWEEN THE LOCATIONS OF THE TWO GERMAN GOVERNMENTS. IT FLOURISHED IN WEST BERLIN, WITHIN A CITY ONCE DIVIDED BETWEEN
OCCUPYING MILITARY FORCES, AND WITH EAST BERLIN SUBJECT TO AN UNFORGETTABLY HARSH RÉGIME. AFTER THE WALL WAS DEMOLISHED, THE
FESTIVAL MOVED FROM THE SITE IT HAD OCCUPIED FROM 1961 TO 1989 TO A SITE NEAR THE POTSDAMERPLATZ, SURROUNDED BY THE FUTURISTIC ARCHI-
TECTURE OF RENZO PIANO. THE NEW SITE IS HIGHLY SYMBOLIC, OCCUPYING PART OF WHAT HAD ONCE BEEN THE "NO MAN'S LAND" BETWEEN DIVIDED
EAST AND WEST BERLIN. THE BERLINALE DIFFERS DECISIVELY FROM THE VENICE AND CANNES FILM FESTIVALS IN ITS FLAIR FOR EXPERIMENTATION
AND, ABOVE ALL, IN ATTRACTING A LARGE AND VERY PASSIONATE AND DEMANDING AUDIENCES OF BERLINERS AND FOREIGN VISITORS.

year

1951	*Four in a Jeep*, directed by Leopold Lindtberg
1951	*Justice Is Done* (aka *Let Justice Be Done*), directed by André Cayatte
1951	*...Sans laisser d'adresse* (*...Without Leaving an Address*), directed by Jean-Paul Le Chanois
1951	*Cinderella*, directed by Wilfred Jackson, Hamilton Luske, and Clyde Geronimi
1952	*One Summer of Happiness*, directed by Arne Mattsson
1953	*The Wages of Fear*, directed by Henri-Georges Clouzot
1954	*Hobson's Choice*, directed by David Lean
1955	*The Rats*, directed by Robert Siodmak
1956	*Invitation To The Dance*, directed by Gene Kelly
1957	*12 Angry Men*, directed by Sidney Lumet
1958	*Wild Strawberries*, directed by Ingmar Bergman
1958	*The Cousins*, directed by Claude Chabrol
1960	*El Lazarillo de Tormes*, directed by César Fernandez Ardavin
1961	*The Night*, directed by Michelangelo Antonioni
1962	*A Kind of Loving*, directed by John Schlesinger
1963	*Bushido*, directed by Tadashi Imai
1963	The Devil (aka *To Bed... Or Not to Bed*), directed by Gian Luigi Polidoro
1964	*Dry Summer* (aka *I Had My Brother's Wife*, Reflections), directed by Metin Erksan
1965	*Alphaville, a Strange Adventure of Lemmy Caution*, directed by Jean-Luc Godard
1966	*Cul-de-sac*, directed by Roman Polanski
1967	*Le départ*, directed by Jerzy Skolimowski
1968	*Who Saw Him Die?*, directed by Jan Troell
1969	*Early Works*, directed by Zelimir Zilnik
1971	*The Garden of the Finzi-Continis*, directed by Vittorio De Sica
1972	*The Canterbury Tales*, directed by Pier Paolo Pasolini
1973	*Distant Thunder*, directed by Satyajit Ray
1974	*The Apprenticeship of Duddy Kravitz*, directed by Ted Kotcheff
1975	*Adoption*, directed by Márta Mészáros
1976	*Buffalo Bill and the Indians*, directed by Robert Altman
1977	*The Ascent*, directed by Larisa Shepitko
1978	*Trout*, directed by José Luis García Sánchez
1978	*What Max Said*, directed by Emilio Martínez Lázaro
1978	*Ascensor*, directed by Tomas Muñoz
1979	*David*, directed by Peter Lilienthal

1980	*Heartland*, directed by Richard Pearce
1980	*Palermo or Wolfsburg*, directed by Werner Schroeter
1981	*Faster, Faster* (aka *Fast, Fast*), directed by Carlos Saura
1982	*Veronika Voss*, directed by Rainer Werner Fassbinder
1983	*Ascendancy*, directed by Edward Bennett
1983	*The Beehive*, directed by Mario Camús
1984	*Love Streams*, directed by John Cassavetes
1985	*Die Frau und der Fremde* (The Woman and the Stranger), directed by Rainer Simon
1985	*Wetherby*, directed by David Hare
1986	*Stammheim*, directed by Reinhard Hauff
1987	*The Theme*, directed by Gleb Panfilov
1988	*Red Sorghum*, directed by Zhang Yimou
1989	*Rain Man*, directed by Barry Levinson
1990	*Music Box*, directed by Costa-Gavras
1990	*Larks on a String* (aka *Larks on a Thread* or *Skylarks on a String*), directed by Jiri Menzel
1991	*The House of Smiles*, directed by Marco Ferreri
1992	*Grand Canyon*, directed by Lawrence Kasdan
1993	*The Women from the Lake of Scented Souls* (aka *Woman Sesame Oil Maker*), directed by Fei Xie
1993	*The Wedding Banquet*, directed by Ang Lee
1994	*In the Name of the Father*, directed by Jim Sheridan
1995	*Fresh Bait* (aka *The Bait*), directed by Bertrand Tavernier
1996	*Sense and Sensibility*, directed by Ang Lee
1997	*The People vs Larry Flint*, directed by Milos Forman
1998	*Central Station*, directed by Walter Salles
1999	*The Thin Red Line*, directed by Terrence Malick
2000	*Magnolia*, directed by Paul Thomas Anderson
2001	*Intimacy*, directed by Patrice Chéreau
2002	*Spirited Away* (aka Miyazaki's *Spirited Away, Sen and the Mysterious Disappearnce of Chihiro*), directed by Hayao Miyazaki
2002	*Bloody Sunday* (aka Sunday), directed by Paul Greengrass
2003	*In This World* (aka *The Silk Road*), directed by Michael Winterbottom
2004	*Head-On*, directed by Fatih Akin
2005	*U-Carmen*, directed by Marc Dornford-May
2006	*Esma's Secret - Grbavica* (aka *Grbavica: The Land of My Dreams*), directed by Jasmila Îbanic
2007	*Tuya's Marriage*, directed by Wang Quan An
2008	*Elite Squad*, directed by José Padilha

GOLDEN GLOBE FOR BEST FILM: DRAMA

THOUGH NOT ENJOYING THE SAME PRESTIGE OF THE OSCARS, OVER TIME THE GOLDEN GLOBE AWARDS HAVE STILL ASSUMED IMPORTANCE IN ANTICIPATING THE OSCARS, SETTING THE PACE FOR THE ACADEMY AWARDS, EITHER CONFIRMING OR DENYING THEM, AS IT WERE. SELECTING THE GOLDEN GLOBE AWARDS WINNERS IS A JURY COMPOSED OF ABOUT ONE HUNDRED HOLLYWOOD-ACCREDITED FOREIGN JOURNALISTS ASSOCIATED WITH THE HOLLYWOOD FOREIGN PRESS ASSOCIATION. THE GOLDEN GLOBE AWARDS FOR FILM WERE INSTITUTED IN 1944 AND THEN EXPANDED TO INCLUDE TELEVISION IN 1956. THE AWARDS ARE MADE IN JANUARY, ABOUT TWO MONTHS BEFORE THE OSCARS. AWARDS ARE GIVEN IN TWO CATEGORIES: THE GOLDEN GLOBE FOR THE BEST DRAMATIC FILM AND THE GOLDEN GLOBE FOR THE BEST COMEDY OR MUSICAL. THE CATEGORIES FOR BEST PERFORMANCE BY A LEADING ACTOR AND ACTRESS HONOR THE SAME TWO CATEGORIES

year

1944	*The Song of Bernadette*, directed by Henry King
1945	*Going My Way*, directed by Leo McCarey
1946	*The Lost Weekend*, directed by Billy Wilder
1947	*The Best Years of Our Lives*, directed by William Wyler
1948	*Gentleman's Agreement*, directed by Elia Kazan
1949	*Johnny Belinda*, directed by Jean Negulesco
1949	*The Treasure of the Sierra Madre*, directed by John Huston
1950	*All the King's Men*, directed by Robert Rossen
1951	*Sunset Boulevard*, directed by Billy Wilder
1952	*A Place in the Sun*, directed by George Stevens
1953	*The Greatest Show on Earth*, directed by Cecil B. DeMille
1954	*The Robe*, directed by Henry Koster
1955	*On the Waterfront*, directed by Elia Kazan
1956	*East of Eden*, directed by Elia Kazan
1957	*Around the World in Eighty Days*, directed by Michael Anderson & John Farrow
1958	*The Bridge on the River Kwai*, directed by David Lean
1959	*The Defiant Ones*, directed by Stanley Kramer
1960	*Ben-Hur*, directed by William Wyler
1961	*Spartacus*, directed by Stanley Kubrick
1962	*The Guns of Navarone*, directed by J. Lee Thompson
1963	*Lawrence of Arabia*, directed by David Lean
1964	*The Cardinal*, directed by Otto Preminger
1965	*Becket*, directed by Peter Glenville
1966	*Doctor Zhivago*, directed by David Lean

1967	*A Man for All Seasons*, directed by Fred Zinnemann
1968	*In the Heat of the Night*, directed by Norman Jewison
1969	*The Lion in Winter*, directed by Anthony Harvey
1970	*Anne of the Thousand Days*, directed by Charles Jarrott
1971	*Love Story*, directed by Arthur Hiller
1972	*The French Connection*, directed by William Friedkin
1973	*The Godfather*, directed by Francis Ford Coppola
1974	*The Exorcist*, directed by William Friedkin
1975	*Chinatown*, directed by Roman Polanski
1976	*One Flew Over the Cuckoo's Nest*, directed by Milos Forman
1977	*Rocky*, directed by John G. Avildsen
1978	*The Turning Point*, directed by Herbert Ross
1979	*Midnight Express*, directed by Alan Parker
1980	*Kramer vs Kramer*, directed by Robert Benton
1981	*Ordinary People*, directed by Robert Redford
1982	*On Golden Pond*, directed by Mark Rydell
1983	*E.T.: The Extra-Terrestrial*, directed by Steven Spielberg
1984	*Terms of Endearment*, directed by James L. Brooks
1985	*Amadeus*, directed by Milos Forman
1986	*Out of Africa*, directed by Sidney Pollack
1987	*Platoon*, directed by Oliver Stone
1988	*The Last Emperor*, directed by Bernardo Bertolucci
1989	*Rain Man*, directed by Barry Levinson
1990	*Born on the Fourth of July*, directed by Oliver Stone
1991	*Dances with Wolves*, directed by Kevin Costner
1992	*Bugsy*, directed by Barry Levinson
1993	*Scent of a Woman*, directed by Martin Brest
1994	*Schindler's List*, directed by Steven Spielberg
1995	*Forrest Gump*, directed by Robert Zemeckis
1996	*Sense and Sensibility*, directed by Ang Lee
1997	*The English Patient*, directed by Anthony Minghella
1998	*Titanic*, directed by James Cameron
1999	*Saving Private Ryan*, directed by Steven Spielberg
2000	*American Beauty*, directed by Sam Mendes
2001	*Gladiator*, directed by Ridley Scott
2002	*A Beautiful Mind*, directed by Ron Howard
2003	*The Hours*, directed by Stephen Daldry
2004	*The Lord of the Rings: The Return of the King*, directed by Peter Jackson
2005	*The Aviator*, directed by Martin Scorsese
2006	*Brokeback Mountain*, directed by Ang Lee
2007	*Babel*, directed by Alejandro Gonzalez Iñárritu
2008	*Atonement*, directed by Joe Wright

year

1952	*An American in Paris*, directed by Vincent Minnelli
1953	With a Song in My Heart, directed by Walter Lang
1955	*Carmen Jones*, directed by Otto Preminger
1956	*Guys and Dolls*, directed by Joseph L. Mankiewicz
1957	*The King and I*, directed by Walter Lang
1958	*Les Girls*, directed by George Cukor
1964	*Tom Jones*, directed by Tony Richardson
1965	*My Fair Lady*, directed by George Cukor
1966	*The Sound of Music*, directed by Robert Wise
1967	*The Russians Are Coming the Russians Are Coming*, directed by Norman Jewison
1968	*The Graduate*, directed by Mike Nichols
1969	*Oliver!*, directed by Carol Reed
1970	*The Secret Of Santa Vittoria*, directed by Stanley Kramer
1971	*M*A*S*H*, directed by Robert Altman
1972	*Fiddler on the Roof*, directed by Norman Jewison
1973	*Cabaret*, directed by Bob Fosse
1974	*American Graffiti*, directed by George Lucas
1975	*The Longest Yard*, directed by Robert Aldrich
1976	*The Sunshine Boys*, directed by Herbert Ross
1977	*A Star Is Born*, directed by Frank Pierson
1978	*The Goodbye Girl*, directed by Herbert Ross
1979	*Heaven Can Wait*, directed by Warren Beatty & Buck Henry
1980	*Breaking Away*, directed by Peter Yates
1981	*Coal Miner's Daughter*, directed by Michael Apted
1982	*Arthur*, directed by Steve Gordon

1983	*Tootsie*, directed by Sydney Pollack
1984	*Yentl*, directed by Barbra Streisand
1985	*Romancing the Stone*, directed by Robert Zemeckis
1986	*Prizzi's Honor*, directed by John Huston
1987	*Hannah and Her Sisters*, directed by Woody Allen
1988	*Hope and Glory*, directed by John Boorman
1989	*Working Girl*, directed by Mike Nichols
1990	*Driving Miss Daisy*, directed by Bruce Beresford
1991	*Green Card*, directed by Peter Weir
1992	*Beauty and the Beast*, directed by Gary Trousdale and Kirk Wise
1993	*The Player*, directed by Robert Altman
1994	*Mrs. Doubtfire*, directed by Chris Columbus
1995	*The Lion King*, directed by Roger Allers and Rob Minkoff
1996	*Babe*, directed by Chris Noonan
1997	Evita, directed by Alan Parker
1998	*As Good as It Gets*, directed by James L. Brooks
1999	*Shakespeare in Love*, directed by John Madden
2000	*Toy Story 2*, directed by John Lasseter, Ash Brannon, and Lee Unkrich
2001	*Almost Famous*, directed by Cameron Crowe
2002	*Moulin Rouge!*, directed by Baz Luhrmann
2003	*Chicago*, directed by Rob Marshall
2004	*Lost in Translation*, directed by Sofia Coppola
2005	*Sideways*, directed by Alexander Payne
2006	*Walk the Line*, directed by James Mangold
2007	*Dreamgirls*, directed by Bill Condon
2008	*Sweeney Todd*, directed by Tim Burton

INDEX

20th Century Fox/Album/Contrasto Page 404   *   20th Century Fox/Aspen/The Kobal Collection Page 312 right   *   20th Century Fox/Paramount/The Kobal Collection Pages 522, 523, 525 bottom   *   20th Century Fox/The Kobal Collection Pages 287, 288, 289, 290, 291, 401, 405, 475, 476-477   *   20th Century Fox Film Corp./Courtesy Everett Collection/Contrasto Pages 78 left, 312 left, 399, 402, 402-403, 477 right, 521, 524-525, 525 top and center   *   ABC/Allied Artists/The Kobal Page 325   *   Accent/RAI/The Kobal Collection Page 11 (6th)   *   Alan Pappe/Time Life Pictures/Getty Images Page 323   *   Album/Contrasto Page 189 top and center   *   Alfred Eisenstaedt/Time Life Pictures/Getty Images Page 153   *   Amblin/Universal/The Kobal Collection Pages 443, 444, 446   *   Andrew Cooper/A Band Apart/Miramax/The Kobal Collection Page 554 left   *   Argos/Oshima/The Kobal Collection Pages 361, 362, 363   *   Band Photo/uppa.co.uk/Photoshot Pages 528-529, 529 bottom   *   Bettmann/Corbis Pages 23, 56-57, 61, 139, 140 bottom   *   Brian Hamill/United Artists/The Kobal Collection Pages 395, 396, 397   *   Bud Fraker/Paramount/The Kobal Collection Page 179 bottom   *   Buena Vista Pictures/Courtesy Everett Collection/Contrasto Page 580 center   *   Buena Vista Pictures/The Kobal Collection Pages 580-581   *   Carolco/The Kobal Collection Pages 424, 425 left, 488, 489 right   *   Century Communications/China Films/Salon Films/Era Int./Album/Contrasto Page 479 top and center   *   Chaplin/United Artists/Album/Contrasto Page 65 bottom   *   Chaplin/United Artists/The Kobal Collection Pages 59, 60, 63, 65 top and center   *   CinemaPhoto/Corbis Pages 207, 209, 383   *   Cineriz/Abum/Contrasto Page 248   *   Collection Cinema/Photo12.com Pages 196-197, 269, 313, 378 bottom, 422, 423, 439 center and bottom, 517   *   Collection CSFF/Rue des Archives Pages 133 top and center, 417 right   *   Columbia/The Kobal Collection Pages 11 (2nd), 55, 56, 57, 109 right, 110, 111, 135, 136 top and left, 137 right, 145, 151, 152 bottom, 180, 186, 187, 237, 239 top, 267, 268 center and bottom, 305, 355, 356 center, 373, 374-375   *   Columbia Pictures/Album/Contrasto Pages 136-137, 462, 463 bottom   *   Courtesy Everett Collection/Contrasto Pages 31, 42 bottom, 45, 46 bottom, 62, 64, 96, 107, 109 left, 115 bottom, 119, 121 right, 127, 128 top, 129 center and bottom, 141, 144, 148, 149 center, 152 center, 164, 171, 173, 175 top, 177, 183 bottom, 184, 185, 189 bottom, 194 left, 200, 201, 204 left, 204-205, 208 top and bottom, 211, 213, 218, 219, 220, 221, 227, 228 center, 229, 234-235, 235, 238 right, 239 bottom, 241, 245, 246, 247, 249, 256, 257, 268 top, 271, 275 center, 280 left, 280-281, 281, 284 top and center, 292 left, 299, 309 center, 310-311, 320, 321 top, 324, 328, 329, 331, 340, 341 top, 346-347, 347, 351 top, 353 bottom, 375 bottom, 416 left, 439 top, 449 right, 453 right and bottom, 454, 455 top and bottom, 470-471, 471 bottom, 473 right, 481, 482, 483 center, 507, 508 right, 509 right, 512 center, 539   *   David James/Universal/The Kobal Collection Page 497   *   David James/Warner Bros/The Kobal Collection Pages 559, 560, 561, 562-563, 563 right   *   Decla-Bioscop/The Kobal Collection Pages 20, 21   *   Dream Works/Courtesy Everett Collection/Contrasto Pages 531, 532, 533 top and bottom   *   Dream Works/Universal/The Kobal Collection Page 534   *   Egon Endrenyi/ Hypnotic/Universal Pictures/The Kobal Collection Page 572 top   *   Embassy/The Kobal Collection Pages 277, 278, 279   *   EMI/ Columbia/Warners/The Kobal Collection Pages 377, 378 top, 379, 380 bottom, 381   *   EMI/Universal/Album/Contrasto Pages 380 top, 382   *   Era International/The Kobal Collection Pages 478, 479 bottom   *   Excelsa/Mayer-Burstyn/The Kobal Collection Page 105   *   Fabian Cevallos/Corbis Sygma/Corbis Page 461   *   FIA/Rue des Archives Page 83 top   *   Film 13/The Kobal Collection Pages 264 left, 265 right   *   Firooz Zahedi/Carolco/The Kobal Collection Page 489 left   *   Francinex/Rizzoli-Amato/The Kobal Collection Page 133 bottom   *   Gérard Rancinan/Sygma/Corbis Page 457   *   Glenn Loney/Everett Collection/Contrasto Page 28 bottom   *   Goskino/Album/Contrasto Pages 28 top, 29 left   *   Goskino/The Kobal Collection Pages 27, 28 right   *   Holly Bower/Paramount/The Kobal Collection Page 364   *   Hulton Archive/Getty Images Pages 34, 52 bottom   *   Iena/Ucil/Cocinor/Album/Contrasto Page 174   *   Irving Lippman/Columbia/The Kobal Collection Page 143   *   Itala Film Torino/The Kobal Collection Pages 18, 19   *   Jaap Buitendijk/Dream Works/Universal/The Kobal Collection Pages 533 center, 534-535, 535 bottom   *   Jasin Boland/Universal/The Kobal Collection Pages 571, 572 center, 573   *   Jay Maidment/Universal/The Kobal Collection Page 572 bottom   *   John Springer Collection/Corbis Pages 97 top, 120, 131 left, 152 top, 165 top left, 231   *   Jolly/Constantin/Ocean/The Kobal Collection Pages 254, 255   *   Ken Danvers/MGM/The Kobal Collection Pages 261, 262 top and center, 263   *   Ken Regan/Orion/The Kobal Collection Page 483 top   *   Ladd Company/Warner Bros/Album/Contrasto Page 435 bottom   *   Ladd Company/Warner Bros/The Kobal Collection Pages 431, 433 right, 434, 434-435, 437   *   Les Film 13/Album/Contrasto Pages 264-265   *   Lucas Film/20th Century Fox/The Kobal Collection Pages 367, 368, 369, 370-371   *   Lucas Film/Coppola Co./Universal/The Kobal Collection Pages 339, 341 center and bottom   *   Lucas Film LTD/Paramount/Album/Contrasto Pages 420 top right, 421 right   *   Lucas Film LTD/Paramount/The Kobal Collection Pages 419, 420 top left and bottom right, 421 left   *   MCA/ Universal Pictures/Courtesy Everett Collection/Contrasto Pages 445, 447 top   *   Melampo Cinematografica/The Kobal Collection Pages 518-519   *   Merie W. Wallace/Warner Bros/The Kobal Collection Pages 565, 566-567   *   MGM/Album/Contrasto Pages 46 center, 270, 296 top   *   MGM/Bull, Clarence Sinclair/The Kobal Collection Page 75   *   MGM/Courtesy Everett

Biography

PAOLO D'AGOSTINI

Journalist and cinema critic, was born in Rome in 1952. He has written articles in the entertainment section of the daily paper *La Repubblica* since its foundation in 1976. One of his many assignments was the creation, from 1999 to 2001, of a website given over to the cinema as part of the Kataweb portal website of Gruppo Editoriale Espresso-Repubblica publishers. Over the years he concentrated on Latin American and East European film-making, and then passed on to Italian cinema, first the great *commedia all'italiana* or so-called Italian comedy, in particular its screen writers, and then the "new" Italian cinema that became popular in the mid-1970s. On each of the above subjects he has written articles for *La Repubblica,* books, and articles in volumes on the movie industry, and has also participated in many conferences and debates.

D'Agostini was president of Sncci, the Italian Critics' Union. He has also served on the screening committee of the Venice Film Festival and of the nominations panel for the Italian Oscar submissions; he has also been a member of many film festival juries, and has taught courses on cinema at La Sapienza University, Rome.